MATHEMATICAL MODELLING OF FOOD PROCESSING OPERATIONS

ELSEVIER APPLIED FOOD SCIENCE SERIES

Microstructural Principles of Food Processing and Engineering
J. M. AGUILERA and D. W. STANLEY

Biotechnology Applications in Beverage Production
C. CANTARELLI and G. LANZARINI (Editors)

Food Refrigeration Processes
ANDREW C. CLELAND

Progress in Sweeteners
T. H. GRENBY (Editor)

Food Gels
P. HARRIS (Editor)

Thermal Analysis of Foods
V. R. HARWALKAR and C.-Y. MA (Editors)

Food Antioxidants
B. J. F. HUDSON (Editor)

Development and Application of Immunoassay for Food Analysis
J. H. R. RITTENBURG (Editor)

Therapeutic Properties of Fermented Milks
R. K. ROBINSON (Editor)

Food Irradiation
S. THORNE (Editor)

MATHEMATICAL MODELLING OF FOOD PROCESSING OPERATIONS

Edited by

STUART THORNE

Department of Food Science,
King's College London, London, UK

ELSEVIER APPLIED SCIENCE
LONDON and NEW YORK

ELSEVIER SCIENCE PUBLISHERS LTD
Crown House, Linton Road, Barking, Essex IG11 8JU, England

WITH 17 TABLES AND 90 ILLUSTRATIONS

© 1992 ELSEVIER SCIENCE PUBLISHERS LTD

British Library Cataloguing in Publication Data

Mathematical modelling of food processing operations.
I. Thorne, Stuart
664

ISBN 1851667415

Library of Congress Cataloging-in-Publication Data

Mathematical modelling of food processing operations/edited by
Stuart Thorne.
    p.   cm.—(Elsevier applied food science series)
    Includes bibliographical references and index.
    ISBN 1-85166-741-5
    1. Food industry and trade—Mathematical models. I. Thorne,
Stuart. II. Series.
    TP370.5.M37 1992   91-38966 CIP
    664—dc20

Photoset by Interprint Ltd, Malta
Printed in Great Britain at the University Press, Cambridge

PREFACE

Until a decade or so ago, the design and operation of most food processing operations was largely empirical, based on personal experience and judgement. Knowledge of flow properties, heat and mass transfer and other properties of foods was very limited, making prediction of the behaviour of food processing operations difficult. The almost universal availability of small, fast computers today has resulted in an enormous expansion of the application of computers to prediction and control of food processing operations.

Most design or development work on food processing operations involves some sort of model or prediction of the behaviour of the process. For example, without prediction of the heating rates of cans of food, sterilisation times and the size or quantity of retorts cannot be calculated. Without prediction of freezing times, commercial freezing lines cannot be built. So, modelling is inherent in food engineering. There is no universal definition of 'mathematical modelling', but in the context of the present volume, it is assumed to be a mathematical description of a food processing operation, implemented on a computer, which allows prediction of the behaviour of food with the intention of improving, optimising or understanding processes.

An important prerequisite of process design and optimisation is an adequate knowledge of the variables that influence the process and of their numerical values. In the frequent absence of adequate published values of process variables, mathematical modelling is often used to predict these too.

The term 'computer modelling' is often encountered, but is an inaccurate description of what mathematical modelling is about. The computer is simply a tool for the very rapid evaluation of mathematical formulae and equations and for producing numerical solutions; it has made modelling of complex processes feasible, but the adoption of computers is really only a jump comparable with that from slide rules to calculators. It is essential to remember that process simulation is mathematical modelling, by the operator, who must describe the process mathematically and convert his model into an algorithm that the computer can evaluate. Computers rarely make mistakes; incorrect results are usually due to programming errors. Since the computer always executes its program according to fixed rules; any error in the program will always occur under similar conditions. As a result of this, erroneous results may be a constant function of the correct result and very difficult to detect.

Computers are machines and can only do what they are programmed to do. When computers were first introduced, it was generally considered that they would replace humans in many applications. But this has not proved to be the case; the abilities and shortcomings of computers and humans are complementary. Computers can perform mathematical calculations extremely rapidly, but in spite of many years' research into 'artificial intelligence', it is still left to the human brain to provide the equations and algorithms that describe the process and to make the deductions and inferences from inadequate data that often prove necessary. If a process can adequately be described mathematically, then even complex equations can be solved rapidly by computer. A major difficulty of mathematical modelling of the behaviour of foods is that we usually have a knowledge of the fundamental equations governing a process, but insufficient information about the behaviour of complex individual foods. Assumptions usually have to be made about the thermal and physical properties and behaviour of foods. For example, it is often assumed that foods are isotropic and homogeneous; that their properties are similar in all directions and do not vary throughout the food. Another common assumption is that thermal and physical properties do not vary with temperature or time. Such assumptions are often acceptable and necessary if a workable model is to be produced. Sometimes, of course, such assumptions cannot be made. In freezing, change of thermal properties with the change of state is the very essence of the process; changes in apparent viscosity can be a controlling factor in heat exchanger design for foods.

Because many assumptions and approximations must be made, it is never possible to obtain a perfect model of any food processing operation, because of the immense complexity of foods. A considerable part of any modelling exercise must usually be devoted to error analysis, to predicting the probabilities of magnitudes of errors in calculation. Because of these considerations, complete reliance can never be placed upon models; the potential hazards of inadequate processing are too great. But they still provide essential information for the design and optimisation of food processing operations, and for 'what if' type investigations. They do not provide any magic solution to problems in food technology, but are one of the most powerful tools available to process design and optimisation. Models are no substitute for adequate experimental investigation and must always be verified experimentally, but they do provide considerable confidence in predicting these experimental results.

My final warning is: remember that models are models and not the actual operation. Yes, they provide essential predictions about processes, but these are only predictions and not the real thing. It is far too easy to say, 'Look what happens when I do this to my process', when what you mean is, 'Look what *my mathematical model predicts* when I do this to my process'. The essential difference between these two statements is that a model is not the real thing and must not be treated as such. No engineer working on a pilot-scale physical model of his process would underrate the problems of scale-up to a full-scale process. The relationship between a mathematical model, which is even more remote from reality, and the actual process is even more tenuous than the relationship between a physical model and the process.

January 1991   STUART THORNE

LIST OF CONTRIBUTORS

D. BURFOOT
   Silsoe Research Institute, Wrest Park, Silsoe, Bedford, MK45 4HS.

M. CHERYAN
   University of Illinois, Department of Food Science, Agricultural Bioprocess Laboratory, 382D Agricultural Engineering Sciences Building, 1302 W. Pennsylvania Avenue, Urbana, IL 61801, USA

T. FURUTA
   Department of Biotechnology, Tottori University, 4-101 Koyamacho-minami, Tottori 680, Japan.

P. GERVAIS
   Ecole Nationale Supérieure de Biologie, Appliquée à la Nutrition et à l'Alimentation, 1, Esplanade Erasme, Campus Universitaire Montmuzard, 21000 Dijon, France

D. J. NICHOLS
   University of Illinois, Department of Food Science, Agricultural Bioprocess Laboratory, 382D Agricultural Engineering Sciences Building, 1302 W. Pennsylvania Avenue, Urbana, IL 61801, USA

J. C. OLIVEIRA
   College of Biotechnology, Catholic University of Portugal, Rua Dr António Bernardino de Almeida, 4200 Porto, Portugal

S. K. SASTRY
   Ohio State University, Department of Agricultural Engineering, 590 Wood Hayes Drive, Columbus, OH 43210-1057, USA

D. SIMATOS
Ecole Nationale Supérieure de Biologie, Appliquée à la Nutrition et à l'Alimentation, 1, Esplanade Erasme, Campus Universitaire Montmuzard, 21000 Dijon, France

R. P. SINGH
Department of Agricultural Engineering, Department of Food Science and Technology, University of California, Davis, CA 95616, USA

J. H. WELLS
Department of Biological and Agricultural Engineering, Louisiana State University Agricultural Center, Louisiana Agricultural Experiment Station, Baton Rouge, LA 70803, USA

CONTENTS

Chapter 1

MODELLING OF MEAT PROCESSING

DEAN BURFOOT

Silsoe Research Institute,
Wrest Park, Silsoe,
Bedford, UK

NOTATION

a	Thickness
A	Cross-sectional area
A_s	Surface area
c	Concentration
C	Specific heat capacity
D	Mass diffusion coefficient
$E(x)$, E_0	Energy at depth x and at the surface, respectively
E_y, E_z	Electric field strength in the y and z directions, respectively
$EHTD$	Equivalent heat transfer dimension (eqn 9)
h	Heat transfer coefficient
H	Enthalpy
H_x, H_z	Magnetic field strength in the x and z directions, respectively
k	Thermal conductivity
l_r, l_z	Cosines in the radial and axial directions
L	Latent heat
M	Weight of meat
N_1, N_2, N_3	Element shape functions in finite element routine
P	Factor in Plank's formula (eqn (8))
$P(x)$, P_0	Power flux at depth x and at the surface, respectively
q	Rate of heat transfer
r	Radial location
R	Factor in Plank's formula (eqn (8))
$[S_m]$	Scattering matrix in transmission line model

2   D. BURFOOT

t	Time
t_{slab}	Freezing time of slab
T	Temperature
T^e	Temperature within a finite element
T_n, T_{n+1}, T'_n	Temperature at locations $n+1$ and n after time t, and temperature at location n after time $t + \Delta t$, respectively
T_1, T_2, T_3	Temperature at nodes 1, 2 and 3 in finite element routine (Fig. 3)
$[T^i_n]$	Incident pulses in a transmission line model
$[_mT^r_n]$	Reflected pulses at the time of the mth iteration in a transmission line model
V	Volume
W	Weighting function
x	Axial distance
x_n, x_{n+1}	Locations n and $n+1$
$[\,]$	Vector
Δt	Time increment
Δx	Axial length increment
α	Attenuation coefficient
ε'	Permittivity
μ	Permeability
ϕ	Empirical factor in eqn (25)
ρ	Density
σ	Conductivity

Subscripts

a	Ambient
f	Freezing
i	Initial
s	Surface
r, x, y, z	Coordinates r, x, y and z

1 INTRODUCTION

The meat industry throughout the world uses a very large range of processing activities particularly heating and refrigeration. Mathematical models are being used to assist in the design of equipment and optimisation of these processes. Most of these models focus on the simulation of heat and mass transfer using analytical or numerical (finite difference, finite element or transmission line) methods. The analytical methods are widely used to simulate cooling and other processes where mass transfer and dimensional changes of the food are small. Plank's semi-empirical model is often used to estimate freezing times, particularly of meat blocks. The finite difference techniques are the most commonly used numerical methods and have been applied to simulate almost all meat processing operations (including chilling, freezing, thawing, storage, cooking and microwave heating). Although such methods are very flexible and applicable to complex problems, none of the existing models accurately predict temperature, mass and dimensional changes of meat during processing. Achieving a better understanding of the mechanisms controlling the changes of meat during processing will lead to improvements in the models. More reliable methods of predicting boundary conditions, such as surface transfer coefficients and air flow patterns, are also required.

The meat industry is the largest sector of the UK food production system with an annual value exceeding £8500 million. Few consumers consider the large range of activities that have to be carried out in the industry to convert a live animal to a consumer product. The principal output of the industry is fresh or frozen red meat and poultry, but increasingly these are being used in further processed products, including pies, cooked meats, paté and ready-prepared meals.

Manufacturing operations vary considerably in scale from very small operations, typically family-owned abattoirs or butchers, to large multi-national organisations. The former may operate very simple processes, whilst the larger manufacturer is increasingly using complex processes and operating at high throughputs. Irrespective of the size of operation, the goals are the same: to produce a safe, high-quality product at an economic price. Mathematical models are increasingly being applied by meat processors to help them achieve these aims. Larger organisations are developing their own models and the smaller producers are using the services of research and consultancy organisations.

Historically, large-scale experimental projects have been carried out to determine optimum processing conditions, for example to minimise weight loss. Approximately 25 years ago some organisations began to use empirical or analytical models to predict heat and mass transfer rates and consequently processing times and weight losses. The empirical models were equations fitted to the experimental data, whilst the analytical models were generally taken directly from engineering applications and involved solving two partial differential equations. For one-dimensional heat and mass transfer the relevant equations are:

$$Cp\frac{\partial T}{\partial t} = \frac{\partial}{\partial x}\left(k\frac{\partial T}{\partial x}\right) \qquad (1)$$

$$\frac{\partial c}{\partial t} = \frac{\partial}{\partial x}\left(D\frac{\partial c}{\partial x}\right) \qquad (2)$$

Equation (1) is sometimes called the Fourier equation and may also be written as:

$$\frac{\partial H}{\partial t} = \frac{\partial}{\partial x}\left(k\frac{\partial T}{\partial x}\right) \qquad (3)$$

Solution of these equations, with appropriate boundary conditions, should yield the time-dependent changes of temperature and water profiles in a product during processing. In practice, the predicted temperatures and moisture profiles were compared with experimental measurements to provided factors, such as equivalent dimensions, which could then be used in the models to produce agreement between experimental and predicted data. The models could then be used to interpolate between the experimental data.

Graphical representation of solutions of eqns (1) and (2) are abundant but, owing to the complexity of analytical solutions, extension to the more complex geometries and variable thermophysical properties encountered in the meat industry is very limited. Although there are moves towards portion control by preparing meats in regular forms, most meat is processed as carcasses or joints. These are irregular in shape with inhomogeneous, and often position- and temperature-dependent, properties. Temperature and mass changes of such materials during processing are difficult to predict using analytical models.

Researchers consequently turned towards mathematical techniques which could more easily handle complicated geometries, temperature- and spatially-dependent properties, and variations in the boundary conditions with time and position. Suitable techniques, including finite difference, finite volume, finite analytic, finite element, boundary integral equation, surface element, and transmission line matrix methods, had already been developed for engineering applications. Schneider (1984) describes the various techniques and the advantages of each when applied to heat transfer problems in engineering applications. However, for meat applications only the finite difference and finite element methods have been used and reported to any extent, with the transmission line method being tried but not widely adopted. All of these methods separate the product into imaginary small, but finite, portions which can be analysed more easily; hence they are known as discrete numerical methods. This chapter describes the basis of the analytical and numerical methods using examples of heat transfer in simple geometries and then looks at some applications studied by researchers and used in the meat industry.

2 MATHEMATICAL METHODS

2.1 Analytical Methods

Solutions to eqn (1) with various boundary conditions may be found in many books (Kern, 1950; Carslaw and Jaeger, 1959; Heldman and Singh, 1981). These solutions are often represented by graphs showing the logarithm of the unaccomplished temperature ratio, $(T_a - T)/(T_a - T_i)$, versus the dimensionless group $4kt/\rho c X^2$ for various values of $2k/hl$ and $2x/l$. Such charts, for example Fig. 1, are available to predict the temperatures in regular geometric shapes such as spheres and infinite slabs or cylinders and are known as Gurney–Lurie charts (Gurney and Lurie, 1923). Dalgleish and Ede (1965) show the mathematical derivation of these solutions and, using the method of Newman (1936), extend the applications to finite bricks and cylinders by noting that

$$\left(\frac{T_a - T}{T_a - T_i}\right)_{x,y,z} = \left(\frac{T_a - T}{T_a - T_i}\right)_x \left(\frac{T_a - T}{T_a - T_i}\right)_y \left(\frac{T_a - T}{T_a - T_i}\right)_z \tag{4}$$

$$\left(\frac{T_a - T}{T_a - T_i}\right)_{x,r} = \left(\frac{T_a - T}{T_a - T_i}\right)_x \left(\frac{T_a - T}{T_a - T_i}\right)_r \tag{5}$$

Consequently the temperature distribution within a brick or cylinder may be determined from the Gurney–Lurie charts for infinite regular-shaped objects.

These analytical solutions are restricted to instances where there is no significant phase change and the material properties and dimensions do not change during processing. They are therefore not strictly applicable to freezing, thawing and cooking processes. However, the analytical approach using unaccomplished temperature plots has been applied extensively to predict or represent experimental data on chilling and cooling times (Pflug *et al.*, 1965; Rolfe, 1967; Earle and Fleming, 1967;

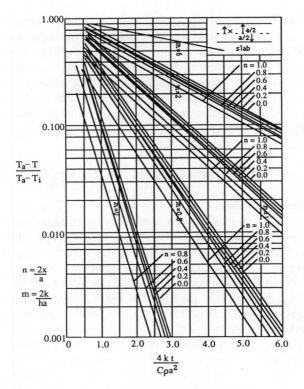

FIG. 1. Gurney–Lurie chart for estimation of temperatures in finite slabs (from Heldman and Singh (1981)).

Fleming and Earle, 1968; Fleming 1970; Bailey and Cox, 1976; Cox and Bailey, 1977; Ramaswamy *et al.*, 1982; Cleland and Earle, 1982a). Similarly measured temperature–time changes during cooking have been reported in a similar form (Carlheim–Gyllenskod, 1970; Sarkin, 1978; Bengtsson *et al.*, 1976).

LeBlanc *et al.* (in press) use 19 different models and Hayakawa (1977) cites others for predicting the freezing times of foods, but it is the Plank (1944) model and modifications of it which form the basis of much of that and other work. To demonstrate the principle of Plank's model, consider a heat balance on an infinite slab initially at a uniform temperature, T_f, which is constant, and allow only steady state heat flow from the freezing boundary to the food surface (Earle, 1959)

Latent heat change = Heat conducted through = Heat convected from
the frozen layer the food surface

$$AL\rho \frac{dx}{dt} = kA \frac{(T-T_s)}{x} = hA(T_s - T_a) \qquad (6)$$

Rearranging these equations and integrating between $x=0$ (the food surface) and $x=a/2$ (the mid-plane) shows that

$$t_f = \text{freezing time} = \frac{L\rho}{(T-T_a)}\left(\frac{a}{2h} + \frac{a^2}{8k}\right) \qquad (7)$$

Plank (1941) further shows that for one-dimensional heat transfer through a slab, cylinder or sphere:

$$t_f = \text{freezing time} = \frac{L\rho}{(T-T_a)}\left(P\frac{a}{h} + R\frac{a^2}{k}\right) \qquad (8)$$

where the value of the factors P and R depend on the product geometry.

Many modifications to Plank's model have been proposed to overcome the assumptions originally imposed, particularly that the food is initially and uniformly at the freezing point and the centre remains at that temperature. Modifications allow for the times prior to initiation of freezing (the prefreezing period) and after freezing (the tempering period) to be estimated and added to Plank's estimate of freezing time (Mascheroni and Calvelo, 1983; De Michelis and Calvelo, 1983; Lacroix and Castaigne, 1987). Researchers in New Zealand have carried out most work in this area, both to estimate prefreezing and tempering times and further to derive modifications allowing for the shape of products and changes in boundary conditions with time (Cleland and Earle, 1979a, 1979b; Loeffen et al., 1981; Cleland and Earle, 1982b; Pham, 1984, 1985a, 1986a, 1986b). Prefreezing and tempering periods may be estimated using the analytical solutions of the Fourier equation without a phase change. Cleland and co-workers introduce another factor into eqn (8), the 'equivalent heat transfer dimensionality' (EHTD), to allow for irregular product shapes such that

$$t_f = \frac{t_{slab}}{EHTD} \qquad (9)$$

The *EHTD* may be calculated theoretically for simple geometries (1 for an infinite slab, 2 for an infinite cylinder, 3 for a sphere) and by relating experimental and predicted freezing times for real products such as meat carcasses. Pham (1985) uses a 'mean conducting path' from the surface to the thermal centre when analysing irregular shapes; but again this needs to be determined by experiment for meat carcasses.

2.2 Numerical Methods

The growing introduction of digital computers has led to major developments in numerical methods for solving heat and mass transfer problems. Three particular numerical methods, finite difference, finite element and transmission line have been applied to meat processing.

2.2.1 Finite Difference Methods

In the finite difference method the meat is subdivided into imaginary segments and heat and mass balances applied to each segment. Figure 2 shows the subdivision carried out on a semi-infinite slab. The

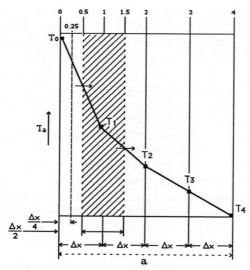

FIG. 2.   Subdivision of a slab for preparation of finite difference approximations of heat balances (adapted from Bailey *et al.* (1974)).

following equations are then used to provide the energy balance on each segment.

$$q = hA_s(T_s - T_a) \quad \text{(through the surface)} \quad (10)$$

$$q = kA \frac{(T_{n-1} - T_n)}{(x_{n-1} - x_n)} \quad \text{(internal flow)} \quad (11)$$

$$q = \rho A \, \Delta x \, C \frac{(T'_n - T_n)}{\Delta t} \quad \text{(accumulation of heat)} \quad (12)$$

An energy balance on a segment away from the surface then produces:

$$kA \frac{(T_{n-1} - T_n)}{(x_{n-1} - x_n)} - kA \frac{(T_n - T_{n+1})}{(x_n - x_{n+1})} = \rho A \, \Delta x \, C \frac{(T'_n - T_n)}{\Delta t} \quad (13)$$

A similar energy balance may be developed at the surface regions and the equations then solved for an initial boundary condition, e.g. $T_n = T_i$, to calculate the temperature changes at each position within the object (Burfoot and James, 1988). The method of solution uses either a repetitive procedure or matrices. The method is known as the explicit finite difference, or Dusinberre (Dusinberre, 1949), method because the temperature, T'_n at time $t + \Delta t$, can be calculated directly from the temperature, T_n at time t.

However, the temperature gradients on the left-hand side of eqn (13) change during the time interval, Δt. In the Crank–Nicholson method (Jenson and Jeffreys, 1977) the temperature gradients are the average values over the time interval:

$$\frac{kA \frac{(T_{n-1} - T_n)}{(x_{n-1} - x_n)} + kA \frac{(T'_{n-1} - T'_n)}{(x_{n-1} - x_n)}}{2} + \frac{kA \frac{(T_n - T_{n+1})}{(x_n - x_{n+1})} + kA \frac{(T'_n - T'_{n+1})}{(x_n - x_{n+1})}}{2}$$

$$= \rho A \, \Delta x \, C \frac{(T'_n - T_n)}{\Delta t} \quad (14)$$

This requires more computing time than the explicit method because twice the number of temperature gradients must be calculated and iterations are required to determine T'_n. Weightings other than 0·5 can be used in eqn (14), for example the effective temperature gradient could be used on one-third of the gradient at time t and two-thirds that at time $t + \Delta t$. A fully implicit method, requiring less computation of the temperature gradients, involves calculating all thermal gradients a time $t + \Delta t$. This reduces the number of temperature gradients which need to be calculated but still requires iteration to determine T'_n.

The thermal properties may also vary with temperature and hence over the time step, Δt. In the explicit method, the thermal conductivity and specific heat are evaluated at time t so that no unknown temperatures are required in the calculation. As with other methods, the density is assumed constant, otherwise the spatial increment, Δx, must be varied to maintain constant mass. With the implicit methods, the thermal properties are evaluated at the temperature and times appropriate to the temperature gradients. Again this increases the computing times and errors can occur when the properties are very temperature-dependent, for example, the specific heat of meat between -4 and $-1°C$. Small time intervals have to be used in any of these 'two time level schemes', which evaluate properties at times t and $t + \Delta t$. A three time level scheme developed by Lees (1966) which evaluates temperatures at times $t - \Delta t$, t and $t + \Delta t$ and has been applied to heat transfer problems by several researchers (Bonacina and Connini, 1973; Cleland and Earle, 1977; Cleland et al., 1982, 1987d). Whilst this method may allow larger time increments to be used, more calculations over each time step are required. Furthermore very small time steps are often required, as with the explicit methods, to ensure accuracy in regions of high thermal gradient.

Finite difference methods are the most widely reported technique used to determine temperatures during processing. These methods have been applied to simulate chilling and cooling (Loginov, 1976; Srinivasa Murphy et al., 1976; Radford et al., 1976; Self and Burfoot, 1986; Fulton et al., 1990), freezing (Cleland and Earle, 1977, 1979a; Cleland et al., 1982; Earle and Earl, 1966; Fleming, 1971a, 1971b; Cullwick and Earle, 1971; Fleming, 1972; Charm et al., 1972; Bonacina et al., 1974; Brisson-Lopes and Domingos, 1979; Bazan and Mascheroni, 1984; Pham, 1985b, 1987a), thawing (Bailey et al., 1974; James et al., 1977; James and Bailey, 1980; Mascheroni, 1982), cooking (Godsalve, 1976; Dagerskog, 1979; Burfoot and James, 1983; Holtz, 1984; Burfoot and Self, 1989), microwave heating (Ohlsson, 1971; Kirk and Holmes, 1975; Nykvist and Decareau, 1976; Self et al., 1990) and retail display (Fulton et al., 1987; James et al., 1988).

2.2.2 Finite Element Methods

The finite element technique originally developed to analyse stresses in engineering components was first applied to the analysis of heat transfer in 1965 (Schneider, 1984). In this method the object is divided into imaginary discrete elements with nodes situated on their boundaries. A temperature distribution is assumed which relates the temperature within the element to the temperature on the boundaries. In effect the method then minimises the sum of the differences between the conducted and accumulated heat in each element. The temperature distributions which satisfy this condition, and provide equality of temperature at the boundaries of elements, then provide the temperature distribution throughout the entire object. The following derivation of one finite element routine, given by De Baerdemaeker *et al.* (1977) shows how the equations are developed for triangular elements which can be used to build up a variety of shapes.

Figure 3 shows the triangular element and coordinate system for which the heat transfer equation may be expressed as:

$$\frac{\partial}{\partial r}\left(rk\frac{\partial T}{\partial r}\right) + \frac{\partial}{\partial z}\left(rk\frac{\partial T}{\partial z}\right) - r\rho C\frac{\partial T}{\partial t} = 0 \tag{15}$$

with a surface boundary condition given by:

$$k\frac{\partial T}{\partial r}l_r + k\frac{\partial T}{\partial z}l_z + h(T - T_a) = 0$$

$$= k\frac{\partial T}{\partial n} + h(T - T_a) \tag{16}$$

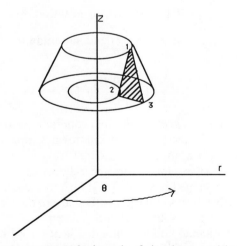

FIG. 3.   Coordinate system and triangular finite element with nodal values (from De Baerdemaeker *et al.* (1977)).

The Galerkin Residual Method is then applied with weighting functions being introduced leading to orthogonality (i.e. multiply both sides of eqn (15) by a function and integrate over the volume of the element):

$$\int \left(\frac{\partial}{\partial r}\left(rk\frac{\partial T}{\partial r}\right) + \frac{\partial}{\partial z}\left(rk\frac{\partial T}{\partial z}\right) - r\rho C\frac{\partial T}{\partial t}\right) W\, dV = 0 \qquad (17)$$

where T is the approximate temperature distribution.

The conduction terms in eqn (17) are then integrated by parts to give

$$\int \left(rk\frac{\partial T}{\partial r}\frac{\partial W}{\partial r} + rk\frac{\partial T}{\partial z}\frac{\partial W}{\partial z} + r\rho C\frac{\partial T}{\partial t}W\right) dV$$

$$+ \int \left(rk\frac{\partial T}{\partial r}l_r + rk\frac{\partial T}{\partial z}l_z\right) W\, dS = 0 \qquad (18)$$

The integral term over the surface is obtained using the divergence theorem which states that the integral of the heat conduction over the objects volume must equal the integral of the heat loss by convection perpendicular to the surface.

The temperature within an element can be related to the temperatures at its boundary, so for a triangular element we can use:

$$\begin{aligned} T^e &= T_1 N_1 + T_2 N_2 + T_3 N_3 \\ &= [T][N] \text{ in vector notation} \end{aligned} \qquad (19)$$

Substituting this formula into eqn (18) and summing the integrals for all the elements gives

$$[K][T] + [C]\frac{\partial [T]}{\partial t} - [F] = 0 \qquad (20)$$

where $[K]$ and $[C]$ depend on the thermal conductivity and heat capacity of the foodstuff, $[T]$ is the matrix of unknown temperatures and $[F]$ includes the values of heat input. Schneider (1984) derives the same equation but defines the matrices for a more general coordinate system showing how to calculate the shape functions ($[N]$) for more complex geometries.

The time derivative in this equation is then approximated using a finite difference scheme. Use of a finite element scheme to minimise the difference between conducted and accumulated heat for estimated temperature changes over time would be too cumbersome and require excessive computing time.

Much has been written on the mathematical and computer code formulation of finite element methods (Schneider,1984; Whiteman, 1973) and they have been applied to simulate some food processing operations. However, they have only been applied in a limited manner to meat processing, exceptions are chilling (Arce *et al.*, 1983), freezing (Cleland *et al.*, 1982, 1984, 1987d; Purwadaria and Heldman, 1982), sterilisation (Mazzola *et al.*, 1986) and cooking (De Baerdemaeker *et al.*, 1977).

2.2.3 Transmission Line Matrix Method

The transmission line method was originally used in the simulation of electronic circuits and electromagnetic fields; however, in 1984 Johns and Pulko (1987) applied it to the heat diffusion equation.

In food applications, the food is considered as a network of nodes connected by transmission lines which carry pulses of heat a finite distance in a finite time (Johns and Pulko, 1987). Resistors, equivalent to the inverse of the thermal conductivity of the food, are located around the nodes while the thermal capacity is represented by the capacitance of the transmission lines (Fig. 4). From the electrical analogy

Impedance of the transmission line = Voltage/Current

$$= \Delta t / \text{Capacitance}$$

$$= \text{Temperature/Heat flux density} \quad (21)$$

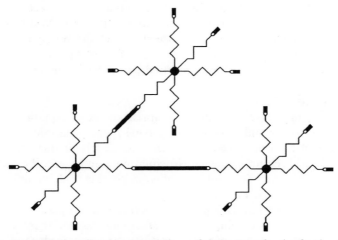

FIG. 4.   Transmission line representation of heat transfer in foods showing resistors and transmission lines (from Johns and Pulko (1987)).

Initially pulses of heat (temperature T^i) are incident at each terminal in the simulated food and these are scattered to create reflected pulses (with temperature T^r). These reflected pulses become incident on neighbouring nodes and so the process is repeated throughout time. Two equations describe this behaviour: the first describes the scattering of the incident pulses using:

$$[_m T^r_n] = [S_m][T^i_n] \qquad (22)$$

and the other describes the connection of resistor terminals, i.e. the transformation of incident into reflected pulses:

$$[_{m+1} T^i] = [C_m][T^r] \qquad (23)$$

The scattering matrix, $[S_m]$, is determined by an energy balance on each node. For a one-dimensional object:

$$S = \frac{1}{R+Z}\begin{bmatrix} R & Z \\ Z & R \end{bmatrix} \qquad (24)$$

where R depends on the thermal conductivity of the foodstuff and spatial increment Δx, and Z depends on the volumetric specific heat capacity (ρC) and the spatial and time increments, Δt and Δx.

The connection matrix defines the connection of nodes and consists of unit values on the leading diagonal to enable heat to move away from a node and unit values off the diagonal to enable pulses to return.

The transmission line method has found little application in the food industry. Its only use in meat processing was the prediction of meat temperature during cooking (Johns and Pulko, 1987) where similar results were obtained to those produced using the Dusinberre method.

2.3 Accuracy and Stability
A complete mathematical model comprises a set of equations used to simulate a process and a method of solving those equations. The aim of any modeller is to produce a model that accurately predicts reality. It is also a practical requirement that the equations can be solved quickly and efficiently. These requirements are often in conflict and examples of this discord are shown in Fig. 5.

The upper solid line is a plot of experimental temperature measurements obtained in a cooling trial. By assuming that the thermal properties of the product are not temperature- or position-dependent, and assuming a regular geometric shape for the product, an analytical solution

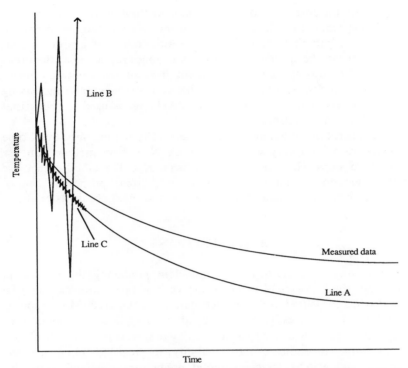

FIG. 5. Typical temperature–time changes predicted using models and illustrating the concepts of accuracy and stability.

(line A) can be generated rapidly. However, the result is not an accurate prediction of reality. The same differential equation, as used in the analytical model, can also be solved using numerical techniques. If very large time steps, or an inappropriate method of solution, are used (line B) then an unstable situation is likely and no solution is produced. Using smaller time steps, or a more stable method (line C), the solution initially oscillates about and then converges to the analytical solution. With the correct choice of time step and method the analytical solution can be duplicated exactly, creating a stable solution; but this is still an inaccurate representation of reality. Sometimes an inappropriate model is used but the predicted data agree with those measured. Such models are generally unreliable and an accurate model of reality can be produced only by increasing the complexity of the model to allow for the shape and complex characteristics of the food.

Even with the correct model and a stable method of solution, accuracy can be lost when the use of large time increments leads to predicted temperatures 'jumping' over the temperature range of a specific heat peak. For meat, the specific heat capacity changes rapidly over the range -4 to $-1°C$ owing to the high latent heat of the ice–water phase transition. Sometimes, a heat balance between the heat entering/leaving the food surface and the internal enthalpy change is used to check that 'jumping' has not occurred.

The explicit finite difference methods generally require very small time steps to ensure, stability while the Crank–Nicholson method can use larger time steps. However, to ensure accuracy all methods must use small time and spatial increments when thermal properties change rapidly with temperature and high thermal and mass gradients exist.

3 APPLICATIONS

The reliability of a mathematical model in predicting the processing times and weight losses of meat during various operations can only be judged when measured and predicted data are compared. Most applications have been investigated under laboratory/pilot-scale conditions, using either meat or a meat substitute (Tylose), and few published data are available to indicate the reliability in 'real-life' circumstances. Several useful articles have compared predictions obtained using different models over the range of conditions found in meat processing and they provide additional information about the application of each type of model.

The majority of the applications are in refrigeration (chilling, freezing, thawing and retail display) whilst the simulation of other processes, for example, cooking and microwave processing, has received less attention.

3.1 Chilling
The aim of primary chilling is to reduce the temperature of the carcass to inhibit the growth of microorganisms, diminish protein denaturation leading to 'drip', restrict evaporative loss and produce the temperatures required for optimum cutting. Rapid chilling is often preferred to increase throughput but, if too fast, may lead to toughness of the meat when finally cooked, consequently there is a need to determine optimum chilling conditions and mathematical models have been developed to assist in this process.

Earle and Fleming (1967) measured the temperature and weight changes of lamb and ewe carcasses in a pilot-scale tunnel and under factory conditions. They found that the temperature measured in the deep leg during pilot-scale tests could be represented by straight lines when presented as log(unaccomplished temperature ratio) versus time. The air temperature used in the denominator of the unaccomplished temperature ratio was not the dry bulb temperature of the air but a value between the dry and wet bulb temperatures; this allowed for the reduction in surface temperature due to drying. It would appear that cooling times could be predicted to within about 10%. Data obtained under factory conditions produced slight curvature of the log-lin temperature–time plots although this data could also be approximated using Gurney–Lurie diagrams.

To predict weight losses, Fleming and Earle (1968) carried out an overall heat balance on the carcass and the equivalent cylinder concept was used to calculate the average bulk and surface temperatures of the carcass. The surface temperature was then used to predict evaporative loss assuming a wet surface. The difference (mean) between measured and calculated weight loss was 3·9% of the weight loss based on data for 51 lambs and 10·9% for 19 ewes. This method of calculating weight loss was found to be reliable when the rate of heat loss was high, but not during the later stages of chilling. The predictions were also very dependent on the equivalent diameter of the cylinder.

Bailey and Cox (1976) used a similar approach to beef chilling. They considered each carcass to be composed of regular shapes and derived relationships, shape factors, which provided agreement between measured temperature–time data and that calculated assuming the deep leg to be an infinite cylinder. For a given temperature in the deep leg, the mean difference between measured and calculated cooling time was within 5%. Brown and James (1988) presented temperature–time data for pig chilling using plots of log(unaccomplished temperature) versus time and again linear relationships were found.

Perjes (1978) suggested that a slab was a better approximate representation of a beef side. However, all the predicted temperatures assumed the characteristic dimension to be 120 mm, based on measurements of the thickness of sides, irrespective of whether a slab, cylinder or sphere model was being used. No attempt was made to determine the dimension which would have produced better agreement between measured and calculated data with each of the models.

Cleland and Earle (1982) produced alignment charts providing similar results to the Gurney–Lurie charts for infinite slabs, cylinders and spheres but using the concept for equivalent heat transfer dimensions (*EHTD*) for other shapes. The lines on their charts were not precisely straight lines but they approximated them as such and consequently there was not exact agreement with the Gurney–Lurie predictions. For regular shapes, their method agreed with analytical solutions of predicted cooling times to within 12%. Comparison of their calculation method with experimental data (Earle and Fleming, 1967; Hodgson, 1966) showed that for beef, ewe and lamb carcasses, $EHTD = 1.33$, 2.13 or 2.5, respectively, but no measure of accuracy of the predictions was given.

Besides the use of Gurney–Lurie plots, numerical methods have also been used to calculate meat temperatures during chilling. Fleming (1970) used a finite difference technique to predict temperatures in a two-dimensional cross-section through the leg of a lamb carcass. However, the results do not compare predicted with measured temperatures during chill conditions but only for freezing when measured and predicted bone temperatures agreed to within 4°C.

Arce *et al.* (1983) used a finite element method with triangular elements and the Crank–Nicholson scheme to predict the loin temperature in a beef carcass during chilling. Predictions were compared with results obtained while chilling five beef sides. Agreement between measured and predicted temperatures could only be achieved by varying the heat transfer coefficient considerably with time (from 85 to 11 W m^{-2} K^{-1}) and by assuming that the ambient temperature was the temperature of the meat measured just beneath the surface. In this way, temperatures measured at two positions in the loin could be calculated to within 3°C throughout chilling.

Other workers have adopted simpler methods to predict product weight losses during chilling. These use a lumped parameter approach whereby overall heat and mass balances are applied and internal temperature gradients are either ignored or allowed for empirically. Califano and Calvelo (1980) found that

$$\text{Percentage weight loss} = (1 - \phi \sqrt[3]{M})\gamma \qquad (25)$$

where M = weight of meat, ϕ = factor found by comparison of measured and calculated data and γ = relationship found from heat and mass balances which depends on the properties and the initial and final temperature of the meat and the air conditions. They used an average specific heat of the meat based on the properties of the fat, lean and bone and the Gurney–Lurie chart was used to determine the average temperature of the carcass at the end of chilling. The average difference between predicted and measured weight losses from beef and lamb carcasses (Fleming and Earle, 1968; Bailey and Cox, 1976; Gac and Tupin, 1964; Golovkin et al., 1955) was 12%.

Pham (1987b) follows a very similar approach, using overall heat and mass balances, but extends the method to operations other than chilling and uses basic psychrometric charts to illustrate the background to the method. Measured weight losses for lamb carcasses (Fleming and Earle, 1968; Longdill and Pham, 1982) were within −30% and +40% of those predicted with a mean difference of 4%. For beef, measured weight losses from Kerens and Visser (1978) agreed with predictions to within −35% and +10% with a mean difference of −15%.

It is clear that the plotting of log(unaccomplished temperature ratio) versus time provides a good method of representing measured data in a form for interpolation, or prediction using comparisons with Gurney–Lurie charts. This method is particularly useful in practice when limited data is available from factory trials and further data can then be estimated by interpolation or extrapolation. The limitation is that processing conditions should be relatively constant. Furthermore, when predictions are required and no measured data is available, the characteristic dimensions recommended in research papers should only be used with the meat properties and heat transfer coefficients specified in that paper. Also the shape and composition of the carcasses being considered should be similar to those used in the research. Using data from various sources in these models can lead to large errors in estimating cooling times. Nonetheless, the log-lin plotting method remains one of the most useful and practical methods of estimating temperature–time relationships during chilling.

Often numerial methods are used in a similar way to the Gurney–Lurie charts with temperatures being predicted in an equivalent cylinder representing a real carcass. The only advantages of numerical methods over charts then become the speed and accuracy of a computer relative to the difficulties of obtaining data from a graph and the ability to include temperature-dependent properties.

Numerical methods also have the capability to predict temperature and weight changes simultaneously. Such calculations would be more difficult using analytical methods. However, such numerical simulations of coupled heat and mass transfer during chilling and verification of the results have not been reported although such computer prediction methods are available (Fulton et al., 1988).

3.2 Freezing

Freezing is the most widely used long-term preservation technique in the meat industry and several methods are used, especially air blast freezing, plate freezing and, to a lesser extent, immersion freezing. In the design of any of these systems, the refrigeration engineer faces a dilemma, whether to design a very fast freezing process using very low temperatures and capable of high throughputs but incurring high operating costs or to use a higher refrigerant temperature and accept longer processing times. Clearly some design methods are required to assist in the selection process, and a major requirement is to estimate the freezing times achievable under different conditions.

No exact analytical solutions of the Fourier equation are available to predict processing times of meat when a phase change occurs, since the properties of the meat then vary considerably with temperature and no single phase change temperature exists. However, an approximate solution to this problem has been developed by Plank (1941) and subsequently modified by many others. Finite difference and finite element methods have also been used to predict freezing times.

Earle (1959) found that the freezing times of boxed veal or beef were predicted by Plank's equation with an error of about 35% and that multiplying the Plank prediction by 10/7 provided much better agreement. He also needed to increase the effective thickness used in the model of the blocks to allow for non-symmetry of temperature profiles. He provided charts to estimate P and R in the Plank model. Herbert and Lovett (1979) later provided a list of correcting factors to Earle's predictions which enable the freezing times of blocks in practical situations to be calculated. Each correcting factor is usually a 15% change of freezing times or the number of hours the freezer fans are not switched on, and allow freezing times to be predicted to within 3 hours of measured values. When plate freezing liver, Creed and James (1983) used a simplified form of Plank's equation relating freezing time to the inverse of the difference between the meat freezing point and refrigerant temperature. Regression constants in the equation were found from their experimental data and provided predictions of freezing time to within 17·8%, although generally much better, when compared to experimental values. They later (Creed and James, 1985) compared the experimental data to comparisons obtained with Cleland and Earle's (1977) modification to the Plank equation and found a maximum error of 1·3 hours in a 10-hour process. Maximum percentage difference between measured and predicted freezing time was 32·7% with a mean of 6·5%. They concluded the errors were due to the use of constant thermal properties in the Plank equation. Hung and Thompson (1983) compared freezing times obtained from the Plank formula with data measured on slabs of Tylose, lean beef and ground beef. The P and R values in Plank's equation were found by comparison with the experimental data to provide predicted times within 4·7% of experimental data.

Plank's formula has been used by many other researchers to predict freezing times of shapes other than slabs. Earle and Fleming (Earle and Fleming, 1967; Fleming and Earle, 1966) determined the equivalent diameters of lamb (9·1 cm diameter) and ewe (10·4 or 13·0 cm diameter) carcasses to be used in Plank's equation. The maximum difference between experimental and predicted freezing times was 27·5% and design monographs to predict freezing times are provided. Freezing times of bricks, finite cylinders and infinite slabs of beef were estimated to within 10% of experimetal data by De Michelis and Calvelo (1983) using Plank's equation to estimate the period of freezing and analytical solutions to the Fourier equation along with Newman's method to predict the prefreezing and tempering periods. The latter agreed with the *EHTD* method of Cleland and Earle and, consequently, this method was adopted, rather than the analytical technique. Lacroix and Castaigne (1987) also examined the prefreezing, freezing and tempering periods. The non-freezing periods were estimated using Gurnie–Lurie charts, analytical solutions of eqn (1), or by an equation previously proposed by them. The time of freezing was estimated using Plank's equation with P and R found from data in Cleland and Earle (1979b) for bricks, Plank (1941) for parallelepipeds and De Michelis and Calvelo (1983) for finite cylinders. Overall freezing times were underestimated by up to 44·4% for slabs. Correcting the formula by calculating freezing times at $x/L = 0·4$ rather than $x/L = 0·5$ (the geometric centre), freezing times of bricks were predicted to within 39·2%. Modifying P and R reduced the error to 16·3%.

Le Blanc *et al.* (in press) compare 19 non-numerical methods for predicting freezing time with their experimental data obtained on french fries. They concluded the methods presented by IIR (1986), Hayakawa *et al.* (1983a, 1983b), Cleland *et al.* (1987b) and Salvadori *et al.* (1987) gave the best agreement (within 10% of measured freezing time) for that particular product. Although not based on tests with meat, this study does indicate some agreement between the non-numerical prediction methods.

Finite difference methods and slab models have been used by several researchers. Cullwick and Earle (1971) modified the heat transfer coefficient to provide the best agreement between measured and predicted temperatures with minced meat slabs; however, the error in predicted temperatures in the frozen region was more than 10°C. The Lees scheme was used by Bonacina and Comini (1971) to estimate to within 0·5°C the temperatures of Tylose slabs during plate freezing but very limited experimental data was provided. Bazan and Mascheroni (1984) later used an explicit finite difference method to show that plate freezing times of blocks of mutton could be predicted to within 16·4% but a regression of the measured times with experimental factors allowed estimates to within 2·1%.

Other workers have used finite difference models to predict the freezing times of shapes other than slabs. Earle and Earl (1966) found measured temperatures of spheres and cubes of minced beef were shorter than predicted using a finite difference model and large errors (>20°C) in temperature in the frozen region were computed. Fleming (1970, 1971b) later used the alternating direction finite difference method to predict temperatures in lamb carcasses. This method uses the explicit and implicit finite difference techniques alternately in the x and y directions to solve the Fourier equation with temperature-dependent properties. Computed bone temperatures were within the range of experimental scatter and the model showed that the region of highest temperature moves away from the bone during freezing; however, computed freezing times were 25% longer than measured. Creed and James (1984) also predicted the freezing times of mutton. They could not use Fleming and Earle's (1966) modification of the Plank formula because they used heavier carcasses. Instead they assumed the carcasses could be represented as cylinders in a finite difference model (Cleland and Earle, 1979a) and produced an average error in predicted freezing time of 12·1%.

A few models of meat freezing have been based on the finite element approach. Purwadaria and Heldman (1982) used heat transfer coefficients based on temperatures measured at the surface of elliptical and trapezoidal shapes of minced beef and compared the predicted internal temperatures with those measured. Temperatures at the position of slowest freezing agreed with measured values for the ellipse within a 95% confidence limit. However, such agreement was not achieved when freezing the trapezoid at low air speeds. Hayakawa et al. (1983a, 1983b) used a finite element method to simulate heat and moisture loss but this only allowed for surface evaporation and not moisture loss from within the food. Predicted temperatures in 2-D bricks of lean beef and finite cylinders of Tylose in cans were within 2·7°C (slabs) and 1·4°C (cylinders) of measured values but only two test results were provided. The heat transfer coefficient was determined from the measured temperatures.

Instead of empirical equations, modifications to Plank's formula, or numerical models, Hayakawa and Bakal (1973) developed an analytical model of the various stages of freezing slabs including prefreezing, partially frozen zone with some meat still unfrozen (first phase change period), partially frozen meat throughout (intermediate phase change), all meat almost completely frozen (second phase change) and the tempering period when all of the meat was frozen. Analytical solutions of the Fourier equation were used to calculate temperatures in the prefreezing period and differential equations were developed and solved to predict the temperatures in the other periods. Temperatures in the precooling and first phase change period were predicted to within $1.3°C$ of those measured in slabs of ground beef, in the intermediate zone to within $11.1°C$, in the second phase change period to within $1.7°C$ and in the tempering period to $2°C$. They recommend use of numerical methods to predict temperatures in the period of intermediate phase change.

Ilicali (1989) also presents an analytical model for predicting freezing times. Analytical solutions of eqn (1) were determined for each direction of heat transfer in a rectangular brick. These solutions, obtained using an effective thermal diffusivity during freezing, were multiplied together using Newman's method to predict the freezing times of bricks. Predictions from the model were compared with experimental data for Tylose (Cleland and Earle, 1979b) and lean beef (De Michelis and Calvelo, 1983; Hayakawa et al., 1983a), and other data reported in the paper for ground beef and mashed potato. Mean differences between predicted and measured freezing times varied between -6.3% and $+2.3\%$ but maximum differences exceeded 15%.

The New Zealand researchers Pham and Cleland and co-workers have produced the most extensive work on predicting freezing times using modifications of Plank's formula and numerical methods. Often the results are compared with data obtained by other workers and their own using minced beef or Tylose.

Plank's formula is based on the assumption that the food freezes at one temperature. Pham (1984) used a 'mean freezing temperature' to account for gradual phase change when meat freezes and used the total enthalpy change during freezing rather than the latent heat in Plank's formula. Prefreezing and tempering times were estimated using a simplified formula. Predicted freezing times were within 24% of values measured on Tylose, lean beef, ground beef, potato and carp (De Michelis and Calvelo,

1983; Cleland and Earle, 1977, 1979a; Hung and Thompson, 1983). The predictions were within −9% to +10% of Cleland and Earle's (1977, 1979a), data. This model was later extended (Pham, 1985a) to predict the freezing times of bricks and comparison made with data on Tylose and lean beef (De Michelis and Calvelo, 1983; Cleland and Earle 1979b). A 'mean conducting path' (*MCP*) was defined which could be estimated from the largest and smallest distance from the surface of an object to the centre or from comparisons with experimental data. Errors in freezing time predictions ranged from −12% to +16%. These methods (Pham, 1984, 1985a) were later simplified (Pham, 1986a) assuming that the resistance to heat transfer was the same during the prefreezing and freezing periods, the enthalpy term in Plank's equation was the enthalpy change over the freezing and tempering periods and the temperature change is the difference between the initial and final meat temperature. Comparisons with 283 values of freezing time obtained with Tylose, lean and ground beef, potato and carp, showed differences of −23% to +24% when some of the experimental freezing data believed to be inaccurate was not used in the comparison. This model was also capable of estimating the effects of fluctuating air temperature during freezing but not variations of heat transfer coefficient.

Pham (1985b, 1987a) also compared freezing time predictions achieved using numerical methods. He concluded that the methods proposed by Comini *et al.* (1974) and Hsiao (1985) were essentially the same and both underestimated freezing times, while the best methods were those proposed by Pham (1985b) and the explicit method based on enthalpy variations (equation (3)). The Lees scheme was found to require too much computing time to handle many of the freezing problems.

Cleland and Earle report on a series of experimental tests with Tylose and minced beef and comparison with freezing times predicted using modified constants in Plank's equation. In the first studies (Cleland and Earle, 1977) they used 1-D slabs and found the *P* and *R* values in Plank's equation from the experimental data. For Tylose, the maximum errors in predicting freezing times with the modified Plank formula was 7·1% with a maximum error of 9·5% when using a three time level finite difference method. For meat, the maximum errors were 4·3% using the Plank method and 9·7% using the finite difference model. The work was later extended to cylinders and spheres (Cleland and Earle, 1979a) and revised values of *P* and *R* were used to give 95% confidence intervals on freezing times of ±5·2% with cylinders and ±3·8% with spheres. For the finite difference method the 95% confidence interval covered measured freezing times to within -8.3% to $+10.5\%$. This work was extended to 3-D slabs (Cleland and Earle, 1979b) and equations to calculate P and R values for slabs, cylinders, spheres and bricks were developed. Predictions of freezing times (95% confidence intervals) were $\pm 10\%$ for bricks, $\pm 5\%$ for slabs and $\pm 7\%$ for cylinders and spheres when compared to their experimental data. They concluded that Plank's formula using their P and R values was at least as accurate as the finite difference method in predicting freezing times. Their prediction method was extended to allow for variations in boundary conditions (Loeffen *et al.*, 1981) using two methods, either numerically integrating the differential equation on which Plank's formula is based or evaluating the Plank predictions over small time intervals. Both methods gave similar predictions of freezing time. The Plank method agreed to within 10% of finite difference predictions of freezing time.

Cleland and Earle (1982) used the 'equivalent heat transfer dimension' concept with Plank's formula and found that freezing times could be predicted to within $\pm 6\%$ (95% confidence interval) for slabs, $\pm 7\%$ for cylinders and $\pm 10\%$ for spheres. They also presented $EHTD$ values for lambs (2·4) and ewes (2·1) by comparison with experimental data.

Subsequently these researchers (Cleland *et al.*, 1982, 1984) compared numerical methods and concluded that finite difference and finite element methods produced little difference in predicted freezing times with errors compared to their Tylose freezing data varying between -16% and $+10\%$ for the finite difference method. However, the accuracy of the model varied with freezing rate: low predictions of freezing time were found at high freezing rates and high predictions at low rates of freezing. They concluded that freezing rate affects the thermal properties of foods owing to variations in rates of nucleation and growth of ice crystals and this was not considered in the determination of the material properties. (Pham (1989) later showed that dendritic growth of ice crystals would be most significant for small products, low heat transfer coefficients, high air temperatures ($> -20°C$) and nucleation temperatures below $-5°C$. However, the effect on freezing times would be generally small in practice and very rarely would crystal growth affect freezing times by more than 10%.) Cleland and co-workers (Cleland *et al.*, 1982, 1984) also suggested that no more improvements in numerical techniques were required to predict freezing times and future research should focus on the mechanisms of freezing and obtaining more experimental data for comparison with the models. In the later paper (Cleland *et al.*, 1984) freezing times of Tylose were predicted to within 15% of measured values but large differences between predicted and measured temperature–time curves were found. The finite element procedure required very large computing times and restricted the testing of this method.

In a series of four papers, Cleland and co-workers compared measured freezing times obtained with Tylose or beef with predictions obtained using Plank's formula with the $EHTD$ and 'mean conducting path' concepts, and with numerical methods. In the first paper (1987a) the freezing times of 2-D and 3-D irregular shapes were determined experimentally. Deformed cylinders, square pyramids, an ovoid, fish shape and spheres were used. In the second paper (1987b) they found the best agreement between measured and predicted freezing times of bricks of Tylose was achieved using the $EHTD$ concept with the slab prediction from Plank's formula (maximum difference in times was 9·7%). Predictions based solely on a finite difference method produced a maximum error of 20·7%. However, comparison with data from De Michelis and Calvelo (1983) showed differences of up to 30·3% between measured and predicted freezing times using the $EHTD$ concept and Plank's formula.

Further predictions of freezing times of regular and irregular shapes were also carried out (1987c) and revised values of $EHTD$ and MCP were determined. Freezing times of bricks were predicted to within 10·1% of measured values using the $EHTD$ method with Plank's equation. Using the same approach to predict the freezing times of irregular 2-D shapes led to a maximum error of 13·5%. The $EHTD$ and MCP approaches produced similar predictions of freezing time. Freezing times of 3-D shapes with ovoid cross-section could not be estimated reliably because insufficient experimental data was available to estimate the $EHTD$ or MCP values.

In the concluding paper, Cleland et al. (1987d) compare predictions obtained using the Lees finite difference method with a full finite element analysis and a simplified finite element method in which constant thermal properties are assumed across an element of the food. For 1-D shapes, and regular 2-D and 3-D shapes, all methods produced similar accuracy compared to experimental data. For bricks, the finite difference and finite element methods produced maximum errors of 20·7% and 24·1%, and for the 2-D shapes the simplified finite element method produced a maximum error of 12·0%. However, computing times were very dependent on the method used: the computer processing time needed to predict the freezing time of a brick was 0·28 hours using the finite difference method and 14 hours using the full finite element method. Only data based on freezing and thawing tests were available for other shapes and these showed a maximum difference between measured and predicted processing times of 58·4%.

Cleland (1986) reviews the methods for predicting freezing times. He found that Plank's original formula underpredicts freezing times by 10% to 40%. For slabs, cylinders and spheres, the methods of Cleland *et al.* (1987b), Pham (1984, 1986b), Hung and Thompson (1983 and De Michelis and Calvelo (1983) are recommended whilst the *EHTD* or *MCP* concepts should be used for predicting the freezing times of 3-D regular shapes. The *EHTD* concept, with *EHTD* values determined by experiment or comparison with finite element predictions are recommended for predictions with irregular shapes. Alternatively approximate values of *EHTD* may be estimated from results determined for similar shapes.

Most research has used simple Gurnie–Lurie charts to estimate prefreezing and tempering times. The use of Gurnie-Lurie charts with effective thermal diffusivities of meats has received little attention for predicting the time of the phase change period. Variations of factors in Plank's formula are most widely used to estimate the phase change period. Such procedures provide reasonable predictions of overall freezing times for regular shapes of Tylose but their accuracy has not been confirmed over a wide range of freezing rates with different forms of meat such as sides, quarters or primal joints. For such non-homogeneous irregular 3-D shapes, the *EHTD* concept can be used to provide estimates of freezing times but only if some measured freezing times are available to determine the factors in Plank's formula.

Finite difference and finite element methods can be used to predict freezing times but the latter requires much computing time and extensive computer programming. The numerical methods, and Plank's formula, require many factors such as heat transfer coefficients and thermal properties to be known. Without knowledge of these variables, freezing times are unlikely to be predicted reliably to within about 35%. Greater reliability with any prediction method can only be achieved by combined pilot-scale or factory testing.

3.3 Thawing

Thawing may be considered as the reverse of freezing but it is inherently a slower process because of the lower thermal conductivity of the thawed meat at the surface of a product. The majority of thawing operations are carried out on carcasses, quarters or blocks using air, water or steam/vacuum techniques. Maximum thawing rate will be achieved using high air, water or steam temperatures but result in high bacterial loads, an unattractive surface or even denaturation (cooking) of the meat surface. Mathematical models are therefore used to simulate and optimise thawing systems.

The majority of thawing predictions use numerical methods. Bailey *et al.* (1974) compared experimental thawing times for pork legs in air, water and vacuum systems against predictions obtained using an explicit finite difference method. They assumed that pork legs over the range 3 to 6 kg could be represented by spheres with radii between 8·7 and 11·9 cm. Measured and calculated thawing times generally agreed to within 15% with a maximum difference of 2·8 hours in a 10-hour process and maximum percentage error of 34%.

James *et al.* (1977) followed the same approach to the thawing of beef quarters. Forequarters (50–70 kg) were simulated as infinite slabs (17·4–20·3 cm) and hindquarters (50–70 kg) as infinite cylinders (14·7–16·7 cm). The maximum difference between measured and calculated thawing times was 27 hours in a 98-hour process and the maximum percentage error was 38%. The same method, using an infinite slab model of meat blocks during thawing (James and Bailey, 1980), showed maximum differences between measured and calculated thawing times of 7 hours in a 46-hour process with a maximum percentage difference of 57%.

Explicit finite difference methods have also been used by others to predict thawing times (Mascheroni, 1982; Mannapperuma and Singh, 1988). Mascheroni (1982) found minimal (0·1%) differences in predicted thawing times of infinite slabs obtained using explicit or Crank–Nicholson finite difference routines. Results obtained using the explicit method were within the range of experimental scatter of data from James and Bailey (1980). These workers used an equivalent heat transfer coefficient at the surface of the meat but, during thawing, moisture condenses on the surface of the meat and may then freeze and thaw prior to evaporation of moisture from this layer and the meat. Mannapperuma and Singh (1988) simulated these phenomena as six stages and consequently estimated the variation in heat transfer coefficient. Thawing times of blocks of Tylose were predicted using an explicit finite difference technique to within 7·7%. As with many predictions of thawing, predicted temperatures differed most from measured values at the surface when ice is changing to water. This result was also found by Suzuki and Singh (1985), who used an analytical solution to the Fourier equation over short time increments so that the thermal properties could be changed during thawing. Few experimental data are given but a maximum difference between measured and predicted temperature was found to be 4·3°C.

Cleland et al. (1987a), as reported earlier, carried out a wide range of experimental freezing and thawing tests with Tylose and in subsequent papers compared the measured data with predicted values. Simple formulae (Cleland et al., 1987b) were used to predict the thawing times of regular shapes: infinite 2-D rods, finite cylinders and rectangular bricks. They assumed products could be represented as 1-D shapes and then calculated the equivalent heat transfer dimensions (EHTD) or mean conducting path (MCP) to allow for the product shape. The thawing time of the 1-D shape (slab) was calculated using a finite difference method. For rectangular bricks, measured and calculated thawing times agreed to within 15% using the EHTD and 13·7% using the MCP method. Thawing times of bricks of minced beef were predicted to within 9·4%. The same approach (Cleland et al., 1987c) was used to predict the thawing times of 2-D and 3-D shapes of both regular and irregular form. For a 'fish' shape the EHTD and MCP methods enabled predictions of thawing and freezing times (individual thawing times not given) to within 28·5% and 24·1% of measured values.

Cleland et al. (1987d) examined the use of numerical methods and also compared the results with their own experimental data (1987a). The three time level Lees scheme was used in all three models: finite difference, full finite element and a simplified finite element scheme assuming constant thermal properties within an element over a time step. They also carried out a heat balance at each time step (equality of heat flow through the surface to the change in internal enthalpy) to ensure that time and spatial increments were not so large as to cause inaccuracies in the numerical predictions. All methods gave similar results when predicting the thawing times of simple 1-D shapes. Maximum differences between measured and predicted thawing times for rectangular bricks were 7·9% (finite difference) and 12·9% (simple finite element) and for irregular 2-D shapes the differences were 11·3% (full finite element) and 21·9% (simple finite element). Only combined predictions for freezing and thawing are given for more complex 3-D shapes.

The simplest procedures for estimating thawing times are based on using appropriate dimensions in numerical simulations of 1-D shapes. The phase changes occurring during thawing restrict the use of simple plots of log(unaccomplished temperature ratio) versus time which were adopted to estimate chilling times. Plank's equation for predicting freezing times can be adapted for thawing and used in the EHTD and MCP approaches of Cleland and co-workers but little has been reported on the reliability of this method in practical thawing applications. Finite

difference and finite element simulations of realistic shapes during thawing are available but no results have been reported to estimate their
accuracy for predicting thawing times of materials such as carcasses or
quarters when the thermal centre of a product is difficult to locate.

3.4 Industrial Storage, Retail Display and Domestic Storage

Most meat spends a period of time in chilled or frozen storage before
processing and retail sale. Much chilled meat is still stored as an
unwrapped carcass and evaporative weight loss is of significant economic
importance. However, there has been little attempt to predict weight loss
in chilled storage. Pham's lumped parameter model (Pham, 1987b; Pham
and Willix, 1984) has been used to predict weight losses from large foods
stored at freezer temperatures, but the majority of frozen meat is wrapped
before storing.

Fresh meats are sold from chilled retail display cabinets and subsequently stored in domestic refrigerators in the household. Experimental
data has shown a relationship exists between the appearance and weight
loss from meat: losses greater than 0.02 g cm^{-2} of surface area lead to an
unattractive appearance and rejection of the meat by the consumer. Such
losses, which depend on the storage conditions, consequently lead to
financial loss by the retailer or consumer. Numerical models have been
developed to predict product temperature and weight loss during retail
and domestic refrigerated storage and subsequently used to improve the
design of display cabinets.

Fulton et al. (1987) used an explicit finite difference method to solve the
coupled heat and mass transfer problem and predict temperature and
weight losses of meat during retail display. After the mass transfer
coefficient in the model had been chosen to minimise the difference
between measured and predicted data, the maximum error was 29%. The
model was used later (James et al., 1988) to show that the average air
conditions over the storage period were more important than the
fluctuations provided that condensation of moisture did not occur on the
meat surface. An extended version of the model (Fulton and Burfoot,
1988) showed that covering meat led to insignificant weight losses when
holding meat at refrigerated or ambient temperatures. Weight losses from
uncovered meat over a 24-hour period agreed with predicted values to
within 8.9% (storage in domestic refrigerator) or 6.1% (ambient of $21\,^{\circ}$C).

When modelling the thin products found in retail display and particularly when mass transfer occurs, very small spatial increments (typically
< 0.3 mm) are needed to ensure reliability of the numerical methods. Such

distances represent only a fraction of the diameter of a meat fibre which will have an array of thermal and mass diffusion property differences across the diameter. Such differences have been ignored in the above models and average properties have been used along with the assumption that losses occur by diffusion alone. The effects of these assumptions have not been quantified and greater reliability of models should be achieved by modelling the real structure of the meat network.

3.5 Cooking

Most meat is cooked on commercial premises or by the consumer before being eaten. Many cooking methods may be used, including forced and natural convection in air, cooking in water or steam, and infrared and microwave heating. The latter is considered in a separate section because it may be used for purposes other than cooking and introduces its own problems of mathematical modelling.

Cooking induces more and larger changes in meat than any other heating or cooling process. Temperature changes during cooking are often large, more than 50°C at the centre of a meat joint, and weight losses are high, lying between 10% and more than 50% of the initial mass of meat. These changes may have substantial effects on the thermophysical properties, dimensions and structure (texture) of the meat. Simulation of such large changes is difficult but nonetheless important to assist in the optimisation of these operations which determine the value of the cooked meat.

In a study to provide consumers with methods of predicting heating times, Carlheim-Gyllenskold (1970) found that in practice, only the size and shape of a meat joint affect the roasting time. Although other researchers suggest that the type of meat, amount of fat and bone, and orientation of the meat fibres also affect cooking times, Carlheim-Gyllenskold produced charts to predict heating times based on a linear relationship between the square root of roasting time and thickness. Comparisons with Gurnie–Lurie type plots for two and three dimensional shapes were considered too complicated for use by the consumer. However, when graphs of log(unaccomplished temperature ratio) versus time/(initial thickness)^2 were produced for meat slices during frying there was a large scatter in the experimental data. When the original slice thickness was replaced by the final thickness the scatter was considerably reduced. Bengtsson et al.(1976) also found a straight line relationship when meat temperature–time changes during roasting of slabs were presented as a Gurnie–Lurie type plot. When roasting from the frozen state, two straight line regions were found. Sarking (1978) also used the Gurnie–Lurie plots to represent the cooking of hams and produced regression equations to describe the relationship.

Almost all other studies of meat cooking, where predicted and measured temperatures have been compared, have used the finite difference methods for simulation, particularly the explicit version. Bengtsson *et al.* (1976) used a 3-D model to predict temperature changes of meat slabs during roasting. From the limited experimental data shown, the maximum difference between measured and predicted temperatures was 4.4°C when the heat transfer coefficient used in the model was determined from the experimental data. They also carried out one of the few attempts to predict moisture profiles in meat during cooking. Thin meat slabs were heated under various combinations of temperature and time and the moisture contents measured. The moisture profiles in thicker 3-D slabs were then estimated by superimposing this data on the predicted temperature profiles of the thicker slabs. Measured and calculated moisture profiles were in good agreement for meat centre temperatures below 40°C but large differences were found at the meat surface when heating to a centre temperature of 70°C.

Godsalve (1976) compared measured meat temperatures with values predicted from a finite difference method and used the comparison to determine the thermal properties. This produced an anomaly that the thermal diffusivity should be $0 \, \mathrm{W \, m^{-2} \, K^{-1}}$ at 100°C and agreement between measured and predicted temperatures in beef cylinders was still poor. The best agreement was achieved assuming a boiling front at 100°C moved through the meat during heating and the position of this boiling front was changed within the model to provide agreement between measured and predicted temperatures at the centre. Finite difference models of spheres were also used to estimate the cooking times of rolled joints but this showed that thermal properties used in the cylinder model did not allow agreement between measured and predicted temperatures. Predictions of temperatures within beef steaks was achieved, assuming they were infinite slabs and by varying the heat transfer coefficient during heating.

Skjöldebrand and Hallström (Skjöldebrand, 1980; Skjöldebrand and Hallström, 1980; Hallström and Skjöldebrand, 1983) describe the mechanisms of heat and mass transfer when cooking meat products and subsequently (Holtz, 1984; Holtz and Skjöldebrand, 1986) used these principles to develop a finite difference prediction model for meat temperatures. The meat was separated into two imaginary regions, the crust and crumb, which were above and below 100°C, respectively. The heat transfer coefficient and thermal conductivity of the crust were determined from measured temperatures. The maximum difference between measured and predicted centre temperatures of meat loaves was 20°C.

Burfoot (1984, 1987) used the explicit finite difference method to predict the temperatures in infinite slabs and cylinders and then used these with the Newman method to predict the temperatures in finite cylinders composed of regions of fat and lean meat. Average dimensions of the joints during heating were used in the model to produce a maximum error in predicted heating time of 37% in a 107-minute heating period. The same model was used (Burfoot and Griffin, 1988) with the raw meat dimensions to predict the temperature of lean meat cylinders of various lengths and diameters in a natural convection oven. Heating times of cylinders greater than 28 mm long were predicted to within 17% of measured values.

Burfoot and James (1988) and Burfoot and Self (1989) predicted the temperatures of finite cylinders of polyethylene terephthalate (PTFE) or meat during mixed forced and natural convection with heat transfer coefficients measured in separate tests using a heat transfer transducer. Measured and predicted lowest internal temperatures over a 5-hour period agreed to within 10°C for the PTFE and 36°C for the meat. Errors of up to 62% were found in predicted heating times of meat joints to 74°C. Townsend et al. (1989a, 1989b) also used a finite difference model of a finite cylinder during heating, but they also allowed for evaporation of moisture from the meat surface. They predicted that cooking time is proportional to the square root of the mass of a joint. Apart from recommendations in cookery books, they did not compare their predictions with measured heating times.

Heating times of cubes in water have been predicted using finite differences with the Newman method (Burfoot and Self, 1988). Root mean square differences between measured and predicted heating times for PTFE cubes were 3·8 s (heating times of 84 to 560 s) while for meat cubes the difference was 33 s (heating times of 139 to 512 s). The model incorporated the cooked dimensions of the meat.

Dagerskog (1979) used a finite difference model to predict the temperature of meat slices during infrared heating. This model assumed an exponential decay of energy from the meat surface. Meat centre and surface temperatures were predicted to within 6 and 10°C, respectively.

Models using analytical or numerical predictions of temperature in regular shapes can be used to estimate the temperature of meat pieces during cooking. However, these methods rely on choosing values of meat dimensions, heat transfer coefficients and thermophysical properties which provide agreement between measured and predicted data. No realistic models have been produced to predict temperature, mass and dimensional changes of meat during cooking. Some researchers have suggested that mass losses may be predicted from solutions of Fick's law (eqn (2)). Using effective diffusion coefficients, it may be possible to predict weight losses from some meat products using this method. For meat joints during roasting, unrealistically high diffusion coefficients would be required to estimate overall weight losses and would not predict the moisture profiles within the meat. During cooking, meat loses more water because of shrinkage than by the pure diffusional mechanisms represented by eqn (2). Unfortunately, insufficient is known about the mechanisms of mass and dimension changes for such knowledge to be applied in a quantitative model. Studies with meat fibres (Offer et al., 1983) have shown that they shrink radially when their temperature reaches 45–60°C and longitudinally between 60 and 90°C. This shrinkage moves water to the surface of the meat where it may evaporate or drip depending on the temperature driving force between the meat surface and the air. Models have been developed at our Institute which allow the finite difference mesh to shrink during heating, but these models have included many empirical factors. More recently, a similar approach has been adopted to simulate the drying of fish (Balaban, 1989). More extensive models of meat during cooking are being considered which will simulate dimensional changes, assuming that meat may be represented by an array of small diameter flexible tubes (Burfoot and Self, 1989), but no results have been published. Although weight losses during cooking are of considerable economic importance to the meat industry, no models are currently available to predict them accurately.

3.6 Microwave Heating

Microwave ovens are now widely accepted in the domestic kitchen with almost 50% of UK, and 90% of US, households having a microwave oven. Similarly microwave tempering of meat, raising the temperature into the range -4 to $-1°C$, has been adopted worldwide. Microwave pasteurisation plants are being introduced to extend the shelf life of chilled products and sterilisation units have been developed for producing 'ambient shelf stable' foods. Microwave heating is a rapidly expanding sector of food processing technology. Design, testing, monitoring and control of microwave plants is hampered by the difficulty and expense of measuring product temperature during microwave processing. Furthermore, methods of measuring the distribution of electromagnetic field strength, which affects heating rates and profiles, are still at the development stage for high power cavities. Mathematical models have been produced to overcome some of these problems and assist in the development of better processing equipment.

Models (Ohlsson, 1971; Kirk and Holmes, 1975; Nykvist and Decareau, 1976, Self *et al.*, 1990; Taoukis *et al.*, 1987) of microwave heating which have compared predicted product temperatures with data measured in meats have assumed that the energy decays exponentially within the product according to

$$E(x) = E_0 e^{-\alpha x} \text{ and consequently } P(x) = P_0 e^{-2\alpha x} \qquad (26)$$

where the exponential term includes the attenuation coefficient (α). These researchers, except Nykvist and Decareau(1976), assumed the microwave field could be represented as a series of beams which were perpendicular to the food surface. Nykvist and Decareau assumed that the beams could be incident at various angles and these were refracted within the food.

Ohlsson (1971) used a finite difference method to predict temperatures within slabs of beef, ham or simulated meat and Kirk and Holmes (1975) used agar/water mixtures. In both cases, the predictions were within the ranges of experimental scatter. Both groups determined the surface power flux in eqn (26) by experiment, using either calorimetric determination or from the measured temperature profiles. Self *et al.* (1990) adopted the same model to predict temperatures in packaged sliced ham (6, 12 or 24 mm thick) and found good agreement, within 5°C, between measured and predicted temperatures at the centre of 6 mm thick slabs but poor agreement, more than 20°C difference, when using the thicker products. Surface power flux was determined by an iterative process to achieve a balance between maximum rated energy output of the magnetrons supplying energy and the enthalpy change of the meat. Temperatures measured at the geometric centre of a pack were up to 34°C lower than those measured near to the edges showing that the assumption of one-dimensional energy transfer was not valid. They also used a lumped parameter model, assuming a uniform temperature within the meat, which was based on an energy balance between maximum rated magnetron energy supply and enthalpy change of the meat. Temperatures predicted with this model agreed to within 6°C of those obtained with the finite difference model for 6 and 12 mm thick products but differences of 25°C were found with the thickest product.

Nykvist and Decareau (1976) also used a finite difference method to predict the temperatures of finite beef cylinders during cooking. Incidence angles of 'microwave beams' were varied to provide agreement between measured and predicted temperatures and surface power flux was determined by calorimetric measurement. Few experimental data are given but the results indicate maximum differences between measured and predicted temperatures of 4·4°C at the geometric centre and 6·7°C at the position of highest temperature.

Taoukis et al. (1987) considered a phase change problem, thawing of cylinders of meat, in a microwave cavity. They assumed an exponential energy decay within the meat and used a numerical or analytical method to predict the temperature distribution in the meat when the surface reached the thawing temperature. The modified isotherm migration method was then used to calculate the temperature profiles during thawing. This method transforms the system variables such that position is a (time- and temperature-) dependent variable. The resulting equations were then solved using finite differences. Power absorbed was determined experimentally. Measured thawing time (56 minutes) was 22% less than predicted.

None of the models considered the variation of field distribution within the microwave cavities yet experimental data shows wide differences in heating of foods according to position in microwave ovens. The electric fields coupled to magnetic fields cause the heating of foodstuffs in microwave cavities. Predictive methods show wide variations of these fields in cavities such as vehicle engine compartments (Christopoulos and Heering, 1989), hypothermia treatment applicators (Lau and Sheppard, 1986; Lau et al., 1986) and around electronic circuits (Railton and McGeehan, in press). Variations within the high-power operations (600 W to 120 kW) found in food heating are also likely to occur (Sheppard, 1989). These electric and magnetic field distributions are governed by Maxwell's equations. These can be represented by a system of six scalar equations, two of which are (Lau and Sheppard, 1986):

$$\frac{\partial H_x}{\partial t} = \frac{1}{\mu}\left(\frac{\partial E_y}{\partial z} - \frac{\partial E_z}{\partial y}\right) \tag{27}$$

$$\frac{\partial E_y}{\partial t} = \frac{1}{\varepsilon'}\left(\frac{\partial H_x}{\partial z} - \frac{\partial H_z}{\partial x} - \sigma E_y\right) \tag{28}$$

For complex microwave cavities containing foods, two numerical techniques are currently being used in the UK to solve these equations: finite difference and transmission line methods. The finite difference approach is currently receiving most support and models are being developed to predict the electromagnetic field distribution around and within foodstuffs, including meats. In these models the field distributions are predicted and their effect on the product temperature is calculated. This heat may be used for mass transfer, be convected, or be conducted within the food and a finite difference routine calculates the result of these traditional heat/mass transfer mechanisms over a given time step. New dielectric and thermophysical properties of the food are then calculated and the field distribution again predicted for the next time step of traditional heat/mass transfer. New predictions of the field distributions are required because they are affected by the properties of the food which vary as the temperature and composition of the food changes. The above procedures are repeated until the required food temperature is reached. This approach uses a finite difference method to solve many coupled equations; the electric and magnetic field distributions are predicted using a routine with much smaller time steps than are used in the heat/mass transfer problem. Fortunately, the field distribution becomes sufficiently stable over a very short time that many iterations within the time step of the heat/mass transfer problem are not required.

The simple assumption of uniform field distribution in a microwave cavity can be used to enable estimates of the temperature rise at the centre of foods during microwave heating. However, such models require estimates of the power density at the surface of a product and this is usually determined by experiment, often from calculations of the enthalpy change of the product based on internal temperature measurements. Subsequent predictions of product temperature using this data will apply specifically to that product and location in the microwave cavity. Consequently, the use of the surface power flux becomes akin to the use of the surface heat transfer coefficient in simple predictions of temperature changes in conventional heat processing: either of these factors may be changed in a model to provide agreement between measured and predicted temperatures at the centre of a product. The simple models allow interpolation with relative reliability between experimental data, whilst more complex models enable predictions over a wider range but require much more effort to develop and test. The choice of model must depend on its ultimate use.

4 CONCLUSIONS

The scientific literature abounds with papers describing the simulation of heating and cooling of meat or a meat analogue under well-controlled

38 D. BURFOOT

laboratory or pilot-scale conditions. Research papers containing mathematical models were particularly prevalent in the 1970s and early 1980s, and some of these models are now being used by research organisations and larger companies to simulate real-life applications. Not surprisingly, for confidentiality and financial gain, there have been fewer reports of commercial applications.

Most attention has focused on refrigeration processes because of their use commercially around the world. However, expertise has tended to concentrate in different countries. The New Zealand industry produces large volumes of frozen lamb and mutton and research by Cleland and co-workers and Pham in New Zealand has consequently focused on models of freezing. The UK workers, Bailey and James, have concentrated more on modelling of chilling and thawing applications, again owing to commercial interest, although subsequent applications in the freezing of meat blocks, quarters and meat products have also been simulated and used in the design of commercial operations. Swedish research over the last two decades, notably by Ohlsson, Hallstrom, Skjoldebrand, and Dagerskog has led to the development of models of heating processes including the use of microwaves. Whilst Swedish researchers have specialised on simulations of heating meat products, such as the meat loaf and meat balls common in Sweden, UK research has tended to simulate the heating of meat joints and processing of prepared foods. Modelling of chilled retail display has also received most attention in the UK where it is widely accepted and where periods of transporting chilled cooked foods are short compared to those required in the US. Research from the US on other applications, although they are not specific to meat, is described elsewhere in this book. Hayakawa, Singh and co-workers have produced several useful models of meat processing techniques including cooling, chilling and thawing.

A wide range of models are being used, including mixtures of different modelling techniques within given simulation packages. 'Rules of thumb' are still widely used by designers and those on the factory floor. Examples include: double the product thickness in a plate freezer and the freezing time increases four-fold; cooking times are typically 30–45 minutes/kg and cooking losses increase by 1% for each 0·6°C temperature rise above 29°C. Few analytical or numerical models have considered the weight losses from meats during processing despite the fact that any change in the weight loss can substantially effect the financial viability of a commercial operation. Individual companies have produced empirical models for their own use.

Analytical solutions of the Fourier equation, or more often the simple representation of factory data in the form of log(unaccomplished temperature ratio) versus time, have been used widely by research organisations to assist designers and users of chilling and cooling equipment. For freezing applications, modifications of Plank's formula are numerous and although they appear simple to use, much care must be taken in the choice of factors required in these models. Many substitute the latent heat value in the original formula for an enthalpy change covering the entire freezing or phase change and tempering periods. Further, the choice of thermal conductivity and heat transfer coefficient used in the formula can lead to wide differences in computed freezing times. Often, the advice of the developer of the model is needed to provide guidance in the use of the formulae. Nonetheless, the use of Plank's equation, or modifications of it, can produce predictions of freezing time which are adequate for some commercial applications.

For the commercial user with little time to fully explore the intricacies of some of the modifications of Plank's formula applicable to more complex situations, there is the choice of using a consultancy or the 'black box' approach. The latter generally involves the purchase of a computer package which uses equations based on Plank's formula or discrete numerical methods to predict processing times and product temperatures. Unfortunately, if the user has little knowledge of the equations used or product thermal properties incorporated into the programs, default values are used which may lead to predictions which are not representative of the process being simulated. There still remains a need for a well-documented and 'menu-driven' suite of computer programs for use by the practitioner in the meat and allied industries.

All mathematical models must include some factors which are pertinent to the particular application, for example heat transfer coefficients and thermal properties, which the user of the model may need to decide for himself. However, the discrete numerical methods require further decisions as to which time and spatial increments should be used in a particular circumstance. Such decisions do require a knowledge of the mathematical technique used to solve the model. Finite difference methods are the most commonly used in the meat industry although each of these requires different stability criteria. However, for problems incorporating a phase change or large temperature or mass gradients, the implicit, three times level, and explicit schemes all require small time and spatial increments. The explicit method is the easiest to program onto a computer but generally provides a slightly less accurate solution to the

Fourier equation than the other methods; however, it is still used in many models. Finite element schemes require the most sophisticated programming if the computer package is to allow for simulations of temperature/mass changes within any food shape. Computing times are large using these schemes and this has led to many researchers concentrating on the finite difference methods. The transmission line method has been used very little in the meat industry and has been mentioned here because some simulations of microwave processing may be developed using this method in the future, and it has been applied to simulate processing of other foodstuffs. The control volume approach described by Patankar (1980) has not been reported openly with reference to meat processing and so was not considered in the present review. However, this approach, which is similar to the finite difference method, is being used by several research organisations.

One of the problems with published models is that many contain large numbers of factors which can be varied to provide agreement between predicted and measured temperatures. Indeed, the more complex the model, and the more limited the available experimental data, the better the agreement which can be achieved between measured and predicted data. Such agreement only demonstrates the reliability of the model over a very restricted range of processing parameters and often the model cannot be used reliably to predict product temperatures under other processing circumstances. A better understanding needs to be developed of the factors used in the models, including heat transfer coefficients and thermal properties, and of the actual mechanisms involved in transferring heat and mass to, from and within meat. Such knowledge is beginning to be developed. Mannapperuma and Singh (1988) have produced a procedure for estimating heat transfer coefficients during thawing, Cleland et al. (1982) have suggested that freezing rate affects the thermal properties of materials, Burfoot and Self (1989) suggest modelling the structure of meat to predict processing times and weight losses and models of field distributions in microwave cavities are being produced to improve the accuracy of models of microwave processing. All of this work is improving our understanding of the mechanisms involved in meat processing and increasing the reliability of predictions. In addition, further work is needed to predict the interactions between meat products and their processing environment. For example, models are required to predict air flow variations within arrays of products and the consequent effects on product temperature, quality and safety.

New mathematical techniques which improve the ease and speed of solving mathematical models should be used when they become available, but more effort now needs to concentrate on three areas. The food scientist needs to understand better the changes of meat structure during processing so that those ideas can be formulated into prediction models. More controlled processes are required from the food engineer so that plant operation can be simulated without the need to consider widely fluctuating processing variables. Simpler models for incorporation into on-line control systems could be then be more easily applied. A further area, food engineering science, is then needed to determine the factors relating heat and mass changes of the meat to the changes in its environment and produce models based on the work of the scientists and engineers. These three approaches would lead to more reliable models and more practical application.

ACKNOWLEDGEMENTS

Many thanks to S. J. James (AFRC Institute of Food Research) and C. Railton (University of Bristol) for their helpful suggestions in the preparation of this manuscript.

REFERENCES

Arce, J. A., Potluri, P. L., Schneider, K. C., Sweat, V. E. & Dutson, T. R. (1983). Modelling beef carcass cooling using a finite element technique. *Trans. ASAE*, **26**, 950–4, 960.

Bailey, C. & Cox, R. P. (1976) The chilling of beef carcasses. *Proc. Inst. Refrig.*, **72**, 76–90.

Bailey, C., James, S. J., Kitchell, A. G. & Hudson, W. R. (1974) Air-, water and vacuum thawing of frozen pork legs. *J. Sci. Fd Agric.*, **25**, 81–97.

Balaban, M. (1989). Effect of volume change in foods on the temperature and moisture content predictions of simultaneous heat and moisture transfer models. *J. Food Proc. Engng*, **12**, 67–88.

Bazan, H. C. & Mascheroni, R. H. (1984). Heat transfer with simultaneous change of phase in freezing boned mutton. *Lat. Am. J. Heat Mass Transfer*, **8**, 55–76.

Bengtsson, N. E., Jakobsson, B. & Dagerskog, M. (1976). Cooking of beef by oven roasting: a study of heat and mass transfer. *J. Food Sci.*, **41**, 1047–53.

Bonacina, C. & Comini, G. (1971). On a numerical method for the solution of the unsteady state heat conduction equation with temperature dependent parameters, *Proc. 13th Int. Cong. Refrig.*, Washington, Vol. 2, pp. 329–36.

42	D. BURFOOT

Bonacina, C. & Comini, G. (1973). On the solution of the nonlinear heat conduction equations by numerical methods. *Int. J. Heat Mass Transfer*, 16, 581–9.
Bonacina, C., Comini, G., Fasano, A. & Primicerio, M. (1974). On the estimation of thermophysical properties in nonlinear heat-conduction problems, *Int. J. Heat Mass Transfer*, 17, 861–7.
Brisson Lopes, J. M. & Domingos, J. J. D. (1979). The numerical computation of freezing processes in bodies of arbitrary shape. *15th Int. Cong. Refrig.*, Venice, 1979, B1-82.
Brown, T. & James, S. J. (1988). Process design data for pork chilling, *Proc. AFRC Institute of Food Research–Bristol*, Subject Day 'Meat Chilling', 23 February, 1988.
Burfoot, D. (1984). Predicting the effect of fat thickness and distribution on the heating times of joints of rolled meat. *Proc. 30th Euro. Meeting of Meat Res. Workers*, Paper 6:31, 312–13.
Burfoot, D. (1987). Effect of thickness and location of minced fat on cooking times and weight losses of composite beef joints. *Int. J. Food Sci. Technol.*, 22, 49–58.
Burfoot, D. & Griffin, W. J. (1988). Effect of dimensions on the heating times and weight losses of cylindrical beef joints. *Int. J. Food Sci. Technol.*, 23, 487–94.
Burfoot, D. & James, S. J. (1983). Problems in mathematically modelling the cooking of a joint of meat, Proc. COST 91 Seminar, Athens, 1983. In *Thermal Processing and the Quality of Foods*, 1st edn, ed. P. Zeuthen *et al.* Elsevier Applied Science Publishers, Barking, pp. 467–72.
Burfoot, D. & James, S. J. (1988). The effect of spatial variations of heat transfer coefficient on meat processing times. *J. Food Eng.*, 7, 41–61.
Burfoot, D. & Self, K. P. (1988). Prediction of the heating times of cubes of beef during water cooking. *Int. J. Food Sci. Technol.*, 23, 247–57.
Burfoot, D. & Self, K. P. (1989). Predicting the heating times of beef joints. *J. Food Engng.*, 9, 251–74.
Califano, A. N. & Calvelo, A. (1980). Weight loss prediction during meat chilling. *Meat Science*, 1980, 5–15.
Carlheim-Gyllenskod, H. (1970). The penetration of salt and heat into foodstuffs while being cooked. *Acta Polytechnica Scandinavica*, Ch. 93, Stockholm, Sweden.
Carslaw, H. S. & Jaeger, J. C. (1959). *Conduction of Heat in Solids*, 2nd edn, Clarendon Press, Oxford.
Charm, S. E., Brand, D. H. & Baker, D. W. (1972). A simple method for estimating freezing and thawing times of cylinders and slabs. *ASHRAE Journal*, 14, 39–45.
Christopoulus, C. & Heering, J. L. (1989). Simulation of the electromagnetic environment inside vehicles. *Proc. 20th ISATA*, Florence, Italy, May/June 1989.
Cleland, A. C. (1986). A review of methods for predicting the duration of freezing processes. In *Food Engineering and Process Applications*, ed. M. Le Maguer & P. Jelen. Elsevier Applied Science, London, pp. 41–53.
Cleland, A. C. & Earle, R. L. (1977). A comparison of analytical and numerical methods of predicting freezing times of foods. *J. Food Sci.*, 42, 1390–5.
Cleland, A. C. & Earle, R. L. (1979a). A comparison of methods for predicting the freezing times of cylindrical and spherical foodstuffs. *J. Food Sci.*, 44 958–63, 970.

Cleland, A. C. & Earle, R. L. (1979b). Prediction of freezing times for foods in rectangular packages. *J. Food Sci.*, **44**, 964–70.

Cleland, A. C. & Earle, R. L. (1982a). A simple method for prediction of heating and cooling rates in solids of various shape. *Int. J. Refrig.*, **5**, 98–105.

Cleland, A. C. & Earle, R. L. (1982b). Freezing time prediction for foods–a simplified procedure. *Int. J. Refrig.*, **5**, 134–40.

Cleland, A. C., Earle, R. L. & Cleland, D. J. (1982). The effect of freezing rate on the accuracy of numerical freezing calculations. *Int. J. Refrig.*, **5**, 294–301.

Cleland, D. J., Cleland, A. C., Earle, R. L. & Byrne, S. J. (1984). Prediction of rates of freezing, thawing or cooling in solids of arbitrary shape using the finite element method. *Int. J. Refrig.*, **7**, 6–13.

Cleland, D. J., Cleland, A. C., Earle, R. L. & Byrne, S. J. (1987a) Experimental data for freezing and thawing of multi-dimensional objects. *Int. J. Refrig.*, **10**, 22–31.

Cleland, D. J., Cleland, A. C. & Earle, R. L. (1987b). Prediction of freezing and thawing times for multi-dimensional shapes by simple formulae: I. Regular shapes. *Int. J. Refrig.*, **10**, 156–64.

Cleland, D. J., Cleland, A. C. & Earle, R. L. (1987c). Prediction of freezing and thawing times for multi-dimensional shapes by simple formulae: II. Irregular shapes. *Int. J. Refrig.*, **10**, 234–40.

Cleland, D. J., Cleland, A. C., Earle, R. L. & Byrne, S. J. (1987d). Prediction of freezing and thawing times for multi-dimensional shapes by numerical methods, *Int. J. Refrig.*, **10**, 32–9.

Comini, G., Del Guidice, S., Lewis, R. W. & Zienkiewicz, O. C. (1974). Finite element solution of non-linear heat conduction problems with special reference to phase change. *Int. J. Numer. Methods Eng.*, **8**, 613–24.

Cox, R. P. & Bailey, C. (1977). Product loads for beef carcass chilling, *Proc. Inst. Refrig.*, **74**, 11–28.

Creed, P. G. & James, S. J. (1983). The freezing times of liver in a vertical plate freezer. *Proc. 16th Int. Cong. Refrig. Paris*, Vol. 4, pp. 145–51.

Creed, P. G. & James, S. J. (1984). The prediction of freezing and thawing times of mutton carcasses. *Proc. 30th Eur. Meeting Meat Res. Workers*, Bristol, 1984, 2:5, 49–60.

Creed, P. G. & James, S. J. (1985) Heat transfer during the freezing of liver in a plate freezer. *J. Food Sci.*, **50**, 285–8, 294.

Cullwick, T. D. C. & Earle, R. L. (1971). Prediction of freezing times of meat in plate freezers. *Proc. 13th Int. Cong. Refrig.*, Vol. 3, pp. 397–401.

Dagerskog, M. (1979) Infra-red radiation for food processing. II. Calculation of heat penetration during infra-red frying of meat products. *Lebensm.-Wiss u.-Technol.*, **12**, 252–7.

Dalgleish, N. & Ede, A. J. (1965). Charts for determining centre, surface and mean temperatures in regular geometric solids during heating or cooling, National Engineering Laboratory Report No. 192, Glasgow, Scotland.

De Baerdemaeker, J., Singh, R. P. & Segerlind, L. J. (1977). Modelling heat transfer in foods using the finite-element method. *J. Food Proc. Engng*, **1**, 37–50.

De Michelis, A. & Calvelo, A. (1983). Freezing time predictions for brick and cylindrical-shaped foods. *J. Food Sci.*, **48**, 909–13, 934.

Dusinberre, G. M. (1949). *Numerical Analysis of Heat Flow.* McGraw-Hill, New York.

Earle, R. L. (1959). Physical aspects of the freezing of cartoned meat. Meat Industry Research Institute of New Zealand Bulletin No. 2.

Earle, R. L. & Earl, W. B. (1966). Freezing rate studies in blocks of meat of simple shape. *Proc. 3rd Int. Heat Transfer Conf.* (1966), 152–8.

Earle, R. L. & Fleming, A. K. (1967). Cooling and freezing lamb and mutton carcasses, 1. Cooling and freezing rates in legs. *Food Technology*, 21, 79–84.

Fleming, A. K. (1970). Physical aspects of meat cooling. *Bull. IIF/IIR Annexe 1970–3*, (Leningrad), 151–60.

Fleming, A. K. (1971a). The numerical calculation of freezing processes, *Proc. 13th Int. Cong. Refrig.*, Vol. 2, pp. 303–11.

Fleming, A. K. (1971b). The numerical calculation of freezing processes, Thesis for Technical Licentiate Degree, Technical University of Norway, Trondheim.

Fleming, A. K. (1972). Freezing processes. *Proc. 14th Meat Ind. Res. Conf.*, Meat Industry Research Institute of New Zealand, pp. 51–4.

Fleming, A. K. & Earle, R. L. (1966). Cooling and freezing of lamb and mutton carcasses. Meat Industry Research Institute of New Zealand Report, October, 1966.

Fleming, A. K. & Earle, R. L. (1968). Cooling and freezing of lamb and mutton carcasses, 2. Weight loss during cooling. *Food Technology*, 22, 100–4.

Fulton, G. S. & Burfoot, D. (1988). Predicting the weight loss and appearance of meat stored under refrigerated or ambient conditions. *Proc. 10th Int. Home Econ. Res. Conf.* (1988), pp. 135–146.

Fulton, G. S., Burfoot, D., Bailey, C. & James, S. J. (1987). Predicting the weight loss from unwrapped chilled meat in retail displays. *XVIIth Int. Cong. Refrig.*, Vienna, 1987, C2–8.

Fulton, G. S., Burfoot, D., James, S. J. & Bailey, C. (1990). Applications of mathematics to heat processing in the meat industry. *Proc. 3rd European Conference on Mathematics in Industry*, University of Strathclyde, 1988. Kluwer Academic Publishers. B. G. Tuebner, Stuttgart, pp. 343–51.

Gac, A. & Tupin, J. P. (1964). Chilling of beef. Bulletin Technique du Gente Rural, No. 69.

Godsalve, E. (1976). Heat and mass transfer in cooking meat, Ph.D. thesis, University of Minnesota Department of Chemical Engineering.

Golovkin, N., Chizov, G. & Alamovski, I. (1955). A trial thermophysical estimation of the process of cooling foods in air. *Proc. 9th Int. Cong. Refrig.*, Vol. 2, Paper 4.414, pp. 4.161–6.

Gurney, H. P. & Lurie, J. (1923). Charts for estimating temperature distributions in heating or cooling solid shapes. *Ind. Eng. Chem.*, 15, 1170–2.

Hallstrom, H. & Skjoldebrand, C. (1983). Heat and mass transport in solid foods. In *Developments in Food Preservation*, Vol. 2, ed. S. Thorne. Applied Science Publishers, London, pp. 61–94.

Hayakawa, K. (1977). Estimation of heat transfer during freezing or defrosting of food. *IIF/IIR Comm C1, C2* (Karlsruhe), 293–301.

Hayakawa, K. & Bakal, A. (1973). Formulas for predicting transient temperatures in food during freezing or thawing. *AIChe Symp. Ser. No. 132*, 69, 14–25.

Hayakawa, K., Nonino, C. & Succar, J. (1983a). Two dimensional heat conduction in food undergoing freezing: predicting freezing time of rectangular or finitely cylindrical food, *J. Food Sci.*, **48**, 1841–8.

Hayakawa, K., Nonino, C., Succar, J., Comini, G. & Del Guidice, S. (1983b). Two-dimensional heat conduction in food undergoing freezing: development of computerized model. *J. Food Sci.*, **48**, 1849–53.

Heldman, D. R. & Singh, R. P. (1981). *Food Processing Engineering*, 2nd edn., AVI Publ., Westport, CT, pp. 124–42.

Herbert, L. S. & Lovett, D. A. (1979). New measurements of cooling times in blast freezers, *Aust. Refrig., Air Cond. Heat*, September, 8–14.

Hodgson, T. (1966). The effect of environmental conditions on the chilling times of meat. *Bull. IIR Annexe-1*, 635–46.

Holtz, E. (1984). Baking of meat products in convection oven—a study of heat and mass transfer. Licentiatavhandling, Lund University, Sweden.

Holtz, E. & Skjoldebrand, C. (1986). Simulation of the temperature of a meat loaf during the cooking process. *J. Food Eng.*, **5**, 109–21.

Hsiao, J. S. (1985). An efficient algorithm for finite difference analyses of heat transfer with melting and solidification. *Numer. Heat Transfer*, **8**, 653–66.

Hung, Y. C. & Thompson, D. R. (1983). Freezing time prediction for slab shape foodstuffs by an improved analytical method. *J. Food Sci.*, **48**, 555–60.

IIR (International Institute of Refrigeration), (1986). *Recommendations for the Processing and Handling of Frozen Foods*, 3rd edn. IIR, Paris.

Ilicali, C. (1989). A simplified analytical model for freezing time calculation in brick-shaped foods. *J. Food Proc. Engng*, **11**, 177–91.

James, S. J. & Bailey, C. (1980). Air and vacuum thawing of unwrapped boneless meat blocks. *Proc. Inst. Refrig.*, **76**, 44–51.

James, S. J., Creed, P. G. & Roberts, T. A. (1977). Air thawing of beef quarters. *J. Sci. Fd Agric.*, **28**, 1109–19.

James, S. J., Fulton, G. S., Swain, M. V. L. & Burfoot, D. (1983). Modelling the effect of temperature and relative humidity fluctuations on weight loss in retail display. *Int. Inst. Refrig. Refrigeration for Food and People*, 1988–3, Brisbane, pp. 111–19.

Jenson, V. G. & Jeffreys, G. V. (1977). *Mathematical Methods in Chemical Engineering*. Academic Press, London pp. 416–21.

Johns, P. B. & Pulko, S. H. (1987). Modelling of heat and mass transfer in foodstuffs. In *Food Structure and Behaviour*, ed. J. M. V. Blanshard & P. Lillford. Academic Press, London, pp. 199–218.

Kerens, G. & Visser, C. J. (1978). Environmental requirements during beef carcass chilling. CSIR (South Africa) Report ME 1597.

Kern, D. Q. (1959). *Process Heat Transfer*. McGraw-Hill Kogakusha, Tokyo, pp. 639–64.

Kirk, D. & Holmes, A. W. (1975). The heating of foodstuffs in a microwave oven. *J. Food Technol.*, **10**, 375–84.

Lacroix, C. & Castaigne, F. (1987). Simple method for freezing time calculations for brick and cylindrical shaped food products. *Can. Inst. Food Sci. Techol. J.*, **20**, 342–9.

Lau, R. W. M. & Sheppard, R. J. (1986). The modelling of biological systems in three dimensions using the time domain finite-difference method: I. The implementation of the model. *Phys. Med. Biol.*, **31**, 1247–56.

Lau, R. W. M., Sheppard, R. J., Howard, G. & Bleehan, N. M. (1986). The modelling of biological systems in three dimensions using the time domain finite-difference method: II. The application and experimental evaluation of the method in hypothermia applicator design. *Phys. Med. Biol.*, **31**, 1257–66.

LeBlanc, D. I., Kok, R. & Timbers, G. E. (in press). Freezing of a parallelepiped food product: II. Comparison of experimental and calculated results. *Int. J. Refrig.*

Lees, M. (1966). A linear three level difference scheme for quasilinear parabolic equations. *Math. Comput.*, **20**, 516–22.

Loeffen, M. P. F., Earle, R. L. & Cleland, A. C. (1981). Two simple methods for predicting food freezing times with time-variable boundary conditions, *J. Food Sci.*, **46**, 1032–4.

Loginov, L. I. (1976). Applying numerical methods for cooling process calculation. *17th Int. Congress on Refrigeration*, Madrid (1976), pp. 717–29.

Longdill, G. R. & Pham, Q. T. (1982). Weight losses from New Zealand lamb carcases from slaughter to market. *IIR Bull. Annexe 1982-1*, 123–32.

Mannapperuma, J. D. & Singh, R. P. (1988). Thawing of frozen foods in humid air. *Rev. Int. Froid*, **11**, 173–86.

Mascheroni, R. H. (1982). The ultilization of numerical methods for the solution of the heat balance during the thawing of meat blocks under industrial conditions, *Lat. Am. J. Heat Mass Transfer*, **6**, 13–29.

Mascheroni, R. H. & Calvelo, A. A. (1982). A simplified model for freezing time calculations in foods. *J. Food Sci.*, **47**, 1201–7.

Mazzola, P., De Cindio, B., Miglioli, L., Massini, R., Dipollina, G., Pedrelli, T. & Romano, V. (1986). Application of the finite-element method to the sterilisation of canned beef homogenate. *Industria Conserve*, **61**, 3–8.

Newman, A. B. (1936). Heating and cooling rectangular and cylindrical solids. *Ind. Eng. Chem.*, **28**, 545–8.

Nykvist, W. E. & Decareau, R. V. (1976). Microwave meat roasting. *J. Microwave Power*, **11**, 3–24.

Offer, G., Restall, D. & Trinick, J. (1983). Water holding in meat. In *Recent Advances in the Chemistry of Meat*, ed. A. J. Bailey. Proc. Symp. organised by Food Chemistry Group of Royal Soc. Chem. and Food Group of Soc. Chem. Ind. held at AFRC Meat Research Institute, April 1983.

Ohlsson, T. (1971). Microwave heating profiles in foods—a comparison between heating experiments and computer simulation. A research note. *Microwave Energy Applications Newsletter*, **4**, 3–8.

Patankar, S. W. (1980). *Numerical heat transfer and fluid flow*. Hemisphere Publishing Corporation, New York.

Perjes, P. (1978). Computational-model for the chilling of suspended meat. *IIF/IIR Commission C2, D1, D2* (Budapest, Hungary), 1978–2.

Pflug, I. J., Blaisdell, J. L. & Kopelman, J. (1965). Developing temperature–time curves for objects that can be approximated by a sphere, infinite plate, or infinte cylinder. *ASHRAE Trans.*, **71**, 238–48.

Pham, Q. T. (1984). Extension to Plank's equation for predicting the freezing times of foodstuffs of simple shapes. *Int. J. Refrig.*, **7**, 377–83.

Pham, Q. T. (1985a). Analytical method for predicting freezing times of rectangular blocks of foodstuffs. *Int. J. Refrig.*, **8**, 43–7.

Pham, Q. T. (1985b). A fast, unconditionally stable finite-difference scheme for heat conduction with phase change. *Int. J. Heat Mass Transfer*, **28**, 2079–84.

Pham, Q. T. (1986a). Freezing foodstuffs with variations in environmental conditions. *Int. J. Refrig.*, **9**, 290–5.

Pham, Q. T. (1986b). Simplified equation for predicting the freezing time of foodstuffs. *J. Food Technol.*, **21**, 209–19.

Pham, Q. T. (1987a). A note on some finite-difference methods for heat conduction with phase change. *Numerical Heat Transfer*, **11**, 353–9.

Pham, Q. T. (1987b). Moisture transfer due to temperature fluctuations, *J. Food Engng*, **6**, 33–49.

Pham, Q. T. (1989). Effect of supercooling on freezing time due to dendritic growth of ice crystals. *Int. J. Refrig.*, **12**, 295–300.

Pham, Q. T. & Willix, J. (1984). A model of food desiccation in frozen storage, *J. Food Sci.*, **49**, 1275–81, 1294.

Plank, R. (1941). Beitrage zur Berechnung und Bewertung der gefriergeschwindigkeit von Lebenmitteln., *Z. ges. kalteind*, **10**, 1–16.

Purwadaria, H. K. & Heldman, D. R. (1982). A finite element model for prediction of freezing rates in food products with anomalous shapes. *Trans. ASAE*, **25**, 827–32.

Radford, R. D., Herbert, L. S. & Lovett, D. A. (1976). Chilling of meat—a mathematical model for heat and mass transfer. *1st Annexe Bull IIR*, (Melbourne), 323–30.

Railton, C. J. & McGeehan, J. P. (in press). Analysis of microstrip discontinuities using the finite difference time domain technique. *IEEE Transactions on Microwave Theory and Techniques.*

Ramaswamy, H. S., Lo, K. V. & Tung, M. A. (1982). Simplified equations for transient temperatures in conductive foods with convective heat transfer at the surface, *J. Food Sci.*, **47**, 2042–7, 2065.

Rolfe, E. (1967). The Chilling and Freezing of Foodstuffs. In '*Biochemical and Biological Engineering Science*', ed. N. Blakebrough. Academic Press, New York. pp. 137–207.

Salvadori, V. O., Reynoso, R. O., De Michelis, A. & Mascheroni, R. H. (1987). Freezing time predictions for regular shaped foods: a simplified graphical method. *Int. J. Refrig.*, **10**, 357–61.

Sarkin, R. J. (1978). Computerized cooking simulation of meat products. *J. Food Sci.*, **43**, 1140–3.

Schneider, G. E. (1984). Discrete methods in heat conduction: a review. In *Advances in Transport Processes*, Vol. III ed. A. S. Mujumdar & R. A. Mashelkar. Wiley Eastern Ltd, New Delhi, India, pp. 118–204.

Self, K. & Burfoot, D. (1986). Predicting the effect of air distribution on cooling time. *IIF/IIR Commission C2* (Bristol), 281–7.

Self, K. P., Burfoot, D., Wilkins, T. J. & James, S. J. (1990). Microwave pasteurisation of pre-packed sliced ham. In *Process Engineering in the Food Industry*: Vol. 2, *Convenience Foods and Quality Assurance*, ed. R. W. Field and J. A. Howell. Elsevier Science Publishers, Barking, pp. 33–44.

Sheppard, R. J. (1989). Browning and crisping theory: could microwaves brown food? *Packaging Technology and Science*, **2**, 63–7.

48 D. BURFOOT

4
Skjoldebrand, C. (1980). Convection oven frying: heat and mass transport between air and product. *J. Food Sci.*, **45**, 1354–8, 1362.
Skjoldebrand, C. & Hallstrom, B. (1980). Convection oven frying: heat and mass transport in the product. *J. Food Sci.*, **45**, 1347–53.
Srinivasa Murphy, S., Krishna Murphy, M. V. & Ramachandran, A. (1976). Heat transfer during air cooling and storing of moist food products—II. Spherical and cylindrical shapes. *Trans. ASHRAE*, **19**, 577–82.
Suzuki, K. & Singh, R. P. (1985). A computer-aided calculation of temperature history during thawing of foods. *Trans. ASAE*, **28**, 1330–5.
Taoukis, P., Davis, E. A., Gordon, J. & Talmon, Y. (1987). Mathematical modeling of microwave thawing by the modified isotherm migration method. *J. Food Sci.*, **52**, 455–63.
Townsend, M. A., Gupta, S. & Pitts, W. H. (1989a). The roast: nonlinear modelling and simulation. *J. Food Proc. Engng*, **11**, 17–42.
Townsend, M. A., Gupta, S. & Pitts, W. H. (1989b). Optimal roasting, *J. Food Proc. Engng*, **11**, 117–45.
Whiteman, J. R. (ed.) (1973). *The Mathematics of Finite Elements and Applications*. Academic Press, London.

Chapter 2

MODELLING OF MEMBRANE PROCESSES

MUNIR CHERYAN and DEBRA J. NICHOLS

Department of Food Science, University of Illinois, Urbana, IL, USA

NOTATION

A	Membrane permeability coefficient
A	Constant in dimensionless mass transfer correlation
A	Virial coefficient in expanded osmotic pressure relationship
A	Membrane area
b	Friction (drag) factor $(1 + f_{23}/f_{21})$
b	Parameter in linear IT (irreversible thermodynamics) model
B	Solute permeability coefficient
B	Constant in cross-flow microfiltration equation
c	Concentration
c	Constant in cross-flow microfiltration equation
$\tilde{c}_2$	$\Delta\pi/(RT\Delta \ln a_2)$, where a is activity
$(c_2)_{\ln}$	Log mean solute concentration difference
C	Concentration
D	Diffusion coefficient
D_p	Particle diameter
f	Friction coefficient
F	Frictional force
G	Gibbs free energy
H	Hydraulic permeability for pore flow $(\varepsilon r^2/8\eta)$
i	Number of ions in osmotic pressure equation
J	Flux
k	Mass transfer coefficient
K	Distribution coefficient
K^*	Hydraulic permeability coefficient

K^{**}	Total water permeability coefficient
K_2	Generalized solute permeability coefficient
K'	Transport coefficient
L	Phenomenological coefficient
L_p	Hydraulic permeability coefficient
L_π	Osmotic permeability coefficient
M	Molecular weight
n	Number of moles of component i
N	Number of moles
P	Pressure
P^*	Diffusive permeability coefficient
ΔP_T	Transmembrane pressure
$\bar{P}_2$	Local solute permeability coefficient $[J_2/(\Delta c_2/\lambda)]_{Jv}=0$
P_h	Specific permeability coefficient
r	Radius
R	Universal gas constant
$\tilde{R}$	Solute rejection $[1-(c_2''/c_2')]$
R	Resistance (to solvent flow)
R_{max}	Maximum solute rejection
t	Tortuosity factor
t	Time
T	Temperature
v	Transverse velocity of liquid
$\bar{v}$	Partial molar volume
V	Volume of liquid through membrane
x	Length
X	Mole fraction
X	Conjugated forces in Onsager relationship
y	Transverse length
α	Specific cake resistance in microfiltration
α	Coefficient in non-linear membrane transport model
α	Exponent of Reynolds number term in dimensionless mass transfer correlation
β	Exponent on Schmidt number term in dimensionless mass transfer correlation
δ	Boundary layer thickness
Δ	Difference between conditions on either side of membrane
ε	Fractional pore area or number of pores per unit area

ε_b	Porosity of bed in microfiltration equation
η	Viscosity
κ	Transport coefficient
λ	Effective membrane thickness
μ	Chemical potential
π	Osmotic pressure
σ	Reflection coefficient $(\Delta P_T/\Delta\pi)_{J_v}=0$
ω	Solute permeability coefficient $(J_2/\Delta\pi)_{J_v}=0$
ρ_L	Density of liquid
ϕ	Dissipation function
ϕ	Ratio of hydraulic permeability to diffusive permeability coefficients in diffusion-flow model

Superscripts

$'$	Interface conditions on high-pressure side of membrane
$''$	Interface conditions on low-pressure side of membrane
b	Bulk fluid conditions
o.	Pure solvent
s	Compressibility coefficient in microfiltration

Subscripts

1	Solvent
2	Solute
3	Membrane
B	Bulk fluid conditions in ultrafiltration
c	Cake of solids built up on microfiltration membrane
F	Feed side of membrane
G	Gel-layer in ultrafiltration
i	Inlet
i	Any component of a mixture
j	Any component other than i of a mixture
m	At the membrane surface
o	Outlet
p	Pore
p	Permeate side of membrane
s	Solute
T	Transmembrane
v	Volume
w	Water

1 INTRODUCTION

Membrane separation processes are based on the ability of semipermeable membranes, of the appropriate physical and chemical nature to
discriminate between molecules primarily on the basis of size, and to a
lesser extent, on shape and chemical composition. A membrane's role is
to act as a selective barrier, enriching certain components in a feed
stream, and depleting it of others. In this regard, the phenomenon is very
similar to 'osmosis', which has been observed and studied for more than
200 years, beginning with the efforts of the French scientist Abbé Nollet
in 1748. However, there was very little interest in the osmosis process
outside the academic, medical and photographic fields until the early
1950s, mostly because membranes capable of withstanding high pressures
while giving both high flux rates and high rejections were not available.
Serious study of reverse osmosis (RO) as a practical tool for the
production of potable water from brackish or saline water began in 1953
when the US Department of the Interior, Office of Saline Water, began
supporting research projects aimed at developing RO technology for
desalination. The first real breakthrough was made by Reid and Breton
in 1959 who, while screening membrane materials for desalination,
discovered that cellulose acetate membranes gave high rejections and
reasonable fluxes (dewatering rates) (Reid and Breton, 1959). Shortly
thereafter, Loeb and Sourirajan (1960, 1962) developed the casting
procedure for asymmetric cellulose acetate membranes and demonstrated
that flux could be greatly improved by making asymmetric rather than
homogeneous membranes.

This landmark event is generally considered the birth of modern
membrane separations technology. Originally termed the 'surface skim-
ming' of sea water or brackish water for the production of pure water by
a non-thermal energy-efficient method, it has, since then, led to a vast
array of applications unmatched by any other processing technique in its
variety. Desalination and water treatment by reverse osmosis is probably
the earliest and best-known application. The decade of the 1970s saw
increasing usage in the chemical process industries (paint, textiles, oil
recovery, pulp and paper). In the 1980s, the most significant inroads made
by this technology were in the food and biotechnology processing
industries, where reverse osmosis (RO) and its sister processes, ultrafiltration (UF) and cross-flow microfiltration (MF), found increasing uses as a
gentle and efficient way of fractionating, concentrating and clarifying a
variety of food and biological systems, from milk products, fruit juices

and alcoholic beverages to fermentation broths, protein fractions and wastewaters.

1.1 Principles

The chemical nature and physical properties of the membrane control which components are retained and which permeate through the membrane. So the distinction between reverse osmosis (RO), ultrafiltration (UF) and microfiltration (MF) and the comparatively newer process, nanofiltration (NF), is somewhat arbitrary, although the mechanisms of transport through each type of membrane may differ and, accordingly, so will the operating strategies for optimum performance. Depending on the chemical nature and physical properties of the membrane (primarily pore size distribution), one can concentrate or dewater by reverse osmosis (RO), fractionate components in solution by ultrafiltration (UF) and clarify slurries or remove suspended matter by microfiltration (MF), as shown schematically in Fig. 1. In all three processes, hydraulic pressure (through a pump) is used to provide the driving force for permeation. In the case of reverse osmosis, it is to overcome the chemical potential difference between the concentrate and the permeate, expressed in terms of the osmotic pressure (see Section 1.2). The process is very simple, involving only the pumping of the liquid mixture across the appropriate

MEMBRANE SEPARATIONS

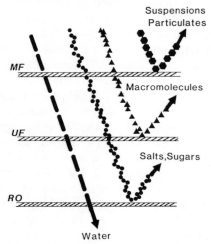

FIG. 1.   Schematic of membrane processes.

membrane. The pressure applied to the feed side increases the thermodynamic activities of the solutes and solvents by an amount proportional to their partial molar volumes. The difference in the thermodynamic activity on either side of the membrane is the driving force for the permeation of solutes and solvent. Relatively pure solvent is withdrawn as the permeate, leaving a concentrated solution (the retentate) on the high-pressure side of the membrane.

The most appealing feature of membrane technology is its simplicity. It involves only the bulk movement (i.e., pumping) of fluids using mechanical energy. In addition, reverse osmosis and ultrafiltration are perhaps the first continuous molecular separation processes that do not involve a phase change or interphase mass transfer. The removal of solvent or water is accomplished without a change in its state from liquid to vapor (as in evaporation) or liquid to solid (as in freeze concentration).

Membrane processes can thus also be operated at ambient temperatures if necessary. This avoids product degradation problems associated with thermal processes, thus resulting in products with better functional and nutritional properties. Membrane processes are frequently run at higher temperatures, however, to lower viscosity and reduce pumping costs and to minimize microbial growth during processing.

For these reasons, energy requirements are low compared to other dewatering processes. Typically, while open-pan evaporation may need over 600 kW h/1000 kg water removed and a 5-7 effect evaporator with MVR requires 37-53 kW h/1000 kg, reverse osmosis for desalination requires 5-20 kW h/1000 kg water removed. Energy consumption by RO for concentrating whole milk to 31% solids was only 6-7 kcal/kg of milk, compared to 70-90 kcal/kg using MVR evaporators and 330 kcal/kg by double-effect evaporators (Cheryan et al., 1987).

There are limitations, however. Membranes cannot take a liquid stream to dryness. In the case of reverse osmosis, it is the osmotic pressure of the concentrated solutes that limit the upper concentration that can be comfortably handled. For example, milk and whey exert an osmotic pressure of about 670 kPa at room temperature. Since RO is commonly conducted at pressures of 2-4 MPa, it means a maximum 3-6 × concentration of milk or whey. However, a combination of innovative engineering design and appropriate membranes has enabled fruit juice processors to obtain concentrates as high as 60°Brix. In ultrafiltration, it is rarely the osmotic pressure, but rather the low mass transfer rates and high viscosity of the concentrate that limits the process.

Skimmilk can quite economically be concentrated to about 36–45% total solids by UF for specific cheesemaking applications.

1.2 Thermodynamics and Osmotic Pressure

Osmotic pressure is a critically important property in reverse osmosis and thus warrants some detailed discussion. It is based upon Gibbs free energy which, on a molar basis, is called the thermodynamic or chemical potential (μ). It is an intensive quantity, i.e., dependent on its nature and concentration, but independent of size of the system. It is a driving force which describes how much the free energy (G) changes when one mole of a component is added to or removed from the system. Therefore, an expression for chemical potential for a single component i at constant pressure and temperature is:

$$\mu_i = [\partial G / \partial n_i]_{P,T} \qquad (1)$$

where n_i is the number of moles of component i. For multicomponent systems each constituent has its own partial contribution to the overall chemical potential.

If a solvent (e.g., water, denoted as component 1) and a solution (e.g., of NaCl) are separated by a semipermeable membrane (i.e., a barrier that allows passage or permeation of water and not of the salt), the chemical potential of the solvent in the pure solvent compartment is μ_1^0, since the mole fraction (X_1) of water is 1·0. On the solution side, however $X_1 < 1$, and thus the chemical potential of water there (μ_1) is less than one. This difference in chemical potential of the water is the 'driving force' for the permeation of water from the high-potential side (the pure water compartment) to the low-potential side (the solution compartment). This phenomena is known as 'osmosis'. The vapor pressure over each side will also differ owing to the presence of solutes in the feed which will reduce the water vapor pressure over the feed solution. This can be related (for dilute solutions) by Raoult's Law:

$$P = X_1 P^o \qquad (2)$$

where P is the vapor pressure of the solution, X_1 is the mole fraction of solvent (water) and P^o is the vapor pressure of pure solvent at solution temperature.

From the preceding equations and the ideal gas law, the following expression can be derived (Cheryan, 1986):

$$\mu_1^0 - \mu_1 = -RT \ln X_1 \qquad (3)$$

To counter the diffusion of pure water down the chemical potential gradient, energy in the form of pressure can be applied to the solution side in order to raise its chemical potential. By definition, the pressure applied to balance the chemical potentials is the osmotic pressure (π). Thus, at equilibrium, the governing equation will be:

$$\mu_1^o - \mu_1 = \pi V_1 = -RT \ln X_1 \qquad (4)$$

where V_1 = the partial molar volume of the solvent.

Figure 2 is a schematic of the osmosis phenomenon. Osmosis will continue until chemical equilibrium is reached, which in theory may never happen since the solution will always have a lower chemical potential by virtue of the solute in it. In practice, with a U-shaped assembly as shown in Fig. 2, the permeation will stop when the head is equal to the apparent osmotic pressure.

Van't Hoff also developed an osmotic pressure relationship by making several assumptions (Cheryan, 1986):

$$\pi = N_2 RT = iCRT/M \qquad (5)$$

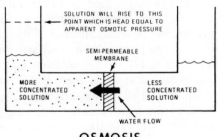

OSMOSIS

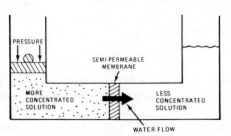

REVERSE OSMOSIS

FIG. 2.   The osmosis and reverse osmosis phenomena.

where N_2 is the number of moles of solute per liter of solution, C is the concentration of solute in grams per liter of solution, M is the molecular weight of solute and i is the number of ions for ionized solutes.

The van't Hoff equation is a gross approximation and is valid only for dilute solutions under ideal conditions. Table 1 illustrates the accuracy of the van't Hoff equation versus the Gibbs equation in predicting osmotic pressures. The van't Hoff model assumes that osmotic pressure increases linearly with molar concentration of the solute, while it actually increases exponentially in most food and biological systems as shown below. Thus it is frequently written in terms of a power series:

$$\pi = A_1 C + A_2 C^2 + A_3 C^3 + \cdots \tag{6}$$

The physical significance of osmotic pressure in reverse osmosis is that it represents the minimum pressure that must be applied to a feed solution in order to obtain any permeation or flux. As will be seen later,

TABLE 1
OSMOTIC PRESSURE OF SUCROSE SOLUTIONS AT 30°C (ADAPTED FROM CHERYAN (1986))

Molality	Osmotic pressure (atm)		
	van't Hoff equation	Gibbs equation	Experimental
0·991	20·3	26·8	27·2
1·646	30·3	47·3	47·5
2·366	39·0	72·6	72·5
3·263	47·8	107·6	105·9
4·108	54·2	143·3	144·0
5·332	61·5	199·0	204·3

the basic model that relates applied and osmotic pressures to flow of solvent through a membrane is, like many transport processes, expressed as the flux (the rate of solvent transport per unit area per unit time), which is the ratio of the driving force to resistance:

$$J = A(\Delta P_T - \Delta \pi) \tag{7}$$

A is a membrane permeability coefficient (the reciprocal of resistance to flow), ΔP_T is the transmembrane pressure and $\Delta \pi$ is the difference in osmotic pressure between the feed solution and the permeate. For example, using the van't Hoff equation, one can calculate for a 1%

solution of NaCl (molecular weight (MW) = 58·5) an osmotic pressure of about 840 kPa. Thus no flux will be obtained unless the pressure is above 840 kPa. This is shown in Fig. 3, which shows typical reverse osmosis performance data. The higher the solute concentration, the higher the osmotic pressure and the higher the applied pressures needed to obtain the required flux (Fig. 3(a)). Owing to differences in their manner of transport, the solvent and solute move through the membrane at different rates (Fig. 3(a) and 3(b)) giving rise to the pattern of rejection observed in Fig. 3(d). The permeate quality will be better at higher pressures and lower concentrations of the solute (Fig. 3(c)).

On the other hand, a 1% solution of sucrose (MW = 360) will have an osmotic pressure of 6·7 kPa and a 1% solution of bovine serum albumin (MW = 60 000) only 0·04 kPa. Therefore much higher pressures have to be applied with the salt solutions than with the protein solution. This is why osmotic pressures are of no consequence in UF or MF, but

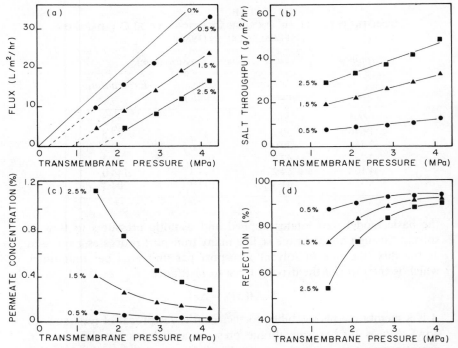

FIG. 3.   Reverse osmosis of salt solutions in a spiral-wound cellulose acetate module at 30°C.

important in RO and NF. This is shown in Fig. 4, which shows typical flux behavior with model solutions of 1% NaCl, 1% lactose and a real liquid food (skimmilk of 9·1% total solids with an osmotic pressure of 670 kPa). As expected, no permeation was observed until the applied pressure was higher than the osmotic pressure. The slopes of the salt and sugar lines are almost the same as the water line. With skimmilk, however, there is a marked deviation from linearity. This is due to 'concentration polarization' of rejected particles, and flux becomes controlled by the mass-transfer characteristics of the system. This explains why turbulence (in the form of higher velocities) has a beneficial effect with skimmilk, but not so with salt or lactose where polarization is less significant.

The osmotic pressure also tells us the approximate limits to a reverse osmosis process. For example, many RO membranes can tolerate only about 4 MPa. This means that in theory, the maximum concentration that can be obtained by RO for the 1% salt solution is $4/0·84 = 4·8 \times 1\% = 4·8\%$, while one should be able to go to much higher concentrations with the sugar and protein solutions, as long as the feed solutions can be pumped. In practice, as will be seen later, the maximum concentration is limited by solubility of the solute, concentration polarization and fouling effects, and economics, i.e., the flux at high concentrations may become too low to be practicable.

There is a paucity of good osmotic pressure data. Some of the data available in the literature is shown in Table 2.

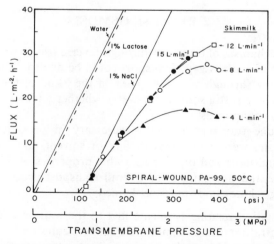

FIG. 4. Reverse osmosis of salt and sugar solutions and skimmilk in spiral-wound composite membrane system (adapted from Cheryan *et al.* (1990)).

TABLE 2
OSMOTIC PRESSURE OF FOOD STREAMS AT ROOM TEMPERATURE

Food	Concentration	Osmotic pressure (psi)
Milk	9% solids-not-fat	100
Whey	6% total solids	100
Orange juice	11% total solids	230
Citrus juice	10°Brix	215
Apple juice	15% total solids	300
Grape juice	16% total solids	300
Coffee extract	28% total solids	500
Glucose	5% w/v	100
Lactose	5% w/v	55
Sodium chloride	1% w/v	125
Sugar beet thin juice	20°Brix	500
Lactic acid	1% w/v	80
Sweet potato waste water	22% total solids	870
Tomato juice	5% total solids	159
	6·8% total solids	201
	9·5% total solids	231
Tomato paste	33°Brix	1000
Perilla anthocyanins	10·6% total solids	330

1 psi = 6·9 kPa.

2 REVERSE OSMOSIS

The exact mechanism of transport through reverse osmosis membranes is still a matter of controversy. Transport could be due to diffusion and/or convective flow through very fine pores in the 'skin' of the asymmetric membrane. There is still some controversy whether a true RO membrane is 'porous' or 'nonporous'.

A membrane transport model is necessary in order to relate the performance (expressed in terms of flux of solvent and solute) to the operating conditions and other measurable properties of the system. To fully describe and understand the overall transport processes involved, the following relationships must be defined:

(1) An equation relating permeate flux to the wall or boundary layer concentration (i.e., a membrane transport equation).
(2) An equation relating the boundary layer concentration to a mass transfer coefficient.

(3) A model describing the mass transfer characteristics of the system in relation to feed solution properties and fluid mechanics of the system.

(4) Equations relating the fluid mechanics to the operating parameters and the flow regime (e.g., turbulent flow, laminar flow—entrance region or fully developed).

Several models attempting to describe the transport phenomena exist in the literature. In most cases, each model has been evaluated for one particular membrane–solute combination and therefore the transport coefficients so obtained may not be applicable to other membrane–solute combinations. Nonetheless, it is important to obtain an understanding of the forces involved and the mechanism by which solutes and solvent are transported through RO membranes, especially for development of suitable membranes and processing systems.

Two very different approaches have been taken in developing RO transport models:

(1) using irreversible thermodynamics to describe the process, and
(2) using physical–chemical–structural descriptions of the RO membrane–solution system.

It should be kept in mind that to be useful, the transport model must be able to predict permeate flux and solute rejection from the transport coefficients characterizing the solution–membrane system and the operating parameters.

2.1 Irreversible Thermodynamics (IT) Transport Models

Irreversible thermodynamics provides a general description of membrane transport that can be used for both RO and UF, since it uses a 'black box' approach leading to phenomenological equations which correlate rejection behavior with macroscopic properties that can be measured. However, since this approach is not model-dependent, it gives no explanation of the flow and separation mechanisms.

In any irreversible process, the dissipation function or rate of entropy production (ϕ) can be expressed as the sum of the products of the flows (fluxes) and the conjugated forces,

$$\phi = \sum_{i=1}^{N} J_i X_i \tag{8}$$

For sufficiently slow processes or small deviations from equilibrium, the Onsager principle states that there is a linear dependence between all fluxes and all forces. This relationship is expressed in the phenomenological equations:

$$J_i = L_{ii}X_i + L_{ij}X_j \tag{9}$$

The Ls are the so-called phenomenological coefficients and the Xs represent the thermodynamic driving forces. This linear law is a generalization of the well-known laws of Fourier, Fick, Poiseuille, Ohm and Darcy in which flux is proportional to a driving force or conjugate force (straight coefficients). In Onsager's phenomenological equations, additional contributions are assumed to be made by non-conjugated forces (denoted by the cross-coefficients) such that any flux (J_i) depends directly linearly on not only its conjugate forces but also the non-conjugate forces.

In an isothermal RO process, two solutions of the same solvent and solute are separated by a membrane. The driving forces are the chemical potential gradients across the membrane, and eqn (9) can be rewritten as:

$$J_1 = -L_{11} \text{ grad } \mu_1 - L_{12} \text{ grad } \mu_2 \tag{10}$$

$$J_2 = -L_{21} \text{ grad } \mu_2 - L_{22} \text{ grad } \mu_2 \tag{11}$$

J_1 is the flux of solvent and J_2 is the flux of solute through the membrane. The external forces in RO are concentration and pressure gradients, both of which appear explicitly in the chemical potential (μ),

$$\text{grad } \mu_i = \left[\frac{\partial \mu_1}{\partial c_i}\right]_{P,T} \text{grad } c_i + \bar{v}_i \text{ grad } P \tag{12}$$

where c_i is the concentration and $\bar{v}_i$ is the partial molar volume of the ith component. Since $L_{12} = L_{21}$, eqn (11) can be written as:

$$J_2 = \left(\frac{L_{12}}{L_{11}}\right)J_1 - L_{22}\left[1 - \left(\frac{L_{12}}{L_{11}}\right)^2 \frac{L_{11}}{L_{22}}\right] \text{grad } \mu_2 \tag{13}$$

To use this approach, the L-coefficients or their equivalents (appropriate ratios) must be determined by experimentation or suitable theories. The L-coefficients should be independent of the fluxes and forces and may be functions of composition. L_{11} can be easily determined from measurements of J_1 when no solute is present, but only when the presence of the solute does not change the membrane characteristics (Johnson et al., 1966).

Several transport models have been derived using the IT approach. These models differ somewhat in their choice of flows, their evaluation of the L-coefficients, their application of local equilibria, etc. Four of the IT models are presented here.

2.1.1 Kedem and Katchalsky's Transport Model

Kedem and Katchalsky (1958) transformed the coupled phenomenological eqns ((12) and (13)) in terms of more practical terms, using three transport coefficients that are easier to experimentally determine:

$$J_v = L_p(\Delta P_T - \Delta \pi) \tag{14}$$

$$J_2 = \omega \Delta \pi + (1 - \sigma) J_v (c_2)_{ln} \tag{15}$$

where J_v is the volume flux through the membrane, J_2 is the solute flux through the membrane, ΔP_T is the pressure difference across the membrane, $\Delta \pi$ is the osmotic pressure difference across the membrane, $(c_2)_{ln}$ is the log mean solute concentration difference across the membrane, L_p is the hydrodynamic permeability coefficient, σ is the reflection coefficient and ω is the solute permeability coefficient.

Since the solute concentration gradient in the membrane is usually large and non-linear, they used a log-mean solute concentration to account for the non-linearity in their linear model.

2.1.2 Spiegler and Kedem's Transport Model

To account for a changing concentration profile at different volume fluxes, Spiegler and Kedem (1966) derived a set of differential flux equations in terms of a local solute permeability coefficient, $\bar{P}_2$, a specific membrane permeability coefficient, P_h, and the reflection coefficient:

$$J_v = P_h \left[\frac{dP}{dy} - \sigma \frac{d\pi}{dy} \right] \tag{16}$$

$$J_2 = \bar{P}_2 \left[\frac{dc_2}{dy} \right] + (1 - \sigma) c_2 J_v \tag{17}$$

Assuming the coefficients, $\bar{P}_2$ and σ, are constant (since they are combinations of the L-coefficients and average solute concentrations which are considered to be constant for a given membrane), the equations can be integrated across the membrane thickness (λ). Volumetric flux and solute flux are:

$$J_v = \frac{P_h}{\lambda}(\Delta P_T - \sigma \Delta \pi) \tag{18}$$

$$J_2 = (1-\sigma)J_v \left[\frac{c_2'' - c_2' \exp[J_v(1-\sigma)\lambda/\bar{P}_2]}{1 - \exp[J_v(1-\sigma)\lambda/\bar{P}_2]} \right] \tag{19}$$

$$\tilde{R} = \sigma \left[\frac{1 - \exp[-J_v(1-\sigma)\lambda/\bar{P}_2]}{1 - \sigma \exp[-J_v(1-\sigma)\lambda/\bar{P}_2]} \right] \tag{20}$$

Thus, solute rejection is a function of volume flux and the parameters ($\bar{P}_2$ and σ), which are assumed to be independent of solute concentration and applied pressure (thus independent of external forces). These parameters can be determined by independent osmotic experiments, in which no pressure is applied to the system, and used in eqn (20) to predict solute rejection. At extremely high pressures, $J_v \to \infty$ and, according to eqn (20), solute rejection (R_{max}) is equal to the reflection coefficient:

$$R_{max} = \sigma \tag{20a}$$

R_{max} provides an indication of the degree of coupling of the solute and solvent fluxes. R approaches 100% as a limit if fluxes are not coupled, since solvent flux through the membrane is usually much larger than solute flux. In case of coupled fluxes, however, an increase in volume flux will increase solute flux proportionately, causing rejection to asymptotically approach a limiting value (R_{max}).

2.1.3 Pusch's Linear IT Model
Pusch (1977) also based his equations on linear phenomenological equations:

$$J_v = L_p(\Delta P_T - \sigma \Delta \pi) \tag{21}$$

$$J_2 = \left[\frac{L_\pi}{L_p} - \sigma^2 \right] L_p \tilde{c}_2 \Delta \pi + J_v(1-\sigma)\tilde{c}_2 \tag{22}$$

where L_p is the hydrodynamic permeability coefficient, L_π is the osmotic permeability coefficient, and σ is the reflection coefficient. A linear relationship between rejection and volume flux can be derived from these equations:

$$\frac{1}{\tilde{R}} = \frac{1}{R_{max}} + \frac{[(L_\pi/L_p) - \sigma^2][1 - R_{max}]L_p\pi'}{(1 - \sigma)R_{max}J_v} \quad (23)$$

When $R_{max} = \sigma$, eqn (23) reduces to:

$$\frac{1}{\tilde{R}} = \frac{1}{R_{max}} + \frac{[(L_\pi/L_p) - R_{max}^2]L_p\pi'}{R_{max}J_v} \quad (24)$$

Since eqn (24) was derived from the general principles of the thermodynamics of irreversible processes without using any particular membrane model, it should have broad applicability in RO where the transport coefficients are independent of pressure and concentration.

2.1.4 Bi-layer IT Models

Spiegler and Kedem's equations were derived for a single-layer membrane. Bi-layer IT models consider asymmetric cellulose acetate membranes as two homogeneous layers in series (Kedem and Katchalsky, 1963; Jagur-Grodzinski and Kedem, 1966; Elata, 1969; Groepl and Pusch, 1970; Jonsson, 1980; Hwang and Pusch, 1981). The reflection coefficient for the whole membrane (σ) is related to the reflection coefficients (σ_a and σ_b) and the solute permeabilities ($\bar{P}_{2a}$ and $\bar{P}_{2b}$) of the two layers through the equation:

$$\frac{\sigma}{\bar{P}_2} = \frac{\sigma_a}{\bar{P}_{2a}} + \frac{\sigma_b}{\bar{P}_{2b}} \quad (25)$$

These models now have six transport coefficients, which can be experimentally determined by measuring the coefficients for one of the layers separately and then for the entire membrane. A homogeneous membrane analog of the porous layer, identical to the skin layer in thickness, can be prepared or removed from an asymmetric membrane by abrasion or hydrolysis. All bi-layer models predict that, at a given volume flux, solute rejection is completely determined by the reflection coefficient and solute permeability coefficient for the skin layer, providing the reflection coefficient for the porous layer is zero. Single-layer models give a good description of rejection versus permeate flux for asymmetric membranes under RO conditions.

2.2 Physical–Chemical–Structural Models

All physical–chemical–structural models use some combination of three parallel transport mechanisms:

(1) Diffusion due to a concentration gradient.
(2) Diffusion due to a pressure gradient.
(3) Hydrodynamic flow through pores.

These models assume a mechanism for transport and then correlate rejection behavior with known or assumed structural properties of the membrane (porosity, pore size, tortuosity) and/or physical–chemical properties of the solution–membrane system (diffusivity, solubility, frictional interactions, etc.). This approach gives more information on the flow and separation mechanisms, depending on the suitability of the chosen model.

2.2.1 Solution–Diffusion Model

The solution–diffusion mechanism attributes solute rejection to large differences in the diffusivity of solvent and solute in the membrane and/or to differences in their solubility in the membrane material. According to this well-known mechanism (Lonsdale et al., 1965, 1971; Banks and Sharples, 1966), both solvent and solute dissolve in the homogeneous nonporous surface layer of the membrane and then diffuse through the membrane in an uncoupled manner. Thus, it is desirable to have membranes with completely nonporous surface layers in which the solubility and diffusivity of the solvent is much higher than those of the solute. All components dissolve in accordance with phase equilibrium considerations and diffuse through by the same mechanisms that govern diffusion through liquids and solids (Lonsdale, 1972). It is assumed that solution processes are rapid enough that equilibrium distributions of solute and solvent between the solutions immediately adjacent to the membrane and the membrane surface are maintained. Under these conditions, the rate of transport of water and solute is proportional to the chemical potential gradients across the membrane. Each component dissolves in the membrane on the high-pressure side and diffuses through the membrane in response to concentration and pressure gradients, without any coupling between the individual fluxes.

The flux of each component (J_i) is given by the product of its mobility, concentration and driving force:

$$J_i = -\left[\frac{D_{im}c_{im}}{RT}\right]\text{grad } \mu_i \qquad (26)$$

where D_{im} is the diffusion coefficient and c_{im} is the concentration of component i within the membrane. The driving force for solvent flux is $\bar{v}_1 (\Delta P_T - \Delta \pi)$, and the solvent flux equation is:

$$J_1 = \left[-\frac{D_{1m}c_{1m}\bar{v}_1}{RT\lambda} \right](\Delta P_T - \Delta \pi) = A(\Delta P_T - \Delta \pi) \tag{27}$$

The influence of pressure on solute transport is neglected so that solute flux across the membrane is:

$$J_2 = \left[-\frac{D_{2m}K_2}{\lambda} \right]\Delta c_2 = B\Delta c_2 \tag{28}$$

where K_2 is the solute distribution coefficient.

According to this model, operating variables (transmembrane pressure, temperature, and feed concentration), membrane thickness, and the water and solute permeabilities ($D_{1m}c_{1m}\bar{v}_1$ and $D_{2m}K_2$) determine flux rates. At constant temperature, the solution–diffusion model uses two parameters, $A(-D_{1m}c_{1m}v_1/RT\lambda)$ and $B(-D_{2m}K_2/\lambda)$, to describe membrane performance. As a membrane constant, A is a measure of water flux through the membrane and the ratio, A/B, is a measure of the rejecting capabilities of the membrane (Lonsdale, 1973). Solute rejection for the solution–diffusion model is:

$$\tilde{R} = \frac{A(\Delta P_T - \Delta \pi)}{A(\Delta P_T - \Delta \pi) + Bc_1''} \tag{29}$$

Both water and solute fluxes are inversely proportional to membrane thickness, but rejection of solute, given by the ratio of the fluxes, is independent of membrane thickness. According to this model, solvent flux increases linearly with net pressure, reaching a maximum rejection (R_{max}) of 1, while solute flux is independent of pressure. This is because no coupling of flows is assumed. This implies that high transmembrane pressures will produce more permeate of better quality. This has generally been observed in practice, although rejection never quite reaches 100% even at very high pressures.

The solution–diffusion model is limited in that it does not allow for convective flow. It has been extended to include a coupling effect and for cases where solvent flux is not linearly proportional to the applied pressure but increases exponentially (Lee, 1975; Paul, 1976; Bo and Stannett, 1976).

2.2.2 Pore Flow Model

Unlike the solution–diffusion model, which represents one extreme in that no coupling of solute and solvent is assumed, pore flow models represent the other extreme in which coupling is a characteristic of viscous flow. This is basically a variant of the early 'sieve' mechanism, in which a semipermeable membrane is visualized as having pores intermediate in size between the solvent and solute molecules. Separation occurs because solute molecules are blocked out of the pores while smaller solvent molecules are able to enter the pores. The sieve mechanism probably accounts in part for the removal of large molecules in UF. However, for RO, in which molecules of approximately the same size are separated, a purely steric explanation for membrane rejection is less plausible.

Merten (1966) developed a model (the 'highly porous transport model') based on volume flux derived from Poiseuille's equation:

$$J_v = \varepsilon v_p = -\frac{\varepsilon r^2 \Delta P_m}{8 \eta t \lambda} \tag{30}$$

where v_p is the center-of-mass pore fluid velocity, ε is the porosity of membrane $(n\pi r^2)$, ΔP_m is the effective pressure difference across the membrane, η is the pore fluid viscosity, n is the number of pores per unit membrane area, r is the pore radius, λ is the membrane thickness and t is the tortuosity factor.

Merten's model includes a tortuosity factor (t) which accounts for twisting of the pores and increases in effective pore length. Solute flux for this model is the sum of solute flux due to convective or bulk movement within the pores and to diffusion of solute through the membrane pores.

Separation of solute and solvent is assumed to occur because the solute concentration in the pore fluid is not the same as that in the feed solution. Assuming chemical equilibria at the solution–membrane interfaces, solute concentration in the pore fluid at each interface is related to the solute concentration in the permeate and feed solutions through equilibrium or partition coefficients.

For Merten's model, solute flux is:

$$N_2 = \frac{v_w}{\varepsilon} \left[\frac{K_2'' c_2'' - K_2' c_2' \exp(v_w t \lambda / \varepsilon D_{21})}{1 - \exp(v_w t \lambda / \varepsilon D_{21})} \right] \tag{31}$$

Solute rejection is:

$$\tilde{R} = 1 - \left[\frac{K_2' \exp(v_w t \lambda / \varepsilon D_{21})}{K_2'' - \varepsilon + \varepsilon \exp(v_w t \lambda / \varepsilon D_{21})} \right] \tag{32}$$

According to these equations the highest rejections will be obtained at the highest volume flux (highest pressure) and the maximum rejection is:

$$R_{max} = 1 - \frac{K_2'}{\varepsilon} \tag{33}$$

The existence of a distribution coefficient different from the water content of the membrane in these equations implies that the membrane affects the equilibrium properties of the pore solution without affecting transport within the pores. Any force (mechanical, chemical, etc.) that affects equilibrium properties should also affect transport. This picture of a highly porous membrane which excludes a solute but allows viscous flow may not be realized in practice and a frictional pore model is more realistic for RO membranes (Merten, 1966).

2.2.3 Frictional Transport Models

In the IT models previously discussed, no attempt was made to define specific interactions between solute, solvent and membrane relative to the phenomenological coefficients. The basic assumption in all frictional models is that, at mechanical equilibrium, the thermodynamic driving forces acting on each particle are exactly balanced by the frictional forces between the particle and all others in the surrounding medium. These frictional forces, F_{ij}, are proportional to the mean relative velocities of the components, i.e.,

$$F_{ij} = f_{ij}(v_i - v_j) \tag{34}$$

where f_{ij} is the friction coefficient between components i and j, and v_i and v_j are the mean linear velocities of components i and j. The total force acting on water and solute can be written as,

$$F_1 = \left(\frac{c_{2m}}{c_{1m}}\right) f_{21}(v_1 - v_2) + f_{13}(v_1 - v_3) \tag{35}$$

$$F_2 = f_{21}(v_2 - v_1) + f_{23}(v_2 - v_3) \tag{36}$$

Belfort (1976) derived relationships between the frictional coefficients and the transport coefficients defined in Spiegler and Kedem's model ($\bar{P}_2$, P_h, σ). It appears that solvent–solute interactions within the membrane are much greater than those in the external solutions and that solute–membrane interactions are much greater than solvent–membrane interactions in hydrophilic membranes where the solvent is water and the solute an electrolyte.

This concept of frictional forces inhibiting movement of solute and solvent within the membrane was used in the derivation of Merten's finely porous model and Jonsson and Boeson's viscous flow-frictional model (see below).

2.2.4 Finely Porous Model

The finely porous model was also developed by Merten (1966) for RO membranes whose transport properties are intermediate between the solution–diffusion and the pore flow models. For dilute solutions, solute flux through the membrane is:

$$N_2 = -\frac{RT}{bf_{21}}\left(\frac{dc_{2m}}{dy}\right) + \frac{c_{2m}v_p}{b} \tag{37}$$

f_{21} is the coefficient for friction between the solute and the solvent and $b(1 + f_{23}/f_{21})$ is defined as a drag factor. Solute–solvent and solute–membrane interactions are important, but not solvent–membrane interactions. Volume flux through the membrane pores is given by a Poiseuille-type equation. The total force acting on the pore fluid includes the frictional force between the solute and the membrane in addition to the applied pressure. The flux equations for the finely porous model are:

$$v_w = \frac{H}{\varepsilon}\left[\frac{1}{1 + \left(\frac{Hf_{23}}{M_2\varepsilon}\right)c_2''}\right]\frac{\Delta P_T}{t\lambda} \tag{38}$$

$$J_2 = \frac{v_w}{\varepsilon b}\left[\frac{K_2''c_2'' - K_2'c_2' \exp[v_w(t\lambda/\varepsilon)(f_{21}/RT)]}{1 - \exp[v_w(t\lambda/\varepsilon)(f_{21}/RT)]}\right] \tag{39}$$

H is the hydraulic permeability of the membrane ($H = \varepsilon r^2/8\eta$) and M_2 is the molecular weight of the solute. Solute rejection is:

$$\tilde{R} = 1 - \left[\frac{K_2' \exp[v_w(t\lambda/\varepsilon)f_{21}/RT]}{K_2'' - b\varepsilon + b\varepsilon \exp[v_w(t\lambda/\varepsilon)(f_{21}/RT)]}\right] \tag{40}$$

Membrane performance is a function of several factors: the equilibrium solubility of the solute in the pore fluid, solute–membrane and solute–solvent interactions, and the velocity of the pore fluid. However, for a given membrane and feed solution, solute rejection depends only on the volumetric flow rate since K_2, b, f_{21} and f_{23} are assumed to be independent of solute concentration. Maximum rejection for this model is:

$$R_{max} = 1 - \frac{K_2'}{\varepsilon} \qquad (41)$$

2.2.5 Combined Viscous Flow–Frictional Model

The combined viscous flow–frictional model is based on the finely porous model, but the distribution or partition coefficient is taken to be the same on both sides of the skin layer (Jonsson and Boesen, 1975). In addition, this model was derived for the effective membrane thickness, λ, or the thickness of skin layer, and the fractional pore volume was corrected for pore tortuosity so that the total pore volume is εt. The flux equations are:

$$v_w = H \left[\frac{1}{1 + \dfrac{H f_{23} c_2''}{\varepsilon M_2}} \right] \frac{\Delta P_T}{t\lambda} \qquad (42)$$

$$N_2 = \frac{K_2 v_w}{b} \left[\frac{c_2'' - c_2' \exp[v_w(t\lambda/\varepsilon)/D_{21}]}{1 - \exp[v_w(t\lambda/\varepsilon)/D_{21}]} \right] \qquad (43)$$

Solute rejection is:

$$\tilde{R} = \frac{(K_2/b - 1) + (1 - K_2/b) \exp[v_w(t\lambda/\varepsilon)/D_{21}]}{(K_2/b - 1) + \exp[v_w(t\lambda/\varepsilon)/D_{21}]} \qquad (44)$$

Maximum rejection for this model is:

$$R_{max} = 1 - \frac{K_2}{b} \qquad (45)$$

The parameters $(1 - K_2/b)$ and $(t\lambda/\varepsilon)$ determined from non-linear parameter estimation procedures should be independent of pressures and concentrations. The parameter $(t\lambda/\varepsilon)$ should also be independent of the type of solute being processed and thus a membrane constant (Jonsson, 1978). This is in accordance with the physical meaning of the parameter—the effective pore length in the membrane skin divided by the pore area.

2.3 Combination Models

The physical–chemical–structural models discussed thus far differ in their description of flow through the membrane (i.e., either purely diffusive flow, purely convection flow through membrane pores, or diffusive and convective flow through membrane pores). The two models presented in this section do not make a distinction among the three types of flow, but merely assume that both diffusive and pore flow or diffusive and convective flow are possible.

2.3.1 Solution–Diffusion–Imperfection Model

Sherwood *et al.* (1967) developed a simple theory of membrane transport based on the assumption that water and solute cross the membrane by the parallel processes of diffusion and pore flow. Solute and solvent dissolve into the water-swollen membrane on the high-pressure side, diffuse across the membrane owing to a chemical potential gradient and desorb from the membrane surface on the low-pressure side. A fraction of the feed solution is assumed to pass through open channels or pores, with negligible change in solute concentration due to diffusion in the pore fluid. The rate of pore flow is proportional to the applied pressure (ΔP_T). In order to have high solute rejections, pore flow must be a small fraction of the total flux.

The flux equations for this model are:

$$N_1 = \kappa_1(\Delta P_T - \Delta\pi) + \kappa_3 \Delta P_T c_1' \tag{46}$$

$$N_2 = \kappa_2 \Delta c_2 + \kappa_3 \Delta P_T c_2' \tag{47}$$

where κ_1 is the transport coefficient for the diffusion of water, κ_2 is the transport coefficient for diffusion of solute and κ_3 is the transport coefficient for pore flow. κ_2 is proportional to the product of the diffusivity of the solute in the membrane and the distribution coefficient for the solute between the solution at the membrane surface and the membrane material. Solute rejection for this model is:

$$\tilde{R} = 1 - \frac{c_1''}{c_2'}\left[\frac{\kappa_2 \Delta c_2 + \kappa_3 \Delta P_T c_2'}{\kappa_1(\Delta P_T - \Delta\pi) + \kappa_3 \Delta P_T c_1'}\right] \tag{48}$$

For dilute solutions ($c_1'' = 1$), rejection is:

$$\tilde{R} = \frac{\kappa_1(\Delta P_T - \Delta\pi)}{\kappa_1(\Delta P_T - \Delta\pi) + \kappa_3 \Delta P_T + \kappa_2} \tag{49}$$

These equations assume only that both solute and solvent cross the membrane by two parallel mechanisms: (i) solute flux is proportional to Δc_2 and water flux is proportional to ($\Delta P_T - \Delta\pi$), and (ii) feed solution is transferred through the membrane at a rate proportional to ΔP_T without any change in solute concentration.

2.3.2 Diffusion–Flow Model

The diffusion–flow model (Yasuda and Lamaze, 1971) assumes that water transport in water-swollen polymer membranes under an applied pressure can occur by both molecular diffusion and bulk flow, depending on the water content of the membrane or the degree of swelling. Solute rejection is due to transport depletion of solute in relation to water rather than the exclusion of the solute by the membrane. Rather than treat pores as capillaries in which the transport of water can be described by Poiseuille's flow equation, a dynamic membrane structure is proposed in which water movement is diffusive at some point in time, and later as viscous flow when the structure changes to a looser geometric arrangement.

Their model uses two types of water permeability coefficients—a hydraulic permeability coefficient (K_1^*) and a diffusive permeability coefficient (P_1^*). The parameter, ϕ, is defined as the ratio of the two permeability coefficients:

$$\phi = \frac{K_1^* RT}{P_1^* \bar{v}_1} \tag{50}$$

Thus membranes can be classified according to their mode of water transport using ϕ. For example, when $\phi = 1$, they are diffusion membranes; $\phi > 1$ as diffusion–flow membranes, and $\phi \gg 1$ as flow membranes.

This model also assumes that whenever water moves through the membrane by diffusion, solute also moves in a diffusive mode. On the other hand, when water moves by viscous flow, there is no solute rejection. The flux equations for this model are:

$$J_1 = \frac{K_1^{**}}{\lambda}(\Delta P_T - \Delta \pi) \tag{51}$$

$$J_2 = \left(\frac{K_1^{**}}{\lambda} - \frac{P_1^* \bar{v}_1}{RT\lambda}\right)(\Delta P_T - \Delta \pi)c_2' + \frac{P_2^* \Delta c_2}{\lambda} \tag{52}$$

in which K_1^{**} is the hydraulic permeability coefficient of the membrane under RO conditions. If water flux is totally diffusive:

$$\frac{K_1^{**}}{\lambda} - \frac{P_1^* \bar{v}_1}{RT\lambda} = 0 \tag{53}$$

Solute rejection is:

$$\tilde{R} = \left[\phi + \frac{P_2^* RT}{P_1^* \bar{v}_1(\Delta P_T - \Delta \pi)}\right]^{-1} \tag{54}$$

If

$$\phi = 1 \tag{55}$$

the model becomes essentially the same as the solution–diffusion model.

2.4 Preferential Sorption–Capillary Flow Models

According to the preferential sorption–capillary flow model postulated by Sourirajan and co-workers (Sourirajan, 1970, 1977; Kimura and Sourirajan, 1967), RO is governed by two distinct factors: (1) an equilibrium effect involving preferential sorption at the membrane surface, which is governed by repulsive or attractive potential force gradients at the membrane surface, and (2) a kinetic effect which is concerned with the movement of solute and solvent molecules through the membrane pores. The kinetic effect is governed by both potential force gradients and steric effects associated with the structure and size of the solute and solvent molecules relative to the membrane pores. Consequently, the chemical nature of the membrane surface and the size, number and distribution of its pores will determine the success of an RO separation process.

For separation, at least one of the components in the feed solution must be preferentially sorbed at the membrane surface. This means that a concentration gradient, arising from the influence of surface forces, must exist at the membrane–solution interface. Preferential sorption at a membrane–solution interface is a function of solute–solvent–membrane material interactions, similar to those governing the effect of structure on the reactivity of molecules. Such interactions arise from the ionic, polar (hydrogen bonding), steric and nonpolar character of each one of the components involved in the RO system. The overall result of these interactions determines the equilibrium condition under which solvent, or solute, or neither is preferentially sorbed at the membrane–solution interface. This equilibrium condition, together with the friction and shear forces affecting the relative mobility of the solute molecule in the membrane pores under the applied pressure gradient, determines the extent of solute separation and solvent flux obtainable in RO with a given membrane under specified operating conditions (Sourirajan and Matsuura, 1984).

For RO systems involving aqueous solutions and polymeric membranes, solutes can be characterized by their ionic, polar, steric, and nonpolar parameters. Numerical data for these parameters for many solutes and CA membranes are given by Sourirajan and Matsuura (1984, 1977a). Unique correlations exist between the above parameters characterizing solutes and their rejection by RO membranes.

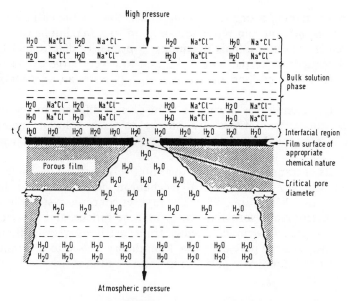

FIG. 5. The preferential sorption–capillary flow mechanism.

Figure 5 is a schematic representation of the preferential sorption–capillary flow mechanism for RO separation of sodium chloride from an aqueous solution. The term 'pore' or 'capillary' refers to any void space (whatever its size or origin) connecting the high- and low-pressure sides of the membrane. The critical pore size for a given membrane–feed solution is not necessarily correlated with the size of the solute and solvent molecules—it is twice the thickness of the preferentially sorbed layer. Thus, this mechanism is not sieve filtration.

Polymeric membranes with low dielectric constants, such as cellulose acetate, repel ions in the close vicinity of the surface which results in the preferential sorption of water. Theories of salt rejection based on the repulsion of ions by membranes with low dielectric constants have also been proposed. Separation occurs when the preferentially sorbed layer is forced through the membrane capillaries under pressure.

This mechanism could explain all the variations in RO separation that have been experimentally observed. In the radial direction, the convective transport of the two ions is unequal. Because the electrical charge has to be zero, a potential gradient is generated which drives the ions opposite to the direction of convection. The overall result is a flow of water from the pore containing a smaller amount of salt than at the entrance of the pore. The membrane can reject salt only up to a maximum value for a given set of conditions. This maximum is primarily determined by the electrical properties of the pore walls, and to a very large extent by the diffusivities of the co-ions and counter-ions (Sourirajan and Matsuura, 1984).

Since RO membranes are made from several different materials and physicochemical parameters are unique to each solution–membrane system, it is reasonable to assume that various rejection mechanisms are possible.

Two sets of transport equations quantitatively describe the preferential sorption–capillary flow (PSCF) mechanism for aqueous solutions (Sourirajan and Matsuura, 1982). The first set concerns systems in which water is preferentially sorbed at the membrane surface, and is basically a capillary or pore flow model. Water transport is by viscous flow, and solute transport is by pore diffusion. Film theory is used to determine the boundary conditions. At a given temperature and pressure, the transport equations are:

$$J_w = A_w \Delta P_T \tag{56}$$

$$J_1 = A_w (\Delta P_T - \Delta \pi) \tag{57}$$

$$J_2 = \frac{D_{2m}(c_2' - c_2'')}{K_2' \lambda} \tag{58}$$

$$v_w = \frac{D_{2m}}{K_2' \lambda} \left[\frac{c_2'}{c_2''} - 1 \right] \tag{59}$$

$$v_w = k \ln \left[\frac{c_2' - c_2''}{c_2^b - c_2''} \right] \tag{60}$$

Permeate flux depends on the magnitude of the preferentially sorbed water layer, the effective thickness of the membrane, the size, number and distribution of pores on the membrane surface, and the operating pressure, temperature and flow conditions in the RO module.

The basic equations appear similar to the solution–diffusion model except for two differences: (1) concentration at the membrane surface on the high-pressure side (c_2') is related to the bulk concentration by the film theory, and (2) explicit expressions for the pure water permeability coefficient and the solute permeability coefficient in terms of the operating variables are required. This is one argument for claiming the PSCF analysis is more realistic than the solution–diffusion model (Sourirajan and Matsuura, 1977b). In the solution–diffusion model there is no pure water permeability constant (A_w); there is no mass transfer coefficient (k) for the high-pressure side of the membrane; there is no means of calculating the boundary layer concentration on the high-pressure side of the membrane; finally, the constant A in the solution–diffusion model cannot be a constant since it must depend on the nature of the solute, solute concentration, and feed flow conditions.

The second set of equations is for the surface force-pore flow model involving preferential sorption of either water or solute at the membrane solution interface. Pores on the membrane surface are treated as circular cylindrical pores with or without a pore size distribution. Solute–membrane interactions, relative to water, are expressed in terms of electrostatic or Lennard–Jones-type surface potential functions. Solute–solvent transport through the membrane pore is governed by these surface forces together with pressure, friction and viscous shear forces. Based on the above considerations, transport equations can be derived in terms of several dimensionless parameters, which are broadly applicable to any single-solute aqueous solution, whether RO or UF, at any given set of operating conditions, provided the pore radius, osmotic pressure data, and surface force and friction force functions are known (Sourirajan and Matsuura, 1984).

2.5 Evaluation and Application of Transport Models

The various IT models use three types of parameters—a hydrodynamic permeability coefficient, a solute permeability coefficient, and the reflection coefficient—to characterize each membrane–solution system. The reflection coefficient (σ) and the solute permeability coefficient strongly depend on the type of solute being processed, and perhaps on the driving forces—pressure and concentration. The hydrodynamic permeability coefficient (L_p or P_h) can also be a function of pressure if the membrane compacts.

It is almost impossible to remain strictly within the range of local transport equations (local equilibrium) as required for the applicability of IT models. Pressure and concentration differences across the membrane are often very large, and the system may be far from equilibrium. Thus fluxes need not be linear functions of the forces, which limits the practical applicability of linear thermodynamic models.

Pusch's linear model is among the easiest of the IT models to evaluate. Kedem and Katchalsky's and Spiegler and Kedem's models each have three transport parameters. The latter is probably a more realistic description of the RO process. The extended IT model, with its six transport parameters, is difficult to use, especially if the partition coefficient (K_2) is not known.

The solution–diffusion model has been widely used, perhaps because it is the simplest. It has only two parameters and the flux equations are linear. It appears to be applicable to very dense membranes in which flux is relatively low and rejection is high. For fairly dense membranes which contain few pores, the solution–diffusion–imperfection model, which uses three transport parameters, may be more realistic than the solution–diffusion model. The concentration profile for Sourirajan's surface force–pore flow model has the same form as the frictional–pore flow models. However, in addition to the basic transport equations, the PSCF model offers a more thorough explanation of membrane transport. Dickson (1988) has discussed the use of the PSCF model to predict performance of CA membranes with a variety of solutes.

2.5.1 Pore Flow or Solution–Diffusion?

To distinguish between pore flow and solution–diffusion, one can study the effect of temperature and pressure on solute and solvent flux. The pore flow model assumes solute flux is pressure–dependent, while the solution–diffusion model assumes it is independent of pressure. For porous membranes, the effect of temperature is due to its effect on viscosity of the solvent. With diffusive membranes, on the other hand, temperature effects reflect the activation energy for diffusion of solvent within the membrane, and thus should show greater changes in solvent permeability with temperature than do microporous membranes.

Rejection data can also be used to distinguish between the two mechanisms. Rejection by many asymmetric membranes approaches an asymptote of less than 100% with increasing pressure, implying that solute and solvent flux must be coupled to some extent. Although most solutes with molecular weights greater than 150 are well rejected by most membranes, some organic solutes are not well rejected (Table 3). Rejection must be influenced by the solubility and diffusivity of the solute in the membrane also, which gives support to the solution–diffusion mechanism. However, the solution–diffusion model still does not account for negative rejections of some solutes such as phenyl compounds (Dickson and Lloyd, 1981) and the effect of pH on rejection of dissociated compounds such as organic acids (Schlicher and Cheryan, 1990) and phenol (Matsuura and Sourirajan, 1973).

TABLE 3
TYPICAL REJECTION CHARACTERISTICS OF A CELLULOSE ACETATE
(CA) AND A THIN-FILM COMPOSITE (TFC) RO MEMBRANE (ADAPTED
FROM CHERYAN (1989))

Solute	Molecular weight	Rejection (%)	
		CA	TFC
Glucose	180	99	>99
$MgCl_2$	203	99	98
$NaHCO_3$	84	98	99
NH_4Cl	54	97	98
$NaNO_3$	85	96	93
NaCl	58	95	99
Ethanol	46	60	75
H_3BO_3	62	56	
Urea	60	27	70
NH_4OH	35	7	
Aniline	93	4	
Phenol	95	-9	
2,4-Dichlorophenol	163	-34	
Lactic acid, pH 2	90	20	90
Lactic acid, pH 5	90	40	99

Another approach is to determine how well experimental data fit the
rejection/pressure relationships predicted by the transport models.They
should be compared on the basis of (1) how well the rejection equation
describes the experimental data, and (2) whether the transport coefficients
or parameters are functions of the driving forces (pressure and concentration). A transport model is useful only if the coefficients are
constant. Otherwise, the model parameters have to be determined experimentally for each new application. When using real pilot-plant or
industrial RO modules to obtain the data, many assumptions and
simplifications are often necessary in order to make quantitative predictions. In addition, the transport models are not directly applicable
to complex solutions and do not handle such phenomena as membrane
hysteresis, membrane compaction and the presence of a concentration
polarization boundary layer (except the PSCF model). Despite these
limitations, however, using simple solutions can help to narrow down
the operating strategy for optimum performance. For example, if it is
determined that the prevailing mechanism is viscous pore flow, then it
is likely that the physical structure of the membrane will determine
its behavior when processing more complex solutions. However, if

diffusive flow mechanisms are dominant, solute–membrane and solvent–membrane forces or the physical–chemical properties of the membrane and the chemical properties of the solution will be the primary factors.

In much of the RO literature, there are few valid comparisons between more than two transport models or with more than one solute. We have conducted a comprehensive theoretical and experimental evaluation of several of these RO models. Cellulose acetate spiral-wound membranes of three different porosities were studied under a variety of experimental conditions using three different model solutes: a salt (NaCl), a sugar (sucrose) and a protein (bovine serum albumin). For evaluation purposes, and for ease of data handling, the models were grouped together as 'linear' or 'non-linear' models. They are shown in their test forms in Tables 4 and 5. The non-linear models all have the same basic form, as shown below:

$$Y = \beta_1 + \beta_2 \exp[-\beta_3 v_w] \qquad (61)$$

In general, the transport coefficients for the linear models were dependent on the driving forces for permeation (concentration and pressure gradients) and on the main ˙operating parameter (temperature). When compared on their ability to predict rejection, no one model gave the best fit for all solute–membrane systems. The non-linear finely porous model had the lowest standard deviations and gave the best fit to most of the data, whereas the one-parameter, solution–diffusion model gave the highest standard deviations. The parameters for the linear models were, for the most part, functions of the driving forces (Nichols and Cheryan, 1986).

It appears that the actual transport mechanism is likely to remain a controversial subject for some time to come. Almost all of the early work in this area focused on cellulose acetate membranes. Thin-film composite membranes have received very little attention, and their transport mechanism is probably quite different from CA membranes, considering the different rejections one obtains with the same solutes (Table 3). Very little has been done with the most recent class of 'loose RO' membranes, those used for nanofiltration. Perry and Linder (1989) have proposed a modification of the Spiegler–Kedem RO model by introducing the Donnan exclusion correction into the driving force term to account for negative salt (NaCl) rejection with NF membranes.

TABLE 4
LINEAR MEMBRANE TRANSPORT MODELS

Transport model	$\tilde{R}$	Test equation	Parameters estimated
Solution–Diffusion (Lonsdale et al. 1965)	$\dfrac{A(\Delta P_T - \Delta\pi)}{A(\Delta P_T - \Delta\pi) + Bc_1''}$	$\dfrac{1-\tilde{R}}{\tilde{R}} = \dfrac{B}{A}\,\dfrac{c_1''}{(\Delta P_T - \Delta\pi)}$	$\dfrac{B}{A}$
Linear I. T. (Pusch, 1977)	$\dfrac{1}{R_{\max}} + \dfrac{(L_\pi/L_p - \sigma^2)(1-R_{\max})L_p\pi'}{(1-\sigma)R_{\max}J_v}$	$\dfrac{1}{\tilde{\tilde{R}}} = \dfrac{1}{R_{\max}} + \dfrac{(L_\pi/L_p - \sigma^2)(1-R_{\max})L_p\pi'}{(1-\sigma)R_{\max}J_v}$ $\dfrac{1}{\tilde{\tilde{R}}} = \dfrac{1}{R_{\max}} + b\,\dfrac{1}{J_v}$	$R_{\max}, b$
Solution–Diffusion–Imperfection (Sherwood et al., 1967)	$\dfrac{\kappa_1(\Delta P_T - \Delta\pi)}{\kappa_1(\Delta P_T - \Delta\pi) + \kappa_3(\Delta P_T) + \kappa_2}$	$\dfrac{1-\tilde{R}}{\tilde{R}} = \dfrac{\kappa_3}{\kappa_1}\,\dfrac{\Delta P_T}{(\Delta P_T - \Delta\pi)} + \dfrac{\kappa_2}{\kappa_1}\,\dfrac{1}{(\Delta P_T - \Delta\pi)}$	$\dfrac{\kappa_3}{\kappa_1},\ \dfrac{\kappa_2}{\kappa_1}$
Diffusion–Flow (Yasuda and Lamaze, 1971)	$\left[\phi + \dfrac{P_2^* RT}{P_1^* \bar{v}_1(\Delta P_T - \Delta\pi)}\right]^{-1}$	$\dfrac{1}{R} = \phi + \dfrac{P_2^* RT}{P_1^* \bar{v}_1}\,\dfrac{1}{(\Delta P_T - \Delta\pi)}$	$\phi,\ \dfrac{P_2^* RT}{P_1^* v_1}$

TABLE 5
NON-LINEAR MEMBRANE TRANSPORT MODELS

Transport model	$\tilde{R}$	Test equation	Parameters estimated
Non-linear IT (Spiegler and Kedem, 1966)	$\dfrac{\sigma - \sigma\exp[-v_w(1-\sigma)\lambda/\bar{P}_2]}{1 - \sigma\exp[-v_w(1-\sigma)\lambda/\bar{P}_2]}$	$\dfrac{1}{1-\tilde{R}} = \dfrac{1}{1-\sigma} - \dfrac{\sigma}{1-\sigma}\exp[-v_w(1-\sigma)\lambda/\bar{P}_2]$ $Y = \beta + (1-\beta)\exp[-\alpha v_w]$	$\beta,\ \alpha$
Viscous Flow–Frictional (Jonsson and Boesen, 1975)	$\dfrac{(K_2/b-1)+(1-K_2/b)\exp[v_w(t\lambda/\varepsilon)/D_{21}]}{(K_2/b-1)+\exp[v_w(t\lambda/\varepsilon)/D_{21}]}$	$\dfrac{1}{1-\tilde{R}} = \dfrac{b}{K_2} + \left(1-\dfrac{b}{K_2}\right)\exp[v_w(t\lambda/\varepsilon)/D_{21}]$ $Y = \beta + (1-\beta)\exp[-\alpha v_w]$	$\beta,\ \alpha$
Finely porous (Merten, 1966)	$1 - \left[\dfrac{K'_2\exp[v_w(t\lambda/\varepsilon)(f_{21}/RT)]}{K''_2 - b\varepsilon + b\varepsilon\exp[v_w(t\lambda/\varepsilon)(f_{21}/RT)]}\right]$	$\dfrac{1}{1-\tilde{R}} = \dfrac{b\varepsilon}{K'_2} + \dfrac{K'_2 - b\varepsilon}{K'_2}\exp[v_w(t\lambda/\varepsilon)(f_{21}/RT)]$ $Y = \beta_1 + \beta_2\exp[-\alpha v_w]$	$\beta_1,\ \beta_2,\ \alpha$

3 ULTRAFILTRATION

3.1 Pressure-Controlled Conditions

The mechanism of transport through UF membranes is generally considered to occur through a sieve-type mechanism and is usually based on the Hagen–Poiseuille model for stream-line flow through channels (in the case of membranes, the pore is considered as a circular channel). This model, which relates pressure drop, viscosity, density and channel dimensions to flow rate, has been analyzed by means of a momentum balance using cylindrical coordinates (e.g., see derivation in Bird et al. (1960)). The form useful in ultrafiltration is:

$$J = \frac{\varepsilon r^2 P}{8 \eta \lambda} \qquad (62)$$

where r is the channel radius (i.e., the mean pore radius), λ is the length of the channel (the membrane skin thickness in this case) and ε is the surface porosity of the membrane (number of pores per unit area). The net driving force (P in eqn (62)) should be ($\Delta P_T - \Delta \pi$). In a dead-end filtration operation as shown in Fig. 6:

$$\Delta P_T = P_F - P_p \qquad (63)$$

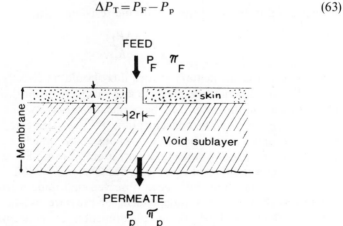

FIG. 6.   Schematic representation of cross-section of UF or MF membrane. P_F is the applied pressure, P_p is permeate back pressure, π_F and π_p are osmotic pressure of feed and permeate side solutions.

In a cross-flow operation, where the feed stream flows parallel to the membrane surface, with an inlet pressure of P_i and an outlet pressure of P_o,

$$P_F = \frac{P_i + P_o}{2} \tag{64}$$

The net osmotic pressure is the difference in osmotic pressure between the feed and permeate sides:

$$\Delta\pi = \pi_F - \pi_p \tag{65}$$

In practice, since UF retains only the high-molecular-weight solids, their contribution to osmotic pressure is negligible, except at very high concentrations (see later). The low-molecular-weight components, on the other hand, should freely permeate through the pores of UF membranes, and their concentrations on either side of the membrane will be similar. Thus $\Delta\pi = 0$ and the net driving force in UF is ΔP_T.

The membrane-specific factors in eqn (62) can be grouped together as a membrane (permeability) coefficient, A:

$$J = \frac{A(\Delta P_T)}{\eta} \tag{66}$$

or expressed in terms of the membrane resistance, R_m:

$$J = \frac{(\Delta P_T)}{\eta R_m} \tag{67}$$

According to this elementary model, flux should be directly proportional to applied transmembrane pressure and inversely proportional to viscosity of the fluid in the pores (i.e., the permeate). Viscosity will be affected by temperature and solids concentration in the permeate, which for a particular application should not change too much except at high concentration factors or during diafiltration. This model has been shown to be true in a number of cases (e.g., see Cheryan (1986)).

However, it has frequently been observed that under certain operating conditions, flux becomes independent of pressure as shown in Fig. 7. This has been ascribed to the phenomenon of 'concentration polarization' (Fig. 8) which is the accumulation of rejected molecules or particles on the surface of the membrane. During ultrafiltration, solute is brought to the membrane surface by convective transport and a portion of the solvent is removed from the fluid. This results in a higher local

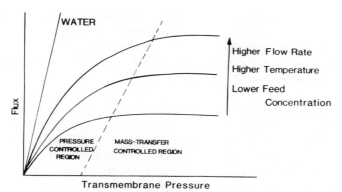

FIG. 7. Generalized correlation between operating parameters and flux in ultrafiltration (adapted from Cheryan (1986)).

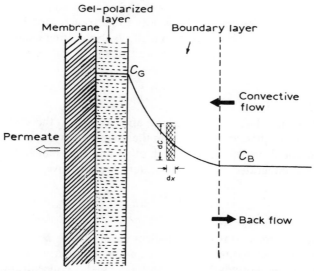

FIG. 8. Concentration polarization during ultrafiltration of colloidal suspensions and macromolecular solutions, showing the built-up gel-polarized layer and boundary layer (adapted from Cheryan (1986)).

concentration of the solute at the membrane surface than in the bulk stream, regardless of whether the solutes are completely or partially rejected. This solute build-up will cause a steep concentration gradient within the boundary layer, resulting in a back-transport of solute into the bulk stream due to diffusion. Eventually a steady state is reached where the two phenomena balance each other. Solute concentration reaches a maximum, the so-called 'gel concentration' (C_G). It is due to this consolidated gel layer that the pressure-independence in Fig. 7 is observed. Flux is no longer controlled by pressure but by the mass transfer characteristics of the system.

3.2 Mass-Transfer-Limited Conditions

One of the simplest and most widely used models for predicting flux in the pressure-independent, mass-transfer-controlled region is the film theory. Its derivation is based on Fick's law of diffusion. As solution is ultrafiltered (Fig. 8), solute is brought to the membrane surface by convective transport at a rate J_s, where

$$J_s = JC_B \tag{68}$$

where C_B is the bulk concentration of the rejected solids. The resulting concentration gradient causes the solute to be transported back into the bulk of the solution due to diffusional effects. Neglecting axial concentration gradients, the rate of back-transport of solute will be given by:

$$J_s = D \frac{dC}{dx} \tag{69}$$

where D is the diffusion coefficient and dC/dx is the concentration gradient over a differential element in the boundary layer. At steady state, the two mechanisms will balance each other and eqns (68) and (69) can be equated and integrated over the boundary layer to give:

$$J = \frac{D}{\delta} \ln \frac{C_G}{C_B} = k \ln \frac{C_G}{C_B} \tag{70}$$

where k is the mass transfer coefficient (D/δ), where D is the diffusion coefficient of the rejected molecules in the boundary layer, δ is the thickness of the boundary layer and C_G is the concentration of the rejected solute on the membrane surface (the so-called 'gel' concentration). Note that in this model there is no pressure term. No effect of pressure has been assumed or implied as far as its effect on flux is concerned. Obviously this model will be valid only in the pressure-independent, mass-transfer-controlled operating region during UF. The flux will be controlled by the rate of back-diffusion (i.e., the movement of rejected solute away from the membrane and back into the bulk stream). Since, in most operations the values of C_G and C_B are fixed by the physicochemical properties of the solute or constraints of the process, flux can be enhanced only by enhancing k as much as possible. This is why attempts at increasing the flux by increasing pressure in this region are self-defeating. After a momentary increase, the flux will drop back to the prior value; indeed, flux may actually decrease at very high pressures.

A number of qualitative relationships correlating the mass transfer coefficient to physical properties, flow channel dimensions and operating parameters exist in the literature. None are wholly satisfactory and thus dimensional analysis is frequently used. Using the π theorem and by analogy with heat transfer, a general correlation of the form below can be obtained:

$$Sh = A(Re)^{\alpha}(Sc)^{\beta} \qquad (71)$$

where Sh is the Sherwood number, a measure of the ratio of convective to molecular mass transfer, Re is the Reynolds number (a measure of the state of turbulence in the system) and Sc is the Schmidt number which provides an indication of the ratio of momentum transfer to mass transfer. A, α and β are constants that depend on the state of turbulence and the development of the velocity and concentration profiles along the channel. For turbulent flow, $A = 0.023$, $\alpha = 0.8$ and $\beta = 0.33$. For laminar flow systems, $A = 1.86$, $\alpha = 0.33$, $\beta = 0.33$.

Despite its limitations, the film theory model has been found to describe the UF process reasonably well, at least in a qualitative manner. In the pressure-independent region, flux decreases in a semi-logarithmic manner with bulk feed concentration. Extrapolation of the flux-concentration line to zero flux gives the C_G value, which according to the theory, should be a property of the solute and not of the membrane–module system. Table 6 lists some C_G values; they are not only useful for process design using eqn (70), but also provide an indication of the maximum concentration attainable by UF. The C_G concept, however, seems to fail with large particles in suspension, i.e., particles that are usually within the microfiltration size range.

Flux is improved by higher turbulence (usually achieved by higher flow rates through the module). This is shown by the positive values of α in eqn (71) (Table 7). Temperature also has a favorable effect as expected from eqns (70) and (71). The model also predicts that, all other factors being equal, modules with smaller channel heights or equivalent hydraulic diameters will result in higher flux. Further, in the laminar flow region, shorter length modules will result in higher flux (Cheryan, 1986).

TABLE 6

C_G VALUES OF SELECTED SYSTEMS (ADAPTED FROM CHERYAN (1986, 1989))

Feed	C_G
Milk (skimmed)	20–25% protein
Milk (whole, 3·5% fat)	9–11% protein
	20–25% fat + protein
Soy extracts (whole, 1% fat)	10% protein
	15–16% fat + protein
Defatted soy extracts	20–25% protein
Whey (acid)	30% protein
Whey (sweet)	20–28% protein
Gelatin	22–30% protein
Egg white	40% protein
Polysaccharides	5–10%
Yeast (*S. cerevisiae*)	300–400 g/liter
Bacteria (*L. bulgaricus*)	800 g/liter
Fungi (*A. niger*)	205 g/liter

TABLE 7

VALUES OF α, THE EXPONENT ON THE REYNOLDS NUMBER TERM IN EQN (71) (ADAPTED FROM CHERYAN (1986, 1989))

Feed	State of turbulence	
Casein (1%)	Laminar	0·5
Milk (skim)	Laminar	0·6
Soy extracts (whole)	Laminar	0·32–0·6
Human albumin	Laminar	0·33–0·6
Immune serum globulin	Laminar	0·67
Whole plasma	Laminar	0·33
Whole blood	Laminar	0·60
Styrene–butadiene	Turbulent	1·11
Yeast (*S. cerevisiae*)	Laminar	0·3
	Turbulent	0·5
Fungi (*A. niger*)	Turbulent	1·1
Bacteria (*L. bulgaricus*)	Laminar	0·3

However, it has been frequently observed that the experimental fluxes obtained are much higher than those predicted from the model (Cheryan, 1986; Porter, 1972). This is especially true with colloidal particles in the feed stream, and under high-shear laminar flow conditions. Part of the reason could be due to inaccuracies in the determination of physical properties, especially under the high-shear conditions prevailing in some membrane modules, and at the high concentrations existing near the membrane wall.

The most elegant explanation comes from Porter (1972) who attributed this 'flux paradox' to back-diffusion from the membrane surface to the bulk stream being greater than expected, and being controlled by factors other than, or additional to, the concentration gradient. This is the 'tubular pinch effect', first noticed in the 1950s with rigid spheres in dilute suspensions. Under certain conditions of flow, particles in a flowing stream migrate away from the walls and reach equilibrium at some eccentric radial position. This is given by the general equation:

$$V_{RM} = f[V, Re, (r_p/R)^a, r/R]$$ (72)

where V_{RM} is the radial migration velocity, V is the average bulk fluid velocity, r is the radial position of particle in the channel, r_p is the particle radius, R is the channel radius and a is a constant, whose value is between 2·84 and 4.

This radial migration of the particles away from the membrane and into the bulk flowing liquid decreases the resistance due to the polarized layer and increases flux. This also explains why the flux paradox is more apparent with colloidal suspensions than with true solutions.

3.2 Osmotic Pressure-Limited Model

Under certain conditions, osmotic pressure may become important even in ultrafiltration. The term in eqn (7) was dropped from consideration since osmotic pressures of macromolecules are small in comparison to applied pressures. However, if concentration polarization is significant, then the concentration of solute on the membrane surface (C_m) may be high enough that osmotic pressure at the membrane surface (π_m) may also become significant. Equation (7) can then become (when $C_p = 0$):

$$J = A(\Delta P_T - \pi_m)$$ (73)

Since π_m is an exponential function of C_m (eqn (6)), a small increase in pressure that causes a corresponding increase in C_m will lead to a large increase in π_m. This will negate the benefit of higher pressures on flux and even reduce flux in some cases. This can be seen in Fig. 4 with skimmilk. Decreases in flux at high applied pressures can be frequently observed with macromolecular feeds in RO; in UF, it is a good indication of osmotic pressure limitations.

Since $\pi_m = f(C_m)$, and, from eqn (70),

$$C_m = C_B \exp(J/k) \tag{74}$$

$$J = A\{\Delta P_T - f[C_B \exp(J/k)]\} \tag{75}$$

Thus those conditions that increase k (higher velocity and temperature, lower concentration) will decrease the value of C_m which will increase the net driving force and thus increase flux.

4 MICROFILTRATION

Modelling of microfiltration is probably the most difficult of all pressure-driven membrane processes. In a qualitative manner, microfiltration appears to follow classic 'cake' filtration models when the equipment is operated as a 'dead-end' filter. On the other hand, when microfiltration modules are operated in the cross-flow mode, the behavior appears to approximate the gel-polarization model, at least qualitatively, except for the semi-logarithmic relationship between flux and solids concentration. Frequently, the line extrapolates to zero flux at solids concentration higher than a mass fraction of 1 or what we know to be unattainably high values.

4.1 Dead-End Microfiltration

For dead-end operations (which may be the mode of operation of choice in selected applications), classic cake filtration models for constant rate filtration and constant pressure filtration have been found to be applicable. In Fig. 9, the total pressure drop across the filter + cake is ΔP, where

$$\Delta P = P_F - P_p = \Delta P_c + \Delta P_m \tag{76}$$

In practice, we can only measure ΔP, and not the individual pressure drops ΔP_c and ΔP_m. Since the flux is the same across both resistances,

$$J = \frac{\Delta P_c}{R_c} = \frac{\Delta P_m}{R_m} \tag{77}$$

where R_m is the resistance of the membrane. The resistance of the cake (R_c) has been found to be a function of several factors:

$$R_c = \frac{\eta \alpha C_B V(\Delta P)^s}{A} \tag{78}$$

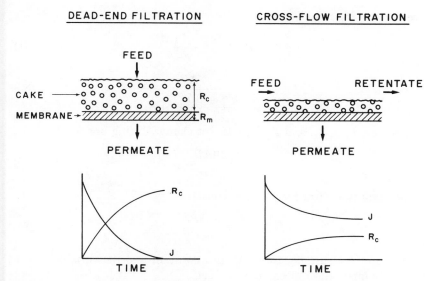

FIG. 9.   Dead-end and cross-flow filtration. The resistance to hydraulic flow through the membrane pores due to the cake is R_c and due to the membrane is R_m. J is the flux.

where C_B is the solids concentration in the feed, α is the specific cake resistance (this appears to be primarily affected by the size of the particles and the porosity of the cake; smaller particles give rise to higher values of a), V is the volume throughput, η is the viscosity of the feed, A is the area and s is the compressibility coefficient, usually taken as zero for incompressible cakes, and 1·0 for perfectly compressible cakes; in practice, it varies between 0·1 and 0·9.

Therefore:

$$J = \frac{\Delta P_c}{\dfrac{\eta \alpha C_B V (\Delta P)^s}{A}} \tag{79}$$

$$\Delta P_c = \frac{J \eta \alpha C_B V (\Delta P)^s}{A} \tag{80}$$

From eqns (76) and (77):

$$\Delta P = J R_m + \frac{J \eta \alpha C_B V (\Delta P)^s}{A} \tag{81}$$

$$J = \frac{dV}{(dt)A} = \frac{\Delta P}{\dfrac{\eta \alpha C_B V (\Delta P)^s}{A} + R_m} \tag{82}$$

In practice, $R_m \ll R_c$, and R_m should not change during operation

$$\frac{dV}{(dt)A} = \frac{A(\Delta P)^{1-s}}{\eta \alpha C_B V} \tag{83}$$

In constant rate filtration, $dV/dt = $ constant.

$$J = \frac{Vt}{A} = \frac{A(\Delta P)^{1-s}}{\eta \alpha C_B V} \tag{84}$$

In constant pressure filtration, ΔP is a constant and the variables are V and t. By integration of eqn (83), we get

$$J = \frac{Vt}{A} = \frac{2A(\Delta P)^{1-s}}{\eta \alpha C_B V} \tag{85}$$

For an incompressible cake, when $s = 0$, the two equations for dead-end filtration ((84) and (85)) state that flux is directly proportional to pressure. This has been shown to be largely true for many systems such as tap water. For most food systems, where s will lie between 0·1 and 0·9, flux will be initially linear with pressure but will reach an asymptotic value at higher pressures. In this respect it is very similar to the ultrafiltration phenomenon. The two equations also state that, for a certain filter and application, a higher volumetric throughput (V) can be obtained if the flux (J) is kept low. Higher temperatures are beneficial primarily because of lower viscosities, which appears in the denominator in the two flux equations.

4.2 Cross-Flow Microfiltration

For cross-flow applications, the beneficial effect of velocity on the resistance of the cake must be incorporated into the model. Murkes and Carlsson (1988) have developed such a model based on sedimentary pipe flow expressions, since it is analogous to cross-flow. For example, in the flow of a suspension in a sedimentary pipe, the settling force is gravity and the driving force for transportation of the particles is the flow velocity. In cross-flow filtration, on the other hand, the 'settling' of the solids on the membrane force is due to the drag experienced by the particles (arising from pressure and convective flow towards the membrane). The 'driving force' for transportation of the particles away from the membrane surface is the cross-flow velocity.

Continuing the analogy with flow of suspensions in a pipe, there will be a critical velocity or Reynolds number below which the suspension begins to settle down, forming a bed at the bottom of the pipe with intermediate regions of stagnant and sliding bed flow. For each suspension concentration, there is a velocity at which the pressure gradient is a minimum, and this velocity marks the transition between flow with a stationary bed and fully suspended flow. If d is the diameter of the pipe or cylinder, D_p the particle diameter and v this critical velocity:

$$v = \frac{c(\Delta P/R_c)}{(a/v + b/v^{0.5} + 0.28)^{0.25}} \tag{86}$$

where

$$a = \frac{21\eta}{D_p \rho_L} \tag{87}$$

$$b = 6(a/21)^{0.5} \tag{88}$$

$$c = 2.43 c_v^{0.33} \left(\frac{2d}{(1 - \varepsilon_b)\rho_L} \right)^{0.5} \tag{89}$$

and c_v is the volumetric concentration of solids, ε_b is the porosity of bed and ρ_L is the density of liquid.

Solving for R_c, we get

$$R_c = \frac{c^2 \Delta P}{(av^3 + bv^{3.5} + 0.28v^4)^{0.5}} \tag{90}$$

Using Darcy's expression for filtrate flux (which is similar to eqn (67)):

$$J = B \frac{\Delta P}{\eta(R_c + R_m)} \tag{91}$$

$$J = \frac{B\Delta P}{\eta} \left(\frac{c^2 \Delta P}{(av^3 + bv^{3.5} + 0.28v^4)^{0.5}} + R_m \right)^{-1} \tag{92}$$

Although this expression appears quite complex and has not been verified, it qualitatively fits much of the microfiltration data observed.

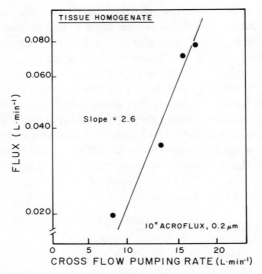

FIG. 10. Effect of cross-flow rate on flux in a Gelman Acroflux microfiltration cartridge (adapted from Tanny *et al.*).

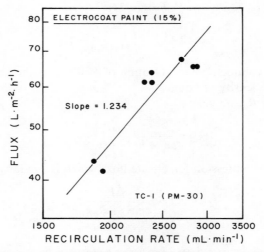

FIG. 11. Effect of recirculation rate on flux in a thin-channel ultrafiltration cell with electrocoat paint of 11% solids (adapted from Porter (1977)).

For example, it predicts the asymptotic relationship between flux and applied transmembrane pressure. Also, at small flow rates, J increases as $v^{1.5}$. Powers on the velocity term greater than 1 have been observed for many microfiltration applications and some UF membranes with colloidal particles (see α values in Table 7; Figs 10 and 11). For high flow rates, on the other hand, where $v \to \infty$, the resistance of the cake (R_c) becomes infinitely small, and the flux is controlled by the resistance of the membrane and independent of velocity. This situation may be difficult to observe in practice. From the definition of the constant c (eqn (89)), it also correctly predicts that flux increases with a decrease in hydraulic diameter of the membrane module, all other factors being kept constant.

5 SUMMARY AND CONCLUSIONS

The design of pressure-driven membrane processes requires a good understanding of the mechanisms of solute and solvent transport through membranes. Developing mechanistic models also requires knowledge of physical properties of the solute–solvent–membrane system. Even the simplest solution–diffusion model for RO requires knowledge of the diffusivities of the solute and solvent in the membrane, the membrane water content, partial molar volume of water and the partition coefficient of solute in the membrane versus the solution. The 'preferential sorption–capillary flow' model also requires Taft numbers and Small's numbers. These are available for simple organic molecules (Sourirajan and Matsuura, 1984) or can be easily estimated. For complex systems, such as those existing in food, it is considerably more difficult.

Ultrafiltration models are much simpler (at least those based on the film theory), but they too require knowledge of diffusivity, viscosity and density of the rejected macromolecule or colloidal particle. These properties should ideally be known under the high shear prevailing in many membrane modules and at the high concentrations existing at the membrane surface. It is of immense interest to determine the physical nature of the 'gel' layer and whether it is a true physical property dependent only on the nature of the solute or on the operating parameters, or both.

Microfiltration (the cross-flow variant using synthetic membranes) has received the least attention. In a qualitative manner, the effect of operating parameters, channel dimensions and physical properties of the

96   M. CHERYAN and D. J. NICHOLS

feed stream are similar in UF and MF. However, considerable theoretical modelling and experimental verification still needs to be done in this membrane process to yield satisfactory quantitative predictions. Thus, the mechanism for selective mass transport is probably different for each situation, depending on membrane structure as well as the nature of the feed and permeating solutions. It is also possible for more than one mechanism to operate simultaneously. A continuum of models may be necessary to fully describe transport through membranes.

REFERENCES

Banks, W. & Sharples, A. (1986) Studies on desalination by reverse osmosis. III. Mechanism of solute rejection. *J. Appl. Chem.*, **16**, 153–8.
Belfort, G. (1976). A molecular frictional model for transport of uncharged solutes in neutral hyperfiltration and ultrafiltration membranes containing bound water. *Desalination*, **18**, 259–81.
Bird, R. B., Stewart, W. E. & Lightfoot, E. N. (1960). *Transport Phenomena*. John Wiley, New York.
Bo, F. & Stannett, V. (1976). On the salt rejection of non-ionic polymeric membranes. *Desalination*, **18**, 113–35.
Cheryan, M. (1986). *Ultrafiltration Handbook*, Technomic, Lancaster, PA.
Cheryan, M. (1989). Membrane separations: mechanisms and models. In *Physical Properties and Computer-Aided Engineering of Food Processing Systems*, ed. R. P. Singh and A. G. Medina. Kluwer Academic, Dordrecht, pp. 367–92.
Cheryan, M., Sarma, S. C. & Pal, D. (1987) Energy considerations in the manufacture of khoa by reverse osmosis. *Asian J. Dairy Res.*, **6**, 143–53.
Cheryan, M., Veeranjaneyulu, B. & Schlicher, L. R. (1990). Reverse osmosis of milk with thin film composite membranes. *J. Membr. Sci.*, **48**, 103–114.
Dickson, J. M. (1988). Fundamental aspects of reverse osmosis. In *Reverse Osmosis Technology*, ed. B. S. Parekh. Marcel Dekker, New York, pp. 1–52.
Dickson, J. M. & Lloyd, D. R. (1981). Solute preferential sorption in reverse osmosis. In *Synthetic Membranes:* Volume II. *Hyper- and Ultrafiltration Uses*, ed. A. F. Turbak. ACS Symposium Series 154, American Chemical Society, Washington, DC, pp. 293–314.
Elata, C. (1969). The determination of the intrinsic characteristics of reverse osmosis membranes. *Desalination*, **6**, 1–12.
Groepl, R. & Pusch, W. (1970). Asymmetric behavior of cellulose acetate membranes in hyperfiltration experiments as a result of concentration polarization. *Desalination*, **8**, 277–92.
Hwang, S. & Pusch, W. (1981). Asymptotic solute rejection in reverse osmosis. In *Synthetic Membranes:* Vol. I, *Desalination*, ed. A. F. Turbak. ASC Symposium Series 153, American Chemical Society, Washington, DC, pp. 253–66.
Jagur-Grodzinski, J. & Kedem, O. (1966). Transport coefficients and salt rejection in uncharged hyperfiltration membranes. *Desalination*, **1**, 327–41.

Johnson, J. S., Dresner, L. & Kraus, K. A. (1966). Hyperfiltration (reverse osmosis). In *Principles of Desalination*, ed. K. S. Spiegler. Academic Press, New York, pp. 346–439.

Jonsson, G. (1978). Methods for determining the selectivity of reverse osmosis membranes. *Desalination*, **24**, 19–37.

Jonsson, G. (1980). The influence of the porous sublayer on the salt rejection and reflection coefficient of asymmetric cellulose acetate membranes. *Desalination*, **34**, 141–57.

Jonsson, G. & Boesen, C. E. (1975). Water and solute transport through cellulose acetate reverse osmosis membranes. *Desalination*, **17**, 145–65.

Kedem, O. & Katchalsky, A. (1958). Thermodynamic analysis of the permeability of biological membranes to non-electrolytes. *Biochim. Biophys. Acta*, **27**, 229–46.

Kedem, O. & Katchalsky, A. (1963). Permeability of composite membranes. Part 3: Series array of elements. *Trans. Faraday Soc.*, **59**, 1941–53.

Kimura, S. & Sourirajan, S. (1967). Analysis of data in reverse osmosis with porous cellulose acetate membranes used. *AIChE J.*, **13**, 497–503.

Lee, C. H. (1975). Theory of reverse osmosis and some other membrane permeation operations. *J. Appl. Polymer Sci.*, **19**, 83–95.

Loeb, S. & Sourirajan, S. (1960). Sea water demineralization by means of semi-permeable membranes. UCLA Engineering Report No. 60.

Loeb, S. & Sourirajan, S. (1962). Sea water demineralization by means of an osmotic membrane. *Advan. Chem. Ser.*, **38**, 117–32.

Lonsdale, H. K. (1972). Theory and practice of reverse osmosis and ultrafiltration. In *Industrial Processing with Membranes*, ed. R. E. Lacey and S. Loeb. Wiley–Interscience, New York, pp. 123–78.

Lonsdale, H. K. (1973). Recent advances in reverse osmosis membranes. *Desalination*, **13**, 317–32.

Lonsdale, H. K., Merten, U. & Riley, R. L. (1965). Transport properties of cellulose acetate osmotic membranes. *J. Appl. Polymer Sci.*, **9**, 1341–62.

Lonsdale, H. K., Cross, B. P., Graber, F. M. & Milstead, C. E. (1971). Permeability of cellulose acetate membranes to selected solutes. In *Permaselective Membranes*, ed. C. E. Rogers. Marcel Dekker, New York.

Matsuura, T. & Sourirajan, S. (1973). Reverse osmosis separation of organic acids in aqueous solutions using porous cellulose acetate membranes. *J. Appl. Polymer Sci.*, **17**, 3661–82.

Merten, U. (1966). Transport properties of osmotic membranes. In *Desalination by Reverse Osmosis*, ed. U. Merten. MIT Press, Cambridge, MA.

Murkes, J. & Carlsson, C. G. (1988). *Crossflow Filtration*. John Wiley, Chichester.

Nichols, D. J. & Cheryan, M. (1986). Evaluation of membrane transport models for reverse osmosis in spiral wound cellulose acetate membranes. *World Congr. III Chem. Engr.* Vol. 3, Society of Chemical Engineers, Tokyo, pp. 208–11.

Paul, D. R. (1976). The solution-diffusion model for highly swollen membranes. *Separation and Purification Methods*, **5**, 33–50.

Perry, M. & Linder, C. (1989). Intermediate reverse osmosis ultrafiltration (RO UF) membranes for concentration and desalting of low molecular weight organic solutes. *Desalination*, **71**, 233–45.

Porter, M. C. (1972). Concentration polarization with membrane ultrafiltration. *I&EC Prod. Res. Devel.*, **11**, 234–48.

Porter, M. C. (1977). Membrane filtration. In *Handbook of Separation Techniques for Chemical Engineers.* McGraw-Hill, New York, pp. 2–103.

Pusch, W. (1977). Determination of transport parameters of synthetic membranes by hyperfiltration experiments. Part I: Derivation of transport relationship from the linear relations of thermodynamics of irreversible processes. *Ber. Bunsenges. Physik. Chem.*, **81**, 269–76.

Reid, C. E. & Breton, E. J. (1959). Water and ion flow across cellulose acetate membranes. *J. Appl. Polymer Sci.*, **1**, 133–43.

Schlicher, L. R. & Cheryan, M. (1990). Reverse osmosis of lactic acid fermentation broths. *J. Chem. Technol. Biotechnol.*, **49**, 129–140.

Sherwood, T. K., Brian, P. L. T. & Fisher, R. E. (1967). Desalination by reverse osmosis. *Ind. Eng. Chem. Fund.*, **6**, 2–12.

Sourirajan, S. (1970). *Reverse Osmosis.* Academic Press, New York.

Sourirajan, S. (1977). Reverse osmosis—a general separation technique. In *Reverse Osmosis and Synthetic Membranes. Theory–Technology–Engineering*, ed. S. Sourirajan. National Research Council of Canada Publications, Ottawa.

Sourirajan, S. & Matsuura, T. (1977a) Transport through reverse osmosis membranes. In *Reverse Osmosis and Synthetic Membranes. Theory–Technology–Engineering*, ed. S. Sourirajan. National Research Council of Canada Publications, Ottawa.

Sourirajan, S. & Matsuura, T. (1977b). Physicochemical criteria for reverse osmosis separations. In *Reverse Osmosis and Synthetic Membranes, Theory–Technology–Engineering*, ed. S. Sourirajan. National Research Council of Canada Publications, Ottawa.

Sourirajan, S. & Matsuura, T. (1982). Science of reverse osmosis—an essential tool for the chemical engineer. *The Chemical Engineer*, **385**, 359–76.

Sourirajan, S. & Matsuura, T. (1984). *Reverse Osmosis and Ultrafiltration.* National Research Council of Canada, Ottawa.

Spiegler, K. S. & Kedem, O. (1966). Thermodynamics of hyperfiltration (reverse osmosis): criteria for efficient membranes. *Desalination*, **1**, 311–26.

Tanny, G. B., Hauk, D. & Merin, U. (1982). Biotechnical application of a pleated cross-flow microfiltration module. *Desalination*, **41**, 299–302.

Yasuda, H. & Lamaze, C. E. (1971). Salt rejection by polymer membranes in reverse osmosis. I. Nonionic polymers. *J. Appl. Polymer Sci., Part A-2*, **9**, 1537–51.

Chapter 3

MOISTURE TRANSFER MODELLING OF A LIQUID FOOD DROPLET ON DRYING

Takeshi Furuta

Department of Biotechnology,
Tottori University,
Koyamacho-minami,
Tottori, Japan

NOTATION

A_a	activity coefficient of flavor	(—)
c_a	mass concentration of flavor	(kg/m³)
c_D	drag coefficient	(—)
c_s	mass concentration of solid	(kg/m³)
c_t	total mass concentration of liquid	(kg/m³)
c_w	mass concentration of water	(kg/m³)
C_{pd}	heat capacity of droplet	(J/K)
C_{pw}	specific heat capacity of water	(J/kg K)
C_{ps}	specific heat capacity of solid	(J/kg K)
d_p	droplet diameter	(m²/s)
$\mathcal{D}_a$	diffusivity of flavor	(m²/s)
$\mathcal{D}_v$	diffusivity of water vapor in air	(m²/s)
$\mathcal{D}_w$	diffusivity of water	(m²/s)
$\mathcal{D}_{wa}$	cross-diffusivity of water and flavor	(m²/s)
E	fraction of moisture removed	(—)
F	flux parameter	(—)
g	gravity acceleration	(—)
h	heat transfer coefficient	(J/m² s K)
H_a	modified activity coefficient	(—)
ΔH_v	heat of evaporation of water	(J/kg)
j_w^s	mass flux relative to dissolved solid	(kg/m² s)
k	mass transfer coefficient of water vapor	(kg/m² s Pa)
k_a	mass transfer coefficient of flavor vapor	(kg/m² s Pa)

99

m	weight fraction of dissolved solid	(—)
n	mass flux	(kg/m^2 s)
n_t	total molar concentration	(mol/m^3)
N	mole flux	(mol/m^2 s)
p_a	partial vapor pressure of flavor	(Pa)
p_w	partial vapor pressure of water	(Pa)
r	radial coordinate	(m)
R	radius of droplet	(m)
$\mathscr{R}$	gas constant	(m^3 Pa/mol K)
T	temperature	(°C or K)
T_a	temperature of air	(°C or K)
T_d	temperature of droplet	(°C or K)
u	velocity of air	(m/s)
u_r	relative velocity of droplet to air	(m/s)
W_w	mass of water	(kg)
x	mole fraction	(—)
α_{Aw}	relative volatility of flavor	(—)
θ	time	(s)
λ	thermal conductivity	(J/m s K)
ρ_a^0	density of flavor	(kg/m^3)
ρ_w^0	density of water	(kg/m^3)
σ	substantial coordinate defined by eqn (26)	(—)
φ	humidity of air	(kg steam/ kg dry air)
ψ_a	flavor retention	(—)
ψ_w	water retention	(—)
ω	mass fraction	(—)
ω_a'	flavor content on dry basis	(—)
ω_w'	moisture content on dry basis	(—)
$\bar{\omega}_w'$	average moisture content on dry basis	(—)

Subscript

a	flavor
d	droplet
e	value at inflation of droplet
s	solid
w	water
0	initial value

Superscript
b   bulk of air stream
i   interface
*   before inflation

1 INTRODUCTION

Drying is one of the most important processes in manufacturing food product, because it both increases the shelf-life of the product by protecting against microbial spoilage and reduces transportation costs. There are many processes used in the drying of food liquids. Spray-drying is one of the most popular methods of obtaining powdered product efficiently from food liquid in a few tens seconds. However, thermal degradation of the nutritious or volatile components is often observed during spray-drying, because of the high temperature of the drying air. To prevent this serious damage to the product, the transport mechanism of the moisture and other chemical species should be understood correctly.

Fine droplets of food liquid are sprayed into the drying chamber through the atomizer and are dried by high-temperature air, involving simultaneous heat and mass transfer. If the vapor pressure of the water on the surface of the droplet is the same as that of pure water, the dynamic equilibrium state obtains, where the evaporation rate remains constant (e.g. surface evaporation period). During this period, the water inside the droplet migrates rapidly enough to maintain surface saturation, and the resistance to mass transfer exists only in the boundary film in the gas phase. As the drying proceeds, the concentration of water near the phase boundary inside the droplet decreases. Since the diffusivity of water in liquid food decreases predominantly with the increase in dissolved solid concentration, the moisture gradient near the surface of the droplet becomes more steep. At this period of drying, the interfacial vapor pressure of water in the gas phase becomes less than that in pure water, and then the droplet temperature begins to rise as the balance between heat income and consumption is disrupted. Thereafter, the drying rate falls, and the resistance to moisture movement exists mainly inside the liquid droplet. If no forced convection exists in the liquid droplet, the drying rate can be mathematically expressed by Fick's differential equation.

In this chapter, the transport of the moisture and the volatile component inside the liquid food droplet will be discussed on the basis of the molecular diffusion theory.

2 EVAPORATION OF A SPRAYED DROPLET OF WATER

Though the drying characteristics of a sprayed droplet show much variation, depending on the nature of the solutes dissolved in the feed liquid, the drying behavior immediately after atomization is quite similar to the evaporation of a pure water droplet if the moisture content of the feed liquid is large enough. Moreover, since a large amount of the removable water can be evaporated in this region, the theoretical calculation for the drying of a pure water droplet has been studied to determine the gross size of the spray-dryer.

As shown in Fig. 1, a water droplet (diameter: d_p) is assumed to move in air with a temperature T_a and a water vapor pressure p_w^b. If the droplet is evaporated at a steady rate, the droplet temperature is constant and equal to the wet-bulb temperature of the air, T_w. Assuming the ideal gas law is valid, the evaporation rate of water N_w can be as:

$$N_w = -\frac{dm}{d\theta} = \pi d_p^2 n_t k(x_w^i - x_w^b) = k\frac{\pi d_p^2}{\mathscr{R}T_a}(p_w^i - p_w^b) = \pi d_p^2\frac{h(T_a - T_w)}{\Delta H_v} \quad (1)$$

where m is the mass of the droplet, x_w mole fraction of water vapor in the air, n_t the total molar concentration of the water vapor and air, p_w^i and p_w^b the water vapor pressure in the gas phase at the interface and the bulk of

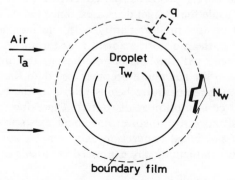

FIG. 1.   Evaporation of water droplet in air stream.

the air, ΔH_v the latent heat of evaporation of water, and h and k are heat and mass transfer coefficients of the droplet, respectively. As the mass of the droplet is equal to $(\pi/6)\rho_w^0 d_p^3$, the equation of change of the droplet diameter is described as:

$$\frac{d(d_p)}{d\theta} = \frac{k}{\mathscr{R}T_a \rho_w^0}(p_w^i - p_w^b) = \frac{h(T_a - T_w)}{\Delta H_v} \tag{2}$$

Since the heat and mass transfer coefficient in eqn (2) depend on the relative velocity between the droplet and the air stream as well as on the droplet diameter, the equation must be solved simultaneously with the equation of motion of the droplet. The following are some calculated examples.

Low Reynolds number of droplet (Masters, 1972; King et al., 1984). If the droplet Reynolds number can be approximated as zero, h and k can be calculated with the following equations.

$$Nu = 2 \cdot 0 \qquad \text{and} \qquad Sh = 2 \cdot 0 \tag{3}$$

where $Nu = h d_p/\lambda$ and $Sh = k d_p/\mathscr{D}_v$ (λ: the thermal conductivity of the air, $\mathscr{D}_v$: the diffusivity of the water vapor in the air). Substituting eqn (3) into eqn (2), the following equation can be obtained.

$$\frac{d(d_p^2)}{d\theta} = \frac{8\mathscr{D}_v}{\mathscr{R}T_a \rho_w^0}(p_w^i - p_w^b) = \frac{8\lambda}{\rho_w^0}\frac{h(T_a - T_w)}{\Delta H_v} \tag{4}$$

Integrating eqn (4) under constant $\mathscr{D}_v$ and T_a, one can obtain

$$\frac{d_p^2}{d_{p0}^2} = 1 - \frac{8\lambda(T_a - T_w)}{d_{p0}^2 \rho_w^0 \Delta H_v}\theta \tag{5}$$

Then, the time for complete evaporation of water droplet θ_e is as follows:

$$\theta_e = \frac{d_{p0}^2 \rho_w^0 \Delta H_v}{8\lambda(T_a - T_w)} \tag{6}$$

Unidirectional downward movement of a droplet in stagnant air (Kerkhof and Schoeber, 1974; Sjenitzer, 1952). The equation of motion of droplet falling vertically in stagnant air is represented as:

$$\frac{du_R}{d\theta} = \frac{\rho_w^0 - \rho_a}{\rho_w^0}g - \tfrac{3}{4}c_D\frac{\rho_a u_R^2}{\rho_w^0 d_p} \tag{7}$$

in which u_R is the relative velocity between the droplet and the air, and c_D is the drag coefficient of the droplet, which is a function of the Reynolds number of the droplet. Since the Reynolds number of the droplet varies continuously, owing to evaporation, eqn (7) must be solved simultaneously with eqn (2). Kerkhof and Schoeber (1974) have solved these equations numerically to obtain the change of droplet diameter and evaporation rate as a function of time. They used the fourth order Runge–Kutta–Gill method to obtain the solution. Sjenitzer (1952) suggested a graphical method which contained several important assumptions. Table 1 shows the comparison between these two results.

TABLE 1
COMPARISON BETWEEN THE RESULTS OF KERKHOF AND SJENITZER (KERKHOF AND SCHOEBER, 1974)

d_p (μm)	Terminal velocity of droplet (m/s)	Descending period		Evaporation fraction	
		Kerkhof (s)	Sjenitzer (s)	Kerkhof	Sjenitzer
100	0·23	0·087	0·090	0·27	0·21
200	0·69	0·22	0·165	0·21	0·14
400	1·66	0·54	0·278	0·19	0·093

It can be seen that there are significant differences between them, especially in descending period and the evaporation fraction in the period, as the initial diameter of droplet becomes large. In recent years, computers have been developed so extensively that, as Kerkhof and Schoeber (1974) mention, the numerical approach is recommended to solve eqn (2) together with eqn (7). Kerkhof and Schoeber (1974) have also calculated the evaporated histories of water droplets in a swirl air flow. They found that the vertical trajectories in the swirl flow showed a little difference from that in unidirectional downward flow.

Miura and Ohtani (1979) calculated the evaporation process of a swarm of water droplets. The calculated results of the air humidity variation along the drying tower, based on their empirical heat and mass transfer coefficients, are in good agreement with the experimental results.

3 THE FUNDAMENTAL EQUATION OF MOISTURE TRANSFER IN A DROPLET ON DRYING

In order to predict the drying rate in the falling rate period, it is necessary to construct a model for the transfer of the water in the liquid phase. For liquid food systems, a useful approximation is that the liquid phase is regarded as a binary system consisting of dissolved solids and water, and that Fick's diffusion equation is applied to describe the movement of the moisture. However, from the mathematical point of view, there remain two major difficulties to the solution of such an equation. One is that the diffusivity of water in the liquid phase is greatly dependent on the moisture content, so that the resultant differential equations are substantially non-linear. The second is that the boundary between the liquid phase and the gas is moving and not invariant in time, since the shrinking or inflation of the droplet takes place during drying.

In recent years, Kerkhof (1975), Schoeber (1976), van der Lijn (1976) and Okazaki *et al.* (1974) have proposed some mathematical models, in which all possible contributions to the moisture transfer are lumped into an effective diffusivity. Furthermore, an equation for the coordinate transformation, which overcomes the difficulty of the moving boundary, was proposed by van der Lijn (1976). The resulting equations have been solved numerically by digital computers, including the change of the temperature of droplet.

3.1 The Moisture Flux Relative to the Reference Component
As shown in Fig. 2, a droplet of liquid food, of which the initial diameter is R_0, is being dried in air at the temperature T_a. For simplicity, the following assumptions are made:

(a) Liquid phase is a binary system—water and dissolved solid— and consists of one phase only.

(b) Transfer of water in the liquid phase takes place by molecular diffusion and no convective movements are taken into account. Spherically symmetric diffusion is also assumed.

(c) No volume contraction takes place upon mixing. Consequently the magnitude of shrinkage is equal to the volume of water evaporated.

(d) No bubbles or crystals appear during drying.

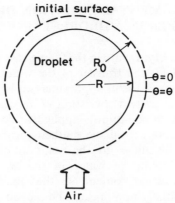

FIG. 2.   Drying of a droplet in air stream.

According to Fick's first law of diffusion in a binary system, the mass flux of water n_w relative to a stationary coordinate can be expressed as (Bird et al., 1960):

$$n_w = (n_w + n_s)\omega_w - \mathscr{D}_w c_t \nabla \omega_w \tag{8}$$

where n_s is the mass flux of dissolved solid relative to the stationary coordinate, ω_w the mass fraction of water ($= c_w/c_t$), c_t the total mass concentration (i.e. density of the droplet) and $\mathscr{D}_w$ the diffusion coefficient of water (Bird et al., 1960). In our system, since the surface of the droplet will move inward as drying proceeds, the mass flux should be described as a reference component (dissolved solid) mass centred coordinate. If j_w^s is defined as the mass flux relative to the movement of dissolved solid, it can be described as (Schoeber, 1986; van der Lijn, 1976; Liou, 1982):

$$j_w^s = c_w(v_w - v_s) = n_w - n_s \omega_w' \tag{9}$$

in which ω_w' is the mass ratio relative to the dissolved solid ($= c_w/c_s$), and v_w and v_s are the mass averaged velocities of the water and the solid, respectively. Expressing eqn (8) in terms of ω_w', one can obtain

$$n_w = n_s \omega_w' - \mathscr{D}_w c_s \nabla \omega_w' \tag{10}$$

From eqns (9) and (10), j_w^s can be rewritten as:

$$j_w^s = - \mathscr{D}_w c_s \nabla \omega_w' \tag{11}$$

For a binary system, where no contraction of volume by mixing takes place, c_s can be given as:

$$c_s = 1/(1/\rho_s^0 + \omega_w'/\rho_w^0) \tag{12}$$

where ρ_w^0 and ρ_s^0 are the partial densities of the water and the dissolved solid, respectively. Substitution of eqn (12) into eqn (11) yields

$$j_w^s = -\mathscr{D}_w \left(\frac{\rho_w^0 \rho_s^0}{\rho_w^0 + \rho_s^0 \omega_w'} \right) \nabla \omega_w' \tag{13}$$

This is the expression of the mass flux, j_w^s, in terms of ω_w'.

3.2 Equation of Continuity

The equations of continuity for the moisture and the dissolved solid in the fixed coordinate system are expressed as:

$$\frac{\partial c_w}{\partial \theta} = -\nabla n_w \tag{14}$$

$$\frac{\partial c_s}{\partial \theta} = -\nabla n_s \tag{15}$$

From the definition of ω_w' and eqns (14) and (15) the time derivative of ω_w' can be given as

$$c_s \frac{\partial \omega_w'}{\partial \theta} = -\nabla n_w + \omega_w' \nabla n_s \tag{16}$$

Furthermore, according to eqn (9), one can obtain

$$j_w^s = n_w - \omega_w' \nabla n_s - n_s \nabla \omega_w' \tag{17}$$

Then, substituting eqn (17) into eqn (16) yields

$$\frac{D\omega_w'}{D\theta} = \frac{\partial \omega_w'}{\partial \theta} + v_s \nabla \omega_w' = -\frac{1}{c_s} \nabla j_w^s = \frac{1}{c_s} \nabla (\mathscr{D}_w c_s \nabla \omega_w') \tag{18}$$

where $D/D\theta$ indicates the substantial time derivative on dissolved solid mass centred coordinate. Since a spherically symmetrical distribution of water content is assumed in the droplet, eqn (18) can be simplified as,

$$\frac{\partial \omega_w'}{\partial \theta} + v_s \frac{\partial \omega_w'}{\partial r} = \frac{1}{c_s r^2} \frac{\partial}{\partial r} \left(\mathscr{D}_w c_s r^2 \frac{\partial \omega_w'}{\partial r} \right) \tag{19}$$

This is the general diffusion equation of water inside the droplet with respect to the reference component fixed coordinate, which is a very convenient way of solving the diffusion problem, even in a shrinking system (Kerkhof, 1975; Schoeber, 1976; van der Lijn, 1976; Liou, 1982).

3.3 Initial and Boundary Conditions

If no concentration gradient of water exists inside the droplet before drying, the initial condition reads:

$$\omega'_w = \omega'_{w,0} \tag{20}$$

where $\omega'_{w,0}$ is the initial value of ω'_w. At the center of the droplet, the symmetry condition holds, that is,

$$\frac{\partial \omega'_w}{\partial r} = 0 \qquad (\text{at } r = 0) \tag{21}$$

Since the rate of evaporation of water at the surface of the droplet is equal to j^s_w, which is equal to the mass flux in the gas film, the boundary condition at the interface can be obtained from eqn (11) as:

$$j^s_w = -\mathcal{D}_w c_s \frac{\partial \omega'_w}{\partial r} = k(p^i_w - p^b_w) \tag{22}$$

where value of p^i_w is a function of water activity and temperature at the surface of the droplet, so that it varies as drying proceeds.

3.4 Equation of Change of Droplet Temperature

The resistance of heat transfer in the media is represented by the Biot number, Bi. If Bi is high in the droplet, a sharp temperature profile is generated, and *vice versa*. However, as expressed in detail by Kerkhof and Schoeber (1974), the value of Bi inside the droplet under the normal drying condition is relatively low in comparison with that in the gas phase. One can, therefore, assume that the temperature distribution inside the droplet is negligible. Consequently, the heat balance gives the following equation for the droplet temperature T_d.

$$C_{pd} \frac{dT_d}{d\theta} = 4\pi R^2 \{ h(T_a - T_d) - j^s_w \Delta H_v \} \tag{23}$$

where C_{pd} is the heat capacity of the droplet and R is the droplet radius at time θ. C_{pd} can be expressed as:

$$C_{pd} = \tfrac{4}{3}\pi R_0^3 \left\{ C_{ps} c_{s,0} + C_{pw} \left[c_{w,0} - \rho_w^0 \left(1 - \frac{R^3}{R_0^3} \right) \right] \right\} \qquad (24)$$

where C_{pw} and C_{ps} are the specific heat capacities of the water and the solid, and $c_{w,0}$ and $c_{s,0}$ are the initial concentration of the water and the solid, respectively. The initial condition of T_d is given as:

$$T_d = T_{d,0} \qquad (\text{at } \theta = 0) \qquad (25)$$

3.5 Transformed Coordinate Based on Dissolved Solid Mass

The set of equations, eqns (19) and (23), with their initial and boundary conditions, cannot be solved analytically, because of the strong dependencies of $\mathscr{D}_w$ on the moisture concentration and temperature, the variation of water activity with the moisture content, and the shrinkage of the droplet. Therefore, we need to use numerical methods for solving the equations. However, since the boundary conditions (eqn (22)) are given at the surface, moving with respect to fixed coordinate, it is very complicated to apply the usual finite difference scheme—by using a grid in a fixed space coordinate—because some complicated interpolation procedures are required to make the finite difference equations at the moving boundary. To overcome the difficulties, van der Lijn (1976) proposed a new transformed space coordinate in which the boundary can be immobilized on drying. The new distance coordinate is defined as:

$$\sigma = \int_0^r c_s r^2 \, dr \qquad (26)$$

Physically, the value of σ means the mass of the dissolved solid inside a sphere of the radius r. With this new coordinate σ, eqn (19) is transformed into

$$\frac{\partial \omega_w'}{\partial \sigma} = \frac{\partial}{\partial \sigma} \left(\mathscr{D}_w c_s^2 r^4 \frac{\partial \omega_w'}{\partial \sigma} \right) \qquad (27)$$

in which r can be derived from eqn (26) as:

$$r = \left\{ \int_0^\sigma 3(\omega_w'/\rho_w^0 + 1/\rho_s^0) \, d\sigma \right\}^{1/3} \qquad (28)$$

Also the initial and boundary conditions read:

$$
\left.
\begin{array}{l}
t=0, \quad 0 \leqslant \sigma \leqslant \sigma_0; \quad \omega_{\mathrm{w}}' = \omega_{\mathrm{w},0}' \\[2mm]
t>0, \quad \sigma=0; \quad \partial \omega_{\mathrm{w}}'/\partial \sigma = 0 \\[2mm]
t>0, \quad \sigma=\sigma_0; \quad -\mathscr{D}_{\mathrm{w}} c_{\mathrm{s}}^2 r^2 \dfrac{\partial \omega_{\mathrm{w}}'}{\partial \sigma} = k(p_{\mathrm{w}}^{\mathrm{i}} - p_{\mathrm{w}}^{\mathrm{b}})
\end{array}
\right\}
\tag{29}
$$

where σ_0 is the value of σ at $r=R$ in eqn (26), and can be regarded as the surface of the droplet in the σ-coordinate. From eqn (26), σ_0 can be related with the total amount of the solid mass in the droplet, as follows:

$$
\sigma_0 = \int_0^R c_{\mathrm{s}} r^2 \, \mathrm{d}r = \int_0^{R_0} c_{\mathrm{s},0} r^2 \, \mathrm{d}r = \tfrac{1}{3} c_{\mathrm{s},0} R_0^3
\tag{30}
$$

where $c_{\mathrm{s},0}$ is the initial concentration of the dissolved solid. Since the total amount of the solid mass in the droplet does not change on drying, σ_0 is invariant with time. This means that, even if the droplet shrinks inward in the real coordinate on drying, the droplet surface can be fixed in the σ-coordinate space, and consequently the drying process can be treated as if the moisture is removed from a non-shrinking solid droplet.

3.6 Dimensionless Formula of Drying Equation
For convenience to the following discussion, eqn (27) is transformed into the following dimensionless equation

$$
\frac{\partial \omega_{\mathrm{w}}'}{\partial \tau} = \frac{\partial}{\partial \xi}\left(D_{\mathrm{r}} X^2 \frac{\partial \omega_{\mathrm{w}}'}{\partial \xi} \right)
\tag{31}
$$

where the dimensionless variables are defined as follows: dimensionless time τ:

$$
\tau = \frac{\mathscr{D}_{\mathrm{w}}^0 c_{\mathrm{s},0}^2}{(\rho_{\mathrm{s}}^0 R_{\mathrm{s}})^2}
\tag{32}
$$

$\mathscr{D}_{\mathrm{w}}^0$ is an arbitrary reference value of the diffusion coefficient and R_{s} and the radius of droplet if all of the water is removed from the droplet. This can be represented by the initial droplet radius R_0, as

$$
R_{\mathrm{s}} = (c_{\mathrm{s},0}/\rho_{\mathrm{s}}^0)^{1/3} R_0
\tag{33}
$$

dimensionless diffusivity, D_r:

$$D_r = \frac{\mathscr{D}_w c_s^2}{\mathscr{D}_w^0 c_{s,0}^2} \tag{34}$$

dimensionless radial coordinate, ξ:

$$\xi = \frac{\sigma}{\sigma_0} = \frac{3}{c_{s,0} R_0^3} \int_0^R c_s r^2 \, dr \tag{35}$$

geometry variable, X:

$$X = 3\left\{ \int_0^\xi \frac{\rho_s^0}{c_s} \, d\xi \right\}^{2/3} = 3\left\{ \int_0^\xi \left(1 + \frac{\rho_s^0}{\rho_w^0} \omega_w' \right) d\xi \right\}^{2/3} \tag{36}$$

The value of ξ represents the solid mass ratio between the mass in a sphere of radius r and the total value. Also X is a measure of the surface ratio of the two spheres of radius r and R. By substitution of these dimensionless variables into eqns (11) or (13), the dimensionless mass flux F is expressed as,

$$F = \frac{\rho_s^0 R_s}{\mathscr{D}_w^0 c_{s,0}^2} j_w^s = -D_r X \frac{\partial \omega_w'}{\partial \xi} \tag{37}$$

F is called the 'flux parameter'. The parabolic partial differential equation of eqns (27) or (31) has been solved by van der Lijn (1976), Kerkhof (1975) and Schoeber (1976), by an implicit finite difference method analogous to the Crank–Nicholson scheme for various concentration-dependent diffusion coefficients.

4 A SHORT-CUT METHOD FOR CALCULATION OF THE DRYING RATE

The drying equation for the droplet developed in the previous section can be solved numerically if the concentration-dependence of the diffusion coefficient is known. However, the calculations are rather cumbersome and time-consuming, and data for the diffusion coefficient under various conditions are very scarce. In this section, some short-cut methods for calculations of the drying rate will be discussed, which have been recently developed by Kerkhof (1975), and Schoeber (1976) and revised by Liou (1982).

4.1 Length of the Constant Rate Period

Let us consider two extreme cases of the surface evaporation rate of water. If the evaporation rate of water from the droplet surface is so slow that the internal water can be transferred enough to maintain the uniform concentration profile, the drying will proceed under a flat water concentration distribution. By simple calculation, the length of the constant rate period θ_c can be obtained (Kerkhof, 1975):

$$\theta_c = \frac{\rho_w^0 R_0}{2j_{w,0}^i}\left[1-\left(\frac{1-c_{w,0}/\rho_w^0}{1-c_{w,c}/\rho_w^0}\right)^{2/3}\right] \tag{38}$$

Introducing two following reduced variables,

$$\Theta_c = \theta_c/R_0^2 \quad\text{and}\quad f = j_{w,0}^i R_0/\rho_w^0 \tag{39}$$

eqn (38) can be rewritten as follows:

$$\Theta_c = \frac{1}{2f}\left[1-\left(\frac{1-c_{w,0}/\rho_w^0}{1-c_{w,c}/\rho_w^0}\right)^{2/3}\right] \tag{40}$$

where $j_{w,0}^i$ is the water flux in constant rate period, and $c_{w,0}$ and $c_{w,c}$ are the mass concentration of water at the start and the end of the constant rate period, respectively. On the other hand, if the rate of evaporation is rapid, a steep concentration profile will be constructed immediately near the surface of the droplet. The gradient of the profile is proportional to the moisture flux $j_{w,0}^i$, and consequently the penetration distance and the amount of water removed from the droplet are inversely proportional to $j_{w,0}^i$. Since the amount of water removed is equal to $\theta_c j_{w,0}^i$, θ_c is inversely proportional to $(j_{w,0}^i)^2$. Using the above reduced variables Θ_c and f, the following relation is derived (Kerkhof, 1975).

$$\Theta_c = K/f^2 \tag{41}$$

where K is a constant. These equations were first derived by Kerkhof (1975; Kerkhof and Thijssen, 1977), who furthermore obtained the relationship between Θ_c and f by numerical calculations under various drying conditions. Fig. 3 illustrates the logarithmic plot of Θ_c versus f for two values of the initial water concentration at 25°C. The points represent the numerical results, and the solid lines and the dotted lines are given by eqns (40) and (41), respectively. Here, the constant K is derived from the numerically calculated value of Θ_c at very high f-value. It is found that eqns (40) and (41) are in good agreement with the numerical results for very high and for very low values of f. Large deviations are found near the intersection points of the two lines. Kerkhof

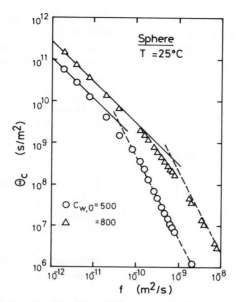

FIG. 3. Correlation of constant drying rate period (after Kerkhof (1975) and Kerkhof *et al.* (1977)).

(1975; Kerkhof and Thijssen, 1977) performed further numerical calculations to determine the dependencies of K on the temperature and initial water content. It was concluded that K could be correlated by the following Arrhenius-type equation.

$$K = K_0 \exp(-\Delta E_k/\mathscr{R}T + K_1 c_{w,0}/\rho_w^0) \qquad (42)$$

where ΔE_k is the activation energy, and K_0 and K_1 are constants. According to Kerkhof (1975), the value of K for a droplet calculated by eqn (42) is equal to that for a slab of the same material. Consequently, if the initial values of the moisture, $c_{w,0}$, the initial droplet temperature, $T_{d,0}$, and the evaporation rate, $j_{w,0}^i$, are known, one can calculate the time length of the constant drying period through eqns (40) to (42).

4.2 The Regular Regime in Isothermal Drying

The concentration distribution inside the media, or the drying rate for a given initial water profile, may be divided into two periods. In the first stage, the drying process is strongly influenced by the initial water distribution. In the second this influence disappears. The latter period of drying is called the 'regular regime', which concept was first introduced by Kondrativ (1964) and Luikov (1968) in order to analyze heat conduction problems with constant thermal diffusivities. Schoeber and Thijssen (1977), Schoeber (1976, 1978), and Liou (1982; Liou and Bruin, 1982) have extended the idea to the drying of homogeneous materials with concentration-dependent diffusivities of water. Figure 4 shows the isothermal drying curve of a slab of an aqueous glucose solution at 30°C, where the flux parameter, F, defined by eqn (37) is illustrated against the average moisture content $\bar{\omega}'_w$. Schoeber (1976, 1978) deduced two important conclusions from the curve:

(a) Though the initial drying rates of the same initial water content are different depending on the drying conditions (e.g. velocity, humidity, etc.), the drying curve gradually converges to a single curve, the 'parent curve', which is independent of the initial drying rates.
(b) Parent curves of different initial water contents coincide asymptotically with a drying curve, the 'grand parent curve'.

The regular regime phenomena can be found in a system where the water activity of the material is nearly equal to unity in the initial period of drying and also the falling rate of drying is limited by the internal diffusion of water. These conditions are fulfilled in aqueous carbohydrate and protein solutions. Schoeber (1976) has solved eqn (31) numerically for

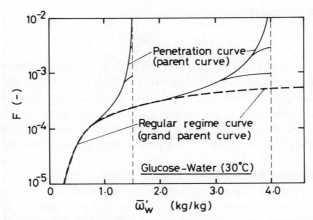

FIG. 4. The regular regime in the isothermal drying curve of aqueous glucose solution (after Schoeber (1976) and Schoeber and Thijssen (1977)).

various cases of concentration-dependent diffusion coefficients. He concluded that the rate of drying can be correlated well by the following dimensionless variable:

$$Sh_d = \frac{2F}{(\bar{\omega}'_w - \bar{\omega}'^i_w)\bar{D}_r} \qquad (43)$$

in which $\bar{D}_r$ is defined as:

$$\bar{D}_r = \frac{1}{(\bar{\omega}'_w - \omega'^i_w)} \int_{\omega'^i_w}^{\bar{\omega}'_w} D_r \, d\omega'_w \qquad (44)$$

where ω'^i_w is the moisture content on the surface of the body. Figure 5 shows some examples correlation results by Sh_d versus $D_r(\bar{\omega}'_w)/\bar{D}_r$ for a spherical, slab and cylindrical material. It is found that the value of Sh_d is nearly constant and independent of the function of the concentration-dependent diffusion coefficient, but that it is dependent on the shape of the material. As a starting point for the calculation, Schoeber (1978) has used the isothermal drying curve of a slab with constant (equilibrium) surface moisture content, since the drying equation for slab includes no explicit terms of shrinkage in its formula. From numerous calculations, he has concluded that the flux parameters (dimensionless moisture flux)

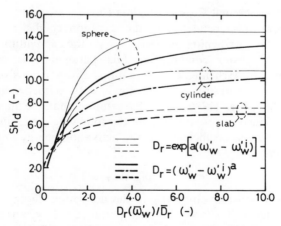

FIG. 5.   Correlation of Shd (after Schoeber (1976) and Schoeber and Thijssen (1977)).

116   T. FURUTA

for spheres or infinite cylinders could be related with the flux parameter
of slab, F_{slab}, as:

$$F = \chi F_{\text{slab}} \tag{45}$$

The conversion factor χ is shown in Fig. 6 as a function of $d \ln F_{\text{slab}}/d \ln (\bar{\omega}'_w - \omega'^i_w)$, which is a measure of the steepness of the moisture concentration profile inside the material.

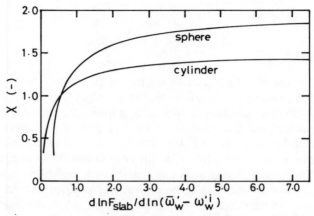

FIG. 6.   Correlation of conversion factor (after Schoeber (1978)).

4.3 The Non-isothermal Regular Regime Curve

If the temperature-dependence of the diffusion coefficient can be described by the Arrhenius equation and the activation energy is independent of water content, the flux parameter, F, can also be described by an Arrhenius-type equation. From extensive numerical calculations of the drying equation for a slab, Schoeber and Thijssen (1977), and Schoeber (1976, 1978) have found that the flux parameter could be described approximately by the following Arrhenius equation, even if the diffusion coefficient and the activation energy are concentration-dependent:

$$F = F^0 \exp(-\Delta E_F/\mathscr{R}T) \tag{46}$$

where F^0 is a constant and ΔE_F is the activation energy for the flux parameter. Figure 7 shows the flux parameter F versus $1/T$ for an aqueous glucose solution. The slope of each line is different and increases as the average moisture content increases. From their numerical results,

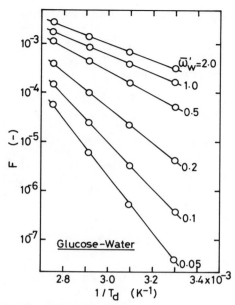

FIG. 7. Arrhenius plot of flux parameter (after Schoeber (1976) and Schoeber and Thijssen (1977)).

non-isothermal regular regime curves can be determined by at least two isothermal drying experiments at different temperatures.

4.4 The Penetration Period

In the initial period of the drying process with constant equilibrium surface water concentration, a sharp concentration gradient is formed near the surface. In this period, however, the change of the moisture content at the center of the material is still negligible and the drying rate can be assumed not to be influenced by the thickness of material. This period of drying is called the 'penetration period', where the penetration length is so short that the diffusion can be regarded as that in a semi-infinite medium (Schoeber, 1976). Using the Boltzmann transformation, the rate of evaporation from the slab surface can be derived from eqn (31) as follows:

$$D_r\left(\frac{d\omega'_w}{d\eta}\right)_{\xi=0} = \beta(\omega'_{w,0} - \omega'^i_w) \tag{47}$$

where β is a constant, and η a new variable defined as:

$$\eta = \frac{1-\xi}{2\sqrt{\tau}} \tag{48}$$

Partial differentiation of η by ξ gives

$$-\frac{\partial \eta}{\partial \xi} = \frac{1}{2\sqrt{\tau}} \tag{49}$$

From eqns (47) and (49) the flux parameter, F, is obtained as

$$F = -D_r \left(\frac{\partial \omega'_w}{\partial \xi} \right)_{\eta=0} = \frac{\beta(\omega'_{w,0} - \omega'^i_w)}{2\sqrt{\tau}} = -\frac{d\bar{\omega}'_w}{d\tau} \tag{50}$$

Therefore,

$$-\frac{d\bar{\omega}'_w}{d\sqrt{\tau}} = \beta(\omega'_{w,0} - \bar{\omega}'^i_w) \tag{51}$$

If the fraction of water evaporated is denoted by E,

$$E = \frac{\omega'_{w,0} - \bar{\omega}'_w}{\omega'_{w,0} - \omega'^i_w} \tag{52}$$

and then from eqns (51) and (52), one can obtain

$$E = \beta\sqrt{\tau} \tag{53}$$

Substitution of eqn (53) into eqn (51) yields

$$FE = \frac{\omega'_{w,0} - \omega'^i_w}{2} \beta^2 = \frac{\omega'_{w,0} - \omega'^i_w}{2} \left(\frac{dE}{d\sqrt{\tau}} \right)^2 = \text{constant} \tag{54}$$

Equation (54) means that only a single combination of F and E is necessary to determine the value of F in the penetration period. Differentiation of eqn (54) by E yields another formula between F and E.

$$\frac{d \ln F}{d \ln(1-E)} = \frac{1-E}{E} \tag{55}$$

Equations (54) and (55) are the equations which characterize the penetration period. It is important to note that these equations hold regardless of the concentration-dependence of the diffusivity. In the penetration period, since the concentration gradient is limited within the thin shell, the diffusion process for a spherical material behaves like a flat plate.

Therefore, only the specific surface has to be taken into account. The flux parameter in this thin shell, F^*, can be derived as (Schoeber, 1978):

$$F^* = \frac{(\rho_s^0/\rho_w^0)(\omega_{w,0}' - \omega_w'^i)}{(1 + \rho_s^0/\rho_w^0)^{1/3} - (1 + \rho_s^0 \bar{\omega}_w'/\rho_s^0)^{1/3}}(EF)_{\text{slab}} \tag{56}$$

However, eqn (56) cannot be applied in the wide range of moisture content, but holds only for the very short diffusion time. From analytical results with constant diffusivities, Schoeber (1978) assumed that the flux parameter, F, could be described as the following equation:

$$F = F^* - \Delta F \tag{57}$$

in which ΔF is approximately constant over the penetration period. He assumed further that ΔF could be correlated by the following F_t which was the value of F at the transition point from penetration region to regular regime.

$$\Delta F = F_t \tag{58}$$

If both the penetration region and the regular regime are connected smoothly, the flux parameter, F_t, is equal for both the penetration period and the regular regime at the transition point. Therefore, from eqns (57) and (58) the following relation can be derived:

$$F^* = 2 \cdot 0 F \tag{59}$$

This means that F_t (and therefore ΔF) can be determined by intersection of the curve of F^* with 2·0 times the regular regime curve. Figure 8 illustrates an example of the graphical determination of penetration curve (Schoeber, 1978). The procedures are as follows:

(1) Determine the regular regime curve by eqn (46).
(2) Draw the ΔF curve by eqn (56).
(3) Draw the curve with an F value double that of the regular regime curve.
(4) Determine F_t by intersection of the curves 2 and 3. Then $\Delta F = F_t$.
(5) Calculate F by eqn (57).

The bold solid line in Fig. 8 is the numerical result and the points indicate the results according to the graphical method mentioned above. The two results are in good agreement.

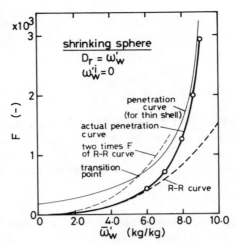

FIG. 8. Graphical determination of penetration curve (after Schoeber (1976, 1978)).

4.5 A Short-Cut Method for the Non-isothermal Drying Curve

During the falling rate period, the temperature of the media will increase rapidly. Under this condition, the drying curve can be calculated on the basis of the isothermal drying curve for the penetration period and the regular regime. From extensive numerical calculations, Schoeber (1976) concluded that under non-isothermal conditions the flux parameter, F, lay in good approximation on the isothermal parent curve for the actual temperature, and that the rate of mass transfer inside the material was independent of temperature history and only a function of the actual temperature. Schoeber (1976, 1978) also found that the relation between the flux parameter and the average moisture content at the end of constant activity period was in good agreement with the penetration curve at the same temperature. On the basis of these two results, he calculated the non-isothermal drying curve of a slab of aqueous glucose solution, which is illustrated in Fig. 9. The points in the figure indicate the results obtained by the short-cut method and the solid line those of the numerical one. Liou (1982; Liou and Bruin, 1982) has extended the Schoeber's method to the case in which the diffusion coefficient of water decreases along the power law of the water content. His results are more analytical than Schoeber's, and it becomes possible to calculate the whole drying rate by a simple calculator.

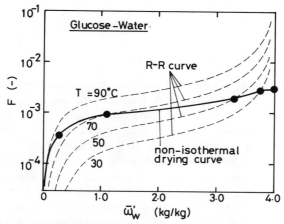

FIG. 9.   Graphical method of non-isothermal drying curve (after Schoeber (1976, 1978) and Schoeber and Thijssen (1977)).

5 THE MECHANISM OF FLAVOR RETENTION IN THE DRYING OF A DROPLET

Good taste and flavor in the spray-dried powder product are the most important quality factors demanded by consumers. The taste of food originates in many kinds of flavor components; they commonly have high relative volatility with respect to water. Therefore, they would be lost from the atomized droplet on spray-drying.

Several comprehensive reviews have been presented on this subject from both theoretical and experimental points of view (King *et al.*, 1984; Bomben *et al.*, 1973; Bruin *et al.*, 1980; King, 1988). The advances of the digital computer have made the numerical simulation of the thermal degradation during drying easier.

In this section, the diffusional transfer of a flavor substance will be discussed on the basis of the selective diffusion theory originally proposed by Thijssen and Rulkens (1968).

5.1 The Selective Diffusion Concept

According to the Rayleigh equation, the fraction of the original flavor content that is retained in the liquid (the flavour retention fraction) is given by the following equation.

$$\psi_a = \left(\frac{\omega_{w,0}}{\omega_{w,\theta}}\right)^{\alpha_{Aw}}$$ (60)

where ψ_a is the retention of the flavour, $\omega_{w,0}$ and $\omega_{w,\theta}$ are the water contents at commencement and at time θ, respectively, and α_{Aw} is the relative volatility of the flavor components. Bomben et al. (1973) have calculated the retention of several popular flavor components and concluded that they disappeared almost completely after 80% of the original water had been evaporated. This means that none of the flavor could have remained in the dried powders. However, in practical spray-drying, the loss of flavor was much less than that estimated by eqn (60). This indicates that the evaporation of the flavor component during drying would be dominantly influenced by the molecular diffusion of the flavor substance inside the droplet.

Thijssen and Rulkens (1968) proposed the 'selective diffusion theory' to explain the greater retention of the flavor components than the estimation by eqn (60). The concept is based on the fact that the rate of transfer of the water and the flavor in the liquid food are not equal but depend strongly on the moisture content. If the water and the flavor inside the droplet can be postulated to migrate as molecular diffusion, their transfer rates may be determined by their molecular diffusivities. As several researchers have pointed out (Menting et al., 1970; Chandrasekaran and King, 1972a; Furuta et al., 1984a), the diffusivity of the flavor is substantially lower than that of water at low moisture content. It is well-known that the droplet surface is covered by a film of low moisture content (case-hardening), as drying proceeds. The dried film behaves as a semi-permeable membrane through which water can permeate more easily than the flavor, and then the flavor substance can be encapsulated inside the droplet.

5.2 Theoretical Formulation of the Selective Diffusion Theory

Mathematical formulations of the selective diffusion concept have been made by several workers (Kerkhof and Schoeber, 1974; Kerkhof, 1975; Rulkens and Thijssen, 1969; Furuta et al., 1983, 1985) on the basis of the diffusion equation of the ternary system (water, flavor component and dissolved solid). As already shown in Fig. 2, a droplet is assumed to be dried in air at the temperature T_a. In addition to the assumptions made in Section 3.1, it is assumed that the concentration of the flavor is extremely low compared with the water and the solid concentration. Then, the equations of change of moisture and the flavor can be formulated on the basis of the thermodynamics of an irreversible process as follows (Kerkhof and Schoeber, 1974; Kerkhof, 1975; Furuta *et al.*, 1983; Chandrasekaran and King, 1972b):

$$\frac{\partial c_w}{\partial \theta} = \frac{1}{r^2} \frac{\partial}{\partial r}\left(\mathscr{D}_w r^2 \frac{\partial c_w}{\partial r}\right) \tag{61}$$

$$\frac{\partial c_a}{\partial \theta} = \frac{1}{r^2} \frac{\partial}{\partial r}\left\{r^2\left(\mathscr{D}_a \frac{\partial c_a}{\partial r} + \mathscr{D}_{wa} \frac{\partial c_w}{\partial r}\right)\right\} \tag{62}$$

where $\mathscr{D}_w$ and $\mathscr{D}_a$ are the diffusivities of water and the flavor, respectively. In eqn (62), the cross-diffusion term $\mathscr{D}_{wa}$, which describes the movement of the flavor by the diffusion of water, is included. According to Kerkhof and Schoeber (1974), $\mathscr{D}_{wa}$ can be derived by the moisture diffusivity $\mathscr{D}_w$ and the flavor diffusivity $\mathscr{D}_a$ as follows, provided that the flavor concentration is extremely low:

$$\mathscr{D}_{wa} = c_a\left\{\mathscr{D}_a\left(\frac{\partial \ln H_a}{\partial c_w}\right) - \mathscr{D}_w \frac{\rho_w^0}{\rho_w^0 - c_w}\right\} \tag{63}$$

where H_a is the modified activity coefficient of the flavor and can be defined as follows:

$$A_a = H_a c_a \tag{64}$$

where A_a is the activity coefficient of the flavor. Chandrasekaran and King (1972a) and Tsujimoto *et al.* (1982) found that H_a was a function of the moisture content only at extremely low concentrations of the flavor.

Since the concentration of the flavor, c_a, is extremely low, it is reasonable to assume that the same equation as eqn (23) is valid for the temperature of the droplet. Assuming the initial moisture content, flavor content and the droplet temperature (i.e. $c_{w,0}$, $c_{a,0}$ and $T_{d,0}$, respectively) are uniform, the initial and the boundary conditions are given as follows:

$$\left.\begin{array}{l} \theta = 0, \ 0 \leqslant r \leqslant R_0; \ c_w = c_{w,0}, \ c_a = c_{a,0}, \ T_d = T_{d,0} \\[2em] \theta > 0, \ r = 0; \ \dfrac{\partial c_w}{\partial r} = 0, \ \dfrac{\partial c_a}{\partial r} = 0 \\[2em] r = R; \ \dfrac{-\mathscr{D}_w}{1 - c_w/\rho_w^0} \dfrac{\partial c_w}{\partial r} = k(p_w^i - p_w^b) \\[2em] -\mathscr{D}_a\left(\dfrac{\partial c_a}{\partial r} + c_a \dfrac{\partial \ln H_a}{\partial c_w} \dfrac{\partial c_w}{\partial r}\right) = k_a(p_a^i - p_a^b) \end{array}\right\} \tag{65}$$

where k_a is mass transfer coefficient of the flavor vapor, p_w^i, p_w^b, p_a^i and p_a^b are the vapor pressure of the water and flavor on the surface of the droplet and in the bulk of the air stream, respectively.

As discussed in Section 3.5, an invariant coordinate should be introduced for the finite difference scheme, since the droplet surface moves inward during drying. For this purpose, the current (fixed) radial coordinate, r, is converted to the substantial (invariant) coordinate, σ, by means of eqn (26). Using dimensionless concentrations $\omega_w' = c_w/c_s$ and $\omega_a' = c_a/c_s$ instead of c_w and c_a, eqns (61), (62) and (65) can be rewritten as follows:

$$\frac{\partial \omega_w'}{\partial \theta} = \frac{\partial}{\partial \sigma}\left(\mathscr{D}_w c_s^2 r^4 \frac{\partial \omega_w'}{\partial \sigma}\right) \tag{66}$$

$$\frac{\partial \omega_a'}{\partial \theta} = \frac{\partial}{\partial \sigma}\left[c_s^2 r^4 \left\{ \mathscr{D}_a \frac{\partial \omega_a'}{\partial \sigma} + \frac{c_s}{\rho_a^0}\left[\left(\frac{\rho_w^0}{\rho_s^0}\right)\mathscr{D}_{wa} + \omega_a'(\mathscr{D}_w - \mathscr{D}_a)\right]\frac{\partial \omega_a'}{\partial \sigma}\right\}\right] \tag{67}$$

$$\left.\begin{array}{l} \theta = 0,\ 0 \leqslant \sigma \leqslant \sigma_0;\ \omega_w' = \omega_{w,0}',\ \omega_a' = \omega_{a,0}',\ T_d = T_{d,0} \\[2mm] \theta > 0,\ \sigma = 0;\ \dfrac{\partial \omega_w'}{\partial \sigma} = 0,\ \dfrac{\partial \omega_a'}{\partial \sigma} = 0 \\[2mm] \sigma = \sigma_0;\ -\mathscr{D}_w c_s^2 R^2 \dfrac{\partial \omega_w'}{\partial \sigma} = k(p_w^i - p_w^b) \\[2mm] -\mathscr{D}_a c_s^2 \left(\dfrac{\rho_w^0}{\rho_a^0}\right)\left[\dfrac{\partial \omega_a'}{\partial \sigma} + c_s \omega_a'\left\{1 - \dfrac{1}{\rho_w^0} - \dfrac{c_s}{\rho_w^0}\dfrac{\partial \ln H_a}{\partial c_w}\right\}\dfrac{\partial \omega_w'}{\partial \sigma}\right] \\[2mm] = k_a(p_a^i - p_a^b) \end{array}\right\} \tag{68}$$

where ρ_a^0 is the density of the flavor. The amount of the moisture and the flavor retained at time θ in the droplet can be evaluated by the following equations.

$$\psi_a = \frac{3}{R_0^3 c_{s,0}}\int_0^\sigma \omega_a'\,d\sigma,\qquad \psi_w = \frac{3}{R_0^3 c_{s,0}}\int_0^\sigma \omega_w'\,d\sigma \tag{69}$$

5.3 Diffusivities of the Moisture and the Flavor
A knowledge of the diffusivities of the moisture and the flavor is essential for the theoretical estimation of flavor retention during drying. Several researchers have made extensive measurements of them. Menting et al.

(1970) measured the diffusivities of moisture and a few kinds of volatile substances in aqueous maltodextrin solutions. The diffusivity of the moisture was measured by the sorption and desorption curves, which were obtained by recording the time history of the weight of the sample placed in the isothermal and isohumetric chamber. To measure the flavor diffusivity, gas chromatography and radioactive tracer techniques were used to get the sorption or desorption curves. Furuta *et al.* (1984a) used a similar method to measure the moisture and the ethanol diffusivities in aqueous maltodextrin solution. They also used the capillary method at high moisture range.

Figures 10 and 11 illustrate the experimental results of Furuta *et al.* (1984a) together with the measurements by Menting *et al.* (1970). At high moisture range, $\mathscr{D}_a$ is greater than $\mathscr{D}_w$. However, if the weight fraction of moisture is less than 0·6, $\mathscr{D}_a$ decreases rapidly and the ratio of these two diffusivities $\mathscr{D}_a/\mathscr{D}_w$ becomes less than 1. Furuta *et al.* (1984a) correlated

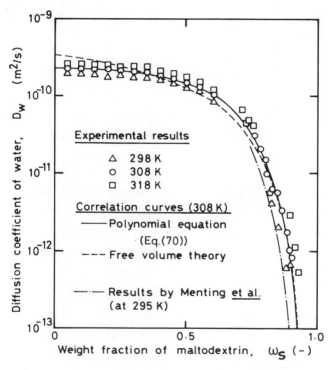

FIG. 10.   Diffusivities of water in aqueous maltodextrin solution.

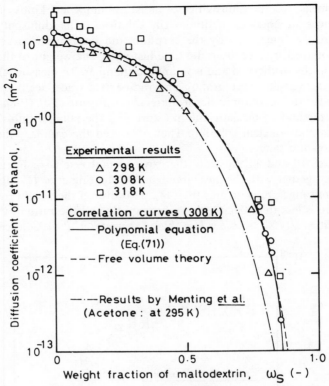

FIG. 11.   Diffusivities of ethanol in aqueous maltodextrin solution.

$\mathscr{D}_w$ and $\mathscr{D}_a$ by the following polynomial functions of the mass fraction of the dissolved solid ω_s.

$$\begin{aligned}
\log \mathscr{D}_w = {} & -5{\cdot}620\,29 + 3{\cdot}7542\omega_s - 86{\cdot}5335\omega_s^2 \\
& + 704{\cdot}872\omega_s^3 - 2853{\cdot}10\omega_s^4 + 6354{\cdot}49\omega_s^5 \\
& - 7952{\cdot}04\omega_s^6 + 5245{\cdot}81\omega_s^7 - 1424{\cdot}05\omega_s^8
\end{aligned} \tag{70}$$

$$\begin{aligned}
\log \mathscr{D}_a = {} & -4{\cdot}82\,361 - 48{\cdot}0705\omega_s + 1213{\cdot}57\omega_s^2 \\
& - 12\,183{\cdot}4\omega_s^3 + 63\,719{\cdot}2\omega_s^4 - 193\,515\omega_s^5 \\
& + 354\,025\omega_s^6 - 384\,787\omega_s^7 + 228\,912\omega_s^8
\end{aligned} \tag{71}$$

The cross-diffusivity $\mathscr{D}_{wa}$ calculated by eqn (63) was always negative, when eqns (70) and (71) are used as $\mathscr{D}_w$ and $\mathscr{D}_a$. This was also found experimentally by Chandrasekaran and King (1972a) for some volatile components in sugar solutions.

5.4 Flavor Retention on Drying of a Single Droplet

Drying a large droplet of pendant shape in hot air, Menting and Hoogstad (1967) studied the retention of flavor on drying. Recently, Furuta *et al.* (1983, 1984b, 1985) have performed similar experiments to confirm the applicability of the selective diffusion concept for flavor retention on drying of a single droplet. The sample solution used was aqueous maltodextrin solution, in which a trace amount of ethanol was mixed as a model flavor substance. A single droplet, was hung at the end of a fine glass filament and placed in well stabilized hot air. The retention of ethanol was measured by gas chromatography at different drying intervals.

Figure 12 shows the typical result of the time history of the flavor retention (i.e. retention of ethanol) ψ_a and residual moisture fraction (i.e.

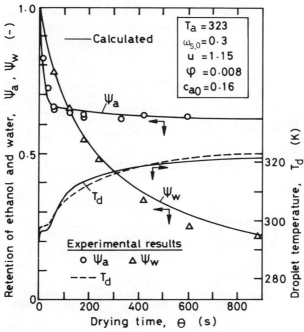

FIG. 12.   Retention of ethanol on drying of a single droplet.

128   T. FURUTA

moisture retention) ψ_w. The temperature history of the droplet T_d is also shown in Fig. 12 by a dashed line. A large part of the total ethanol loss takes place in the initial period of drying, where the droplet temperature T_d is nearly constant and equal to the wet-bulb temperature. This means that the surface evaporation period is the most important for the flavor retention. The retention of ethanol remains almost unchanged after the initial period of drying. However, the water inside the droplet continues to evaporate. The solid lines in Fig. 12 are the numerical results by eqns (66) through (68), where the diffusion coefficients in eqns (70) and (71) were used for calculations. The numerical results are in good agreement with the experiments. It can be concluded that the selective diffusion theory can estimate quantitatively the flavor retention of the drying of a single droplet. From microscopic observation, Furuta et al. (1983) found that the droplet was covered by an opaque dry film (case-hardening) after the initial period of drying. From these results, it was assumed that the ethanol was encapsulated by the film because the diffusivity of the flavor through the film was quite low at such low moisture content.

The effect of the initial dissolved solid concentration (initial maltodextrin concentration) $\omega_{s,0}$ on the ethanol retention is shown in Fig. 13. As several researchers have pointed out, the initial solid content has an

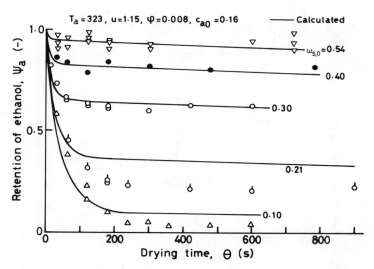

FIG. 13.   Effect of initial maltodextrin content on retention of ethanol.

appreciable effect on flavor retention. The solid lines in the figure are the
calculated results based on the selective diffusion theory.

Figure 14 shows the influences of the drying air temperature T_a on
the flavor retention. The final values of ψ_a increases as T_a increases.
Intuitively, this seems to be contradictory. However, at high air temperature the case-hardening begins to cover the droplet surface immediately
after the beginning of the drying, so that the interval of the initial drying
period becomes shorter and then much of the flavour remains in the
droplet.

The effect of air velocity and humidity on the final value of ψ_a are
illustrated in Fig. 15. Air humidity has an important influence on ψ_a. The
theoretical results in the figures are also in good agreement with the
experiments.

Numerical examples of ethanol concentration profiles inside the droplet during drying are illustrated in Figs. 16 and 17 (Furuta *et al.*, 1983). In
the case of $\omega_{s,0} = 0 \cdot 1$, the gradient near the surface of the droplet becomes
less steep as drying proceeds. However, after 220 s, the gradient becomes
steeper again. The time roughly corresponds to the time at which the
ethanol retention begins to remain constant. Furthermore, the concentration of ethanol in the central region of the droplet increases after this
time. This can be explained by the dry film selectively allowing the
moisture but not the ethanol to permeate. In the case of $\omega_{s,0} = 0 \cdot 54$, the

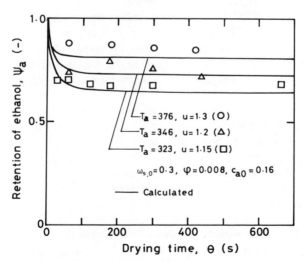

FIG. 14.   Effect of air temperature on retention of ethanol.

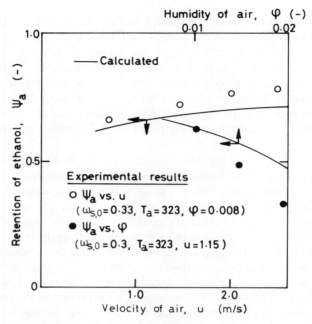

FIG. 15.   Effect of air velocity and humidity on retention of ethanol.

maximum value appears in the concentration profile of the ethanol, as shown in Fig. 17. The maximum value, which has been also found experimentally by Chandrasekaran and King in the case of the drying slab solution, results from the shrinkage and cross-diffusion effect in eqn (62). The radial position of the maximum moves inward as drying proceeds and then disappears in the final stage of the drying.

By computer simulations, Kerkhof and co-workers (Kerkhof, 1975; Kerkhof and Schoeber, 1974; Kerkhof and Thijssen, 1977) studied the influences of the process variables on the retention of flavor. They found that flavor retention was strongly dependent on the interval of the initial period of drying, and that flavor retention increases under intensive drying conditions, that is, at high air temperature, low air humidity, high initial solid content and high air velocity.

5.5 Flavor Retention with Expansion of the Droplet

If the temperature of the droplet exceeds its boiling point, the droplet expands during drying. The morphology of the inflation of the droplet is

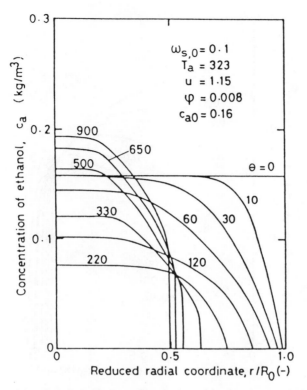

FIG. 16.   Concentration profile of ethanol in droplet ($\omega_{s,0} = 0.1$).

so complicated that thorough understanding of the phenomenon has not been achieved yet. Wijlhuizen *et al.* (1979) analyzed theoretically the enzyme inactivation of a hollow droplet on spray-drying. Furuta *et al.* (1984b, 1985) simplified the inflation of the droplet as shown in Fig. 18. According to their model, the droplet shrinks in the initial period of drying. When the central vapor pressure of the water exceeds atmospheric pressure, they assumed that the droplet expanded abruptly and a single bubble of radius R_i was formed coaxially inside the droplet. Thereafter, the outer surface of the droplet shrinks on drying with the inner radius R_i remaining constant. For the concentration profile of the moisture and the flavor inside the shell region at the inflation of the droplet, Furuta *et al.* (1984b, 1985) proposed two extreme models: a perfect mixing model in which the concentration profiles of the moisture and the flavor inside the shell region are supposed to be

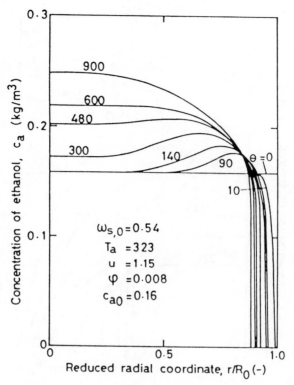

FIG. 17.   Concentration profile of ethanol in droplet ($\omega_{s,0}=0.54$).

uniform owing to the perfect mixing (PM model), and the non-mixing
model where the concentration profiles are assumed to be proportional to
that just before the inflation (NM model). The boundary condition for
each model can be represented as follows.

PM model

$$\left.\begin{array}{l} \theta=\theta_e,\ R_{in}\leqslant r\leqslant R_{out};\ c_w=c_{w,e},\ c_a=c_{a,e},\ T_d=T_{d,e} \\ \theta>\theta_e,\ r=R_{in};\ \dfrac{\partial c_w}{\partial r}=0,\ \dfrac{\partial c_a}{\partial r}=0 \end{array}\right\} \quad (72)$$

where R_{out} is the outer radius of the droplet just after the inflation, θ_e is
the time of the inflation and other subscript 'e' means the average value
after the inflation.

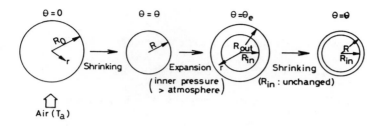

FIG. 18. Drying model of expansion of droplet.

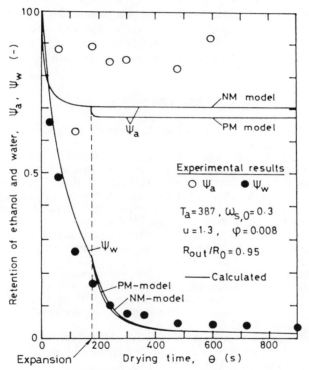

FIG. 19. Ethanol retention of expanding droplet.

NM model

$$\left.\begin{array}{l} \theta = \theta_e, \quad R_{in} \leqslant r \leqslant R_{out}; \quad c_w r = c_w^* r^*, \quad c_a r = c_a^* r^*, \quad T_d = T_{d,e} \\[2mm] \theta > \theta_e, \quad r = R_{in}; \quad \dfrac{\partial c_w}{\partial r} = 0, \quad \dfrac{\partial c_a}{\partial r} = 0 \end{array}\right\} \quad (73)$$

where $r^* = (r^3 - R_{in}^{*})^{1/3}$ and the superscript '*' means the value just before the inflation.

Figure 19 shows the comparison of the theoretical results with the experimental ones under the drying condition of $T_a = 114°C$ and $\omega_{s,0} = 0.3$. The ratio of R_{out}/R_0 was determined by observation. The theoretical value of ψ_a is lower than the measurements, though the calculated results of ψ_w are in good agreement with the experimental values. It is noticed that the difference between the PM model calculations and the NM model calculations is small for both ψ_a and ψ_w.

REFERENCES

Bird, R. B., Stewart, W. E. & Lightfoot, E. N. (1960). *Transport Phenomena*, 3rd edn. John Wiley, New York.

Bomben, J. L., Bruin, S. & Thijssen, H. A. C. (1973). Aroma recovery and retention in concentration and drying of foods. *Adv. Food Research*, Vol. 20, ed. C. O. Chichester, E. M. Mrak & G. F. Stewart. Academic Press, New York, 2–111.

Bruin, S. & Luyben, K. Ch. A. M., (1980). Drying of food materials: a review of recent developments. In *Advances in Drying*, Vol. 1, ed. A. S. Mujundar. Hemisphere Publishing, New York, pp. 155–215.

Chandrasekaran, S. K. & King, C. J. (1972a) Multicomponent diffusion and vapor–liquid equilibria of dilute organic components in aqueous sugar solutions. *AIChE Journal*, **18**, 513–19.

Chandrasekaran, S. K. & King, C. J. (1972b). Volatile retention during drying of food liquid. *AIChE Journal*, **18**, 520–6.

Furuta, T., Tsujimoto, S., Okazaki, M. & Toei, R. (1983). Effect of drying on retention of ethanol in maltodextrin solution during drying of a single droplet. *J. Drying Techn.*, **2**, 311–27.

Furuta, T., Tsujimoto, S., Makino, H., Okazaki, M. & Toei, R. (1984a), Measurement of diffusion coefficients of water and ethanol in aqueous maltodextrin solution. *J. Food Engr.*, **3**, 169–86.

Furuta, T., Tsujimoto, S., Okazaki, M. & Toei, R. (1984b). Retention of volatile component in a single droplet during drying. In *Engineering and Food*, Vol. 1, ed. B. M. Mckenna. Elsevier Applied Science Publishers, London, pp. 33–9.

Furuta, T., Okazaki, M. & Toei, R. (1985). Flavor retention of a single droplet under various drying conditions. In *Drying '85*, ed. A. S. Mujumdar. Hemisphere Publishing, New York, pp. 338–45.

Kerkhof, P. J. A. M. (1975). A quantitative study of the effect of process variables on the retention of volatile trace components in drying. Ph.D. thesis, Eindhoven University of Technology, The Netherlands.

Kerkhof, P. J. A. M. & Schoeber, W. J. A. H. (1974). Theoretical modeling of the drying behaviour of droplets in spray dryers. In *Advances in Preconcentration and Dehydration of Foods*, ed. A. Spicer. Applied Science Publishers, London, pp. 349–97.

Kerkhof, P. J. A. M. & Thijssen, H. A. C. (1977). Quantitative study of the effects of process variables on aroma retention during the drying of liquid foods. *AIChE Symposium Series*, No. 163, Vol. 73, pp. 33–46.

King, C. J. (1988). Spray drying of food liquid and volatiles retention. In *Preconcentration and Drying of Food Materials*, ed. S. Bruin. Elsevier Science Publishers, Amsterdam, The Netherlands, pp. 147–62.

King, C. J., Kieckbusch, T. G. & Greenwalt, C. G. (1984). Food-quality factors in spray drying. In *Advances in Drying*, Vol. 3, ed. A. S. Mujundar. Hemisphere Publishing, New York. pp. 71–120.

Kondrativ, G. M. (1964). *Regular Thermal Regime*. Gostekhizdat, Moscow (as cited by Luikov (1968)).

van der Lijn, P. (1976). Simulation of heat and mass transfer in spray drying. Ph.D. thesis, Agricultural University of Wageningen, The Netherlands.

Liou, J. K. (1982). An approximate method for nonlinear diffusion applied to enzyme inactivation during drying. Ph.D. thesis, Agricultural University of Wageningen, The Netherlands.

Liou, J. K. and Bruin, S. (1982). An approximate method for the nonlinear diffusion problem with a power relation between diffusion coefficient and concentration. I, Computation of desorption time. *Int. J. Heat and Mass Transfer*, **25**, 1209–20.

Luikov, A. V. (1968). *Analytical Heat Diffusion Theory*. Academic Press, New York.

Masters, K. (1972). *Spray Drying*. Leonard Hill, London.

Menting, L. C. & Hoogstad, B. (1967). Volatile retention during the drying of aqueous carbohydrate solution. *J. Food Sci.*, **32**, 87–90.

Menting, L. C., Hoogstad, B. & Thijssen, H. A. C. (1970). Diffusion coefficients of water and organic volatiles in carbohydrate–water systems. *J. Food Technol.*, **5**, 111–26.

Miura, T. & Ohtani, S. (1979). Characteristics of heat transfer in a concurrent spray dryer. *Kagaku Kougaku Rombunshu* (in Japanese), **5**, 130–5.

Okazaki, M., Shioda, K., Masuda, K. & Toei, R. (1974). Drying mechanism of coated film of polymer solution. *J. Chem. Eng. Japan*, **7**, 99–105.

Rulkens, W. H. & Thijssen, H. A. C. (1969). Numerical solution of diffusion equations with strongly variable diffusion coefficients. *Trans. Inst. Chem. Engrs*, **47**, T292–8.

Schoeber, W. J. A. H. (1976). Regular regimes in sorption process. Ph.D. thesis, Eindhoven University of Technology, The Netherlands.

Schoeber, W. J. A. H. & Thijssen, H. A. C., (1977). A short-cut method for the calculation of drying rates for slabs with concentration-dependent diffusion coefficient. *AIChE Symposium Series*, No. 163, Vol. 73, pp. 12–24.

136   T. FURUTA

Schoeber, W. J. A. H. (1978). A short-cut method for the calculation of drying rates in the case of a concentration-dependent diffusion coefficient. *Proceedings of 1st Int. Drying Symp.*, ed. A. S. Mujumdar, Hemisphere Publishing, New York, pp. 1–9.

Sjenitzer, F. (1952). Spray drying. *Chem. Eng. Sci.*, **1**, 101–17.

Thijssen, H. A. C. & Rulkens, W. H. (1968). Retention of aromas in drying food liquid. *De Ingenieur*, **80**, 45–56.

Tsujimoto, S., Matsuno, R. & Toei, R. (1982). Vapor–liquid equilibrium of dilute aroma component in aqueous solution of non-volatile food-related substance. *Kagaku Kougaku Rombunsyu*, (in Japanese), **8**, 103–6.

Wijlhuizen, A. E., Kerkhof, P. J. A. M. & Bruin, S. (1979). Theoretical study of the inactivation of phosphotase during drying spray drying of skim-milk. *Chem. Eng. Sci.*, **34**, 651–60.

Chapter 4

MODELLING OF WATER RELATIONS IN FERMENTATION PROCESSES

P. Gervais and D. Simatos

*Ecole Nationale Supérieure de Biologie,
Appliquée à la Nutrition et à l'Alimentation,
Dijon, France*

INTRODUCTION

Water has existed on Earth since its origin. The organization of life was conditioned by the presence of this inorganic element and its particular properties. In fact, water is a major component of animal and plant cells since it constitutes 70–95% of the total mass of the organisms and since it is essential to their functioning. Cellular exchanges take place between solutions and water is the only molecule whose exchanges through the membrane are essentially passive according to the pressure gradient.

The roles of water in biological systems are numerous and the mechanisms of action and interaction of this molecule with organic molecules are not yet totally elucidated. There are two fundamental functions which can be distinguished:

- Solvent function, on the level of the organism as well as of the cell, provides nutrients and scavenges wastes, or metabolites, under the dissolved form.
- Structural function, which is implicated in the stability and the function of the biological structures organized at the molecular and cellular levels. At the molecular level, the role of water in the stabilization of the structure of the biopolymers, such as proteins, nucleotides and carbohydrates, was recognized about twenty years ago (Schwan, 1965; Kuntz, 1971). At the cellular level, the role of water molecules in the stabilization of the lamellar structure of the plasmic membranes and thus in the preservation of membrane permeability has been shown (Crowe *et al.*, 1982; Wolfe and Steponkus, 1983; Quinn, 1985). In the intracellular medium, the molecules

of water linked with other molecules, such as polyols, sugars or enzymes, contribute to the maintenance of the cellular volume, especially when the cell is placed in a hypertonic medium and particularly during desiccation or freezing conditions (Mazur *et al.*, 1981).

From these different functions, we can understand why water is essential to cell metabolism and why the cellular exchanges occur in aqueous medium. In fact:

- If the quantity of water becomes insufficient and does not allow a good diffusion of solutes and gas, the cell metabolism slows, or can stop, because of a lack of substrates or through too high a concentration of inhibitive metabolites in or near the cell.
- If the intracellular or extracellular quantity of water does not allow the maintenance of the functional properties of some enzymes (Todd, 1972), their inactivity creates a disequilibrium in the metabolic chain of the cells.
- In the same way, if the transfer of water induced by water stress leads to a denaturation of the mechanical structure of the plasmic membrane, all the properties of permeability and transport through the membrane are affected and the cell is then perturbed (Wolfe and Steponkus, 1983; De Loecker *et al.*, 1987).

The part played by each of these patterns in the modification of the metabolism of the cells placed in hypertonic media must be defined. It is evident that the physicochemical nature of the extracellular medium, the type of cell studied, and the gradient of the osmotic pressure, as well as interactions with other parameters, temperature, diffusion, etc. must be considered.

This chapter intends to identify and model the influence of the conditions of the medium hydration on microbial development. In microbiology, especially for liquid fermentations, water parameters are rarely considered; nevertheless, they are directly implicated in cell exchanges.

First, some physical parameters, relating to the water state of the medium and implicated in the variations of metabolism, will be examined for homogeneous and heterogeneous media.

Then, the mechanisms of the action of water at the cellular level will be discussed and mathematical models will be proposed for cultures of filamentous fungi on agar-agar support, and of yeasts in liquid medium.

I Dynamic and Thermodynamic Properties of Water in Biological Systems

1 INTRODUCTION

There are numerous parameters which describe the energy state of water in a homogeneous medium (liquid, gas, vapour) or in a heterogeneous one. Generally, two types of parameters can be listed:

- Thermodynamic parameters allow the energy state of water equilibrium to be characterized in the systems studied. The difference between the energy states of water in two systems brought together will be the mainspring of water transfer between the two systems. The thermodynamic equilibrium concept must be specified, notably for biological systems which in nature are not in equilibrium. The evolution of biological systems is very slow compared with chemical systems, and the implication of such an evolution on thermodynamic water status can generally be neglected.
- Dynamic or kinetic parameters allow the resistance of the medium to water transfer to be characterized. The diffusion of solutes, as well as their cellular absorption, takes place in an aqueous medium. The solution properties interact in these transfers, particularly the diffusional properties of water. In fact, the dynamic properties of water molecules are modified when they are near other molecules. The diffusion laws are deduced from the atomic theory of brownian movement established by Einstein. The relation between flow and concentration gradient is given by Fick's law and the coefficient of proportionality is called the diffusion coefficient, or diffusivity; its value is closely dependent on the concentration of water in the medium.

In fact, these two types of parameters, although fundamentally different, are always related to the water content of the medium and so are dependent. Nevertheless, this degree of dependence is extremely variable and the limiting factors for the transfer of water in a system can have, depending on the circumstances, a kinetic or thermodynamic origin.

2 THERMODYNAMIC PARAMETERS

A thermodynamic analysis of a hydrated equilibrated system was carried out by Griffin (1981). From the two fundamental laws of thermodynamics and considering temperature (T) and partial molar volume of water $(\bar{V}_w)$ as constants the parameters generally used may be defined and related as follows.

2.1 The Chemical Water Potential
The chemical water potential of a system is equivalent to the partial free energy of water:

$$\left(\frac{\delta G}{\delta n_w}\right)_{T,P,n_j} = \mu_w = \bar{G}_w \tag{1}$$

where

P = pressure,
w = water suffix,
n = number of moles,
j = solute suffix,
G = free energy,
$\bar{G}_w$ = partial molar free energy of water,
μ_w = water chemical potential in the solution.

The potential difference can be estimated in relation to a standard reference state.

— For a solution:

$$\mu_w - \mu_w^0 = \bar{V}_w(P - \pi) \tag{2}$$

with

$$\pi = RT\left(\frac{C}{M} + A_2 C^2 + A_3 C^3 + \cdots\right) \tag{3}$$

— For a porous solid:

$$\mu_w - \mu_w^0 = \bar{V}_w(P - \tau) \tag{4}$$

with $\tau = h\rho g$
— For a heterogeneous system (solutes and porous solids):

$$\mu_w - \mu_w^0 = \bar{V}_w(P - \pi - \tau) \tag{5}$$

where

μ_w^0 = chemical potential of pure water,
π = osmotic pressure,
C = solute concentration,
M = solute molar weight,
A_i = ith virial osmotic coefficient,
R = perfect gas constant,
$\overline{V}_w$ = partial water molar volume,
τ = suction,
h = capillary rise,
ρ = volumetric mass of water,
g = mass acceleration.

2.2 Water Potential of a System

Water potential (Ψ) of a system is defined by:

$$\Psi = \frac{\mu_w - \mu_w^0}{\overline{V}_w} \qquad (6)$$

It has the dimensions of energy per volume unit (Pa), which is equivalent to a pressure, and provides the difference between the water chemical potentials (related to the partial molar volume of water) of the studied (μ_w) and the reference (μ_w^0) systems.

The water potential, Ψ, can be separated into the sum of terms of different origins:

$$\Psi = \Psi_P + \Psi_S + \Psi_m \qquad (7)$$

with $\Psi_P = P$, water potential pressure (hydrostatic pressure), $\Psi_S = -\pi$, osmotic water potential (solute effect: osmotic pressure), and $\Psi_m = -\tau$, matrix water potential (solid matrix effect: adsorption, capillarity).

Other terms, such as temperature or gravity, can affect the water energy state when they vary in the system; this is not often the case in biological systems, where only two components Ψ_S and Ψ_m can describe the systems most of the time. The distinction between Ψ_S and Ψ_m is especially valid at the macroscopic level; at the molecular level, the same physicochemical phenomena (adsorption, size effects) are implicated.

2.3 Water Activity

The water activity concept is frequently used to describe the vapour phase (water vapour) which behaves like a perfect gas. The water activity of a solution is given by:

$$a_w = \frac{P_w}{P_w^0} = \gamma_w X_w \tag{8}$$

where P_w is the partial pressure of water vapour equilibrated with the solution, P_w^0 is the partial pressure of water vapour above pure water in the same conditions, X_w is the water molecular fraction, and γ_w is the water activity coefficient (dependent on the concentration).

Guggenheim (1967) demonstrated the relation between the chemical potential and water activity:

$$\mu_w - \mu_w^0 = RT \ln a_w \tag{9}$$

and so, according to eqn (6)

$$\Psi = \frac{RT \ln a_w}{\bar{V}_w} \tag{10}$$

2.4 Water Properties in Ideal and Non-Ideal Solutions

Water molecules interact differently according to the nature of the solution. The degree of hydrophobicity, like the degree of ionization intervene.

In terms of energy, the water properties in a solution are related to solute–solute, solute–solvent and solvent–solvent molecular interactions. The hydration phenomenon corresponds to water–solute interactions and it can be studied alone at solute concentrations corresponding to an infinite dilution where the solute–solute interactions therefore become negligible. For electrolyte solutions, this dilution threshold can be estimated using the Debye–Hückel law; for non-electrolytes, an objective method of estimation does not yet exist.

The thermodynamic reference for the hydration term is the ideal solution, which presents no interaction between water and solute molecules. From this model, some deviations are observed which can be attributed to three types of phenomena:

- Solute molecular size versus the solvent molecular size. Flory (1953) using the theory of the 'liquid network', showed that binary solution entropy, and consequently eventual deviation from an ideal solution, depends on the respective size of the solvent and solute molecules.
- Solute molecule hydration or solvation.
- Other molecular interactions (solute–solute).

2.5 Water Properties in the Presence of Insoluble Substances

In the case of insoluble substances, the previous types of interactions can occur depending on the chemical nature of the polymers, hydrophilic for cellulose and hydrophobic for PTFE (Teflon) and the cellulose gels. But, in addition, the energy state of water is closely dependent on the geometry of the medium and especially on the dimensions of the pores.

Fisher and Israelachvili (1979) showed that the thermodynamic properties of liquids trapped in microscopic pores can be described by the Kelvin equation, the basis of the nucleation theory, for pore sizes as small as 4 nm. The Kelvin equation can be written:

$$\ln \frac{P_w}{P_w^0} = \frac{M_w}{\rho_w RT} \left(-\frac{\sigma}{r_m} - (P_w - P_w^0) \right)$$

where r_m is the radius of the curve of the water meniscus in the pore, σ is the surface tension at temperature T, and ρ_w is the water volumetric weight.

$P_w - P_w^0$ is negligible for σ/r_m so:

$$\frac{RT \ln a_w}{M_w} = -\frac{\sigma}{\rho_w r_m} \quad \text{and then} \quad \frac{RT \ln a_w}{\bar{V}_w} = -\frac{\sigma}{r_m} = \Psi$$

In this case, the energy state of water is dependent only on the curve radius of the meniscus, and then on the particles or pore size of the material. Thus, in moist sand where the curve radius of the water meniscus is 1.5×10^{-5} m, the corresponding water potential is $\Psi_m = -10$ kPa. If the sand is dried so that the curve radius is equal to 7.5×10^{-6} m, the water potential becomes $\Psi_m = -20$ kPa.

In most cases, the porosity of heterogeneous systems is modified during drying or hydration (bulking). Nevertheless, for a definite water content, the matrix water potential provides an account of liquid–gas and solid–liquid interactions, generated by very thin pore size (capillarity), which can belong to biological structures (membranes, macromolecules).

3 DYNAMIC PARAMETERS

Dynamic parameters allow the water resistance to transfer in a medium to be characterized. The parameters used are the coefficients of the rotational and translational diffusion of water. These coefficients are related to the friction coefficient by Einstein's equation:

$$D = \frac{kT}{\xi}$$

where D is the diffusion coefficient of a particle in a liquid, ξ is the friction coefficient, k is Boltzmann's constant, and T is the temperature.

The hydrodynamic model permits one to calculate ξ: in the case of a sphere with a radius a, for the translational diffusion $\xi = 6\pi a\eta$ and for the rotational diffusion $\xi = 8\pi a^3\eta$ ($\eta =$ liquid viscosity). Nevertheless, this model describes the diffusion of large molecules (Kovarskii et al., 1972) better.

Water content is a parameter which represents the diffusional properties of a slightly hydrated medium. In fact, in the case of the study of the rotational diffusivity of the solute molecules (Le Meste and Voilley, 1988), as in the case of the translational diffusivity of water molecules (Simatos and Karel, 1988), the relation proposed between diffusivity and water content is established for definite scales of water content.

Viscosity and temperature of the vitreous transition (T_g) (Slade and Levine, 1985) are also used to characterize the solutions for their biological properties kinetically.

The no-frozen-water quantity of a solution, a predictive parameter of the conservation of living cells during freezing (Mazur et al., 1981), is also a kinetic parameter (Franks, 1984).

The thermodynamic and kinetic parameters of a medium are linked by the water content. Nevertheless, this link, represented by the sorption isotherm of the medium, can be formalized by the equations for simple model systems. In most cases, this link can only be established experimentally.

Previous studies concerning the a_w influence on solute diffusivity (Voilley and Le Meste, 1985; Guilbert et al., 1985) show that the link is complex and extremely variable according to the type of solute. Other works (Bruin and Luyben, 1980) confirm that the water diffusivity in polymer solutions is essentially dependent on the water content of solutions. Le Meste and Voilley (1988) even show an antagonism between the kinetic and thermodynamic parameters, since in solutions of maltodextrins with the same water content in a model, the probe mobility decreases parallel to the increase of the a_w of the corresponding solutions. This conclusion is based on the fact that for the same water content the increase of a solute molecular weight leads to a decrease of the probe diffusivity in the solution parallel to the increase of the water activity.

4 CONCLUSION

A unique factor allowing both the energy state of water and its solvent properties in a heterogeneous system to be represented does not exist. Nevertheless, it seems possible to draw general conclusions. For dilute solutions, the solute diffusion is not a limiting factor. The solute nature has only a small influence. If the solvent and the solute molecules are of comparable sizes, there is little deviation from Raoult's law. In this case, thermodynamic factors allow the water transfer in the system to be predicted.

For more concentrated solutions, homogeneous or heterogeneous, the above hypotheses do not hold; the diffusion phenomena can become limiting according to the sorption properties of the solutes or solids. The physico chemical nature of the molecules can then interfere.

For certain enzymatic activities, which can be developed over almost the whole scale of water content (5% to 100% w/w) (Bouanda, 1983) or of water activity (Goldberg, *et al.* 1988), the previous considerations are particularly important in the understanding of these systems.

For microorganisms' activity which requires high water content, as high water activity levels, there may be a hierarchy in the action of kinetic and thermodynamic parameters on the cellular physiology.

II Influence of the Hydration of the Culture Medium on Microbial Physiology and Metabolism

1 INTRODUCTION

The control of parameters such as temperature, pH and oxygen concentration is generally required for submerged and solid state fermentations, although the basic mechanisms of their biological actions are not well understood.

An increase in temperature will modify the molecular configuration by breaking van der Waals or hydrogen bonds and so lead to denaturation of biological molecules such as enzymes, proteins and DNA. This action is described by the Arrhenius equation for enzymes; but the application of this equation to the whole microorganism is not valid. The heat transfer properties of different parts of microorganisms are not well-known, and these properties vary with temperature. Moreover, there is an important interaction between temperature and water activity dependence of microorganisms due to the water calorific property. A kinetic model which relates the rate constant of death of microbial cells to water activity (a_w) and temperature has been proposed (Moser, 1988) using the following equation

$$k = k_\infty a_w \exp - \frac{E_A a_w}{RT}$$

where the constants k_∞ and E_A are calculated from the experimental values of a_w. MacMeekin et al. (1987) have proposed a kinetic approach to the temperature dependence of microorganisms. Such kinetic models have also been developed for pH and O_2 effects on microorganisms (Andreyeva and Biryukov, 1973). In spite of the lack of structured information, all these parameters undoubtedly have an influence on cell metabolism and could be measured and controlled by using existing and acute sensors such as thermometers, pH meters and oxymeters.

The effect of water activity or water potential of a medium on microorganisms, on the other hand, is well-known. The introduction of the water activity concept (and then of the water potential) in microbiology dates from 1953 (Scott). This parameter has been and still is widely used as a predictive criterion of microorganic physiological functions and thus, of food preservation (although physicochemical factors such as non-enzymatic oxidations also intervene). Ben-Amotz and Avron (1978) have used the water activity or osmotic pressure influence to increase the glycerol production by unicellular algae. So the influence of water activity (a_w) on the physiology of microorganisms is a well-known phenomenon. Nevertheless if there are numerous observations there are less explanations. For some years, the systematic utilization of this parameter was debated by specialists to qualify the water situation of a medium (Lilley, 1985; Franks, 1985). For these authors, the thermodynamic considerations were insufficient to explain the water availability in a medium. Kinetic parameters should also be included. The respective influence of kinetic and thermodynamic parameters in fermentation media should be investigated.

2 INFLUENCE OF THE THERMODYNAMIC PARAMETERS OF THE CULTURE MEDIUM ON MICROBIAL ACTIVITY

It is recognized that there is no active water transport in cells and that water moves freely according to the gradient of the water potential. A thermodynamic model relating the energy equilibrium of intracellular and extracellular media has been developed by many authors, for example, Griffin (1981) and Steudle *et al.* (1983).

At equilibrium, the equality between water potentials can be written as the following equation:

$$\Psi^E = \Psi^C = \Psi^{mb} = \Psi^P$$

where Ψ^E is the water potential of the outer medium, Ψ^C is the cellular water potential, Ψ^{mb} is the water potential of the membrane, and Ψ^P is the water potential of the protoplasm.

Ψ^P variations with Ψ^E are in a typical scale per species. For xerotolerant species, Ψ^P can decrease to $-40\,\text{MPa}$ without damaging the cells. The protoplasmic water potential, Ψ^P, can be decomposed as follows:

$$\Psi^P = \Psi_p^P + \Psi_s^P + \Psi_m^P$$

where $\Psi^P = P - \pi - \tau$ and P is the hydrostatic pressure, π is the osmotic pressure, and τ is the suction pressure.

Ψ_s^P and Ψ_m^P are the water osmotic and matrix potentials of the protoplasm, and Ψ_p^P is the turgor potential of the protoplasm created by the plasmic membrane and the cellular walls. This latter potential corresponds to the pressure that initiates the cellular plasmolysis. For most filamentous fungi, $\Psi_p^P \approx 1\,\text{MPa}$, a value which can rise $3\,\text{MPa}$ for xerotolerant species.

An increase in the osmotic pressure in the extracellular medium (e.g., by increasing solute concentration) is at the origin of a cell response characterized by two successive phases (Zimmermann, 1978).

- A passive phase of water exit, the length of which is estimated in seconds and which is characterized by cellular volume and cellular turgor potential decreases. The variations of the turgor potential are

related to cellular volume modifications through the elastic properties of the cellular walls, defined by the elastic volumetric coefficient,
ε, according to the equation:

$$\Delta P = \varepsilon \frac{\Delta V}{V}$$

where P is the turgor or hydrostatic pressure, V is the cellular
volume, and ε is the volumetric coefficient of elasticity.

This coefficient ε is related to turgor pressure and cellular volume
and can vary from 5 to 600 bars according to species and pressure
conditions. Therefore, in the case of cells with walls, this phase of
osmoregulation is controlled not only by the hydraulic permeability
in the cell membrane, but also by the elastic properties of cell walls.
This first phase can lead, in the case of large gradients of osmotic
pressure, to either an exit of most of the free water from the cell and
thus to a metabolically inert cell which can survive for long periods,
or to cellular death essentially due to the alteration of the membrane
properties (Cudd and Steponkus, 1987).

• A second phase of compensation during which there is an access of
solutes from the outer medium or a synthesis of intracellular solutes.
This accumulation of organic solutes in response to an osmotic
stress is related to microorganisms, plant and animal cells (Gilles,
1975; Hellebust, 1976; Luard, 1982) and allows the cell to recover its
initial volume.

The turgor potential of the cell seems to interact in the growth
mechanisms of microorganisms. Indeed a growing cell constitutes a
system of non-equilibrium and the intracellular medium is slightly
hypertonic versus the extracellular medium. During growth, the
concentration of intracellular solutes increases and then the Ψ_s^p
(osmotic water potential of the protoplasm) decreases, leading to a
water entrance in the cell intended to re-equilibrate the system and
then to an increase in volume. Such an increase is still more
important when the walls become more elastic as for the mechanism
of yeast budding.

During the stationary phase of the growth of the microorganisms,
the tugor potential is still constant and the system can be considered
in equilibrium.

Numerous authors have reviewed the influence of the water activity
of the culture medium on the survival, the growth and the metabolism

of microorganisms cultivated on different types of medium (Mossel, 1975; Troller, 1980; Christian, 1981; Griffin, 1981; Richard-Molard *et al.*, 1982; Gould, 1985; Jakobsen, 1985; Hahn-Hägerdal, 1986).

3 INFLUENCE OF WATER ACTIVITY ON THE DEVELOPMENT OF MICROORGANISMS

3.1 Growth

The characteristic shape of the curve (Fig. 1) relating water activity of the medium to the growth of a microorganism, estimated by the measurement of the radial extension rate on agar-agar medium for filamentous fungi, or by the measurement of cell division number for yeasts in liquid medium, has been known since the work of Scott (1957). The optimum growth occurs in a medium in which the water activity is clearly less than 1, corresponding to a water potential scale between -0.1 MPa and -10 MPa (osmophilic).

Esener *et al.* (1981) have tried to relate growth kinetics to the water activity of the media in a model. From their data, it is evident that biosynthesis is less efficient at a reduced a_w level. They found an optimum

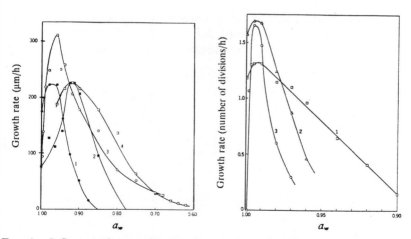

FIG. 1.   Influence of a_w on the growth rate (*A*) of filamentous fungi (1, *Aspergillus niger* at 20°C; 2, *A. glaucus* at 20°C; 3, *A. amstelodami* at 25°C; 4, *Xeromyces bisporus* at 25°C) and (B) of bacteria (1, *Staphylococcus aureus* at 30°C; 2, *Salmonella newport* at 30°C, *Vibrio metschnikovi* at 30°C) (from Scott, 1957).

a_w level less than 1 for the yield of biomass relative to substrate. Such an optimum is confirmed by plotting the thermodynamic efficiency parameter, η, given previously by Roels (1980) versus a_w, (Fig. 2). This parameter η describes the efficiency of the growth process by considering its irreversibility

$$\eta = Y_{sx}/Y'_F$$

where Y_{sx} is the biomass yield on a substrate (mole/mole) and Y'_F is the maximum value of Y_{sx} using the second law of thermodynamics. During a cultivation, the specific substrate consumption rate q_s can be related to the a_w of the medium by using the following Pirt's model (1965):

$$q_s = [\mu/Y_{sx}^{max}] + m_s$$

where μ is the specific growth rate, Y_{sx}^{max} is the maximal yield on substrate (mole/mole), and m_s is the maintenance coefficient ((mole/mole)/h). Previous workers, Stouthamer and Bettenhaussen (1973) showed that both parameters Y_{sx}^{max} and m_s were a function of a_w. This assumption prevented the construction of a thermodynamic model.

The results that we obtained on the growth of *Trichoderma viride* TS and the *Penicillium roqueforti* confirmed these observations (Gervais *et al.*, 1988c) (Fig. 3).

Radial extension rate. Growth kinetics which are presented in Figs 4 and 5 for the two fungi confirmed that the colony diameter was linearly time-dependent (Trinci, 1969). The regression lines calculated were always

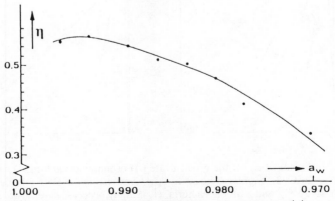

FIG. 2.   Thermodynamic efficiency versus water activity.

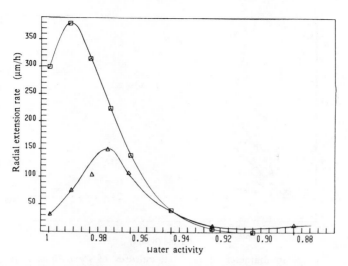

FIG. 3. Influence of the substrate water activity on the radial extension rate of *Trichoderma viride* TS (□) and of *Penicillium roqueforti* (△).

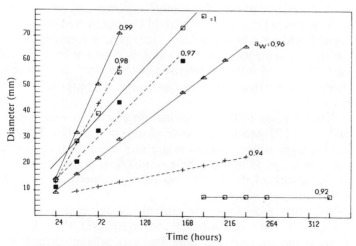

FIG. 4. Change in diameter of mycelial cultures of *Trichoderma viride* TS of different a_w values. (For a confidence level equal to 0·95, confidence intervals are all smaller than ±5·5 mm.)

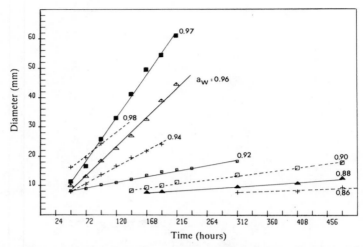

FIG. 5. Change in diameter of mycelial cultures of *Penicillium roqueforti* of different a_w values. (For a confidence level equal to 0·95, confidence intervals are all smaller than ± 6 mm.)

significantly correlated at the 99% level to experimental values. For each water activity, a mean extension rate could be approached using the slope of the corresponding regression line. The radial extension rate values were then related to the water activity value as shown in Fig. 3. The shape of the curves obtained was characteristic of the answer of a microorganism growth to a variation of water potential as proposed previously (Griffin, 1981).

For *Trichoderma viride* TS, the optimal water activity value for growth was found to be 0·99; below 0·90 no development occurred. These values allowed this fungus to be classified in a group constituted of moderately water-sensitive fungi. Moreover, these results have been confirmed by a study of the growth of this fungus led on sugar-beet pulp (Grajek and Gervais, 1987a).

For *Penicillium roqueforti*, the optimal water activity value was found to be 0·97 and development occurred over the whole range studied. However, at 0·90 the time lag was greater than five days. This fungus could be classified as a xerotolerant species. Otherwise, for the whole range of water activities studied, growth occurred faster in *Trichoderma viride* TS than in *Penicillium roqueforti*. The maximal radial extension rate values were 390 and 140 μm/h, respectively. This difference could be attributed to the nature of the microrganisms while the culture parameters, such as temperature and pH, were optimized. The addition of glycerol to the medium led to a maximum dilution of the nutrients elements of c. one-third for the lowest a_w values. It was verified by preliminary experiments that such a dilution of Morton's medium (Morton, 1960) did not significantly modify the radial extension rate.

Model construction. The model was designed using energy considerations. Using nutrients and gas, the microorganism could use an amount of energy, E_t, that could not be considered as a limitant during the fermentations studied. Energy E_t was defined as a variable which took a definite value for given environmental conditions and time interval; in the present conditions,

$$E_t = k \text{ (joules)} \tag{1}$$

This energy was used for the metabolic activity of the fungus and can be divided into 'maintenance' energy, E_m, and growth energy, E_g.

Growth energy. After a certain time interval, t, the fungus increased its biomass of M. The engaged energy is linearly related to the biomass synthesized:

$$E_g = k_1 M \tag{2}$$

Since M is proportional to the rate of the mycelium length increase, v,

$$E_g = k_2 v \text{ (joules)} \tag{3}$$

This mycelial length rate can be estimated by the measurement of the radial extension rate when the development does not follow the preferential direction.

Maintenance energy. The maintenance energy increases as the stress intensities applied to microorganisms increase. In optimal culture conditions, this energy (in joules) is reduced to E_{m0}, and the growth of the fungus is then controlled by the intrinsic characteristic of the organism which is considered to have balanced growth:

$$E_m = E_{m0} + E_{m\psi} + E_{m\theta} + \cdots \tag{4}$$

where E_{m0} is the minimal maintenance energy value, $E_{m\psi}$ is the energy necessary in non-optimal water conditions, and $E_{m\theta}$ is the energy necessary in non-optimal thermic conditions.

Other factors such as ionic forces and pressure can generate energy consumption. Some physiological transformations, such as sporulation, also require the use of specific energy.

In the experiment, all environmental conditions were kept constant at optimal value except water conditions, so that only $E_{m\psi}$ had to be considered. Moreover, the radial extension rate was measured only in the apical peripheral zone where no sporulation was observed and thus sporulation energy did not have to be taken into account in the proposed model. This observation was confirmed by the analysis of Figs. 4 and 5 which did not show any breakdown in the linear change of growth when sporulation began to occur in the culture (between 70 and 100 h culture).

It has been shown (Luard and Griffin, 1981) that optimal water conditions require a slight water potential difference between the inner medium of the microorganism and the external medium. When placed in different water potential conditions, the cell, in order to prevent passive exit of water, adapts its inner water potential by synthesizing compatible solutes as sugars and polyols or by facilitating diffusion of entering solutes. So the energy used to prevent osmotic shock must be related to the water potential difference between the optimal value for growth and the value of the medium used:

$$E_m\psi = k_3(\psi - \psi_0) = k_4 \ln \frac{a_w}{a_{w0}} \qquad (5)$$

where a_w is the water activity value of the medium, a_{w0} is the optimal growth water activity of the medium, ψ is the water potential value of the medium, and ψ_0 is the optimal water potential value.

From previous equations,

$$E_t = E_m + E_g = E_{m0} + k_4 \ln \frac{a_w}{a_{w0}} + k_2 v$$

E_t and E_{m0} are constant, so

$$v = A \ln \frac{a_w}{a_{w0}} + v_m \qquad (6)$$

where v_m is the maximal radial extension rate value (m/s), and A is a constant (m/s).

Model evaluation. The experimental values agreed with the eqn (6) for both fungi within a range of water activity values between 0·94 and c. 1.

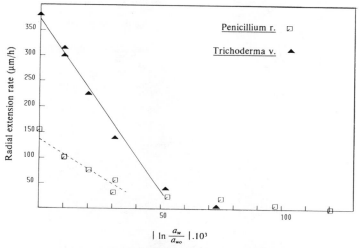

FIG. 6.   Application of the model to experimental data.

The correlation coefficients of the regressions proposed in Fig. 6 were 0·96 for *P. roqueforti* and 0·99 for *T. viride* TS. The two parameters V_m, representative of the balanced radial extension rate, and A, representative of the physiological resistance to a water stress, have been calculated for each mould:

—   *T. viride* TS
$A = -7 \times 10^3 \ \mu m/h$
$V_m = 390 \ \mu m/h$
—   *P. roqueforti*
$A = -3 \times 10^3 \ \mu m/h$
$V_m = 140 \ \mu m/h$

This model was tested (Fig. 7) on results proposed by other authors (Scott, 1957; Anand and Brown, 1968) for unicellular organisms cultivated in submerged media and seemed to be very predictive for such cultures.

Similar results were obtained during the development of *Trichoderma viride* TS on beet pulps. This microorganism is a hydrolysing agent of this substrate through its cellulases (Grajek and Gervais, 1987b).

3.2 Sporulation

Results obtained on the sporulation of these two previous species are presented in Fig. 8. A final numeration of the spores was performed after

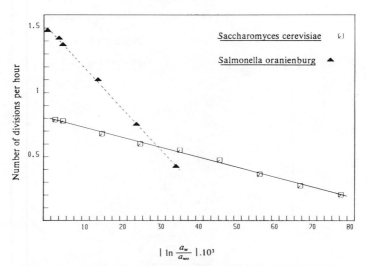

$$\left| \ln \frac{a_w}{a_{wo}} \right| .10^3$$

FIG. 7. ►Application of the model to data in the literature.

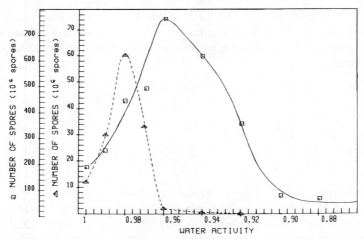

FIG. 8.   Influence of the substrate water activity on the sporulation intensity of *T. viride* TS ($\triangle$) and of *P. roqueforti* ($\square$).

10 days of culture. For the two fungi, sporulation did not occur in the youngest mycelial filaments, particularly in the peripheral zone. The intensity of sporulation was weaker for *Trichoderma viride* TS than for *Penicillium roqueforti*, certainly due to the pH conditions. The

sporulation of *Trichoderma viride* TS (Fig. 8) attained a maximum for $a_w = 0.98$ and the values decreased above as well as below this value. For both fungi, optimal a_w values for sporulation were slightly lower than optimal values for growth. Nevertheless for *Trichoderma viride* the minimal a_w value allowing sporulation (c. 0.96) was greater than for growth (c. 0.92).

A cyclic sporulation versus time of *T. viride* TS was observed in Petri dishes and confirmed in a larger Petri dish (16 cm diameter) maintained at 0.98 a_w value, as shown in Fig. 9. The rhythmic activity of filamentous fungi is a well-known phenomenon (Lysek, 1977) which can be exogenous, i.e. due to environmental stimuli (light, temperature), or endogenous, i.e. created by the fungus itself. Although *Trichoderma viride* species have been known to sporulate after short exposure to blue light (Betina and Zajakova, 1978), the period of the observed oscillations was not related to the exposure variations. Thus a circadian rhythm initiated by the water activity of the medium may be postulated.

Maximum sporulation values of *Penicillium roqueforti* were obtained at a_w of 0.96 as shown in Fig. 8. No periodicity in sporulation was observed for that species.

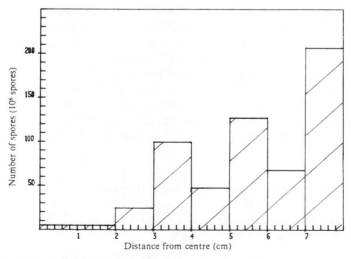

Fɪɢ. 9. Sporulation of *Trichoderma viride* TS observed on a Petri dish ($a_w = 0.98$) after 300 h.

3.3 Germination

The germination of a mould spore is a physiological reaction of a resting cell to modifications of the environmental conditions. The resting state of a spore is controlled by the internal presence of metabolic blocks, nutrient penetration barriers, self-inhibitors, and low water content (Smith, 1978). After a certain time lag, three successive structural changes are observed during germination (Gottlieb, 1978): the swelling of the mould spore, the emergence of a germ tube, and the elongation.

Water is a predominant part of germination, and hydration of the medium is an important parameter (Snow, 1949). Germination has been observed in pure water for *Alternaria* and *Cladosporium* (Dickinson and Bottomley, 1980). *Penicillium frequentans* and *Trichoderma viride* have been identified as strains with self-feeding spores (Sheridan and Sheeman, 1980). However, other authors have shown that the conidia of *P. notatum* and *T. lignorum* need carbon and nitrogen to germinate (Martin and Nicolas, 1970). When the water availability is limited, the water activity (a_w) of the medium strongly influences the mould development (Gervais *et al.*, 1988a). This parameter is widely used for quantifying the availability and the energy state of water. Nevertheless, a_w alone cannot explain the biological variations; when the medium a_w is adjusted by solutes the nature of the solute has an effect (Beuchat, 1983).

Only a few authors have tried to describe germination of conidia as a function of time. An empirical model for spore germination of *Alternaria solani* has been described, and further extended in order to develop a complex box model of germination (Waggoner and Parlange, 1975). A model proposed for conidial germination in *Colletotrichum graminicola* (Lapp and Skoropad, 1976) fitted the data well, but the parameters had little biological significance. The model proposed in a recent work (Gervais *et al.*, 1988b) was based on the observation of germination kinetics and the parameters involved take the physiology of germination into account.

Theoretical analysis of germination. Germination of a mould spore is considered as a classical first-order system where the basic hypothesis is the proportionality between the rate of germination and the corresponding number of ungerminated conidia:

- At time $t=0$ all the spores (N_0) are ungerminated and after time lag t_0, conidia begin to germinate.

- At time t, N spores germinate and the basic hypothesis allows to write:

$$\frac{dN}{d(t-t_0)} = k(N_0 - N) \qquad (7)$$

where k = constant of velocity.
- After integration

$$(N_0 - N) = e^{-k(t-t_0)} a \qquad (8)$$

where a = constant of integration.
- At $t = t_0$, $N = 0$ and then $a = N_0$

$$\frac{N}{N_0} = 1 - e^{-k(t-t_0)} \qquad (9)$$

- With $k = 1/\lambda$, and introducing a maximum ratio of germination K, the final equation is:

$$\frac{N}{N_0} = K(1 - e^{-(t-t_0)/\lambda}) \qquad (10)$$

where N/N_0 is the ratio of germinated spores at time t.

The model is described by three parameters:

- K = maximum ratio of germination
- t_0 = time lag
- λ = time constant, corresponding to the time needed to reach 63% of the maximum germination (K). Then $1/\lambda$ is an estimation of the rate of germination.

In order to study the influence of medium hydration on germination, conidia of *Penicillium roqueforti* and *Trichoderma viride* TS were produced on modified Morton's medium (Morton, 1960), diluted to one-quarter strength and solidified with 15 g of agar per litre. The medium was buffered to pH 5·0, and the water activity value was 0·97 to produce conidia from *P. roqueforti*, and 0·98 from *T. viride* TS as shown previously (Gervais *et al.*, 1988b).

To study the influence of hydration, glycerol was used as the water activity depressor because of its well-known compatible solute properties (Hocking and Pitt, 1979). Preliminary measurements showed that spores of the strains studied need oxygen to germinate, and that this could occur on a water–glycerol–agar mixture.

The medium was poured as thin layer (5 ml medium/dish) into a Petri dish (80 mm diameter). Cultures were inoculated by rubbing approximately 0·01 ml of the spore suspension on the medium until complete absorption of inoculum water by the medium. Three Petri dishes of a fixed a_w value were stored into a translucent polyethylene food storage box containing 200 ml of an appropriate water–glycerol solution to control the relative humidity of the atmosphere.

The criterion used for germination was the observation of a germ tube of length at least 1·5 times the diameter of the spore examined (Martin and Nicolas, 1970).

Application of the model. One of the three repetitions observed for each fungus and for the same a_w is shown for $a_w = 0·99$, $a_w = 0·95$, and $a_w = 0·92$ in Fig. 10. Both the observed data and the theoretical line produced by the regression of the data using eqn (10) are presented. The mean of the three values used for the same a_w cannot be used to validate the model owing to the variations in the time lag between repetitions.

The application of the model was validated as follows: for each water activity value, each fungus, and each value, the fit of the regression line was calculated with a chi-square test and was found to be highly significant (1% level). Thus, eqn (10) may interpret the germination data using the three parameters K, t_0, and λ of a real biological significance.

Influence of water on conidial germination. In order to study the influence of the water activity of the medium on germination, the mean values of the parameters K, t_0, and λ for each a_w are presented in Table 1 for *P. roqueforti* and *T. viride* TS. The minimum a_w values for germination observed were 0·90 for *T. viride* TS and 0·86 for *P. roqueforti*. Complete germination of *P. roqueforti* (100%) was observed for a_w values ranging from 0·98 to c. 1 and *T. viride* TS at 0·98 to 0·99 a_w. For lower a_w values, percentages of maximum germination decreased regularly.

The shortest time for germination occurred between 0·94 and c. 1 for *T. viride* TS, with a minimum at 0·99, and for *P. roqueforti* between 0·95 and 0·99, with a minimum at 0·98. The same limits of water activity were observed for the highest rates of germination, evaluated by $1/\lambda$. Maxima were then at 0·97 for *T. viride* TS and at 0·99 for *P. roqueforti*. *P. roqueforti* germinated more rapidly and more completely than *T. viride* TS at all a_w values studied.

The water activity value of the medium, close to 1, was not a good hydration condition for the germination of either fungus. Important

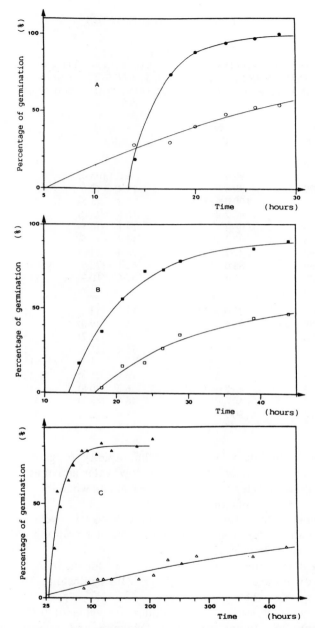

FIG. 10. Germination kinetics of (A) *P. roqueforti* (●) and *T. viride* TS (○) at $a_w = 0.99$; (B) *P. roqueforti* (■) and *T. viride* TS (□) at $a_w = 0.95$; (C) *P. roqueforti* (▲) and *T. viride* TS (△) at $a_w = 0.92$.

TABLE 1

MEAN VALUES OF THE EQN (10) PARAMETERS (K, t_0, AND λ) FOR THE GERMINATION OF (A) *P. ROQUEFORTI*, AND (B) OF *T. VIRIDE* TS. CONFIDENCE INTERVALS OF THE MEAN VALUES FOR A CONFIDENCE LEVEL EQUAL TO 0·90 ARE PRESENTED IN BRACKETS

Parameter water	K (%)		t_0 (h)		λ (h)	
A						
≈1	99·4	(1·7)	58·6	(68·0)	44·7	(53·1)
0·99	99·6	(0·7)	14·4	(2·6)	3·6	(1·3)
0·98	100·0	(0·0)	8.2	(3·5)	6·1	(1·4)
0·97	96·2	(5·0)	10·6	(1·0)	4·7	(0·9)
0·96	96·4	(6·8)	13·1	(0·5)	7·1	(3·1)
0·95	92·2	(1·9)	12·9	(0·6)	8·2	(2·9)
0·92	82·7	(3·6)	28·4	(4·0)	21·6	(9·3)
0·90	88·0	(18·8)	62·1	(72·6)	76·2	(91·7)
0·88	35·2	(15·9)	157·6	(10·9)	147·7	(188·6)
B						
≈1	85·6	(14·9)	11·3	(3·2)	21·3	(12·3)
0·99	98·6	(4·2)	5·3	(9·0)	28·4	(13·2)
0·98	100·0	(0·0)	9·9	(2·7)	23·5	(7·9)
0·97	74·6	(22·2)	13·1	(1·1)	11·9	(4·8)
0·96	67·6	(14·7)	12·7	(1·7)	15·9	(7·1)
0·95	58·9	(4·8)	16·5	(1·8)	12·8	(9·4)
0·94	43·8	(4·8)	16·2	(0·8)	19·1	(4·3)
0·92	44·6	(26·6)	46·8	(48·7)	448·3	(272·0)
0·90	20·7	(7·4)	21·6	(12·5)	313·7	(340·6)

variations in the time lag and in the rapidity of germination were observed. The high mean values at the low water activities (below 0·92), indicated difficulties for the conidia to germinate when the environmental conditions became unfavourable.

In general, water activity values from 0·94 to 0·99 were favourable to the germination of *P. roqueforti*; and the most favourable values for *T. viride* TS were 0·94 to c. 1.

The use of the three parameters K, t_0, and λ for the model was justified by the study of the correlation coefficients: no significant relationship was observed between these parameters.

P. roqueforti germinated at minimum a_w value of 0·86, which was higher than 0·83 found previously (Magnan and Lacey, 1984) with glycerol–agar medium. But the absence of nutrients reduces the range of a_w values where germination and growth are possible (Snow, 1949).

The influence of the low water activity values on germination is not well understood (Charlang and Horowitz, 1974). The loss of an essential substance for germination from *Neurospora crassa*, *Aspergillus nidulans* and *P. chrysogenum* at low water activity has been suggested (Charlang and Horowitz, 1971, 1974). According to Gottlieb (1978) water allows the diffusion of self-inhibitors out of the spore. In all cases, the membrane permeability is important. Dehydration of the membrane would produce a molecular rearrangment of phospholipids leading to a rigidification and a loss of permeability of the membrane (Quinn, 1985). The rearrangement would occur at an a_w value which corresponds to the minimum water activity value observed for germination.

If germination is allowed by the diffusion of self-inhibitors out of the spore, the concentration of inhibitors in the conidia would be inversely proportional to the water content of the medium, until the equilibrium water content (W_0) or water activity (a_{w0}) is reached. This value which corresponds to the maximum germination ratio of the fungus is equal to 0·98 for both fungi (Table 1). So below a_{w0}, the K parameter of the germination (see eqn (10)) would be related to the water content of the medium by the following equation:

$$K = AW \qquad (11)$$

where A is the constant of proportionality and W is the water content.

If K_0 is the maximal value of the parameter K corresponding to a water content of W_0

$$K_0 = AW_0 \qquad (12)$$

From (11) and (12)

$$K = -A(W_0 - W) + K_0 \qquad (13)$$

Equation (13) was compared to the experimental data in Fig. 11. The correlation coefficients of the corresponding regression were significant (1% level). This type of model would be interesting, but has still to be confirmed.

This work confirms the results of Christian (1981) which show that the latency time is little influenced by the nature of the a_w depressor. Nevertheless, germination kinetics seem strongly to be linked to the nature of the used solute. For the same activity of the solution, the lower the water activity coefficient, γ, (<1), the more the solute deviates from Raoult's law, and spore germination can occur.

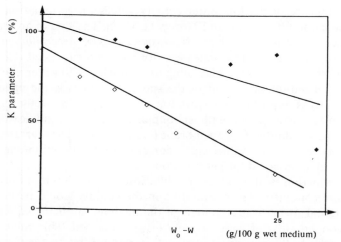

FIG. 11.   Influence of water content on K parameter of eqn (13); *P. roqueforti* (◆), *T. viride* TS (◇).

4 WATER ACTIVITY AND METABOLITE PRODUCTION

The production of principal or secondary metabolites is also dependent in numerous cases on the water energy state in the medium which can be evaluated by thermodynamic parameters. Thus, in the case of the ethanol production by yeasts in liquid medium (Panchal and Stewart, 1980), the optimal water activity for the ethanol production is appreciably less than 1. The toxin production by filamentous fungi cultivated on solid support is also related to the medium a_w; thus the ochratoxin A production by *Penicillium viridicatum* is optimal for an a_w of 0·87 (Northolt *et al.*, 1984).

Some hypotheses have been made on the influence of a decreased water activity on the metabolism of microorganisms. By using increasing concentrations of dextran and polyethylene-glycol (Hahn-Hagerdäl *et al.*, 1982) the initial ethanol production rate was increased by 50%. A new metabolic cycle of glycerol initiated by high concentrations in glycerol was discovered by Ben-Amotz and Avron (1981) in the halophilic alga *Dunaliella*. The result of this cycle is to transfer redox equivalents from NADH to NADPH at the expense of one ATP. The enzyme of this cycle was found to be specific and had a very high K_m to glycerol.

Since an increased synthesis of β-carotene was found to follow the decrease in a_w, it could be postulated that the intracellular accumulation of glycerol starts the glycerol cycle with results in a transfer of redox equivalents from NADH to NADPH which favours biosynthesis pathways and particularly β-carotene synthesis.

The synthesized solutes responsible for osmoregulation, called compatible solutes, are essentially polyols, amino acids and ions. The organic solutes thus defined interfere with enzymatic activities and are generally very water-soluble. With regard to the speed of some syntheses in response to a water stress (3 minutes for the isofluoride synthesis by *Ochromonas malhamensis*) (Kauss, 1974), it seems that these syntheses are due to the activation of previous enzymatic systems. This activation seems to be initiated by the membrane since it has been demonstrated that these enzymatic systems do not depend on the pressure. Furthermore, numerous works have demonstrated that transfers through the membranes are directly related to turgor pressure (Gutknecht and Bisson, 1977; Hüsken *et al.*, 1978).

4.1 Water Activity and Enzymatic Reactions

Water activity can act through the osmoregulation process of the cell or through a direct enzymatic action, as previously described by numerous authors (Nishio *et al.*, 1979; Beuchat, 1983; Kim 1985). We confirmed such a direct action by a study on enzymatic activity related to the mass of enzyme produced versus water activity.

The influence of water activity (a_w) on the biosynthesis of polygalacturonase, D-xylanase and β-glucosidase in a solid culture system of *Trichoderma viride* was studied. It was found that the production of enzymes was strongly affected by the water activity of the substrate and the nature of the a_w depressor used. The maximum polygalacturonase and D-xylanase production occurred at $a_w = 0.99$ whereas β-glucosidase formation was favoured at $a_w = 0.96$–0.98. The influence of water activity on the catalytic effect of enzymes using sodium chloride, glycerol and sorbitol as a_w depressors was also investigated (Figs 12 and 13).

In spite of the importance of the water activity, and owing to the lack of a sensor, there is no way to control water potential or osmotic pressure in order to optimize metabolic production in classical fermentation processes.

Only a few applications need be noted, such as for glycerol production by *Dunaliella* (Avron and Ben-Amotz, 1979) or for glutamic acid production by *Corynebacterium glutamicum melassecola* (Dubreuil, 1985).

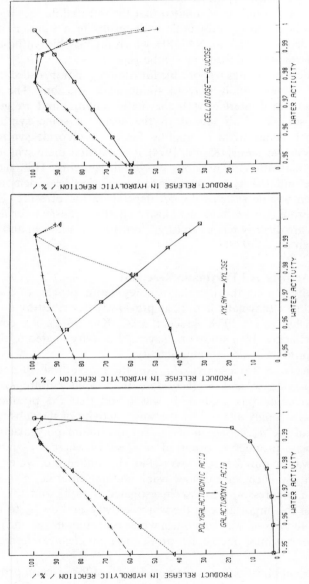

FIG. 12. Effect of water activity on product release in a hydrolytic reaction using enzyme solution from *Trichoderma viride* TS; a_w depressors: NaCl, □; glycerol, △; sorbitol, +.

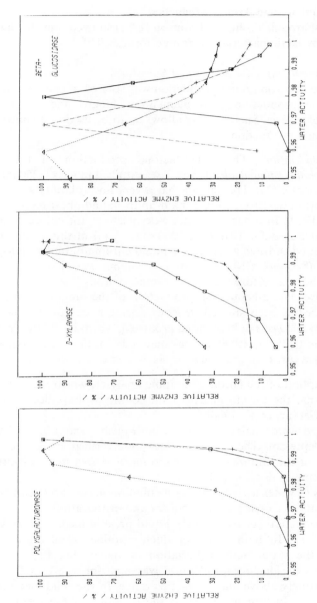

FIG. 13.   Effect of water activity on the production of enzymes by *Trichoderma viride* TS in solid-state fermentation; a_w depressors: NaCl, □; glycerol, △; sorbitol, +.

4.2 Water Activity and Aroma Production

In the case of aroma, Troller and Stinson (1981) showed that the diacetyl production by lactic bacteria is favoured for $a_w = 0.95$.

4.2.1 Experiments on Solid and Liquid Substrates

The influence of a_w on aroma production was studied in two systems: the methyl-ketone production of a filamentous fungus and the lactone production of a yeast. Such a study allows a_w to be used as a controlling factor of aroma production.

- *In liquid media.* The γ-decalactone production of the yeast *Sporidiobolus salmonicolor* F and T was studied in flasks (250 ml) and in a fermenter (2 l). This lactone has a very low volatility so that the main part of the production remains in the liquid phase (Gervais and Battut, 1989). In order to extract γ-decalactone, the culture medium was centrifuged for 10 min at 4000 rpm. 50 ml of this medium was then filtered through a separative liquid chromatographic non-polar column (Sep-pak C18, Waters). The column was then eluted with 2 ml of hexane, before chromatographic analysis.

- *On gelose.* The 2-heptanone production of the fungus *Trichoderma viride* TS has been studied in Roux flasks. A continuous aeration (50 ml/h) allowed the heptanone produced, which is a highly volatile compound (Tallu, 1986) to be analysed. In this case, sequential headspace chromatographic analysis was used (Gervais *et al.* 1988b).

The description of the chromatographic analyser, which was the same for both aroma, and the chromatographic conditions have been reported previously (Gervais *et al.*, 1988b).

The selected water activity values in both media were obtained using glycerol as depressor. The fixed a_w values were verified at the beginning and the end of the culture using a hygrometer (Novasina, Switzerland) and an osmometer (Roebling, Germany).

Variations of water activity during incubation never exceeded 0·01 for all cultures studied, owing to metabolism and evaporation.

Aroma production versus a_w of the liquid or solid media are shown in Figs 14 and 15. In both cases, production values were dramatically affected by the water activity variation of the media. In the liquid medium, the γ-decalactone production was high for $a_w = 0.99–0.97$ and decreased strongly above and below this range. In the solid medium the 2-heptanone production increased as the a_w value of the medium decreased. Such results were obtained by the analysis of the extracellular

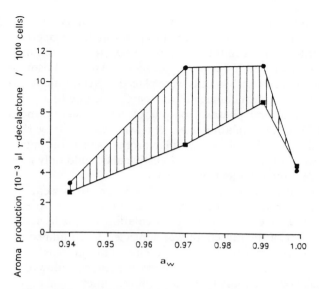

FIG. 14.   Influence of a_w on aroma production (■) and aroma release (●) by *S. salmonicolor* cultivated for 20 days on a liquid medium. (The shaded area corresponds with the accumulated aroma).

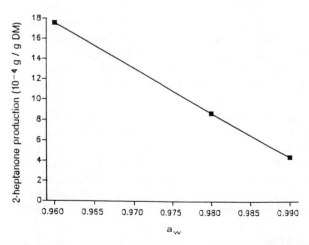

FIG. 15.   Influence of a_w on aroma production by *T. viride* TS cultivated for 5 days on a solid medium. (DM, dry matter).

medium and resulted from the excretion availability of the cell which combines intracellular production and permeability properties.

In order to distinguish these two properties, the intracellular content in aroma was examined in further experiments. An initial osmotic phase of water input occurred when cells were placed in hypotonic media. In order to prevent mechanical damage of the membrane due to a greater volume expansion, a second phase of output of active osmotic molecules also occurred. The accumulation intensity was evaluated by the difference between the quantity of extracellular aroma before and after the hypotonic stress. This method is not exhaustive and could only give a fraction of the intracellular content of molecules.

In the solid substrate the effects of a water stress were studied on a culture of *Trichoderma viride* TS initially at $a_w = 0.99$. After 5 hours of culture, the relative humidity of the circulating air was fixed at 0.80. Thus, the aerial part of the mycelium was subjected to an immediate stress. In the liquid substrate a process of successive dilutions was set up in flasks as well as in a fermenter. A preliminary experiment allowed the dilution time to be fixed at 3 hours in order to prevent interaction of the growth of the microorganism with the aroma analysis.

Results, presented in Fig. 16 for the solid substrate, show that a decrease in water potential causes a drastic decrease in extracellular heptanone production. Hydration properties of the medium and especially the water activity are therefore involved in the aroma production of the fungus. The return of the initial hydration conditions after 10 hours of aeration at a relative humidity of 80% corresponded to an increase in aroma production. Accumulation of the aroma during the stress period related to the osmoregulation of the fungus is represented by the shaded area.

For the liquid substrate, the intracellular accumulation was studied by diluting the media. Each initial culture medium (from $a_w = 0.94$ to $a_w \simeq 1$) was diluted in water to reach comparative level of water activity ($\simeq 1$). In all cases this dilution of the medium led to an increase of the release of γ-decalactone especially for the values of 0.97–0.99 as shown in Fig. 14. In this range the same γ-decalactone quantity was produced by the yeasts with a maximum accumulation occurring at $a_w = 0.97$ which corresponds to severe osmotic conditions. The release of aroma due to dilution decreased for high a_w values ($\simeq 1$) as well as for low water activity values (0.94).

The osmotic effect of the accumulation of aroma inside cells has recently been demonstrated by experimental evidence of the presence of

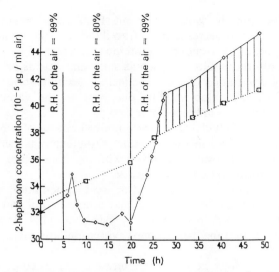

FIG. 16. Influence of hydric stress on aroma production by *T. viride* TS; ◇, with stress; □, without stress. (The shaded area corresponds with the accumulated aroma. RH, relative humidity.)

this compound in the cell. This was done by grinding the cells with a glass bead cell homogenizer. It may be concluded that most γ-decalactone released by the cell occurred when the water activity ranged between 0·97–0·99 and decreased above and below this range. This decrease corresponds to an enzyme inhibition which could be induced as much by too high as by too low a water potential level, as previously reported (Grajek and Gervais, 1987b).

4.2.2 Osmoregulation Mechanisms

Thus in both types of medium, it seems that the extracellular aroma production rate is influenced by the amount of hydration of the medium. When the external osmotic pressure is increased, cells have to equilibrate their inner medium with the outer medium to prevent an osmotic stress due to passive exit of water. Three ways are possible: facilitating diffusion of small solutes like glycerol across the membrane, synthesizing molecules in the inner medium or modifying the permeability of the membrane. Heptanone and γ-decalactone synthesis can be related to this osmoregulation in living cells. However, it has been verified that γ-decalactone accumulation plays only a very minor role in this osmoregulation. Maximum intracellular concentration of this compound could be evalu-

20ated to 200 ppm v/v, which is about 1000 times smaller than the quantity necessary to decrease the intracellular a_w from about 1 to 0·97. So the main part of the osmoregulation must be assumed by the synthesis or transport of other molecules such as salts, aminoacids or polyols.

The observed variation of the γ-decalactone accumulation in the range 0·97–0·99 of the a_w value may be due only to the variation of cell permeability under the influence of a_w.

It may also be concluded that maximum cell release of heptanone and γ-decalactone occurs when the a_w value of the external medium is low enough to generate an osmotic gradient with the inner cell medium, but it is not too low to inhibit enzyme kinetics.

Variation of water activity in liquid or solid fermentation media could lead to great modifications in intracellular accumulation and in extracellular excretion of aroma produced by yeasts or moulds. Enzyme inhibition and cell membrane permeability variation are involved in such mechanisms.

This conclusion may be of great interest in the attempt to optimize metabolite production such as aroma, antibiotics, enzymes by means of a_w control. A recently developed sensor that allows the continuous measurement of the osmotic pressure of a liquid medium could be used with this aim (Gervais, 1989).

It could be of interest to maintain a high cell concentration in metabolites during a concentrated step of the culture on solid as well as in liquid substrates in order to release the aroma during a following diluted step. The use of permeabilizing agents could also be envisaged.

4.2.3 Aroma Production Related to the Age of Filamentous Fungi Mycelium

In a recent work (Gervais and Sarrette, 1990) it was shown that the aroma production by microorganisms is dependent not only on physicochemical factors like pH, temperature (Latrasse et al., 1985) or water activity (Gervais et al., 1988d), but also on the physiological state of the fungus. The cells of a filamentous fungus are not independent and their activity is dependent on their concentric position in the colony and thus on their age (Cole, 1986). The fact that fungal hyphae are growing in the apical zone has been established by various methods (Bartnicki-Garcia, 1973), and some experiments have shown that membrane synthesis activity reaches a maximum in an annular band behind a non-extensible cap (Burnett, 1968). Yanagita and Kogane (1962) described three concentric zones of different physiological states in a mould colony. In the same way, we observed that the sporulation of *Trichoderma viride* is cyclic and follows circadian rhythms (Gervais *et al.*, 1988c).

We have recently tried to relate the aroma production of *T. viride* TS to the physiological state of a circular colony (Gervais and Sarrette 1990).

Aroma production measurements. In order to follow the change of aroma production of a colony without spoiling the mycelium, headspace chromatographic analysis was used. The circulating air carried the aroma to the gas chromatograph.

It was also necessary to study the aroma production of different areas of a colony and a special apparatus was designed which enabled the aroma production of different rings of mycelium to be estimated; this apparatus is shown in Fig. 17. An opened Petri dish containing a colony was set on a support; the partitioned box was applied to the colony; then the colony was cut into concentric areas which were independent. Each concentric area presents two openings: the first permits aeration of the mycelium, and the second conducts the air carrying the volatile compounds to the gas chromatograph.

Before starting the aeration, it was necessary to wait for 20 minutes after applying the partitioned box to the colony, in order to accumulate enough aroma for the analysis. After this time of accumulation and before injecting, the area studied was aerated for 5 seconds with a flow rate of 50 ml/min. Thus the index of aroma production used for a ring is the cumulative quantity obtained for each compartment after 20 minutes of culture, measured after 5 seconds of aeration in 1 ml of the outlet gas, and related to the area unit. By using headspace chromatographic analysis, described by Gervais and Sarrette (1990), each ring of the colony could be analysed.

Study of the reactor aeration. Measurements of aroma production were dependent on aeration conditions of the apparatus. In a previous study the elaboration of aeration models enabled us to study the residence time distribution of a volatile tracer in a reactor (Gervais *et al.*, 1986).

If the aeration is homogeneous, the change of aroma concentration versus time in response to a Dirac impulse can be fitted by a first-order equation as follows:

$$C = \frac{A}{\lambda} e^{-t/\lambda} \tag{14}$$

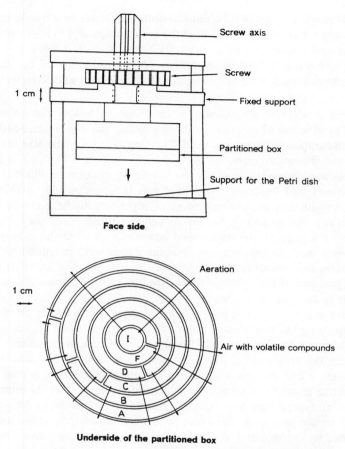

FIG. 17. Apparatus enabling the aroma production of different areas of a mycelial colony to be differentiated.

where C is the tracer concentration at instant t inside the reactor, A is a constant proportional to the concentration injected, and λ is the time constant of the system (min). Lambda (λ) has to be compared with the expected mean residence time t_a which is equal to the ratio of the total volume of the reactor (V) to the inlet flow rate of the total volume of the gas. Comparison of both λ and t_a values allows analysis of the aeration pattern of the reactor by the relation $V_{used} = V_{total}(t_a/\lambda)$ where V_{used} is used volume, and V_{total} is total volume.

In order to reach a perfect mixed reactor ($t_a = \lambda$), the gas vector flow rate can be modified. In the previous case an air flow rate of 50 ml/min was required.

Such an approach would be helpful, in the case of headspace chromatographic analysis of gases issued from the metabolism of micro-organisms. Indeed, in order to have representative samples of the micro-organisms production, the gas vector intensity must afford a perfect gas mixing in the reactor. A general method intended to verify the homogen-ization of aeration in solid substrate fermentation could also be extracted from this work.

Differentiation of the aroma production of a colony. It is necessary to balance the aroma production by a surface unit in order always to compare the same area of mycelium for each water activity. Figure 18 shows the change of aroma production for a same surface unit as a function of time and the position of mycelium. According to the previous results, and for each area studied, the maximum aroma production occurred at the lower a_w value 0·96.

Nevertheless for each a_w value the maximum aroma production first occurred in the centre of a colony, and moved from the centre to the periphery of the colony as a wave.

Variations in mycelium density cannot explain this change of aroma production. According to Gillie (1968), the mycelium density decreases only slightly towards the periphery of a colony, and this variation could not explain our results. The concentric localization of the mycelium of a same age may explain the variations of aroma production. For each water activity and each day, the age of the area which produced the maximal aroma production by surface unity was determined directly by using growth kinetics. The radial growth rate of the my-celium was a constant for each a_w value; so the distance of a mycelium fraction from the periphery or from the centre could be converted into time and thus could give the age of the considered fraction. Maximum aroma production always occurred around 3·4–6·5 days (average 4·6 days). This result shows that there is a relation between aroma production and a particular physiological state of the mycelium which occurred after about 4·6 days of culture. According to this mechanism, a model intended to explain the aroma production by a mould colony can be proposed. This model enables us to calculate the aroma production of a certain area of a colony as a function of its place in the colony.

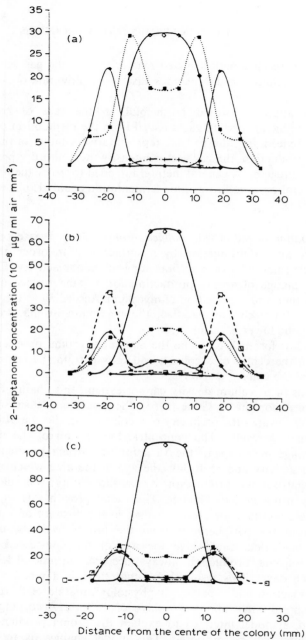

FIG. 18. Aroma production of a culture as a function of time and mycelial development in a Petri dish. ×, 4 days: +, 5 days; ◇, 6 days; ■, 7 days; ◆, 8 days; □, 9 days. (A) $a_w = 0.99$; (B) $a_w = 0.98$; (C) $a_w = 0.96$.

At a fixed time, we can assume that the aroma production around the maximum zone follows a Normal law:

$$P(r) = k \exp - \left[\frac{1}{2} \left(\frac{m-r}{\alpha} \right)^2 \right]$$

where $P(r)$ is the aroma production of a mycelium circle set at a distance r from the colony centre, m is the distance from centre where aroma production is at a maximum, k, a constant, corresponds to the maximum production, and α is a constant.

At time t, m can be deduced from the growth versus time equation: $m = a(t - 4 \cdot 6) + b$, where t represents the time in days, and a, b are coefficients that vary with a_w. Thus

$$P(r) = k \exp \left[-\frac{1}{2} \left(\frac{a(t - 4 \cdot 6) + b - r}{\alpha} \right)^2 \right]$$

α can be calculated from experimental data.

During our experiments, the annular bands studied were too thick to know precisely the experimental aroma production versus r change. There is still no experimental evidence for the coherence of this model.

CONCLUSION

Water is a protean molecule whose properties are due to hydrogen bond specificity. This conformation gives to water the fundamental roles of solvent and structurant in biological systems.

So, the hydration level of the culture medium is a fundamental parameter for the physiology of a microorganism. The transfer of water molecules between intracellular and extracellular media follows the water potential gradient. This passive exchange leads to a mechanical deformation of the cell and particularly to the variation of the surface of the plasmic membrane or to the variation of the turgor pressure. The microorganism reacts to these variations by activating the cellular mechanisms which are energy-consuming and which enable it to limit these effects. The influence of the water potential of the medium on microorganism development and metabolite biosynthesis, which follows from these observations, has been clearly demonstrated in this paper both on the radial growth of filamentous fungi, and on yeast multiplication and also on aroma and enzyme production by these microorganisms.

In the case of dilute media, which are characteristic of most liquid fermentations, we showed that colligative parameters related to the thermodynamic state of water are extremely influential on the physiological evolution of the microorganisms. This observation can be explained through the following properties of dilute solutions.

• Water content is high and the diffusion of solutes is not a limiting factor.
• Molecular interactions are very few, the solutions are quite ideal and the nature of the solute does not interfere.

Otherwise, the previous results underline the determinant role of the plasmic membrane as an osmotic cellular sensor. It seems necessary to deepen the study of the biochemical and physicochemical modifications to the membrane induced by an osmotic shock for a better understanding of the observed physiological modifications.

REFERENCES

Anand, J. C. & Brown, A. D. (1968). Growth rate patterns of the so-called osmophilic and non-osmophilic yeasts in solutions of polyethylene glycols. *J. Gen. Microbiol.*, **52**, 205–12.

Andreyeva, L. N. & Biryukov, V. V. (1973). Analysis of mathematical models of the effect of pH on fermentation processes and their use for calculating optimal fermentation conditions. *Biotechnol. Bioeng.*, **4**, 61–76.

Avron, M. & Ben-Amotz, A. (1979). Metabolic adaptation of the alga *Dunaliella* to low water activity. In *Strategies of Microbial Life in Extreme Environments*, ed. M. Shilo. Dahlem Konferenzen, Berlin, pp. 83–91.

Bartnicki-Garcia, S. (1973). Fundamental aspects of hyphal morphogenesis. In *Microbial differentiation*, ed. J. M. Ashworth and J. E. Smith. Cambridge University Press, London, pp. 245–67.

Ben-Amotz, A. & Avron, M. (1978). On the mechanism of osmoregulation in *Dunaliella*. In *Developments in Halophilic Microorganisms*, Vol. I: *Energetics and Structure of Halophilic Microorganisms*, ed. S. R. Caplan and M. Ginzburg. Elsevier–North-Holland Biomedical Press, Amsterdam, pp. 529–36.

Ben-Amotz, A. & Avron, M. (1981). Glycerol and β-carotene metabolism in the halotolerant alga *Dunaliella*: a model system for biosolar energy conversion. *T.I.B.S.*, November, 297–9.

Betina, V. & Zajacova, J. (1978). Inhibition of photo-induced *Trichoderma viride* conidiation by inhibitors of RNA synthesis. *Fol. Microbiol.*, **23**, 460–4.

Beuchat, L. R. (1983). Influence of water activity on growth, metabolic activities and survival of yeasts and moulds. *J. Food Prot.*, **46**, 135–41.

Bouanda, R. (1983). Contribution to the study of the enzymatic activity in little hydrated medium: influence of the mobility of the substrate. Thesis, third cycle, ENSBANA, Dijon, France.

Bruin, S. & Luyben, K. Ch. A. (1980). Drying of food materials: a review of recent developments. In *Advances in Drying*, Vol. 1, ed. A. Mujumdar. Hemisphere, London, pp. 155–215.

Burnett, J. H. (1968). Spore liberation, dispersal and germination. In *Fundamentals of Mycology*, Vol. 3. Edward Arnold, London, pp. 145–87.

Charlang, G. W. & Horowitz, N. H. (1971). Germination and growth of *Neurospora* at low water activities. *Proc. Nat. Acad. Sci.*, **68**, 260–2.

Charlang, G. W. & Horowitz, N. H. (1974). Membrane permeability and the loss of germination factor from *Neurospora crassa* at low water activity. *J. Bact.*, **117**, 261–4.

Christian, J. H. B. (1981). Specific solute effects on microbial water relations. In *Water Activity: Influences on Food Quality*, ed. L. B. Rockland and G. F. Stewart. Academic Press, London, pp. 825–54.

Cole, G. T. (1986). Models of cell differentiation in Conidia fungi. *Microbiol. Rev.*, **50**, 95–9.

Crowe, J. H., Crowe, L. M. & Deamer, D. W. (1982). Hydration dependent phase changes in biological membrane. In *Biophysics of Water*, ed. F. Franks and S. Mathias. Wiley, Chichester, 295–9.

Cudd, A. & Steponkus, P. L. (1987). Osmotic dehydration-induced lamellar to hexagonal-II phase transitions in liposomes of rye plasma membrane lipids. In *Cryo 87:24th Annual Meeting*, Society for Cryobiology, Edmonton, Canada.

De Loecker, R., Penninckx, F. & Kerremans, R. (1987). Osmotic effects of rapid dilution of cryoprotectants: I, Effects on human erythrocyte swelling. *Cryo-Lett.*, **8**, 131–6.

Dickinson, S. & Bottomley, R. (1980). Germination and growth of *Alternaria* and *Cladosporium* in relation to their activity in the phylophane. In *Trans. Br. Mycol. Soc.*, **74**, 309–19.

Dubreuil, P. (1985). Kinetics and modelisation of the glutamic fermentation. Thesis for Doctor-Engineer, Institut National Polytechnique de Lorraine, Nancy, France.

Esener, A. A., Roels, J. A. & Kossen, N. W. F. (1981). *Biotechnol. Lett.*, **3**, 15.

Fisher, L. R. & Israelachvili, J. N. (1979). Direct experimental verification of the Kelvin equation for capillary condensation. *Nature*, **277**, 548–9.

Flory, P. J. (1953). Statistical thermodynamics of polymer solutions. In *Principles of Polymer Chemistry*, ed. P. J. Flory. Cornell University Press. Ithaca, pp. 495–540.

Franks, F. (1984). *Water*. The Royal Society of Chemistry, London.

Franks, F. (1985). Water and aqueous solutions: recent advances. In *Water Properties of Food*, ed. D. Simatos and J. L. Multon. Martinus Nijhoff, Dordrecht, pp. 1–23.

Gervais, P. (1989). New sensor allowing continuous water activity measurements of submerged or solid-substrate fermentations. *Biotechnol. Bioeng.*, **33**, 266–71.

Gervais, P. & Battut, G. (1989). Water potential and γ-decalactone production in yeasts. *Appl. Env. Microbiol.*, **55**, 2939–43.

Gervais, P. & Sarrette, M. (1990). Influence of age of mycelium and water activity of the medium on aroma production by *Trichoderma viride* TS grown on solid-substrate. *J. Ferment. Bioeng.*, **69**, 46–50.

Gervais, P., Bazelin, C. & Voilley, A. (1986). Patterns of aeration in a solid substrate fermentation through the study of the residence time distribution (R.T.D.) of a volatile tracer. *Biotechnol. Bioeng.*, **28**, 1540–3.

Gervais, P., Bensoussan, M. & Grajek, W. (1988a). Water activity and water content: comparative effects on the growth of *Penicillium roqueforti* on solid substrate. *Appl. Microbiol. Biotechnol.*, **27**, 389–92.

Gervais, P., Fasquel, J. P. & Molin, P. (1988b). Water relations of fungal spore germination. *Appl. Microbiol. Biotechnol.*, **29**, 586–92.

Gervais, P., Molin, P., Grajek, W. & Bensoussan, M. (1988c). Influence of the water activity of a solid substrate on the growth rate and sporogenesis of filamentous fungi. *Biotechnol. Bioeng.*, **31**, 457–63.

Gervais, P., Belin, J. M., Grajek, W. & Sarrette, M. (1988d). Influence of water activity on aroma production by *Trichoderma viride* TS growing on a solid substrate. *J. Ferment. Technol.*, **66**, 403–7.

Gilles, R. (1975). Mechanisms of ion and osmoregulation. In *Marine Ecology*, ed. O. Kinne. Wiley–Interscience, Chichester, Vol. 2, Part 1, pp. 259–347.

Gillie, O. J. (1968). Observations on the tube method of measuring growth rate in *Neurospora crassa*. *J. Gen. Microbiol.*, **51**, 185–94.

Goldberg, M., Parvaresh, F., Thomas, D. & Legoy, M. -D. (1988). Enzymatic ester synthesis with continuous measurement of water activity. *Biochim. Biophys. Acta*, **957**, 359–62.

Gottlieb, D. (1978). In *The Germination of Fungus Spores*, ed. D. Gottlieb. Meadowfield Press, Durham, pp. 1–11.

Gould, G. W. (1985). Present state of knowledge of a_w effects on microorganisms. In *Properties of Water in Foods*, ed. D. Simatos and J. L. Multon. Martinus Nijhoff, Dordrecht, pp. 229–45.

Grajek, W. & Gervais, P. (1987a). Effect of the sugar-beet pulp water on the solid-state culture of *Trichoderma viride* TS. *Appl. Microbiol. Biotechnol.*, **26**, 537–41.

Grajek, W. & Gervais, P. (1987b). Influence of water activity on the enzyme biosynthesis and enzyme activities produced by *Trichoderma viride* TS in solid-state fermentation. *Enzyme Microb. Technol.*, **9**, 658–62.

Griffin, D. M. (1981). Water and microbial stress. *Adv. Microb. Ecol.*, **5**, 91–136.

Guggenheim, E. A. (1967). *Thermodynamics: An Advanced Treatment for Chemists and Physicists*, 5th edn. North-Holland, Amsterdam.

Guilbert, S., Giannakopoulos, A. & Cheftel, J. C. (1985). Diffusivity of sorbic acid in food gels at high and intermediate water activities. In *Properties of Water in Foods*, ed. D. Simatos and J. L. Multon. Martinus Nijhoff, Dordrecht, pp. 314–57.

Gutknecht, J. & Bisson, M. A. (1977). Ion transport and osmotic regulations in giant algal cells. In *Water Relations in Membrane Transport in Plants and Animals*, ed. A. M. Jungreis, T. Hodges, A. M. Kleinzeller and S. G. Schulz. Academic Press, New York, pp. 3–14.

Hahn-Hägerdal, B. (1986). Water activity: a possible external regulator in biotechnical processes. *Enzyme Microb. Technol.*, **8**, 322–7.

Hahn-Hägerdal, B., Larsson, M. & Mattiasson, B. (1982). Shift in metabolism towards ethanol production in *Saccharomyces cerevisiae* using alterations of the physical–chemical environment. *Biotechnol. Bioeng. Symp.* **12**, 199–202.

Hellebust, J. A. (1976). Osmoregulation. *Ann. Rev. Plant Physiol.*, **27**, 485–505.

Hocking, A. D. & Pitt, J. I. (1979). Water relations of some *Penicillium* species at 25°C. *Trans. Br. Mycol. Soc.*, **732**, 141–5.

Hüsken, D., Steudle, E. & Zimmermann, U. (1978). Pressure probe technique for measuring water relations of cells in higher plants. *Plant Physiol.*, **61**, 158–63.

Jakobsen, M. (1985). Effect of a_w on growth and survival of Bacilliaceae. In *Properties of Water in Foods*, ed. D. Simatos and J. L. Multon. Martinus Nijhoff, Dordrecht, pp. 259–72.

Kauss, H. (1974). Osmoregulation in *Ochromonas*. In *Membrane Transport in Plants*, ed. U. Zimmermann and J. Dainty. Springer, Berlin, pp. 90–4.

Kovarskii, A. L., Wasserman, A. M. & Buchachenko, A. L. (1972). The study of rotational and translational diffusion constants for stable nitroxide radicals in liquids and polymers. *J. Magn. Resonance*, **7**, 225–37.

Kuntz, I. D. (1971). Hydration of macromolecules: hydration of poly-peptides, Polypeptides conformation in frozen solutions. *J. Amer. Chem. Soc.*, **92**, 514–18.

Lapp, M. S. & Skoropad, W. P. (1976). A mathematical model of conidial germination and appressorial formation for *Colletotrichum graminicola. Can J. Bot.*, **54**, 2239–42.

Latrasse, A., Degorce-Dumas, J. R. & Leveau, J. Y. (1985). Production d'arômes par les microorganismes. *Sci. Aliments*, **5**, 1–26.

Le Meste, M. & Voilley, A. (1988). Influence of hydration on rotational diffusivity of solutes in model systems. *J. Phys. Chem.*, **92**, 1612–16.

Lilley, T. H. (1985). Water activity as a thermodynamic device: definitions and assumptions. In *Water Activity: A Credible Measure of Technologial Perform-ance and Physiological Viability*, Discussion conference of the Royal Society of Chemistry, Cambridge, pp. 1–6.

Luard, E. J. (1982). Growth and accumulation of solutes by *Phytophthora cinnamomi* and other lower fungi in response to changes in external osmotic potential. *J. Gen. Microbiol.*, **128**, 2583–90.

Luard, E. J. & Griffin, D. M. (1981). Effect of water potential on fungal growth and turgor. *Trans. Br. Mycol. Soc.*, **76**, 33–40.

Lysek, G. (1977). Circadian rhythms. In *The Filamentous Fungi*, Vol. 3, ed. J. E. Smith and D. R. Berry. Edward Arnold, London, pp. 376–88.

MacMeekin, T. A., Chandler, R. E., Doe, P. E., Garland, C. D., Olley, J., Putros, S. & Ratkowsky, D. A. (1987). Model for combined effect of temperature and salt concentration/water activity on the growth rate of *Staphylococcus xylosus*. *J. Appl. Bacteriol.*, **62**, 543–50.

Magnan, N. & Lacey, J. (1984). Effects of temperature and pH on water relations of field and storage fungi. *Trans. Br. Mycol. Soc.*, **82**, 71–81.

Martin, J. F. & Nicolas, G. (1970). Physiology of spore germination in *Penicillium notatum* and *Trichoderma lignorum. Trans. Br. Mycol. Soc.*, **55**, 141–8.

Mazur, P., Rall, W. F. & Rigopoulos, N. (1981). Relative contributions of the fraction of unfrozen water and of salt concentration to the survival of slowly frozen human erythrocytes. *Biophys. J.*, **36**, 653–75.

182   P. GERVAIS and D. SIMATOS

Morton, A. G. (1960). The induction of sporulation in mould fungi. *Proc. Royal Soc. London*, **153**, 548–69.

Moser, A. (1988). Temperature dependence, water activity and enthalpy/entropy compensation. In *Bioprocess Technology, Kinetics and Reactors* ed. A. Moser. Springer Verlag, New York, pp. 198–204.

Mossel, D. A. A. (1975). Water and micro-organisms in foods: a synthesis. In *Water Relation of Foods*, ed. R. B. Duckworth. Academic Press, New York, pp. 347–61.

Nishio, N., Tai, K. & Nagai, S. (1979). Hydrolase production by *Aspergillus niger* in solid-state cultivation. *Eur. J. Appl. Microbiol. Biotechnol.*, **8**, 263–70.

Northolt, M. D., Van Egmont, H. P. & Paulsch, W. E. (1984). Ochratoxine A production by some fungal species in relation to a_w and temperature. *J. Food Prot.*, **42**, 485–90.

Panchal, C. J. & Stewart, G. G. (1980). The effect of osmotic pressure on the production and excretion of ethanol and glycerol by a brewing yeast strain. *J. Inst. Brew.*, **86**, 207–10.

Pirt, S. J. (1965). The maintenance energy of bacteria in growing cultures. *Proc. R. Soc. London*, **163B**, 224–31.

Quinn, P. Y. (1985). A lipid phase separation model of low-temperature damage to biological membranes. *Cryobiology*, **22**, 128–46.

Richard-Molard, D., Bizot, H. & Multon, J. L. (1982). Water activity, essential factor of the microbiological evolution of foods. *Sci. Aliments*, **2**, 3–17.

Roels, J. A. (1980). Application of macroscopic principles to microbial metabolism. *Biotechnol. Bioeng.*, **22**, 2457–514.

Schwan, H. P. (1965). Electrical properties of bound water. *Ann. N.Y. Acad. Sci.*, **125**, 344–54.

Scott, W. J. (1953). Water relations of *Staphylococcus aureus* at 30°C. *Aust. J. Biol. Sci.*, **6**, 549–64.

Scott, W. J. (1957). Water relations of food spoilage microorganisms. *Adv. Food Res.*, **7**, 83–127.

Sheridan, J. J. & Sheeman, P. J. (1980). Development of a technique for the germination of the fungal spores. *Irish J. Agricult. Res.*, **19**, 155–9.

Simatos, D. & Karel, M. (1988). Characterization of the condition of water in foods: physico-chemical aspects. In *Food Preservation by Moisture Control* ed. C. C. Seow. Elsevier Applied Science, London. pp. 1–41.

Slade, L. & Levine, H. (1985). Intermediate moisture systems; water as plasticizer. In *Water Activity: A Credible Measure of Technological Performance and Physiological Viability*, Discussion conference of the Royal Society of Chemistry, Cambridge, pp. 24–27.

Smith, J. E. (1978). Asexual sporulation in filamentous fungi. In *The Filamentous Fungi*, Vol. 3, ed. J. E. Smith and D. R. Berry. Edward Arnold, London, pp. 214–35.

Snow, D. (1949). The germination of mould spores at controlled humidities. *Ann. Appl. Biol.*, **36**, 1–13.

Steudle, E., Tyerman, S. D. & Wendler, S. (1983). Water relations of plant cells. In *Effects of Stress on Photosynthesis*, ed. R. Marcelle, H. Clijsters and M. Van Poucke. Martinus Nijhoff, The Hague, pp. 95–109.

Stouthamer, A. H. & Bettenhaussen, C. (1973). Utilization of energy for growth and maintenance in continuous and batch cultures of microorganisms. *Biochim. Biophys. Acta*, **301**, 54–69.

Tallu, B. (1986). Aroma production. Postgraduate in Food Sciences, University of Clermont-Ferrand.

Todd, G. W. (1972). Water deficits and enzymatic activity. In *Plant Responses and Control of Water Balance*, Vol. 3: *Water Deficits and Plant Growth*, ed. T. T. Kozlowski. Academic Press, New York, pp. 177–216.

Trinci, A. P. J. (1969). A kinetic study of the growth of *Aspergillus nidulans* and other fungi. *J. Gen. Microbiol.*, **57**, 11–24.

Troller, J. A. (1980). Influence of water activity on microorganisms in foods. *Food Technol.*, **5**, 76–82.

Troller, J. A. & Stinson, J. V. (1981). Moisture requirements for growth and metabolite production by lactic acid bacteria. *Appl. Environ. Microbiol.*, **42**, 682–7.

Voilley, A. & Le Meste, M. (1985). Aroma diffusion: the influence of water activity and of molecular weight of the other solutes. In *Properties of Water in Foods.*, ed. D. Simatos and J. L. Multon. Martinus Nijhoff, Dordrecht, pp. 357–73.

Waggoner, P. E. & Parlange, J. Y. (1975). Slowing of spore germination with changes between moderately warm and cold temperatures. *Phytopathology*, **65**, 551–3.

Wolfe, J. & Steponkus, P. L. (1983). Tension in the plasma membrane during osmotic contraction. *Cyro-Lett.*, **4**, 315–22.

Yanagita, T. & Kogane, F. (1962). Growth and cytochemical differentiation of mold colonies. *J. Gen. Appl. Microbiol.*, **8**, 201–13.

Zimmermann, U. (1978). Physics of turgor and osmoregulation. *Ann. Rev. Plant Physiol.*, **29**, 121–48.

Chapter 5

THE MODELLING OF SCREW EXTRUSION PROCESSES

Jorge C. Oliveira

*College of Biotechnology,
Catholic University of Portugal,
Porto, Portugal*

1 INTRODUCTION

The principles of screw extrusion have been known for decades. However, the use of screw extruders as HTST (high temperature, short residence time) devices is a relatively recent development in food technology.

Screw extruders have been used in polymer processing for some time and are now well described and studied in that field. Initially, food extrusion processing was based in the same equipment and principles, but has now evolved into an area of engineering of its own.

Many applications of food extrusion are still being developed and many more will be in the near future. This means that the emphasis of most research work is on the development of new products and new applications. A point has not been reached where work on the fundamentals of food extrusion is able to describe scientifically the whole process. This inability to describe the process and understand well the phenomena that occur inside an extruder is a major drawback for its adequate modelling. Just like the process itself, the modelling has evolved from the achievements of plastic screw extrusion theory. It is thought that the special case of extruding foods is on the verge of separating off on its own as well.

Owing to the limitations of a text of this nature, the development of extruder models, from the several steps of plastic extrusion modelling to the applicability of these principles to food extrusion, will not be considered here. This subject was described by Oliveira (1989). In this chapter, the modelling of food extruders will be considered simply as it is thought that it should be approached, with the benefit of past experience.

There are several possible designs of screw extruders. For modelling purposes they can be divided into three major categories: single-screw, co-rotating twin-screw, and counter-rotating twin-screw. The basis of modelling each of the processes is similar and it is therefore a sensible choice to limit a short text on this subject to the first design, although it is not currently the most important. When applying the principles outlined here to twin-screw extrusion, the most relevant additional factor to consider is the geometry of the extruder. Booy (1978) gives a good description of this situation. Readers are also referred to Booy (1980) for a simple description of a flow model.

Basically, an extruder is a device where a material contained in a chamber is forced out through a small die. In a screw extruder, this is achieved by one or two rotating screws. Depending on the size of the die and on the screw speed, it is evident that the material will be subjected to an increasing pressure and that the viscous energy dissipation will be high. Both temperature and pressure will rise considerably in a screw extruder. The material will also be subjected to considerable shear. Therefore, in an extruder, pressure, temperature and shear are all high. Under these conditions, food products can be cooked and/or sterilized very rapidly; indeed one would expect the destruction of the material if the residence time at those severe conditions was too great.

The existence of a complex shear field depending strongly on the interaction between the food and the extruder screws and barrel makes the environment inside the extruder unique. Extruded products can be very different from comparable products produced by any other method.

In most extruder applications, the material is fed solid (although a water feed can be mixed at the entrance in some cases), melts as it moves in the extruder and dries again after being compressed through the die, losing moisture as it expands in the atmosphere. Therefore, one would have three zones in an extruder: the solids conveying zone, the transition zone, where the material would be a mixture of solid and liquid phases, and a final metering zone where all the material is fluid. It is in this last zone that take place the most relevant changes that extrusion is designed for; it is known as the cooking zone in cooking extruders.

In plastic extrusion, this description is enough: the polymer is conveyed, melts and is extruded. It is self-evident that an extruder cannot melt more than it can convey or extrude more that it can melt and therefore the modelling of an extruder should involve modelling of the three different zones. The transition zone is actually the more critical because the melting process has to be adequately described. However, the importance of the metering zone is reflected in the fact that in most cases the extrusion rate is actually controlled by this zone. Therefore, modelling the metering zone is an approximation to the modelling of the whole extruder that in many cases is close enough to reality (Pearson, 1985).

This assumption is still necessary in food extrusion because the process is complicated by the more complex changes that occur in the material during extrusion: the structure of molecules can be significantly affected (e.g. starch gelatinization) and bioreactions may take place (e.g. breakdown of macromolecules). These changes will affect the properties of the material and therefore the extrusion process. The cooking zone, being a unique environment, as already pointed out, is not yet completely understood. This means that the transition zone would be an even more complex situation; the material is not simply melting. Melting models are already fairly complex (Pearson, 1985) and there is no way yet to describe this zone in a food extruder. In any case, the gain in accuracy might not justify the effort, so such development may be a second priority.

In this chapter, it will also be assumed that the barrel is ungrooved and that in the metering zone the extruder flight height and pitch are constant. Screws with reverse elements are not considered. They are used to improve mixing and can be modelled just like normal screw elements. As the approach is the same, the problem is not considered in this chapter.

2 FUNDAMENTAL EQUATIONS

2.1 Mass and Momentum Balances

As one would expect of an engineering problem, the modelling of an extruder results from applying the principles of conservation of mass, momentum and energy to a generic infinitesimal volume and then integrating the resulting balances over the whole domain. Also, it is evident that the mass and momentum balances will be adequate for an isothermal situation while the additional energy balance is otherwise necessary.

The material being extruded flows in the channel defined by the screw root, screw flights and barrel, against a pressure gradient, due to the drag force exerted by the screw(s). Extruded materials are very viscous and laminar flow can be expected. The momentum balance will therefore be expressed by the fundamental equations of motion. These result simply from applying Newton's law (force = mass × acceleration) for a three-dimensional system. In its general form, the equation of motion can be written precisely in that form, that is, as three relationships (one for each dimension) between the components of the stress tensor and the rate of strain tensor (the velocity component and its derivatives). By doing this, one is not implying any rheological behaviour or model to the material; these can be individualized by considering the rheological model as an addition to the equations of motion.

It is good practice to individualize the equations of motion from the rheological model, since the latter is of crucial importance. It is important to identify the assumptions and consequent conclusions resultant from the rheological model assumed from the ones arising from the flow model itself.

Because of the geometry of the screw(s), the equations of motion should be applied with cylindrical coordinates (Darby, 1976):

$$\rho\left(V_r\frac{\partial V_r}{\partial r}+\frac{V_\phi}{r}\frac{\partial V_r}{\partial \phi}-\frac{V_\phi^2}{r}+V_z\frac{\partial V_r}{\partial z}\right)$$

$$=-\frac{\partial P}{\partial r}+\left(\frac{1}{r}\frac{\partial}{\partial r}(r\tau_{rr})+\frac{1}{r}\frac{\partial \tau_{r\phi}}{\partial \phi}-\frac{\tau_{\phi\phi}}{r}+\frac{\partial \tau_{rz}}{\partial z}\right)+\rho g_r \quad (1)$$

$$\rho\left(V_r\frac{\partial V_\phi}{\partial r}+\frac{V_\phi}{r}\frac{\partial V_\phi}{\partial \phi}+\frac{V_r V_\phi}{r}+V_z\frac{\partial V_\phi}{\partial z}\right)$$

$$=-\frac{1}{r}\frac{\partial P}{\partial \phi}+\left(\frac{1}{r^2}\frac{\partial}{\partial r}(r^2\tau_{r\phi})+\frac{1}{r}\frac{\partial \tau_{\phi\phi}}{\partial \phi}+\frac{\partial \tau_{\phi z}}{\partial z}\right)+\rho g_\phi \quad (2)$$

$$\rho\left(V_r\frac{\partial V_z}{\partial r}+\frac{V_\phi}{r}\frac{\partial V_z}{\partial \phi}+V_z\frac{\partial V_z}{\partial z}\right)$$

$$=-\frac{\partial P}{\partial z}+\left(\frac{1}{r}\frac{\partial}{\partial r}(r\tau_{rz})+\frac{1}{r}\frac{\partial \tau_{\phi z}}{\partial \phi}+\frac{\partial \tau_{zz}}{\partial z}\right)+\rho g_z \quad (3)$$

where

ρ	= density (kg/m^3)
V_i	= velocity component (m/s)
P	= pressure (Pa)
τ_{ij}	= stress tensor component (N/m^2)
g_i	= acceleration of gravity component (m/s^2)
r	= radial direction
ϕ	= angular direction
z	= down-channel direction

(The equations for rectangular coordinates can be found in Appendix I.)

The mass balance yields simply the continuity equation, which is actually of little interest in many cases. This equation is presented in Appendix I.

By writing the equations in this way, one is not assuming any type of rheological behaviour in particular. This will be introduced when the shear stress tensor is related to the rate of strain tensor, by the rheological model (the components of the rate of strain tensor can be found in Appendix I).

For a general case, it is evident that there is no analytical solution for the set of equations written. In fact, as will be found later, only in very particular cases there will be such solutions. Therefore, for most cases, extrusion modelling must be numerical.

Numerical methods can be developed to solve practically any problem. Speed of calculation is becoming less of a worry with the continuous development of computational hardware. However, this does not solve the difficulties that tend to arise when applying numerical methods to complex systems of equations. Stability and the physical meaning of the results are problems of great concern. It is not surprising that authors working on extrusion modelling (e.g. Martin, 1969) have found such problems, even with systems resulting from simplifications of the general eqns (1) to (3).

The existence of more complex and precise solutions does not preclude the usefulness of simplified approaches. In some cases, approximations may be valid, and for these it is certainly more adequate to use simpler equations, easier to use and with less need for checking the validity and stability of the solutions.

In most cases, flow can also be assumed to be laminar, since extruding material is normally a very viscous paste. It is therefore adequate to consider the more common approximations and see what simplifications will be possible, what equations are obtained and then how best to solve them. The boundary conditions will then be established as well.

There are two main types of approximations:

— those resulting from the geometry of the problem;
— those arising from the rheological model used.

The first type demand separate treatment of single- and twin-screw extruders. Before considering these matters, one should examine the non-isothermal situation, that is, the energy balance.

2.2 Energy Balance

Adequate consideration of the heat transfer problem is complex. In general, many terms have to be considered: heat transfer by conduction in the material and in the flights, convection in the down-channel and cross-channel direction (since V_y is zero for laminar flow, there is no heat transfer by convection in the radial direction—heat is transferred by conduction) and viscous shear dissipation. The convective terms are particularly difficult to include properly, since experimental data on this in a real extruder are very difficult to obtain. Work is being carried out on this subject (Steffe and Ofoli, 1989), but at the moment most models available have to consider small cross-channel and down-channel Graetz numbers, as pointed out by Pearson (1985) (that is, the relationship between length of the convection path and of the conduction one is so large that all heat is transferred by conduction, in this case, radially). Some exceptions include the work by Yates (1968) who considered a large down-channel Graetz number (though still assuming a small cross-channel Graetz number) with the lubrication approximation and the work published by Jepson (1953) who assumed both Graetz numbers to be large, but admitted the lubrication approximation and Newtonian behaviour.

This subject is being studied by some research groups and new developments are being obtained constantly. There are different possible approaches. A review of the most relevant ones is given in Van Zuilichem (1990). Most can be reduced to an application of the fundamental equations of heat transfer, which also includes the recent approach by Mohamed and Ofoli (1990). These equations are given by Bird, Stewart and Lightfoot (1960) in a similar way to the fundamental equations of flow considered in this text.

In order to avoid a too complex problem, it is possible to consider that the heat accumulated in an infinitesimal volume of fluid is the sum of the heat transferred by conduction in the radial direction and the heat generated by viscous dissipation. Under these conditions, the equation for rectangular coordinates reduces to:

$$\rho C_p v_x \frac{\partial T}{\partial x} = +\frac{\partial}{\partial y}\left(k\frac{\partial T}{\partial y}\right) + \mu_a\left[\left(\frac{\partial V_x}{\partial y}\right)^2 + \left(\frac{\partial V_z}{\partial y}\right)^2\right] \qquad (4)$$

where

C_p = heat capacity (J/kg °C)
T = temperature (K)
k = thermal conductivity (J/s m °C)

μ_a = apparent viscosity (kg/m s)
y = up-channel direction (from the screw root to the barrel)
z = down-channel direction

A similar equation can be written for cylindrical coordinates (Bird, Stewart and Lightfoot, 1960).

Usual boundary conditions for the y direction are the temperature at the screw root and at the barrel. It is possible to consider the use of hollow screws for cooling or heating with these boundary conditions. However, the most usual case is that heating or cooling only occur at the barrel wall. In this situation, one may note that viscous shear dissipation corresponds in terms of heat transfer to an internal generation of heat. Therefore, the maximum value for the temperature occurs in the fluid and at steady state $\partial T/\partial y = 0$ at the screw root surface. The boundary conditions will then be $y = 0: \partial T/\partial y = 0$ and $y = h: T = T_b$, T_b being the temperature at the barrel wall.

For the x direction only one boundary condition would suffice. Some authors (Pearson, 1985) suggest the temperature at the flight wall, but there is a physical difficulty in accepting such a condition. For one thing, if the temperatures at the screw root and barrel are different, there will be a temperature gradient in the flights, that is, one value for the boundary condition for each radial position. Moreover, since the width of the flight is usually considerably smaller than its height, heat transfer in the flights in the x direction would be much faster than in the y direction. In such situation, the temperature at the flight wall is controlled by the fluid and cannot be preset just from the temperatures at the barrel and screw root. It therefore seems better to consider as a boundary condition $y = h: \partial T/\partial x = 0$. This boundary condition is established for a value of y instead of x, but this creates no problem. It will be shown later how eqn (4) can be solved with this boundary condition.

3 SINGLE-SCREW EXTRUDERS

3.1 Geometrical Considerations

As mentioned in the introduction, it will be assumed that the channel depth and width are constant. The geometry of a single-screw extruder of this type is sketched in Fig. 1. It should be noted that this geometry corresponds to a single-flighted screw. There are other possibilities, but these reduce to more than one channel in parallel and are therefore treated in the same way.

192   J. C. OLIVEIRA

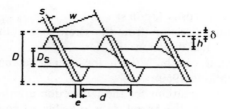

FIG. 1. Geometry of a single-flighted single-screw extruder. d, distance between screw flights, in the direction of the barrel; D, internal diameter of the barrel; D_s diameter of the screw root; e, width of the screw flight wall, in the direction of the barrel; h, channel depth—screw flight height; s, width of the screw flight wall, in the cross-channel direction; w, channel width—distance between flights in the cross-channel direction; α, angle of the screw flights, measured at the tip; δ, gap between the screw flights and the barrel.

The geometrical approximations that can be made are:

(a) *Negligible curvature.* This is applicable if the ratio D_s/h is large. In this case the channel can be visually unrolled. The simplification is that the geometry becomes rectangular (see Fig. 2). Although this may seem a slight improvement, the equations for this geometry are simpler and the model obtained easier to use.

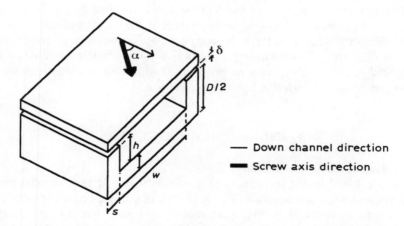

FIG. 2. Geometry of a single-screw extruder channel, with negligible curvature effects. Note that the barrel wall and the channel between the flights move at a relative angle α.

(b) *Negligible flight effects.* This is applicable if the ratio w/h is large. In this case, the effects of the screw flights in the flow are negligible. This will be a similar situation to the flow between parallel, infinite, plates. Under such conditions the velocity at *all points* is horizontal (parallel to the screw axis and barrel). This is known as the lubrication approximation.

There is an obvious simplification in the fact that the velocity, which otherwise would be bidimensional, is unidimensional.

In real situations, both approximations are usually valid for shallow channel extruders. There is also the possibility of curvature effects being negligible while the lubrication approximation cannot be used. The opposite is, however, quite unlikely, as it would require a very small extruder.

Another usual consideration relates to the relative movement between screw and barrel. The real situation in an extruder is that the barrel is stationary and the screw rotates. However, problems defined by initial boundary values equal to zero are simpler to solve in some situations and therefore the opposite is assumed: the screw and therefore the channel between flights are stationary and the barrel wall slides over the flights. For the rectangular geometry, the velocity is therefore equal to πDN (N being the real screw rotational speed), at an angle with the channel direction. This situation is actually perfectly equivalent and is always used in extruder modelling.

3.2 Flow Models

In general, it can be said that the fluid does not move in the radial direction and therefore V_r or V_y (depending on the geometry) are zero. Also, for fully developed flow, the velocity components do not vary in the z direction, which means that $\partial V_i/\partial z = 0$. A further simplification arises from the fact that compared to the velocities and forces in action in an extruder, the effect of gravity can be neglected.

Applying these simplifications to the equations of motion yields the basic models. For negligible curvature (rectangular coordinates):

$$\frac{\partial P}{\partial x} = \frac{\partial \tau_{xx}}{\partial x} + \frac{\partial \tau_{xy}}{\partial y} \tag{5}$$

$$\frac{\partial P}{\partial y} = \frac{\partial \tau_{xy}}{\partial x} \tag{6}$$

$$\frac{\partial P}{\partial z} = \frac{\partial \tau_{xz}}{\partial x} + \frac{\partial \tau_{yz}}{\partial y} \qquad (7)$$

For negligible flight effects, $\partial V_i / \partial x = 0$. Therefore, for the lubrication approximation the problem reduces to:

$$\frac{\partial P}{\partial x} = \frac{\partial \tau_{xy}}{\partial y} \qquad (8)$$

$$\frac{\partial P}{\partial z} = \frac{\partial \tau_{yz}}{\partial y} \qquad (9)$$

For cylindrical coordinates, the appropriate equations can similarly be written.

The solution will depend on the rheological model used, that is, on the relationship between the stress tensor components and the velocity components and its derivatives.

3.3 Rheological Models

Rheological models provide a relationship between the stress tensor and the rate of strain components and can be written as:

$$\tau_{ij} = \mu_a \Delta_{ij} \qquad (10)$$

μ_a being the apparent viscosity function.

The simplest model is obviously Newtonian behaviour. This has been widely used because of its simplicity, and in fact most published work on food extrusion considers this approximation (Oliveira, 1989; Harper, 1989). Extruded material can hardly be expected to be well described by such a simple model and significant errors arise from its use. However, because of its simplicity it is still an important tool for extrusion modelling, since it provides analytical solutions to the equations described. Further comments will be made on this subject regarding the comparison of results predicted by different models.

For a Newtonian fluid:

$$\tau_{ij} = \mu \Delta_{ij} \qquad (11)$$

where μ is the viscosity

The simplest non-Newtonian model is the power law (Ostwald–de Waele equation). Given the fact that it accounts for the variation of the apparent viscosity with the shear rate, it is widely used in spite of its limitations. This model can be written as (Darby, 1976):

$$\tau_{ij} = C \ II^{(n-1)/2} \Delta_{ij} \tag{12}$$

where C is the fluid consistency index, n is the fluid behaviour index, and II is the second invariant of the rate of strain tensor.

The apparent viscosity is $\mu_a = C \ II^{(n-1)/2}$.

Most published work has involved one of these two models. There is, however, another possible model, defined by the Herschel–Bulkley equation, which considers the existence of a yield stress, a common feature of many foods. Noting that for an isotropic material the yield stress in all directions will be the same, one may involve only one more parameter than with the power law, obtaining:

$$\tau_{ij} = C \ II^{(n-1)/2} \Delta_{ij} + \tau^0 \qquad (\text{for } \tau_{ij} \geqslant \tau^0) \tag{13}$$
$$\tau_{ij} = 0 \qquad (\text{for } \tau_{ij} < \tau^0)$$

where τ^0 is the yield stress.

The apparent viscosity is $\mu_a = C \ II^{(n-1)/2} + \tau^0/\sqrt{(II)}$. (Please see note in Appendix I).

The use of models that describe the rheological behaviour of food materials more adequately would have a significant effect in the development of extrusion by using modelling techniques. In fact it can be argued that inaccuracy in extrusion models is due more to inadequate description of the material rheology than to the flow equations. There are some interesting developments of which the most promising seem to be those that include the time–temperature and strain histories in the apparent viscosity function (Steffe and Ofoli, 1989). The complex rheological behaviour of most foods (Rao, 1977; Rizvi and Rao, 1986) includes thixotropicity in many cases. Also, biochemical reactions frequently occur during extrusion (Linko et al., 1983). This leads to flow being affected by factors such as time–temperature and strain histories, besides temperature and shear rate (and also the rate of biochemical reactions eventually taking place). Some promising models have been proposed by Morgan et al (1988), Ofoli, et al. (1987), Remsen and Clark (1978), Janssen (1986) and Morgan et al. (1979).

The way such models can be easily incorporated is by defining the apparent viscosity function. The flow models must be solved numerically. For each point of the numerical integration, the apparent viscosity must be calculated. This procedure may not be as simple as it seems, since, as the material history influences the apparent viscosity, the model may become intrinsic in its general form. Obviously, simplifications can in some cases be made to yield a final result that will in any case allow the study of the influence of material history in the flow.

Another problem that can be raised subsequently is that, if the material history affects the rheological behaviour, the approximation of considering only the metering zone of the extruder is contradictory. Once again, it seems that it is not possible to approach every problem in one go. Efforts made step by step will in the end pay off.

The other complex characteristic of food extrusion referred to is that most processes are designed to cook the material, that is, there will be complex biochemical reactions taking place. Some attempts have been made to include this process (e.g. Gomez and Aguilera, 1984; Diosady *et al.*, 1985), but their applicability is very limited by the proper definition of some parameters introduced, related to the cooking process.

It must also be noted that complex models tend to be individualized, that is, most were studied and are applicable only to a single type or class of food materials.

It is clear that the use of such models is very promising, but much remains to be done and tested experimentally. For the purpose of this text, however, it is adequate to use the three models initially described. This procedure gives examples of the use of the flow models with rheological models following a similar approach to the one that can be used for any rheological model and will in any case cover practically all cases of modelling considered in food extrusion literature.

For non-isothermal extrusion, the dependence of viscosity on temperature must be accounted for. Models have been developed that include this variation in terms of apparent viscosity (Harper, 1989). Some models also exist to account for the variation with moisture content, but these are of no concern to this text since variations in this property will not be considered. Temperature dependence of the apparent viscosity function is well described by an exponential function and therefore one can use the expression:

$$\mu_a = \mu_a^0 \exp[-\beta(1/T - 1/T^0) \tag{14}$$

where β is the heat sensitivity coefficient of the apparent viscosity in K^{-1}. μ_a^0 is therefore the apparent viscosity at the reference temperature T^0. Both μ_a^0 and β are assumed to be temperature-independent.

3.4 Extruder Models

The following models will be considered:

Model 1:   Newtonian behaviour
N. nC. U   Negligible curvature effects
           Unidimensional flow (lubrication approximation
           valid)

Model 2:   Newtonian behaviour
N. nC. B   Negligible curvature effects
           Bidimensional flow (lubrication approximation not
           valid)

Model 3:   Newtonian behaviour
N. C. U   Relevant curvature effects
           Unidimensional flow

Model 4:   Non-Newtonian (power-law) behaviour
nN. nC. U Negligible curvature effects
           Unidimensional flow

Model 5:   Non-Newtonian (power-law) behaviour
nN. nC. B Negligible curvature effects
           Bidimensional flow

Model 6:   Non-Newtonian (Herschel–Bulkley) behaviour
nN'. nC. U Negligible curvature effects
           Unidimensional flow

Note. For easier reference, the models are also referred to by code letters, with the following meaning:

    N = Newtonian behaviour
   nN = non-Newtonian behaviour—power law
  nN' = non-Newtonian behaviour—Herschel–Bulkley
    C = Curvature effects
   nC = negligible Curvature effects
    U = Unidimensional flow
    B = Bidimensional flow

3.4.1 Model 1
(Newtonian, Negligible Curvature, Unidimensional)

Isothermal flow. This model is obtained by combining eqns (8) and (9) with eqn (11). The result is:

$$\frac{\partial P}{\partial x} = \mu \frac{\partial^2 V_x}{\partial y^2} \tag{15}$$

$$\frac{\partial P}{\partial z} = \mu \frac{\partial^2 V_z}{\partial y^2} \tag{16}$$

It must be noted that the two equations are independent, which is a characteristic due to the Newtonian model assumed. Therefore, only (16) is required for determining the flow in the extruder.

Having assumed fully developed flow, all derivatives in relation to z are zero. Therefore,

$$\frac{\partial}{\partial z}\left(\frac{\partial P}{\partial x}\right) = \frac{\partial}{\partial z}\left(\frac{\partial P}{\partial y}\right) = \frac{\partial}{\partial z}\left(\frac{\partial P}{\partial z}\right) = 0$$

$$\frac{\partial}{\partial x}\left(\frac{\partial P}{\partial z}\right) = \frac{\partial}{\partial y}\left(\frac{\partial P}{\partial z}\right) = \frac{\partial}{\partial z}\left(\frac{\partial P}{\partial z}\right) = 0$$

and therefore, $\partial P/\partial z$ is a constant. From this conclusion it follows that:

$$\frac{\partial P}{\partial z} = \frac{\Delta P}{Z} \tag{17}$$

Z being the total length of the channel, that is, of the metering zone, since it was assumed that this zone controls the flow. From geometrical considerations, $L = Z \cos \alpha$, L being the length of the metering zone, measured in the direction of the screw axis. This is usually a better variable to use and therefore:

$$\frac{\partial P}{\partial z} = \frac{\Delta P \cos \alpha}{L} \tag{18}$$

Equation (16) can be integrated straightforwardly with the two boundary conditions. Recalling that it was assumed that the screw is stationary and the barrel rotates, these are simply that $V_z = 0$ at $y = 0$ and $V_z = \pi DN \sin \alpha$ at $y = h$ (neglecting the gap δ). The velocity profile is therefore:

$$V_z = \pi DN \sin \alpha \frac{y}{h} + \frac{\Delta P \cos \alpha}{2\mu L}(y^2 - yh) \tag{19}$$

The net volumetric flow (Q) is by definition $\int V_z \, dA$:

$$Q = w \int_0^h V_z \, dy = \pi D N w \sin \alpha \frac{h}{2} - \frac{w \Delta P \, \cos \alpha}{12 \mu L} h^3 \qquad (20)$$

It should be noted that the first term is the contribution to flow arising from the drag between the barrel and screw (drag flow) and the second term the one resulting from the pressure gradient (pressure flow), of opposite directions.

This equation is usually condensed by naming the velocity at $y = h$ as $U_z (U_z = \pi D N \sin \alpha)$ and introducing the following parameter:

$$a = \frac{h^2 \Delta P \, \cos \alpha}{6 \mu L \pi D N \, \sin \alpha} \qquad (21)$$

Equation (20) becomes:

$$Q = w h U_z (1 - a)/2 \qquad (22)$$

The parameter a has an obvious meaning, comparing eqs (20) and (21); it is the ratio between pressure flow and drag flow. If no externally induced pressures are imposed on either end of the screw, a varies between zero for unrestricted discharge and 1 for a completely closed extruder.

It must be noted that it was assumed that the extruder net flow was obtained as a result of only the drag and pressure flows in the channel. However, recalling the extruder geometry in Fig. 1, there will be a leakage flow through the gap between the screw flights and the barrel (δ), induced by the pressure gradient. This will be small compared to drag flow and is often neglected. It is possible to consider it independently, but it is necessary to assume that it will not affect the velocity gradient in the channel. This subject will be developed later. At the moment, it may be noted that if leakage flow is significant, then a will be less than 1 in a completely closed extruder, being smaller the higher the importance of leakage flow.

Although eqn (15) is not necessary for computing the output flow, it will yield the transverse velocity profile, which is relevant for the determination of mixing, heat transfer and power consumption in an extruder.

Equation (15) can be integrated straightforwardly like eqn (16), since it can be proved that $\partial P/\partial x$ is constant in a similar way to the one shown for $\partial P/\partial z$, yielding:

$$V_x = \pi DN \cos \alpha \frac{y}{h} + \frac{1}{2\mu} \frac{\partial P}{\partial x}(y^2 - yh) \tag{23}$$

Unlike $\partial P/\partial z$, $\partial P/\partial x$ cannot be measured experimentally and is not a good parameter to work with. However, if there is no leakage flow, the net volumetric flow in the x direction must be zero and therefore:

$$\int_0^h V_x \, dy = 0 \tag{24}$$

Integrating eqn (23) and equalling to zero yields:

$$\frac{\partial P}{\partial x} = - \frac{6\mu\pi DN \cos \alpha}{h^2} \tag{25}$$

Mohr *et al.* (1957) analysed the cross-flow in extruders for the first time. The influence of leakage is more significant in this case. Mohr and Mallouk (1959) have analysed this situation and have obtained experimental evidence for the inclusion of the influence of leakage in the cross-channel velocity profile. The ratio between pressure and drag flow in the cross direction was represented as c (a parameter similar to a), defined therefore by:

$$c = \frac{h^2}{6\mu\pi DN \cos \alpha} \frac{\partial P}{\partial x} \tag{26}$$

Introducing this parameter into eqn (23) yields:

$$V_x = \pi DN \cos \alpha [(1 - 3c)(y/h) + 3c(y/h)^2] \tag{27}$$

The parameter c was then found to be given by:

$$c = \frac{(1 - \delta/h) - \dfrac{[(\delta/h)^3 (\mu/\mu_1) e\pi D]}{e \tan \alpha}}{1 + \dfrac{[(\delta/h)^3 (\mu/\mu_1)w]}{e \cos \alpha}} \tag{28}$$

where μ_1 is the viscosity in the gap δ. It is usual to represent it differently from the viscosity in the channel (μ) because temperature and shear rate conditions in the gap may be very different from those in the channel. Usually, δ is much smaller than h, δ/h is much smaller than 1 and then

(28) reduces simply to:

$$c = 1 - \delta/h \tag{29}$$

Non-isothermal flow. For this case, it is necessary to consider the heat transfer eqn (4) coupled with eqns (15) and (16), with the viscosity defined as a function of temperature with eqn (14).

The problem is now more complex since all equations must be solved simultaneously. Furthermore, it is still necessary to use eqn (24) to determine $\partial P/\partial x$.

However, eqn (4) must be simplified. If the lubrication approximation is assumed, then the ratio h/w is very small. Radial heat transfer is therefore very fast and there will be no temperature gradient in the x direction. This is also evident since the velocity depends on the viscosity that is a function of the temperature; the velocity would vary in the x direction if there was a temperature gradient in this direction, contradicting the lubrication approximation. Equation (4) becomes:

$$\frac{\partial}{\partial y}\left(k\frac{\partial T}{\partial y}\right) + \mu\left[\left(\frac{\partial V_x}{\partial y}\right)^2 + \left(\frac{\partial V_z}{\partial y}\right)^2\right] = 0 \tag{30}$$

It is not possible to solve these equations analytically. This particular set of equations is, however, relatively simple to solve by finite differences. Some details of this method are given in Appendix II. Dividing the domain 0–h into n intervals, there will be $n+1$ points $y(i)$. Each interval Δy will be equal to h/n. Using this numerical method, one will determine the values of all variables (V_x, V_z, T) at all points.

For a generic point, i, the finite differences approximation leads to the following equations (see Appendix II):

$$k\left[\frac{T(i+1) - 2T(i) + T(i-1)}{(\Delta y)^2}\right] + \mu(i)\left[\left(\frac{V_x(i+1) - V_x(i-1)}{2\Delta y}\right)^2\right.$$

$$\left. + \left(\frac{V_z(i+1) - V_z(i-1)}{2\Delta y}\right)^2\right] = 0 \tag{31}$$

$$\frac{\partial P}{\partial x} = \mu(i)\frac{V_x(i+1) - 2V_x(i) + V_x(i-1)}{(\Delta y)^2} \tag{32}$$

$$\frac{\partial P}{\partial z} = \mu(i) \frac{V_z(i+1) - 2V_z(i) + V_z(i-1)}{(\Delta y)^2} \qquad (33)$$

$$\mu(i) = \mu^0 \exp[-\beta(1/T(i) - 1/T^0)] \qquad (34)$$

Note. The sign of eqn (31) is '+' for barrel heating and '−' for barrel cooling.

$\partial P/\partial x$ is a parameter that will be obtained by verifying eqn (24). This equation must also be solved numerically, since the function $V_x(y)$ is now a discrete set of points. If an odd number is chosen for n, there will be an even number of intervals and Simpson's rule can be used. Equation (24) becomes:

$$\frac{\Delta y}{3} \left[\pi DN \sin \alpha + 2 \sum_{i=1,3}^{n-2} V_x(i) + 4 \sum_{i=2,4}^{n-1} V_x(i) \right] = 0 \qquad (35)$$

The boundary conditions will yield the values for initiating the resolution of the set of equations. These are:

$y = 0: V_x(0) = 0$ [1] $: V_z(0) = 0$ [2] $: T(1) = T(0)$ [3]

$y = h: V_x(n) = \pi DN \cos \alpha$ [4]$: V_z(n) = \pi DN \sin \alpha$ [5]$: T(n) = T_b$ [6]

The resolution of the problem is as follows. An initial estimate for $\partial P/\partial x$ is taken. This can be the value for isothermal extrusion, defined in eqn (25), for μ at T_b.

From boundary condition [3], once $T(0)$—the temperature at the screw root—is known, $T(1)$ is known. Initially, the value of T_b can be assumed (isothermal extrusion). It is also necessary to assume values for $V_x(1)$ and $V_z(1)$, which can be the ones for isothermal extrusion, defined by eqns (19) and (23) for the value $y = h/n$. Equations (32) and (33) can then be solved for point 1 (for a value of μ obtained from eqn (34), yielding $V_x(2)$ and $V_z(2)$. With these values, eqn (31) for point 1 can be used to yield $T(2)$. The process is then repeated for all points until $n-1$. At this stage, values will be obtained for $V_x(n)$, $V_z(n)$ and $T(n)$. If they differ from the boundary conditions [4, 5, 6], new estimates for $T(0)$, $V_x(1)$ and $V_z(1)$ will be generated and the process repeated.

In the end, eqn (35) is checked. If the error is not acceptable, a new estimate for $\partial P/\partial x$ is generated, initiating the overall process.

In such resolutions, the generation of new estimates used is either the relaxation or the secant method (Oliveira, 1989; Zamodits, 1964; Martin, 1969).

This procedure has the advantage of being very simple to implement in a basic microcomputer and it converges rather quickly, since the initial estimates are usually not far from the solution. More elegant and faster procedures are however possible, by applying some more mathematics. Convergence problems are only likely to occur if inadequate intervals are used for Δy or in the generation of new estimates for $T(0)$, $V_x(1)$ or $V_z(1)$.

3.4.2 Model 2 (Newtonian, Negligible Curvature, Bidimensional)

Isothermal Flow. This model is obtained by combining eqns (5) to (7) with eqn (11). The result is:

$$\frac{\partial P}{\partial x} = 2\mu \frac{\partial^2 V_x}{\partial x^2} + \mu \frac{\partial^2 V_x}{\partial y^2} \tag{36}$$

$$\frac{\partial P}{\partial y} = \mu \frac{\partial^2 V_x}{\partial x \partial y} \tag{37}$$

$$\frac{\partial P}{\partial z} = \mu \frac{\partial^2 V_z}{\partial x^2} + \mu \frac{\partial^2 V_z}{\partial y^2} \tag{38}$$

It can be noted that the three equations are independent. Therefore, as in Model 1, it is only necessary to solve eqn (38) to obtain the output flow.

It was discussed in connection with the previous model that the velocity profile and the flow in a Newtonian fluid can be seen to be the simple subtraction of the drag and pressure-induced movements independently.

For drag flow, eqn (38) for $\partial P/\partial z = 0$ can be solved with boundary conditions:

$$x = 0: V_z = 0; \ x = w: V_z = 0; \ y = 0: V_z = 0; \ y = h: V_z = \pi D N \sin \alpha$$

This equation was first solved by Rowel and Finlayson (1922) and the solution was written by Carley and Strubb (1953) as:

$$V_{zd} = 4\pi D N \sin \alpha \sum_{i=1}^{\infty} \frac{1-(-1)^i}{2i} \sin[i\pi(x/w)] \frac{\sinh[i\pi(y/w)]}{\sinh[i\pi(h/w)]} \tag{39}$$

where the subscript 'd' refers to drag flow.

For the pressure flow, eqn (38) can be solved with boundary conditions:

$$x = 0: V_z = 0; \ x = w: V_z = 0; \ y = 0: V_z = 0; \ y = h: V_z = 0$$

It must be noted that it is still true that $\partial P/\partial z$ is constant and therefore equal to $\Delta P \cos \alpha / L$.

An equation of this type was first solved by Boussinesq (1868) and later adapted by Gore and McKelvey (1958) in the form:

$$V_{zp} = \frac{1}{\mu}\frac{\partial P}{\partial z}\left[\frac{y^2}{2} - \frac{yh}{2} + \frac{4h^2}{\pi^3}\sum_{i=1}^{\infty}\frac{1-(-1)^i}{2i^3}\sin\left(\frac{i\pi y}{h}\right)\frac{\cosh\left[\dfrac{i\pi(2x-w)}{2h}\right]}{\cosh\left[\dfrac{i\pi w}{2h}\right]}\right] \tag{40}$$

where the subscript 'p' denotes pressure flow.

The velocity profile V_z is obtained by subtracting eqn (40) from eqn (39).

The volumetric flow rate is by definition:

$$Q = \int_0^h \int_0^w V_z \,dx\,dy \tag{41}$$

Integration of eqns (39) and (40) leads to:

$$Q = \frac{whU_z}{2}F_d - \frac{wh^3\,\Delta P\cos\alpha}{12\mu L}F_p \tag{42}$$

This is the usual, simplified way of writing the result of the integration, by using the so-called shape factors F_d and F_p, for simplicity. These factors are:

$$F_d = \frac{16}{\pi^3(h/w)}\sum_{i=1}^{\infty}\frac{1-(-1)^i}{2}\frac{\tanh\left[\dfrac{i\pi(h/w)}{2}\right]}{i^3} \tag{43}$$

$$F_p = 1 - 192(h/w)\pi^{-5}\sum_{i=1}^{\infty}\frac{1-(-1)^i}{2i^5}\tanh\left[\frac{i\pi}{2(h/w)}\right] \tag{44}$$

The factors F_d and F_p are a function of h/w only, hence their name. It can be seen that when h/w becomes very small F_d and F_p become equal to 1. For this situation, the lubrication approximation is valid and therefore eqn (42) becomes equal to eqn (20) and Models 1 and 2 are the same. For this reason, writing the model in the form of eqn (42) is very convenient since the importance of the flight effects can be indicated by the deviation of F_d and F_p from 1.

To obtain the cross-channel velocity profile (V_x) would require the solution of eqn (36). Just as in Model 1, this equation is very similar to the one that yielded the down-channel velocity, but it must be noted that

$\partial P/\partial x$ cannot be shown to be constant in this case. This equation has not been the subject of great attention, even though it will be required for the solution of the energy balance and therefore for non-isothermal extrusion. There are no analytical solutions for this equation in literature. However, one may note that eqn (36) is very similar to eqn (38) (if $\partial P/\partial x$ were constant). It is therefore possible to determine the solution from adapting the one for eqn (38), verifying the boundary conditions and the equation itself. This would lead to:

$$V_{xd} = 4\pi DN \cos \alpha \sum_{i=1}^{\infty} \frac{1-(-1)^i}{2i} \sin[i\pi(x/w)] \frac{\sinh[i\pi\sqrt{2}(y/w)]}{\sinh[i\pi\sqrt{2}(h/w)]} \quad (45)$$

$$V_{xp} = \frac{1}{\mu} \frac{\partial P}{\partial x} \left[\frac{y^2}{2} - \frac{yh}{2} + \frac{4h^2}{\pi^3} \sum_{i=1}^{\infty} \frac{1-(-1)^i}{2i^3} \sin\left(\frac{i\pi y}{h}\right) \frac{\cosh\left[\frac{i\pi(2x-w)}{2^{1\cdot5}h}\right]}{\cosh\left[\frac{i\pi w}{2^{1\cdot5}h}\right]} \right] \quad (46)$$

The velocity profile V_x given by subtracting eqn (46) from eqn (45) verifies the differential eqn (36) and the boundary conditions, for both drag and pressure flows (the result must obviously be a subtraction between both terms, otherwise the net flow in the cross direction would not be zero).

The problem that arises from this approach is that the result obtained has to be studied carefully. In fact, the resultant expression has two series, that although convergent, tend to a value that depends on x. It can be shown that the value of $\partial P/\partial x$ would be a sinusoidal function, with a maximum at $x=h/2$. However, as would be expected, it is independent of y.

Therefore, the solution previously described is incoherent with the assumptions made to obtain it and cannot be used. It is necessary to solve eqn (36) by finite differences, considering $\partial P/\partial x = P_x(x)$.

It should be emphasized that recurring to the fact that there is no net flow in the cross-channel direction precludes the consideration of the effect of leakage flow in the gap between flights and barrel on the flow in the channel.

It can be noted that eqn (37) is totally irrelevant for the problem, as it does not bring any significant information: it would only allow the determination of $\partial P/\partial y$, which is of no great concern. It can, however, be borne in mind for the fact that this model predicts a pressure difference along the channel height (the y direction) resulting from the flow characteristics, which Model 1 does not indicate.

Non-isothermal flow. The problem of non-isothermal flow for Model 2 is more complex yet than the one for Model 1. The fact that the model is bidimensional does not only complicate the problem by the fact that variables are now bidimensional but also by the fact that eqn (30) can no longer be used—eqn (4) is the simplest one for the heat balance that can be applied to this model.

In fact, if the velocity V_x varies with x, from eqn (4), the temperature will vary with x, even if convection in the cross-channel direction is neglected and if both flight walls have the same temperature distribution. It is obviously possible to simplify the problem by neglecting this variation, implying that the heat accumulated in an element of fluid in the x direction is much smaller than the one that is being transferred radially by conduction and the one being generated by viscous dissipation. This is likely to be acceptable in many cases, but it is still viable to tackle the problem with eqn (4) using numerical methods. The domain is divided into n points in the y direction and m in the x direction. x will be a set of discrete points $x(j)$ varying from $x(0)$ to $x(m)$ and y will become a set of discrete points $y(i)$ varying from $y(0)$ to $y(n)$.

Applying finite differences, the equations for Model 2 will be:

$$\rho C_p V_x(j, i)\frac{T(j+1, i)-T(j-1, i)}{2\Delta x} = +k\frac{T(j, i+1)-2T(j, i)+T(j, i-1)}{(\Delta y)^2}$$

$$+\mu(j, i)\left[\left(\frac{V_x(j, i+1)-V_x(j, i-1)}{2\Delta y}\right)^2 + \left(\frac{V_z(j, i+1)-V_z(j, i-1)}{2\Delta y}\right)^2\right] \quad (47)$$

$$P_x(j)=2\mu(j, i)\frac{V_x(j+1, i)-2V_x(j, i)+V_x(j-1, i)}{(\Delta x)^2}$$

$$+\mu(j, i)\frac{V_x(j, i+1)-2V_x(j, i)+V_x(i-1, j)}{(\Delta y)^2} \quad (48)$$

$$\frac{\partial P}{\partial z}=\mu(j, i)\frac{V_z(j+1, i)-2V_z(j, i)+V_z(j-1, i)}{(\Delta x)^2}$$

$$+\mu(j, i)\frac{V_z(j, i+1)-2V_z(j, i)+V_z(i-1, j)}{(\Delta y)^2} \quad (49)$$

$$\mu(j. i)=\mu^0 \exp[-\beta(1/T(j, i)-1/T^0)] \quad (50)$$

The boundary conditions will be:

$y = 0: V_x(j, 0) = 0$ [1] $\qquad : V_z(j, 0) = 0$ [2]

$T(j, 1) = T(j, 0)$ [3] $\qquad : y = h: V_x(j, m) = \pi DN \cos \alpha$ [4]

$V_z(j, m) = \pi DN \sin \alpha$ [5] $\qquad : T(j, m) = T_b$ [6]

$x = 0: V_x(0, i) = 0$ [7] $\qquad : V_z(0, i) = 0$ [8]

$x = w: V_x(n, i) = 0$ [9] $\qquad : V_z(n, i) = 0$ [10]

$y = h: T(i, h) = T(i, h - 1)$ [11]

For the determination of the values of $P_x(j)$, an equation similar to eqn (35) can be used, applicable at all points $x(j)$ from $j = 1$ to $m - 1$:

$$\frac{\Delta y}{3} \left[\pi DN \sin \alpha + 2 \sum_{i=1,3}^{n-2} V_x(j, i) + 4 \sum_{i=2,4}^{n-1} V_x(j, i) \right] = 0 \qquad (51)$$

Boundary condition [11] is actually redundant since condition [6] already implies that $\partial T/\partial x$ is zero at $y = h$. However, this does not create any problem for the solution of the set of equations, since an iterative procedure is necessary in any case. It should be noted that the same could be said for other boundary conditions for this direction. As an example, from the symmetry conditions, $\partial T/\partial x = 0$ at $x = w/2$. This condition is also implied by the velocity profile in the x direction. From the two boundary conditions set for V_x it is evident that at $x = w/2$ V_x has a maximum and the velocity profile V_x in relation to x is symmetrical. The same can be said for V_z. From eqn (47), the temperature profile in relation to x must therefore be symmetrical as well. The boundary condition resulting from the symmetry condition does not bring any new information.

The straightforward procedures for solving the equations would be as follows. All values for the temperature at $y = h$ are known from boundary condition [6]. Initial estimates for $T(j, n - 1)$ are required: these can be simply T_b at all points j, which would be the case for isothermal extrusion. Initial estimates for all velocities $V_x(j, n - 1)$ and $V_z(j, n - 1)$ are also required: these can be the ones for isothermal extrusion, given by eqns (39), (40), (45) and (46). Estimates must obviously verify boundary conditions [9] and [10]. Further estimates must be made for $P_x(x)$, which can be all equal to the value for Model 1, isothermal extrusion (eqn (25)). Equations (48) and (49) are then solved for $i = n - 1$, for all j points, generating the values for $V_x(j, n-2)$ and $V_z(j, n-2)$. Equation (47) can then be solved for all values of j to yield $T(j, n-2)$. Once this is achieved, the values of T, V_x and V_z at row $n-2$ are all known. This process can therefore be repeated until row 1. The resolution of this row will yield the values for row 0, which allow the comparison with boundary conditions 1, 2 and 3. If these are not satisfied within an acceptable error, new estimates for the variables in row $n-1$ will be generated. In the end, eqn (51) must be checked for all points from 1 to $m-1$ and if the error is too large at a given point, a new estimate is generated and the process reinitiated.

This process is not as complex as it may seem, because each estimate for a variable at a point $(j, n-1)$ will result in a comparison for the value at point $(j, 0)$ independent of all others and new estimates are then generated independently as well. It is possible that convergence has been achieved for some values of j while to others new estimates are still needed. It seems evident that the ones to converge faster will be the points close to the walls and the last one the centre. The overall process converges usually, since the initial estimates are normally close to the solution. For a better description of the method, Fig. 3 gives an outline of the procedure described.

The method for generating new estimates can be the relaxation or the secant method, as for Model 1, but it is advisable to choose the size of a step in any method to ensure speedy convergence of the iterative procedure. It is a possibility to use different step sizes at different values of j.

The solution of this model using a straightforward finite differences approach clearly starts to present some rather cumbersome algorithms of resolution. Although for this Newtonian case the approach does normally work well, it can be anticipated to take considerable computing time. Therefore, it is desirable to consider other possible approaches, more elaborate, but leading to better equations in terms of speed of convergence and stability.

There are two possibilities widely used in polymer extrusion; One is obviously to use finite elements (Klein, 1975). The second approach is to reduce the complexity of the system (which can be done in conjunction with the first option as well). This can be achieved by introducing the streamline function (Ψ).

The streamline function will be in this case a bidimensional variable $\Psi_{(x,y)}$. By definition, its value is constant along a line of flux: streamlines of the fluid flux are lines having a constant value of Ψ. These lines will therefore

1. Data reading

2. Make $T(j, n) = T_b$ for $j = 0$ to m
   $V_x(j, n) = U_x$ and $V_z(j, n) = U_z$ for $j = 1$ to $m - 1$
   $V_x(0, i) = 0$; $V_x(m, i) = 0$; $V_z(0, i) = 0$; $V_z(m, i) = 0$ for $i = 0$ to n

3. Make $P_x(j) =$ value for Model 1, isothermal extrusion

4. Make $T(j, n-1) = T_b$ for $j = 0$ to m
   $V_x(j, n-1) =$ same as for isothermal extrusion for $j = 1$ to $m - 1$
   $V_z(j, n-1) =$ same as for isothermal extrusion for $j = 1$ to $m - 1$

5. For $i = n - 1$ to 1 (step -1)

6.   For $j = 1$ to $m - 1$

7.   Determine $\mu(j, i)$ with eqn (50)

8.   Determine $V_x(j, i-1)$ with eqn (48)
           $V_z(j, i-1)$ with eqn (49)

9.   Determine $T(j, i-1)$ with eqn (47)
           END LOOP
       END LOOP

10. For $j = 1$ to $m - 1$

11.   Check if $|V_x(j, 0)| <$ error. If not generate new estimate for
$$V_x(j, n-1)$$
        $|V_z(j, 0)| <$ error. If not generate new estimate for
$$V_z(j, n-1)$$
        $|T(j, 1) - T(j, 0)| <$ error. If not generate new estimate
        for $T(j, n-1)$
        END LOOP

12. If any new estimate was generated, return to step 5

13. For $j = 1$ to $m - 1$

14.   Check if $|$eqn $51| <$ error. If not, generate new estimate
        for $P_x(j)$

15.   END LOOP

16. IF any new estimate for $P_x(j)$ was generated, return to step 5

14. END.

FIG. 3.   Outline of the resolution of Model 2 for non-isothermal extrusion.

be perpendicular to the velocity profiles at all points. The derivatives of the streamline function can therefore be related to the velocities V_x and V_z.

This means that the set of equations needed to define the problem is decreased by one. The variables to be determined will be simply T and Ψ. In such cases, it is also usual to use the equation in the y direction as well and assume P as a variable, instead of working around with P_x.

This approach was quite successfully used by Martin (1969).

3.4.3 Model 3 (Newtonian, Curvature, Unidimensional)

Isothermal flow. This model is defined by exactly the same equations as Model 1 (N.nc.U), written in cylindrical coordinates.

These equations were first solved by Booy (1964). The result was compared with the flat-plate, allowing for the determination of correction factors. This procedure is quite convenient because it follows a very similar approach to the one of model 2 (N.nC.B), that permits the immediate visualization of how far the result is from the negligible curvature assumption.

The result is therefore:

$$Q = \frac{whU_z}{2} F_{cd} - \frac{wh^3 \Delta P \cos \alpha}{12\mu L} F_{cp} \tag{52}$$

where F_{cd} and F_{cp} are the curvature effects factors for drag and pressure flow, respectively, found by Booy (1964) to be equal to:

$$F_{cd} = \frac{K(\Omega)F(\Omega)\tan^2\beta}{(1-\Omega)\sin^2\beta\,[F(\Omega)-2G(\Omega)\tan^2\beta]} \tag{53}$$

$$F_{cp} = \frac{3G(\Omega)F(\Omega)\tan^2\beta}{2(1-\Omega)^3\sin^2\beta\,[F(\Omega)-2G(\Omega)\tan^2\beta]} \tag{54}$$

where

$$\beta = \pi/2 - \alpha$$
$$\Omega = D_s/D$$
$$K(\Omega) = 1 + \frac{2\Omega^2\ln\Omega}{1-\Omega^2}$$
$$G(\Omega) = (1-\Omega^2)\left[1 - \left(\frac{2\Omega\ln\Omega}{1-\Omega^2}\right)^2\right]$$
$$F(\Omega) = (\Omega^2 - 1)\left[1 + \Omega^2 + \frac{(1-\Omega^2)}{\ln\Omega}\right]$$

It must be noted that the helix angle, α, varies with the diameter as given by the direct trigonometric relation $\tan \alpha = d/(\pi D\cdot)$ where $D\cdot$ represents the diameter at any point, between D_s and D. Booy's procedure has the advantage of being developed for the value at the barrel diameter, D (that is, neglecting the gap δ), which is more convenient to use since it is the one usually quoted in extruder dimensions.

Many authors have suggested consideration of both shape and convergence factors to describe a model where both flight edges and curvature effects are important (Mohr *et al.*, 1957; Gore and McKelvey, 1958; Squires *et al.*, 1959; Harmann and Harper, 1974; Harper, 1981). The suggestion is to combine the two factors linearly, using $F'_d = F_d \times F_{cd}$ and $F'_p = F_p \times F_{cp}$ in the flow equation. In fact, this has become quite a standard procedure.

As previously mentioned, Booy (1964) did not consider bidimensional flow and hence the application of F_d and F_p factors linearly combined results solely from an intuitive approach. Anyway, for consistency, F_d and F_p factors used should be the ones determined for a mean width w'. Booy (1964) has suggested for this case $w' = \pi(D - h) \cos \alpha$. This minimizes the errors of combining linearly the two factors.

It cannot be expected that several correction factors can be combined in this way rigorously, since the resulting equation would not verify all the different assumptions made to develop each of them. In fact, Hami and Pittman (1980) showed that the use of F'_d and F'_p overestimates curvature effects. The only correct way to consider both curvature and flight edges effects is, obviously, to solve Model 2 for equations written in cylindrical coordinates.

Non-isothermal flow. For this case, there would not be an analytical solution as for Model 1 (N.nC.U). The solution of this problem would once again be exactly like that for Model 1, for equations written in cylindrical coordinates. For such a model, the use of cylindrical coordinates will not bring any significant additional difficulty for the resolution of the model.

3.4.4 Model 4 (Non-Newtonian, Negligible curvature, Unidimensional)

Isothermal flow. This model will be described by combining eqns (8) and (9) with eqn (12). The result will be:

$$\frac{\partial P}{\partial x} = \frac{\mathrm{d}}{\mathrm{d}y}\left[C \sqrt{(II)^{n-1}} \frac{\mathrm{d}V_x}{\mathrm{d}y} \right] \tag{55}$$

$$\frac{\partial P}{\partial z} = \frac{d}{dy}\left[C\sqrt{(II)}^{n-1}\frac{dV_z}{dy}\right] \tag{56}$$

with:

$$\sqrt{(II)} = \sqrt{\left[\left(\frac{dV_x}{dy}\right)^2 + \left(\frac{dV_z}{dy}\right)^2\right]}$$

It can be noted that the equation in the z direction can no longer be solved on its own to determine the flow, because of the dependence of the apparent viscosity on both velocity profiles (through the value of the second invariant of the rate of strain tensor). This set of equations can only be solved numerically.

This problem was first approached by Zamodits (1964) who provided an elegant solution.

From this point onwards, for simplicity reasons, $\partial p/\partial x$ and $\partial p/\partial z$ will be represented by P_x and P_z. It should be recalled that for this geometry (as for Model 1—N.nC.U), both these parameters are constants, P_x being unknown and P_z being given by eqn (18).

Equations (55) and (56) can be integrated straightforwardly, yielding:

$$P_x(y - y_1) = C\sqrt{(II)}^{n-1}\frac{dV_x}{dy} \tag{57}$$

$$P_z(y - y_2) = C\sqrt{(II)}^{n-1}\frac{dV_z}{dy} \tag{58}$$

where y_1 and y_2 are the limits of integration. These will be the stress neutral surfaces, that is, the values of y at which dV_x/dy and dV_z/dy are zero, respectively and will become parameters of the model.

At this stage, it is convenient to introduce dimensionless variables:

$$Y = y/h : U = V_x/U_x : W = V_z/U_z \tag{59}$$

Substituting in eqns (57) and (58) yields:

$$hP_x(Y - Y_1) = C\sqrt{(I_2)}^{n-1}\left(\frac{\pi DN}{h}\right)^n \cos\alpha\frac{dU}{dY} \tag{60}$$

$$hP_z(Y - Y_2) = C\sqrt{(I_2)}^{n-1}\left(\frac{\pi DN}{h}\right)^n \sin\alpha\frac{dW}{dY} \tag{61}$$

where:

$$I_2 = \cos^2 \alpha \left(\frac{\mathrm{d}U}{\mathrm{d}Y}\right)^2 + \sin^2 \alpha \left(\frac{\mathrm{d}W}{\mathrm{d}Y}\right)^2$$

This notation was used for similarity and does not obviously mean that I_2 is II in dimensionless form.

The value of I_2 may be expressed in function of Y_1, Y_2 and P_x instead of $\mathrm{d}U/\mathrm{d}Y$ and $\mathrm{d}W/\mathrm{d}Y$, obtaining more manageable equations. Squaring and adding together eqns (60) and (61) with some manipulation leads to:

$$I_2 = \left(\frac{h}{C}\right)^{2/n} \left(\frac{h}{\pi DN}\right)^2 [(Y-Y_1)^2 P_x^2 + (Y-Y_2)^2 P_z^2]^{1/n} \qquad (62)$$

Substituting this result in eqns (60) and (61) and making for simplicity:

$$F(Y) = [(Y-Y_1)^2 P_x^2 + (Y-Y_2)^2 P_z^2]$$

yields:

$$\frac{\mathrm{d}U}{\mathrm{d}Y} = \left(\frac{h}{C}\right)^{1/n} (Y-Y_1) \frac{hP_x}{\pi DN \cos \alpha} [F(Y)]^{[(1-n)/(2n)]} \qquad (63)$$

$$\frac{\mathrm{d}W}{\mathrm{d}Y} = \left(\frac{h}{C}\right)^{1/n} (Y-Y_2) \frac{hP_z}{\pi DN \sin \alpha} [F(Y)]^{[(1-n)/(2n)]} \qquad (64)$$

These two equations can now be integrated straightforwardly:

$$U = \frac{hP_x}{\pi DN \cos \alpha} \int_0^Y \left(\frac{h}{C}\right)^{1/n} (Y-Y_1) [F(Y)]^{[(1-n)/(2n)]} \, \mathrm{d}Y \qquad (65)$$

$$W = \frac{hP_z}{\pi DN \sin \alpha} \int_0^Y \left(\frac{h}{C}\right)^{1/n} (Y-Y_2) [F(Y)]^{[(1-n)/(2n)]} \, \mathrm{d}Y \qquad (66)$$

There are three unknown parameters in these equations: Y_1, Y_2 and P_x. The boundary conditions of the model state that for $Y=1$, $U=W=1$. Then, from eqns (65) and (66):

$$1 = \frac{hP_x}{\pi DN \cos \alpha} \int_0^1 \left(\frac{h}{C}\right)^{1/n} (Y-Y_1) [F(Y)]^{[(1-n)/(2n)]} \, \mathrm{d}Y \qquad (67)$$

$$1 = \frac{hP_z}{\pi DN \sin \alpha} \int_0^1 \left(\frac{h}{C}\right)^{1/n} (Y-Y_2) [F(Y)]^{[(1-n)/(2n)]} \, \mathrm{d}Y \qquad (68)$$

Also, using eqn (24):

$$\int_0^1 \int_0^Y \left(\frac{h}{C}\right)^{1/n} (Y-Y_1)\,[F(Y)]^{[(1-n)/(2n)]}\,dY\,dY = 0 \tag{69}$$

Equations (67), (68) and (69) will allow the determination of the three parameters of the model. With the values obtained the velocity profiles will then be determined from eqn (65) and (66). The volumetric flow rate is by definition $\int w V_z \, dy$ and can therefore be computed from the V_z velocity profile, as usual.

In order to solve the equations, a finite differences approach may again be used. The problem is in this case unidimensional, with the variables varying only in the y direction. This domain in divided into n points. If an odd number is chosen for n, Simpson's rule may then be used for solving integrals.

To obtain the values of P_x, Y_1 and Y_2, an iterative procedure will be required. Equations (67), (68) and (69) can be manipulated to isolate the parameters and provide a recurrence formula for generation of new estimates. The result is:

$$P_x = \frac{\dfrac{\pi D N \cos\alpha}{h}}{\displaystyle\int_0^1 \left(\frac{h}{C}\right)^{1/n} Y[F(Y)]^{[(1-n)/(2n)]}\,dY - Y_1 \int_0^1 \left(\frac{h}{C}\right)^{1/n} [F(Y)]^{[(1-n)/(2n)]}\,dY} \tag{70}$$

$$Y_2 = \frac{\displaystyle\int_0^1 \left(\frac{h}{C}\right)^{1/n} Y[F(Y)]^{[(1-n)/(2n)]}\,dY - \dfrac{\pi D N \sin\alpha}{h P_z}}{\displaystyle\int_0^1 \left(\frac{h}{C}\right)^{1/n} [F(Y)]^{[(1-n)/(2n)]}\,dY} \tag{71}$$

$$Y_1 = \frac{\displaystyle\int_0^1 \int_0^Y \left(\frac{h}{C}\right)^{1/n} Y[F(Y)]^{[(1-n)/(2n)]}\,dY\,dY}{\displaystyle\int_0^1 \int_0^Y \left(\frac{h}{C}\right)^{1/n} [F(Y)]^{[(1-n)/(2n)]}\,dY\,dY} \tag{72}$$

The initial estimates for these parameters may be the values for Newtonian flow (Model 1—N.nC.U). For P_x, eqn (25) is used. Y_1 and Y_2 had not been considered before, but their values for Newtonian flow are easily found from their definition.

Non-isothermal flow. For this case, the equations and resolution of the model are exactly the same as for isothermal flow, with the important difference that C is no longer constant, but depends on the temperature. For each point in the integration, the energy equation must be used to determine the local value of C.

The equations of the model are therefore added with the result of applying eqn (12) to eqns (30) and (14), using dimensionless variables and then applying eqn (62):

$$\frac{kT_b}{h^2}\frac{d^2\Theta}{dY^2}+\left(\frac{h^{n+1}}{C}\right)^{1/n}[F(Y)]^{[(n+1)/(2n)]}=0 \qquad (73)$$

$$C=C^0\exp[-\beta'(1/\Theta-1/\Theta^0)] \qquad (74)$$

The dimensionless variable for temperature is defined by $\Theta = T/T_b$, and therefore $\beta' = \beta/T_b$. The boundary conditions are that for $Y=0$, $d\Theta/dY=0$ and for $Y=1$, $\Theta=1$.

The solution will require writing the equations in finite difference form, similarly to what has been previously shown. An odd number of points n must be chosen for dividing the domain, so that Simpson's rule can be used to evaluate the integrals in eqns (67), (68) and (69) (and for determining the flow in the end).

The initial estimate for the temperature profile will be $\Theta = 1$ at all points (isothermal extrusion). With this estimate, an iterative procedure will yield Y_1, Y_2 and P_x, just as in isothermal extrusion. Velocity profiles will then be computed from eqns (65) and (66). With these, eqn (73) can be solved (this will require a small iterative loop due to the type of boundary conditions—just as for Model 1). The result will be a new temperature profile. This process will be repeated until two temperature profiles are sufficiently close (that is, all points i from 0 to $n-1$ differ in two estimates less than a predetermined error). This procedure means that for each estimate of the temperature profile a set of equations similar to the one of the isothermal model must be solved.

Once again, because extrusion is usually not very far from iso-thermal, the initial estimates are usually not far from the solution and convergence usually occurs within reasonable computational time. However, this procedure does start to become rather cumbersome and problems of stability are possible. In such cases the only viable alternative is to use a different approach, either more sophisticated numerical methods of finite differences or then to develop the solution using finite elements.

216   J. C. OLIVEIRA

3.4.5 Model 5 (Non-Newtonian, Negligible Curvature, Bidimensional)

Isothermal flow. At this level, extrusion modelling starts to produce
sets of equations that present some problems to be solved. There
is no escape from a complex numerical problem. The simplest possible
solution is that suggested by Martin (1969), who reduced the number
of equations by using the streamline function and then devised an
algorithm to solve the equations in finite differences, using iterative
procedures.

At this moment, it is possible to use instead the general approach, that
is, to consider that at each point in the extruder there will be an apparent
viscosity function. In this case, it will be simply given by the Ostwald–de
Waele equation, but for any general case, the procedure would be as
described below.

The equations of the model will be obtained by combining eqns (5), (6)
and (7) with eqn (12). The general equations for an extruder model can be
written as:

$$P_x = 2\frac{\partial}{\partial x}\left(\mu_a \frac{\partial V_x}{\partial x}\right) + \frac{\partial}{\partial y}\left(\mu_a \frac{\partial V_x}{\partial y}\right) \tag{75}$$

$$P_z = \frac{\partial}{\partial x}\left(\mu_a \frac{\partial V_z}{\partial x}\right) + \frac{\partial}{\partial y}\left(\mu_a \frac{\partial V_z}{\partial y}\right) \tag{76}$$

Therefore:

$$P_x = 2\frac{\partial\mu_a}{\partial x}\frac{\partial V_x}{\partial x} + 2\mu_a\frac{\partial^2 V_x}{\partial x^2} + \frac{\partial\mu_a}{\partial y}\frac{\partial V_x}{\partial y} + \mu_a\frac{\partial^2 V_x}{\partial y^2} \tag{77}$$

$$P_z = \frac{\partial\mu_a}{\partial x}\frac{\partial V_z}{\partial x} + \mu_a\frac{\partial^2 V_z}{\partial x^2} + \frac{\partial\mu_a}{\partial y}\frac{\partial V_z}{\partial y} + \mu_a\frac{\partial^2 V_z}{\partial y^2} \tag{78}$$

(which reduces to eqns (36) and (38) when μ_a is constant).
For the power law:

$$\mu_a = C\left[2\left(\frac{dV_x}{dx}\right)^2 + \left(\frac{dV_x}{dy}\right)^2 + \left(\frac{dV_z}{dx}\right)^2 + \left(\frac{dV_z}{dy}\right)^2\right]^{[(n-1)/2]} \tag{79}$$

Writing the equations in finite differences yields:

$$P_x(j) = 2\frac{\mu_a(j+1,i) - \mu_a(j-1,i)}{2\Delta x} \frac{V_x(j+1,i) - V_x(j-1,i)}{2\Delta x}$$

$$+ 2\mu_a(j,i)\frac{V_x(j+1,i) - 2V_x(j,i) + V_x(j-1,i)}{(\Delta x)^2}$$

$$+ \frac{\mu_a(j,i+1) - \mu_a(j,i-1)}{2\Delta y} \frac{V_x(j,i+1) - V_x(j,i-1)}{2\Delta y}$$

$$+ \mu_a(j,i)\frac{V_x(j,i+1) - 2V_x(j,i) + V_x(j,i-1)}{(\Delta y)^2} \qquad (80)$$

$$P_z(j) = \frac{\mu_a(j+1,i) - \mu_a(j-1,i)}{2\Delta x} \frac{V_z(j+1,i) - V_z(j-1,i)}{2\Delta x}$$

$$+ \mu_a(j,i)\frac{V_z(j+1,i) - 2V_z(j,i) + V_z(j-1,i)}{(\Delta x)^2}$$

$$+ \frac{\mu_a(j,i+1) - \mu_a(j,i-1)}{2\Delta y} \frac{V_z(j,i+1) - V_z(j,i-1)}{2\Delta y}$$

$$+ \mu_a(j,i)\frac{V_z(j,i+1) - 2V_z(j,i) + V_z(j,i-1)}{(\Delta y)^2} \qquad (81)$$

with:

$$\mu_a(j,i) = C(j,i)\left\{2\left[\frac{V_x(j+1,i) - V_x(j-1,i)}{2\Delta x}\right]^2\right.$$

$$+ \left[\frac{V_x(j,i+1) - V_x(j,i-1)}{2\Delta y}\right]^2 + \left[\frac{V_z(j+1,i) - V_z(j-1,i)}{2\Delta x}\right]^2$$

$$\left. + \left[\frac{V_z(j,i+1) - V_z(j,i-1)}{2\Delta y}\right]^2\right\}^{(n-1)/2} \qquad (82)$$

For isothermal flow, $C(j, i)$ is actually a constant, at all points—this will not be true for non-isothermal flow only.

It can be seen that there would not be a straightforward solution for these equations. The resolution would start at point $i=n$, for all j, in a similar way to the one described for Model 2 (N.nC.B), for non-isothermal flow (the reason for this is important only for the non-isothermal case because of the boundary conditions that have been established for the energy equation). When applying the equations to point i, velocities at points $i-1$ and $i-2$ appear in the equations (this is because of the variation of μ_a that requires the calculation of μ_a at point j, $i-1$). Therefore, given the values at i it would not be possible to determine the ones at $i-1$ without the ones for $i-2$. This means that all $m \times n$ equations would need to be solved simultaneously.

There is one possibility of avoiding this problem that does not involve a departure from the philosophy adopted in this text of devising a straightforward solution whenever possible. Finite differences are descriptions of the derivatives of a function that become exact when Δx and Δy become zero (see Appendix II). It was said that the formulae adopted were more precise, but it can be recalled that there are other possibilities. For instance, for the extremes, it was not possible to determine the first derivative in the same way—the derivative to the right or to the left must be used. At any other point, such expressions would yield a value that would be exact only when Δ became zero—otherwise, the derivatives to the right and to the left would differ by a given value. The real value of the derivative would be included within these two and the expression used provides a best estimate. However, if one assumes this error and uses derivatives to the right or to the left *in the apparent viscosity function*, it is enough to avoid the problem mentioned and find a straightforward solution for the model.

Equation 82 is substituted by:

$$\mu_a(j,i)=C(j,i)\left\{2\left[\frac{V_x(j+1,i)-V_x(j,i)}{\Delta x}\right]^2 \right.$$

$$+\left[\frac{V_x(j,i+1)-V_x(j,1)}{\Delta y}\right]^2+\left[\frac{V_z(j+1,i)-V_z(j,i)}{\Delta x}\right]^2$$

$$\left.+\left[\frac{V_z(j,i+1)-V_z(j,i)}{\Delta y}\right]^2\right\}^{(n-1)/2} \tag{83}$$

Straightforward solution of eqns (81), (82) and (83) is similar to the procedure described for non-isothermal flow for Model 2 (N.nC.B).

Initial estimates for $P_x(j)$ are needed—these can be the ones given by eqn (25) (better initial estimates would be the ones generated by Model 2, if available).

From the boundary conditions, $V_x(j, n)$ and $V_z(j, n)$ are known for $j = 1$ to $m - 1$. $V_x(0, i)$, $V_z(0, i)$, $V_x(m, i)$ and $V_z(m, i)$ for $i = 0$ to n are also known from the boundary conditions. Initial estimates for $V_z(j, n-1)$ can be generated by eqns (39) and (40) and for $V_x(j, n-1)$ by eqn (23) (once again, values obtained by Model 2 would be better, if available). Applying eqns (80), (81) and (83) at point $n-1$ (for $j = 1$ to $m-1$) will yield the velocities at point $n-2$. It must be noted that for each value of j a system of two non-linear equations must be solved to obtain both $V_x(j, n-2)$ and $V_z(j, n-2)$. This is a particular complexity of this procedure compared to previous ones, although it is fairly simple to overcome it since a simple iterative method (e.g. Newton–Raphson) can be used. The procedure is repeated until $i = 1$, when the values of $V_x(j, 0)$ and $V_z(j, 0)$ will be obtained. These can be compared with the boundary conditions and new estimates for $V_x(j, n-1)$, $V_z(j, n-1)$ are generated. After convergence has been obtained, eqn (51) is checked for $j = 1$ to $m-1$ and new estimates for $P_x(j)$ are generated if necessary.

Clearly, the model benefits from simplifying it with the use of the streamline function. Martin (1969) described an optimized algorithm.

Non-isothermal flow. For the case of non-isothermal flow, the model must be complemented with eqn (4), since $C(j, i)$ is a temperature-dependent variable, according to eqn (14).

Using finite differences, these equations become identical to eqns (47) and (50). Once again, the model is similar to Model 2 (N. nC. B), with μ substituted by eqn (79).

The straightforward solution of the model is similar, with the exception already noted in isothermal flow: the velocities are not computed independently but by solving a system of two non-linear equations. The procedure can therefore be described by Fig. 3, with steps 7 and 8 substituted by the simultaneous resolution of eqns (80), (81) and (83). This procedure could raise some stability problems, which would lead to a great use of computational time to ensure convergence. The best possible alternative (besides the Martin (1969) algorithm) is to use finite elements. This would generate a model that could fit well most rheological models, in general terms, which would be quite powerful.

3.4.6 Model 6 (Non-Newtonian, Negligible Curvature, Unidimensional)
Model 6 is similar to Model 4 (nN. nC. U), with a different equation for
the apparent viscosity function. The model is therefore defined by eqns (8)
and (9) combined with eqn 13. The result is:

$$P_x = \frac{\partial \mu_a}{\partial y} \frac{\partial V_x}{\partial y} + \mu_a \frac{\partial^2 V_x}{\partial y^2} \tag{84}$$

$$P_z = \frac{\partial \mu_a}{\partial y} \frac{\partial V_z}{\partial y} + \mu_a \frac{\partial^2 V_z}{\partial y^2} \tag{85}$$

$$\mu_a = C \, (II)^{(n-1)/2} + \frac{\tau^0}{\sqrt{(II)}} \tag{86}$$

$$II = \left(\frac{\partial V_x}{\partial y}\right)^2 + \left(\frac{\partial V_z}{\partial y}\right)^2 \tag{87}$$

where C, n and τ^0 are parameters of the rheological model.

It can be seen that there will be no simple solution like Zamodits's
procedure (see Section 3.4.4) on account of the apparent viscosity function.
Therefore, the model is already sufficiently complex for the general
procedure (described in Section 3.4.5) to be the only possible solution.

The resolution of this model will follow a similar approach to the one
described for Model 5. The same can be said of any other rheological
model: any model can be used with that type of procedure.

Therefore, the conclusion is that there are possible simplified results
only for Newtonian behaviour or for power-law behaviour with negligible curvature and negligible flight effects.

3.5 Use of Extruder Models in Food Extrusion
Published results of extruder models in food extrusion are very limited.
Models other than Newtonian have only recently been used. At present,
however, research groups, both at universities (such as Wageningen
Agricultural University, Netherlands) and at companies (such as CLEX-
TRAL, France) are working on different aspects of food extrusion
modelling. Main concerns besides flow prediction are residence-time
distribution (which can also be studied independently) and energy requirements.

Two examples of reported results on the application of mathematical
modelling to food extrusion that are symptomatic are the works of Tsao
et al. (1976) and Harmann and Harper (1974). These authors tested

results with doughs and used Newtonian models. They obtained most predicted outputs within 20% of the experimental ones, which is a rather poor result compared to that achieved in polymer extrusion. The apparent viscosity was determined independently of the extruder results.

This type of procedure is typical of the approach used for applying Newtonian models to food extrusion. The relatively poor agreement between predicted and experimental results is then attributed to non-Newtonian behaviour and/or slippage (Tsao *et al.*, 1976).

There are, however, important comments to be made. The authors mentioned have used the standard procedure at the time of linearly combining correction factors for bidimensional flow, curvature effects and end effects. The danger of such procedure has already been pointed out (see Section 3.4.3). Tsao *et al.* (1976) could have checked the influence of this procedure quite easily by considering not only the overall model with all correction factors but also other models, more simplified (that is, test Models 1, 2 and 3 simultaneously, besides any other model of interest). The use of several models for result analysis instead of only one chosen *a priori* is suggested since this allows the identification of what phenomena are relevant in any given practical case. This will be of great assistance when discussing deviations between theory and experience.

Another aspect, more subtle and therefore less well-identified previously, is the determination of the apparent viscosity. This is in fact merely a way to determine a Newtonian parameter for a Newtonian model, by optimizing the difference between the real non-Newtonian results and the Newtonian prediction. However, if this is done independently, such a parameter will be the best fit for the rheometer, but not necessarily for the extruder. This is shown in Oliveira (1989). Kroesser and Middleman (1965) have shown that the procedure adopted by Tsao *et al.* (1976), among others, leads to gross overestimations of the flow rate, sometimes as large as 50%. Kroesser and Middleman (1965) suggested a model for minimizing this error, by developing it from the beginning with the knowledge that the apparent viscosity is a parameter for a non-Newtonian fluid. This model, however, assumes both curvature and flight edges effects to be negligible. Oliveira (1989) has shown how the apparent viscosity value affects model results and how it is possible to obtain good agreement between Newtonian models and experimental results for the extruder characteristic curve, by using an optimum value for the apparent viscosity.

Extruder characteristic curves (that is, plots of the output flow versus the pressure difference) predicted by Newtonian models are straight lines.

Therefore, it is always possible to have a Newtonian model describing experimental results with reasonable correlation factors. However, it must be noted that the apparent viscosity only changes the slope—the intercept (value of the flow for zero pressure difference) cannot be changed. Oliveira (1989) has shown that Newtonian models overestimate this value in any case, since they overestimate drag flow.

Generally, non-Newtonian behaviour accounts for deviations of the Newtonian theory from experimental results, just as geometrical factors do. Once again, it seems very helpful to use several models for result analysis to clearly identify what factors are important.

Alternative ways to this type of modelling approach were tried, namely response surface analysis (e.g. Olkku and Vainionpaa, 1980) and residence-time distribution modelling from direct tracer measurements (e.g. Van Zuilichem *et al.*, 1988, Jager *et al.*, 1988, 1989, 1990, 1991).

3.6 Die Characteristic Curves

Flow models yield the velocity profiles and the output flow. Plots of the flow versus the pressure difference are the extruder characteristic curves. The operating point of an extruder is defined by the extruder and die characteristic curves—the intercept of both curves is obviously the operating point of a given extruder operating with a given die.

The pressure drop through the die is the sum of three pressure drops: at the entrance of the die, along the die channel and across the die orifice. In order to simplify the equations, it is generally assumed that the third component is much larger than the others and then the pressure drop through the die is approximately equal to the pressure drop across the orifice, an assumption that is usually good enough.

Dies and orifices can have many different shapes and, currently, given the variety of products produced by food extruders, there are complex die designs. The most common, and simpler still, is the cylindrical orifice die. Other shapes that can be treated mathematically with similar simplicity are rectangular slits and annular rings.

The modelling of the flow in the die is therefore simplified to the modelling of fluid flow in pipes and ducts.

The application of the fundamental equations of motion for Newtonian fluids yields:

$$Q = K \frac{\Delta P}{\mu} \qquad (88)$$

where K is the so-called die characteristic, which has different expressions for different geometries. For instance, for cylindrical orifices, the result is the well-known Hagen–Poiseuille equation, with:

$$K = \frac{D_o^4}{128 L_o} \tag{89}$$

where L_o and D_o are the length and diameter of the orifice, respectively (for other die geometries, see Pearson (1985)).

Note that applying eqn (88) in a Newtonian flow model, for isothermal extrusion, yields an equation of the type of (for Model 2):

$$Q = \frac{A F_d N}{1 + B F_p / K} \tag{90}$$

where F_d and F_p are the correction factors, N the screw rotational speed and A and B groups defined by (according to eqn (42)):

$$A = \frac{w h \pi D \sin \alpha}{2}$$

$$B = \frac{w h^3 \cos \alpha}{12 L}$$

Hence, the output flow is independent of viscosity for isothermal extrusion of Newtonian fluids, which is an important conclusion.

Die characteristic curves for non-Newtonian fluids are easy to determine from the equations of motion. For example, for a cylindrical orifice, only τ_{rz} is non-zero and one obtains for a power-law model:

$$\Delta P = \frac{4 C L_o}{D_o} \left[\frac{3n+1}{n} \frac{8Q}{\pi D_o^3} \right]^n \tag{91}$$

An important remark must be made regarding the use of these equations for the die flow. The use of the fundamental equations of motion has neglected end effects in the orifice. This is a good approximation only for values of L_o/D_o greater than 100 (Pearson, 1985). However, it is easy to incorporate end effects if necessary by defining the equivalent length (L_e). Instead of using the real length L_o, one uses $L_o' = L_o + L_e$. For Newtonian fluids, for instance, it is easy to show that $L_e = D_o/6$ (Pearson, 1985). For other rheological behaviours appropriate results can be obtained.

224   J. C. OLIVEIRA

While it was said that for non-Newtonian fluids the use of an optimum value for the apparent viscosity in extruder models is possible with a reasonable correlation, the same cannot be said for the die characteristic curve. In fact, errors arising from using for the die the same value of the apparent viscosity as the one used for the extruder can be very significant. This is actually not surprising, since die flow is a pressure flow and in an extruder drag flow is important (usually, the most important). Situations are therefore quite different and the value that fits well one does not fit the other.

For non-Newtonian fluids, it is always better to use an adequate non-Newtonian equation for the die—even if a Newtonian model will be used for the extruder. This does not raise any special problem, since for die flow the analytical solution of the equations exists and is simple.

Illustration of what has been said is given in Fig. 4, where for a laboratory Brabender extruder and a non-Newtonian dough extruder and die characteristic curves are plotted, for several models (data for this plot was obtained from Oliveira (1989)). Operating points are intersections of curves 1, 2 or 3 with curves 4 and 5.

Curiously enough, the error arising from using Newtonian behaviour

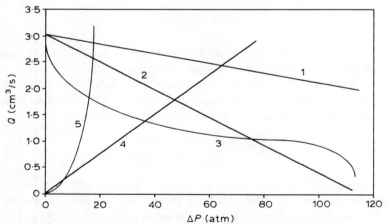

FIG. 4. Examples of extruder and die characteristic curves. 1–Extruder characteristic curve: Model 2 (N. nC. B), for the apparent viscosity determined from drag flow ($\mu_a = 383$ kg/m s). 2–Extruder characteristic curve: Model 2 (N. nC. B), for an optimized apparent viscosity ($\mu_a = 264$ kg/m s). 3–Extruder characteristic curve: Model 4 (N. nC. U), for $C = 1720$ kg/m s$^{(2-n)}$, $n = 0.338$. 4–Die characteristic curve for Newtonian behaviour ($\mu_a = 264$ kg/m s). 5–Die characteristic curve for power-law behaviour ($C = 1720$ kg/m s$^{(2-n)}$, $n = 0.338$).

versus non-Newtonian is much bigger in the die flow model than in the extruder one.

3.7 Leakage Flow

If the gap δ is sufficiently large, there will be a leakage flow, between the flight edges and the barrel, which cannot be neglected. This would affect the flow profile in the channel itself. In terms of the models, it prevents the use of some equations that were needed, as mentioned in the text. The problem must be solved in an integrated manner and becomes quite complex. For this reason, the most sensible approach currently is to neglect it. Models based on residence-time distribution would not have this problem, which is a clear advantage of this method. Many authors have assumed instead that leakage flow is independent of the channel flow and vice versa. If this approach could be used, then one would simply subtract leakage flow from channel flow to obtain the total flow (e.g. Squires *et al.*, 1959; Harper, 1981). This solution would perhaps be useful for some purposes. For instance, as the extruder wears, the gap increases and a model that includes leakage flow would give an indication of the variation of the extruder performance with time (Oliveira, 1989).

However, the independent analysis of leakage flow has further gross approximations: flow is assumed to be fully developed, end effects are neglected, the flow is considered to be equal to the flow in an annular ring of gap δ, with the pressure being the same around the whole circumference. Unfortunately, all these assumptions are unrealistic. The ratio between the gap, δ, and the screw flight width, s, is not small enough (by far) for flow to be fully developed, let alone to neglect end effects. Also, along one turn of the screw flight, the pressure increases significantly in the metering zone. Although the same can be said for both sides of the flights and hence the pressure difference does not vary so much, the flow is unlikely to be the same at all points, along one turn of the flight.

Much more experimental analysis is required to analyse leakage flow adequately and ensure what assumptions can be used and what models can be applied, even for considering leakage flow to be independent.

APPENDIX I: FUNDAMENTAL EQUATIONS

A good description and the mathematical deductions can be found in the literature (e.g. Darby, 1976; Bird, Stewart and Lightfoot, 1960).

The following equations are valid for *steady-state fully developed flow.*

I.1 Energy Equation (for constant heat conductivity)

I.1.1 Rectangular Coordinates

$$\rho C_\rho \left(V_x \frac{\partial T}{\partial x} + V_y \frac{\partial T}{\partial y} + V_z \frac{\partial T}{\partial z} \right) = k \left[\frac{\partial^2 T}{\partial x^2} + \frac{\partial^2 T}{\partial y^2} + \frac{\partial^2 T}{\partial z^2} \right] + \mu_a(\text{II})$$

I.1.2 Cylindrical Coordinates

$$\rho C_\rho \left(V_r \frac{\partial T}{\partial r} + \frac{V\phi}{r} \frac{\partial T}{\partial \phi} + V_z \frac{\partial T}{\partial z} \right) = k \left(\frac{1}{r} \frac{\partial}{\partial r} \left(r \frac{\partial T}{\partial r} \right) + \frac{1}{r^2} \frac{\partial^2 T}{\partial \phi^2} + \frac{\partial^2 T}{\partial z^2} \right] + \mu_a(\text{II})$$

I.2 Equations of Motion (Conservation of Momentum)

I.2.1 Rectangular Coordinates

(x component):

$$\rho \left[V_x \frac{\partial V_x}{\partial x} + V_y \frac{\partial V_x}{\partial y} + V_z \frac{\partial V_x}{\partial z} \right] = -\frac{\partial P}{\partial x} + \frac{\partial \tau_{xx}}{\partial x} + \frac{\partial \tau_{xy}}{\partial y} + \frac{\partial \tau_{xz}}{\partial z} + \rho g_x$$

(y component):

$$\rho \left[V_x \frac{\partial V_y}{\partial x} + V_y \frac{\partial V_y}{\partial y} + V_z \frac{\partial V_y}{\partial z} \right] = -\frac{\partial P}{\partial y} + \frac{\partial \tau_{xy}}{\partial x} + \frac{\partial \tau_{yy}}{\partial y} + \frac{\partial \tau_{yz}}{\partial z} + \rho g_y$$

(z component):

$$\rho \left[V_x \frac{\partial V_z}{\partial x} + V_y \frac{\partial V_z}{\partial y} + V_z \frac{\partial V_z}{\partial z} \right] = -\frac{\partial P}{\partial z} + \frac{\partial \tau_{xz}}{\partial x} + \frac{\partial \tau_{yz}}{\partial y} + \frac{\partial \tau_{zz}}{\partial z} + \rho g_z$$

I.2.2 Cylindrical Coordinates

Cylindrical coordinates are included in the text as eqns (1), (2) and (3).

I.3 Components of the Rate of Strain Tensor

I.3.1 Rectangular Coordinates

$$\Delta_{xx} = 2 \frac{\partial V_x}{\partial x} \qquad \Delta_{yy} = 2 \frac{\partial V_y}{\partial y}$$

$$\Delta_{xy} = \frac{\partial V_x}{\partial y} + \frac{\partial V_y}{\partial x} \qquad \Delta_{yz} = \frac{\partial V_y}{\partial z} + \frac{\partial V_z}{\partial y}$$

$$\Delta_{xz} = \frac{\partial V_x}{\partial z} + \frac{\partial V_z}{\partial x} \qquad \Delta_{zz} = 2 \frac{\partial V_z}{\partial z} \qquad \textit{Note.} \ \Delta_{ij} = \Delta_{ji}$$

I.3.2 Cylindrical Coordinates

$$\Delta_{rr} = 2\frac{\partial V_r}{\partial r} \qquad\qquad \Delta_{\phi\phi} = 2\left[\frac{1}{r}\frac{\partial V_\phi}{\partial \phi} + \frac{V_r}{r}\right]$$

$$\Delta_{r\phi} = \frac{1}{r}\frac{\partial V_r}{\partial \phi} + r\frac{\partial (V_\phi/r)}{\partial r} \qquad\qquad \Delta_{\phi z} = \frac{\partial V_\phi}{\partial z} + \frac{1}{r}\frac{\partial V_z}{\partial \phi}$$

$$\Delta_{rz} = \frac{\partial V_r}{\partial z} + \frac{\partial V_z}{\partial r} \qquad\qquad \Delta_{zz} = 2\frac{\partial V_z}{\partial z} \qquad\qquad Note.\ \Delta_{ij} = \Delta_{ji}$$

I.4 Second Invariant of the Rate of Strain Tensor

I.4.1 Rectangular Coordinates

$$II = 2\left[\left(\frac{\partial V_x}{\partial x}\right)^2 + \left(\frac{\partial V_y}{\partial y}\right)^2 + \left(\frac{\partial V_z}{\partial z}\right)^2\right] + \left(\frac{\partial V_y}{\partial x} + \frac{\partial V_x}{\partial y}\right)^2 + \left(\frac{\partial V_z}{\partial y} + \frac{\partial V_y}{\partial z}\right)^2$$

$$+ \left(\frac{\partial V_x}{\partial z} + \frac{\partial V_z}{\partial x}\right)^2$$

I.4.2 Cylindrical Coordinates

$$II = 2\left[\left(\frac{\partial V_r}{\partial r}\right)^2 + \left(\frac{1}{r}\frac{\partial V_\phi}{\partial \phi} + \frac{V_z}{r}\right)^2 + \left(\frac{\partial V_z}{\partial z}\right)^2\right] + \left(\frac{\partial V_r}{\partial z} + \frac{\partial V_z}{\partial r}\right)^2$$

$$+ \left(r\frac{\partial (V_\phi/r)}{\partial r} + \frac{1}{r}\frac{\partial V_r}{\partial \phi}\right)^2 + \left(\frac{1}{r}\frac{\partial V_z}{\partial \phi} + \frac{\partial V_\phi}{\partial z}\right)^2$$

I.5 Rheological Models Used

Any rheological model can be written as:

$$\tau_{ij} = \mu_a \Delta_{ij}$$

The different models will be defined by the apparent viscosity function.

I.5.1 Newtonian Model

$$\mu_a = \mu - \text{viscosity}$$

I.5.2 Power Law (Ostwald–de Waele) Model

$$\mu_a = C\ II^{(n-1)/2}$$

where C is the fluid consistency index, n is the fluid behaviour index, and II is the second invariant of the rate of strain tensor.

I.5.3 Hershel–Bulkley Model

$$\mu_a = C\, II^{(n-1)/2} + \frac{\tau^0}{\sqrt{(II)}} \qquad \text{(for } \tau > \tau^0\text{)}$$

$$\mu_a = 0 \qquad \text{for } (\tau < \tau^0)$$

where τ^0 is the yield stress.

Note. The apparent viscosity is related to the shear rate $\dot{\gamma}$ and not to the second invariant of the rate of strain tensor. However, such an expression would not yield a scalar quantity when using the components of the vectors, which on the other hand the apparent viscosity must be. For this reason, the invariants of the rate of strain tensor (that is, functions that are independent of the systems of axis) are used instead. There are three invariants. For incompressible fluids, the first invariant is zero. For viscometric flow, since only one component of the velocity vector is non-zero, the third invariant is also zero and only the second invariant exists. In such case, the shear rate is equal to the square root of the second invariant:

$$\gamma = \sqrt{(II)}$$

For other cases, where more than one component of the velocity vector are non-zero, however, the influence of the third invariant must be neglected (Darby, 1975), mainly on account of lack of knowledge of the opposite. Overall, the only possible approach is to consider that the shear rate is equal to the square root of the second invariant of the rate of strain tensor. In most cases this is a good approximation.

I.5.4 Variation with Temperature

The most usual approach for the inclusion of temperature dependence in the rheological models described is to consider that the apparent viscosity function varies exponentially with the temperature, which can be written as:

$$\mu_a = \mu_a^0 \exp[-\beta(1/T - 1/T^0)]$$

where T^0 is the reference temperature (K), μ_a^0 is the value of the apparent viscosity at the reference temperature (kg/m s) and β is the sensitivity of the apparent viscosity to temperature (1/K).

APPENDIX II: NUMERICAL RESOLUTION OF THE FLOW EQUATIONS

(a) Finite Differences

Any set of differential equations can be solved numerically. The basis of all numerical methods is to divide the domain into a series of discrete points—a mesh. The mesh can have any dimension. Its size will be related to the accuracy of the result and also to convergence problems (it is always possible to ensure convergency by using a sufficiently small size of the mesh elements, but this could imply significant computational needs and time). Values for one or two points in the mesh are usually known from the boundary conditions. Calculation will start at one extreme, usually where the boundary value is known. In order to calculate the values at subsequent points, algebraic equations or functions will be used. In some cases, it is not possible to solve each individually and therefore the solution will involve solving a system of algebraic equations.

In the finite differences method, the algebraic equations used to relate one point in the mesh to the others result from linearizing the differential equation. This leads to equations that can also be seen to result from the definition of derivatives.

Let us consider a multivariable function **f**. For one of the independent variables Ω, the domain of Ω can be divided into n points. There will be $n+1$ values of Ω from $\Omega(0)$ to $\Omega(n)$, each related to a value of the function **f** in that point, from $f(0)$ to $f(n)$. The size of each interval $(\Delta\Omega)$ will be equal to $[\Omega(n)-\Omega(0)]/n$. There are several methods for defining the derivatives and the one used in this text is presented. For a first derivative of **f** in relation to Ω, at a point i one can write:

$$\frac{\partial f}{\partial \Omega} = \frac{f(i+1)-f(i-1)}{2\Delta\Omega}$$

This equation corresponds to approximating the first derivative at point i by the slope of the line passing by the points immediately before and after $(i-1$ and $i+1)$. This approximation becomes the exact value of the derivative, by definition, when $\Delta\Omega \to 0$.

The above expression can be used at all points but the extremes, where the first derivative is given by

$$\left.\frac{\partial f}{\partial \Omega}\right|_{i=0} = \frac{f(1)-f(0)}{\Delta\Omega} \quad \text{or} \quad \left.\frac{\partial f}{\partial \Omega}\right|_{i=n} = \frac{f(n)-f(n-1)}{\Delta\Omega}$$

For the second derivative at point i:

$$\frac{\partial^2 f}{\partial \Omega^2} = \frac{f(i+1) - 2f(i) + f(i-1)}{(\Delta\Omega)^2}$$

This expression results from the definition of second derivative as the difference between the first derivatives at point i to the left and to the right ($[f(i) - f(i-1)]/\Delta\Omega$ is the derivative to the left and $[f(i+1) - f(i)]/\Delta\Omega$ the derivative to the right; similar expressions to the first derivative at the extremes of the domain).

There is no estimate for the value of the second derivative at the extremes.

Derivatives in relation to other independent variables and cross derivatives are calculated following exactly the same principles.

(b) Finite Elements

As with finite differences, this method is based in dividing the domain into a series of points. The values of the variables in question at each point of the mesh are related by algebraic equations. In finite elements, these do not relate directly to the differential equations. Instead, there are some functions which are used.

Problems would be solved by using a commercially available package, such as ANSYS. The job of the user trying to solve a specific problem is to define those functions from the differential equations of his own problem. This procedure would be too lengthy to include in this text. The reader is referred to texts on this particular subject.

REFERENCES

Bird, R., Stewart, W. & Lightfoot, E. (1960). *Transport Phenomena*. John Wiley and Sons, New York.

Booy, M. (1964). *J. Eng. Ind.*, **86**, 22.

Booy, M. (1978). *Polym. Eng. Sci.*, **18**, 973.

Booy, M. (1980). *Polym. Eng. Sci.*, **20**, 1220.

Boussinesq (1868). *Mathematiques Pures et Appliquées*, 2nd series, **13**, 377.

Carley, J. & Strubb, R. (1953). *Ind. & Eng. Chem.*, **45**, 970.

Darby, R. (1976). *Viscoelastic Fluids*, Chem. Proc. Eng. Series, Vol. 9. Marcel Dekker, New York.

Diosady, L., Paton, D., Rosen, N., Rubin, L. and Athanassoulias. C. (1985). Degradation of wheatstarch in a single screw extruder: mechano-kinetic break-down of cooked starch. *J. Fd. Sci.*, **50**, 1697–706.

Gomez, R. & Aguilera, J. (1984). A physicochemical model for extrusion of corn starch. *J. Fd. Sci.*, **49**, 40–4.

Gore, W. & McKelvey, J. (1958). Theory of screw extruders in *Rheology–Theory and Applications*, Vol. 3, ed. F. Einrich. Academic Press, New York.

Hami, M. & Pittman, H. (1980). *Polym. Eng. Sci.*, **20**, 339.

Harmann P. & Harper, J. (1974). *J. Fd. Sci.*, **39**, 1099.

Harper, J. (1981). *The Extrusion of Foods*, Vol. 1, CRC Press, Boca Raton, FL.

Harper, J. (1989). Food extrusion. In *Food Properties and Computer Aided Engineering of Food Processing Systems*, ed. R. P. Singh, A. Medina. NATO ASI Series E, Vol. 168. Kluwer Academic, Dordrecht, pp. 271–98.

Jager, T., Van Zuilichem, D., De Swart, J. & Van't Reit, K. (1991). Residence Time Distributions in Extrusion-Cooking: Part 7—Modelling of a Corotating, Twin Screw Extruder Fed with Maize Grits. *J. Fd. Eng.*, **14**, 185–202.

Janssen, L. (1986). Models for cooking extrusion. in *Food Engineering and Process Applications*, Vol. 2, *Unit Operations*, ed. M. Le Maguer & P. Jelen. Elsevier Applied Science Publishers, pp. 115–29.

Jepson, C. (1953). *Ind. & Eng. Chem.*, **45**, 992.

Klein, I. (1975). *Polym. Eng. Sci.*, **15**, 444.

Kroesser, F. & Middleman, S. (1965). *Polym. Eng. Sci.*, **5**, 230.

Linko, P., Linko, Y. & Olkku, J. (1983). Extrusion cooking and bioconversions, *J. Fd. Eng.*, **2**, 243.

Martin, B. (1969). Numerical studies of steady state extrusion processes. Ph.D. thesis, University of Cambridge.

Mohammed, I. & Ofoli, R. (1990). *J. Fd. Eng.*, **12**, 145.

Mohr, W. & Mallouk, R. (1959). Extrusion. In *Processing of Thermoplastic Materials*, ed. E. Bernhardt. Reinhold, New York.

Mohr, W., Saxton, R. & Jepson, C. (1957). *Ind. & Eng. Chem.* **49**, 1857.

Morgan, R., Steffe, J. & Ofoli, R. (1988). A generalized rheological model for extrusion of protein doughs. *J. Fd. Proc. Eng.* (in press).

Morgan, R., Suter, D. & Sweat, V. (1979). Modelling the effects of temperature–time history, temperature, shear rate and moisture on apparent viscosity of defatted soy flour doughs. ASAE Paper No. 79–6002, St Joseph, Michigan.

Ofoli, R., Morgan, R. & Steffe, J. (1987). A generalized rheological model for inelastic fluid foods. *J. Texture Studies*, **18**, 213–30.

Olkku, J. & Vainionpaa, J. (1980). Response surface analysis of HTST extrusion of a texturized starch/protein/sugar paste., in *Food Process Engineering*, Vol. 1, ed. P. Linko, V. Malkki, J. Olkku and J. Lannkan. Elsevier Applied Science Publishers, London.

Oliveira, J. (1989). Mechanisms of machine wear in the extrusion cooking of foods. Ph.D. thesis, University of Leeds. Chapter 4, The mathematical modelling of single screw extrusion processes.

Pearson, J. (1985). *Mechanics of Polymer Processing*. Elsevier Applied Science Publishers, London.

Rao, M. A. (1977). Rheology of liquid foods. A review. *J. Texture Studies*, **8**, 135–68.

Remsen, C. & Clark, J. (1978). A viscosity model for cooking dough. *J. Fd. Proc. Eng.*, **2**, 39–61.

232   J. C. OLIVEIRA

Rizvi, S. & Rao, M. A. (1986). *Engineering Properties of Foods*. Marcel Dekker, New York, pp. 1–48.
Rowell, H. & Finlayson, D. (1922). *Engineering*, **114**, 606.
Squires, P. Mohr, W., Mallouk, R. and McKelvey, J. (1959). Extrusion. In *Processing of Thermoplastic Materials*, ed. E. Bernhardt. Reinhold, New York.
Steffe, J. & Ofoli, R. (1989). Food engineering problems in rheology and non-Newtonian fluid mechanics. In *Food Properties and Computer Aided Engineering of Food Processing Systems*. ed. R. P. Singh & A. Medina. NATO ASI Series E, Vol. 168. Kluwer Academic Dordrecht, pp. 313–16.
Taso, T., Harper, J. & Repholz, K. (1976). *AIChemE Symposium Series*, **172**, 142.
Van Zuilichem *et al.* (1988). *J. Fd. Eng.*, **8**, 109.
Van Zuilichem, D., van der Lan, E. and Kulpar, E. (1990). The development of a heat transfer model for twin screw extruders. *J. Fd. Eng.*, **11**, 187–208.
Yates, B. (1968). Temperature development in single screw extruders. Ph.D. thesis, University of Cambridge.
Zamodits, H. (1964). Extrusion of thermoplastics. Ph.D. thesis, University of Cambridge.

Chapter 6

MODELLING THE CONTINUOUS STERILISATION OF PARTICULATE FOODS

SUDHIR K. SASTRY

Department of Agricultural Engineering,
Ohio State University,
Columbus, OH,
USA

NOTATION

A	Area (m^2)
B	Body force vector in fluid momentum equation (N/m^3)
C	Concentration of chemical component ($kg\,mol/m^3$)
C_p	Specific heat ($J/kg\,°C$)
d	Diameter (m)
D	Differential operator in substantial derivative; or diffusion coefficient (m^2/s)
E_a	Activation energy (J/kg-mol)
F	Volume fraction of material possessing a residence time below a specified value
F	Force vector (N)
F_0	Lethality (minutes at $121°C$)
Fr_p	Particle Froude number (defined in eqn (38))
h	Convective heat transfer coefficient ($W/m^2\,°C$)
h_m	Convective mass transfer coefficient (m/s)
I	Moment of inertia ($kg\,m^2$)
k	Thermal conductivity ($W/m\,°C$)
k_i	Reaction rate constant of species i [$(kg\,mol)^{1-n}\,s^{-1}$]
k_{0i}	Frequency factor (s^{-1})
K	Consistency coefficient ($Pa\,s^n$)
m	Mass (kg); or temperature coefficient of electrical conductivity ($°C^{-1}$)
M	Mass flux ($kg\,mol/m^3\,s$)

$\mathbf{M}$ Momentum flux (N/m^3)

n Flow behaviour index, number of particles, or order of chemical reaction

n_i Number of particles of a specific size or residence time; or reaction order of species i

$\mathbf{n}$ Unit normal vector

Nu Nusselt number ($h_{fp}d_p/k_f$)

p Pressure (Pa)

Pr Prandtl number ($\mu C_{pf}/k_f$)

q Energy transfer rate (W/m^3)

q''' Energy generation rate (W/m^3)

$\mathbf{q}_r$ Radiative energy flux (W/m^2)

r Ratio of mean reduced residence times of dispersed and continuous phases (defined in eqn (36))

R Universal gas constant ($J/kg\,mol\,K$), or electrical resistance (ohms)

R_m Rate of change of concentration of a chemical component via reaction

Re Reynolds number ($V_{fm}d_t\rho_f/\mu$)

Re_g Generalised Reynolds number, given by:

$$\frac{\rho_f V_{fm}^{2-n} d_t^n}{2^{n-3} K \left(\dfrac{3n+1}{n}\right)^n}$$

t Time, or residence time (s)

t_r Reduced time

T Temperature (°C or K)

$\mathbf{T}$ Torque (N m)

T_1 Lag time (reduced)

T_2 Time constant (reduced) of residence–time distribution (F) curve

U Overall heat transfer coefficient ($W/m^2\,°C$)

$\mathbf{v}$ Velocity vector (m/s)

V Volume (m^3); or voltage (volts)

V_{fm} Mean fluid velocity (m/s)

V_m Mean velocity (m/s)

x Particle size (m), or length coordinate (m)

Z Temperature rise required to achieve one log cycle decrease in thermal death time (min)

Δ	Increment
μ	Viscosity (Pa s)
Φ	Viscous energy dissipation (W/m^3)
ρ	Density (kg/m^3)
σ	Electrical conductivity (ohm m)$^{-1}$
Ω	Angular velocity (rad/s)

Subscripts not specifically used in context of above list

a	Activation
b	Bulk
c	Cold zone, or continuous phase
d	Dispersed phase
dasher	Dasher of SSHE
f	Fluid
g	Generalised
ht	Holding tube
hx	Heat exchanger
i	Index representing particle or chemical species
j	Index representing particle, or segment of ohmic heater
m	Mean, bulk fluid, or mass transfer
max	Maximum
n	Normalized
ND	Nondimensionalised
p	Particle
P	Process
pli	Particle–liquid interface
r	Radiative (in relation to heat transfer), or via reaction (in relation to mass transfer), or representative particle (in relation to models), or reduced (in relation to time)
ref	Reference value of a variable
s	Surface
S	Slowest-heating
st	Steam
t	Tube
T	At temperature T
w	Wall
0	Reference value of a variable
∞	Bulk fluid

Superscripts

n Index of increment of length along system

n_i, n_j Order of reaction with respect to chemical component i or j

T   Transpose of matrix

'''   Generation rate

‾   Mean

1 INTRODUCTION

Continuous sterilisation of foods followed by aseptic packaging has shown considerable promise in production of high-quality shelf-stable foods at reduced package cost. The technology has gained widespread acceptance for liquid foods, however, the assurance of a safe thermal process for most liquid–particle mixtures remains a challenge. The main difficulty lies in accurately determining the temperature at the coldest location within the suspension. For conventionally canned foods, this is a relatively simple task. However, for a continuously flowing suspension of particles, current technology does not permit accurate determination of cold zone temperatures without significant alteration in the flow and heat transfer characteristics within the material. Consequently, mathematical modelling appears to be the best approach to the prediction of cold zone temperatures during processing. Indeed, this is one of the infrequent instances in which the development of a technology depends largely on the effectiveness of process models. As in all cases involving modelling, experimental verification is necessary.

The objective of this chapter is to discuss the mathematical problems involving the continuous sterilisation of particulate suspensions, the means of solution of these problems, and the simplifying assumptions used in the solution procedures. The typical process systems under consideration are those involving scraped-surface heat exchangers (SSHEs) for product heating, a holding tube for providing residence at process conditions, and a cooling section involving (typically) SSHEs for product cooling, as illustrated in Fig. 1. In some instances, tubular heat exchangers may be substituted for SSHEs, although this does not change the mathematical formulation of the conduction heat transfer problem. One system which involves a significant departure from the conventional systems described above, is the ohmic, or electroconductive, heating system which involves internal energy generation within the product. The mathematical problem for these situations will also be discussed. The discussion will include some

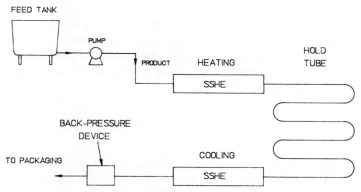

FIG. 1. Schematic diagram of a typical aseptic processing system for liquid–particle mixtures.

of the recent models published in the literature, and the important points of consideration involving thermal process evaluation.

2 MATHEMATICAL PROBLEM FORMULATION

When a liquid–solid mixture flows through a tube, heat, mass and momentum are continuously transferred between fluid and particles, as well as between individual particles. In addition, heat and momentum are transferred across system walls (Fig. 2). The transport phenomena are coupled, and the resulting problem is one of great complexity. Solutions are possible only by making a series of conservative simplifying assumptions, and relying on experimental data regarding certain key parameters.

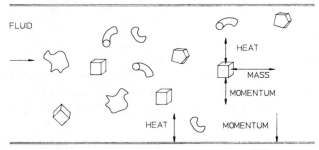

FIG. 2. Illustration of heat, mass and momentum exchange within an aseptic processing system.

2.1 Sterility Requirements

To keep the problem in perspective, the basic reason for modelling involves the determination of the coldest-location temperature within the slowest-heating particle, such that sufficient lethality (F_0) is accumulated to permit commercial sterilisation with respect to microorganisms of public health significance. Lethality may be expressed as:

$$F_0 = \int_0^{t_p} 10^{[T_c(t) - 121 \cdot 1]/Z} \, dt \qquad (1)$$

where the use of $121 \cdot 1°C$ as a reference temperature is common practice, although the general concept of the F-value permits definition of any other reference temperature. In the above equation, T_c refers to the coldest-location temperature within the particle. Integration of eqn (1) over the process time yields the accumulated lethality, which must be sufficient to provide a microbiologically safe product. Thus our objective is the determination of the function $T_c(t)$ over the entire process. The central philosophy underlying this means of process evaluation is that of destruction (to commercial limits) of the most-heat-resistant microorganism that is assumed to be *always* located at the coldest location. In situations where the coldest location changes over time, it is desirable to consider that location which results in the minimum accumulated value of F_0; however, this carries with it the unproven assumption that microorganisms do not change positions within a solid object. The safest approach in such situations would be to calculate lethality based on the coldest temperature regardless of location.

Since temperature prediction is the primary target, the logical starting point is the thermal energy transfer problem. This will be considered in the succeeding section.

2.2 Energy Transfer

2.2.1 Scraped-Surface Heat Exchanger

With the basic criteria established, the primary problem to be solved is that of energy transfer. The problem in this case, reduces to the following equation for the liquid, assuming that the thermodynamically interactive Dufour flux is negligible

$$\rho_f C_{pf} \frac{DT}{Dt} = \nabla \cdot (k_f \nabla T) + q''' - p\nabla \cdot \mathbf{v} - \nabla \cdot \mathbf{q}_r + \Phi - q_p \qquad (2)$$

The derivative on the left-hand side is the substantial derivative, defined as:

$$\frac{DT}{Dt} = \frac{\partial T}{\partial t} + \mathbf{v}.\nabla T$$

The first term on the right-hand side of eqn (2) represents the heat transferred by conduction through the fluid; the second term is the energy generation rate, which is negligible except under ohmic or microwave heating conditions; the third term represents work done by the fluid on its surroundings, and is zero for the present case involving an incompressible fluid. The fourth term ($\nabla.\mathbf{q}_r$) represents radiative heat transfer, which is generally negligible for food fluids. The fifth term (Φ) is that of viscous dissipation, which may be significant for viscous fluids processed in scraped-surface heat exchangers, but is likely to be negligible in other situations; and the sixth term (q_p) is the energy transferred to the particles in the suspension. Elimination of negligible components in eqn (2) yields the following relation for a fluid in a scraped-surface heat exchanger:

$$\rho_f C_{pf} \frac{DT}{Dt} = \nabla.(k_f \nabla T) + \Phi - q_p \tag{3}$$

where the viscous dissipation function Φ for an incompressible fluid is given by (Bird et al., 1960):

$$\Phi = (\mu/2)[\nabla \mathbf{v} + \nabla \mathbf{v}^T] : \nabla \mathbf{v} + \nabla \mathbf{v}^T] \tag{4}$$

For a non-Newtonian power-law fluid, the viscosity term may be represented by an apparent viscosity, given by:

$$\mu = K \mid \sqrt{[\nabla \mathbf{v} + \nabla \mathbf{v}^T] : [\nabla \mathbf{v} + \nabla \mathbf{v}^T]} \mid^{n-1} \tag{5}$$

The apparent viscosity is temperature-dependent, and must be considered as such for purposes of modelling. A commonly used expression for this dependence is (Rao et al., 1981):

$$\mu = \mu_0 \, e^{E_a/RT} \tag{6}$$

The energy transfer to the particles is given by:

$$q_p = \sum_i (h_{fpi} A_i / V)(T_{bf} - T_{spi}) \tag{7}$$

where i represents the particle in question. At any point in the system, the fluid contains particles of various different residence times in the system.

Consequently, the value of surface particle temperature (T_{spi}), area (A_i) and convective coefficient (h_i) would vary from particle to particle. The value of the particle surface temperature must be determined separately for each individual particle, by the solution to the conduction heat transfer equation:

$$\nabla.(k_{pi}\nabla T_{pi}) = \rho_{pi} C_{ppi} \partial T_{pi}/\partial t \qquad (8)$$

subject to the surface condition

$$k_{pi}\nabla T_{pi}.\mathbf{n} = h_{fpi}(T_{spi} - T_{bf}) \qquad (9)$$

Finally, the eqn (3) is subject to the wall boundary condition:

$$U(T_{bf} - T_{sw}) = k_f \nabla T_f.\mathbf{n} \qquad (10)$$

For several reasons, simultaneous solution of eqns (3) (subject to condition (10)) and (8) (subject to condition (9)) is not simple. First, the velocity fields necessary for computation of the substantial derivative (DT/Dt) and the viscous dissipation function (Φ) are unknown, and can only be found from simultaneous solution of the even more complex momentum transfer problem (discussed later). Second, the particle surface temperatures (T_{spi}) require solution of the conduction heat transfer equation for *each* particle, based on an understanding of the distribution of residence times in the system, an exercise that is likely to be computationally taxing given the large numbers of particles that occur in real systems. Thirdly, the fluid-to-particle interfacial heat transfer coefficients are largely unknown; and experiments to determine them are difficult (solid–liquid momentum transfer based solutions may have potential, but these are also of a high degree of difficulty). Finally, except for a few isolated studies (Dail, 1989), rheological properties of food fluids as functions of temperature are not well characterised.

2.2.2 Holding Tube

Within the holding tube, the heat transfer equations stay the same with the exception that the viscous dissipation term drops out of the fluid energy eqn (3), yielding:

$$\rho_f C_{pf} \frac{DT}{Dt} = \nabla.(k_f \nabla T) - q_p \qquad (11)$$

The problem and boundary conditions remain qualitatively the same, with changes in the actual values of medium temperature (T_{bf}) and overall heat transfer coefficient (U). The solution to the equations in general form still remains complex.

2.3. Momentum Transfer

2.3.1 Scraped-Surface Heat Exchanger

The transfer of momentum between liquid and particles has a significant impact on the trajectories and velocities of individual particles, and would therefore dictate not only particle residence times, but relative fluid/particle velocities and fluid-to-particle convective heat transfer coefficients. The basic equations affecting momentum transfer in the field are the continuity equation and the equations of motion, as follows.

Continuity (incompressible fluid)

$$\nabla . \mathbf{v} = 0 \tag{12}$$

Momentum (three equations in mutually perpendicular directions)

$$\rho \frac{D\mathbf{v}}{Dt} = -\nabla p + \mathbf{B} + \nabla . \{\mu[\nabla \mathbf{v} + \nabla \mathbf{v}^{\mathrm{T}}]\} - M_{\mathrm{p}} \tag{13}$$

The derivative on the left-hand side is the substantial derivative of the velocity vector, discussed earlier in relation to temperature. The terms on the right-hand side are as follows: the first term due to pressure gradient; the second due to body forces, the third due to viscous forces, and the fourth due to transfer of momentum from solid particles to the liquid. The typical boundary condition used for these relations is that of no-slip at the walls and particle–liquid interfaces. Thus the following relations apply:

$$\mathbf{v}|_{\text{wall}} = 0 \tag{14}$$

$$\mathbf{v}|_{\text{pli}} = \mathbf{v}_{\text{ps}} \tag{15}$$

$$\mathbf{v}|_{\text{dasher}} = \mathbf{v}_{\text{dasher}} \tag{16}$$

where the subscripts 'pli' and 'ps' refer to the particle–liquid interface, and the solid particle surface, respectively. Condition (15) has been specified using the consideration that the particle surface velocity (with respect to a stationary reference frame) may vary over its surface owing to rotational motion.

A number of comments may be made regarding the momentum transfer problem represented by eqns (12) and (13), subject to conditions

(14) to (16). First, the relations are applicable to laminar flows only, although the use of eddy diffusivities could render the equations applicable in an averaged sense to turbulent flow. However, for most food fluids used as particulate carriers, high viscosity is the norm, and laminar flow is generally a safe assumption. The second point is that the apparent viscosity used in the equations of motion (13), is *temperature-dependent*, resulting in a coupling of these equations to the energy equations discussed earlier. Third, the no-slip boundary condition is an approximation, and may not necessarily be valid in all instances. The slip phenomenon has received some attention in relation to coaxial cylinder viscometry (Rao, 1989), but data on slip coefficients in process equipment are generally unavailable. Finally, the above equations cannot be solved without knowledge of the concentration and velocity distributions of the solid particles; consequently particle momentum equations need to be solved to provide this missing link.

The particle momentum equations may be developed in cases where the solids may be approximated as nondeformable rigid bodies. For each particle, linear and angular momentum equations in three dimensions yield the following:

Linear momentum (three equations)

$$m_{pi} \frac{d\mathbf{v}_{pi}}{dt} = \sum \mathbf{F}_i \qquad (17)$$

Angular momentum (three equations)

$$I_{pi} \frac{d\Omega_{pi}}{dt} = \sum \mathbf{T}_i \qquad (18)$$

where the subscript i refers to the individual particle. For situations involving deformable particles, the problem is more complex, and a thorough treatment has been provided by Goldsmith and Mason (1967) with special reference to blood cells.

In principle, eqns (17) and (18) must be written for every particle in the suspension, and the entire set solved simultaneously with the fluid momentum eqns (12) and (13), and the energy equations discussed earlier. Additional complications are introduced by the necessity to consider the interactions and collisions between individual particles, and between particles and system boundaries. These problems pose considerable difficulties for the following reasons. First, the computation of many-body interactions remains a challenge. Most models, including those of

Durst *et al.* (1984) are based on small, noninteracting particles. Brady and Bossis (1985) have used their method of Stokesian dynamics to compute the interactions of a number of spheres in a Newtonian solvent. While this represents a significant advance in the field, the particles are still considered to be far removed from any boundaries. This does not include considerations of temperature-variable rheological properties and simultaneous solution with the energy equations. The second difficulty arises from the treatment of the physical properties of the particles during collisions. The recent studies of Davis *et al.* (1986) provide insight into the collision of two elastic bodies within a liquid; however, food particles are likely to exhibit non-linear viscoelasticity, complicating this situation further. A third level of complexity arises from the fact that each particle would experience a change in its properties based on its time and temperature of processing. While this change could be calculated from considerations of reaction kinetics; it is necessary to know the time–temperature and velocity history of each particle as well as the appropriate kinetic parameters in order to do so.

Given the difficulties involved in this type of modelling, the undaunted modeller would do well to consider whether the relative benefits justify the effort before embarking upon such an enterprise. The prediction of particle trajectories and velocities would be a useful accomplishment; however, the lack of information on physical characteristics of food materials at process temperatures, slip phenomena and the onset of turbulence within the fluid could render the most sophisticated models inaccurate. Since some of the required information is potentially obtainable by experimentation, the rationale for an all-inclusive model would seem weak from a practical standpoint. However, the challenge exists, and may be accepted by some 'because it is there'.

2.3.2 Holding Tube
Within the holding tube, the problem statement remains largely unchanged, with the exception that the dasher no longer exists, and condition (16) becomes unnecessary. The forces acting on the particle in tube flow would be different when considering bends in the piping.

2.4 Mass Transfer
Mass transfer has generally been a neglected topic during thermal sterilisation; however, mass transfer does occur in the form of diffusion and exchange of nutrients, flavour and other components between the liquid and particulate media. Since these factors greatly affect the quality

of the end product; mass transfer considerations are necessary for process optimisation purposes.

Mass transfer considerations gain further importance when one considers the possibility of bacterial spore diffusion through porous tissue. Data are generally lacking on this aspect of sterilisation processes, since the conservative and preferred approach has been the assumption of spores being located at the cold spot. A number of other interactions may occur. Food tissue which permits free transport of mass may also be considered to possess higher effective thermal conductivities than nonporous tissue. For starchy particles, starches may leach into the fluid and increase its viscosity during the process. The movement (or lack thereof) of residual tissue gases creates peculiar problems. When the release of these gases could cause thermal boundary layer disruption and enhance fluid-to-particle heat transfer, it is also possible for stagnant air pockets to retard heat transfer. Finally, mass transfer considerations take on significance in the light of the nightmarish scenario illustrated by Cerny (1989) where a bacterial spore may be located within an oil droplet during processing, resulting in negligible lethal effect, followed by post-process dislodgement of the spore from the oil into a nutritious microenvironment.

With the exception of nutrient diffusion (addressed by Schwartzberg and Chao (1982), Garrote et al. (1984, 1989), and Tomasula and Kozempel (1989), among others), none of the above phenomena has received much attention in the food engineering literature, and the basic information needed to develop meaningful models is unavailable. Further, the consideration of some of these phenomena (such as increased effective conductivity) is not likely to yield a conservative model. Finally, phenomena such as starch leaching may be conservatively accounted for by considering the carrier viscosity to be that associated with the processed rather than the raw product. Thus modeling of mass transfer is likely to be helpful primarily in optimising product quality rather than in process safety assurance.

Although the generalised driving force for mass transfer is the chemical potential, species concentration can be used as a reasonable assumption if Soret, Dufour and other cross-species diffusion effects are negligible, as is the case in many food processes (Hayakawa and Rossen, 1977). The equations for mass transfer within the fluid (both for the swept surface heat exchanger and the holding tube) then reduce to:

$$\frac{DC_i}{Dt} = \nabla \cdot (D_{mfi} \nabla C_i) + R_{mi} \pm M_{pi} \tag{19}$$

where the terms on the right-hand side are, left to right, the diffusion rate of component i, the generation rate of component i via reaction (R_{mi}), and the rate of exchange of the component with the particles (M_{pi}). The rate of reaction within the fluid depends on the particular kinetics of synthesis or degradation of species i, as well as the temperature. For many food-related applications, the following relations may be useful (Saguy and Karel, 1980):

$$R_{mi} = \left(\frac{dC_i}{dt}\right)_r = k_i C_i^{n_i} C_j^{n_j} \dots \tag{20}$$

with the temperature-dependence being described by the Arrhenius relation:

$$k_i = k_{0i} e^{-E_{ai}/RT} \tag{21}$$

The rate of exchange of component i between liquid and particles is determined by considering the interfacial mass transfer relation between fluid and the solid particles:

$$M_{pi} = \sum_j (h_{mji} A_{ji}/V)(C_{bfi}(t) - C_{spji}) \tag{22}$$

where j represents the particle in question, and i the chemical species. At this point, the similarity between the heat and mass transfer problems represented by eqns (7) and (22) may be noted. The constraints applicable to the heat transfer problem also apply to that of mass transfer. The particle surface concentration (C_{spji}) must be determined from the solution of the diffusive transport equation into each individual (jth) particle:

$$\nabla \cdot (D_{mpji} \nabla C_{pji}) + R_{mpji} = \partial C_{pji}/\partial t \tag{23}$$

subject to the surface condition

$$D_{mpji} \nabla C_{pji} \cdot \mathbf{n} = h_{mji}(C_{spji} - C_{bfi}(t)) \tag{24}$$

Finally, the eqn (19) is subject to the wall boundary condition:

$$D_{mfi} \nabla C_i \cdot \mathbf{n} = 0 \tag{25}$$

The mass transfer problem is also linked to the heat and momentum transfer problems, since the fluid velocity and temperature profiles need to be known for computation of the substantial derivative and reaction rate terms in eqn (19). The similarity between the heat and mass transfer problems implies similar difficulties in solution, although the mass transfer problem must be solved separately for each component of commercial importance. The difficulties of solving the heat and momentum transfer problems have already been detailed; thus it goes without saying that the additional solution of mass transport problems is not simple.

3 PROBLEM SIMPLIFICATION AND SOLUTION APPROACHES

While the difficulties involved in the above problems need not be reiterated, it is possible to achieve insight into most practical situations by making a number of simplifying assumptions. Since our primary objective is the achievement of process safety, particularly at the cold points (interiors of individual food particles), the primary equation of importance is the energy transport equation within an individual particle (eqn (8) subject to condition (9)). Solution of the mass transfer problem could be considered of lower priority, since: (1) it is weakly coupled to the heat transfer problem; (2) it would either (a) result in a nonconservative impact on sterilisation calculations, or (b) where the impact is conservative (as with starch leaching), be addressable by suitable factors of safety. The solid–liquid momentum transfer problem is of a high degree of difficulty, and rigorous solutions may not justify the effort. Further, the major motivation behind an understanding of the momentum transfer problem is the prediction of residence-time distributions and particle–fluid interfacial heat transfer coefficients—both of which may be at least partially handled by experimental techniques. Consequently, the problem of sterilisation reduces to the solution of heat transfer problems. Since the fluid temperature is generally measurable, or can be estimated by using various simplifying assumptions, the main problem to be solved is the conduction heat transfer equation for the most insufficiently heated particle. The boundary condition would be time-dependent, and could be determined from the location of the particle in the system.

At this stage, it is worthwhile considering the factors that result in an insufficiently heated particle. The rate of heating of a particle in an aseptic system is a function of (a) particle size and thermophysical properties, (b) residence time within the system, and (c) fluid-to-particle heat transfer coefficient for the particle in question. Obviously, large particles with high specific heats and densities, and low thermal conductivities, would tend to heat slowly. Fast-moving particles would have had little exposure time to hot fluid to permit them to heat up to process temperature. Finally, particles with low surface heat transfer coefficients would tend to be heated slowly. The most insufficiently heated particle in a system is likely to be that which exhibits the combination of characteristics listed above that are conducive to slow, inadequate heating. It is difficult, however, to conceive that all three factors could simultaneously have adverse effects, for a number of reasons. One is that fast-moving particles are likely to possess higher fluid-to-particle heat transfer coefficients than slower-moving particles. Another point is that high-density particles that might heat slowly are likely to settle near the bottom of the holding tube, and consequently move at slow velocities, resulting in long residence times. The result is that trade-offs must be made somewhere between conservatism and realism, in order to keep the technology viable.

The problem to be solved is then the conduction heat transfer equation, (eqn (8)) which may be rewritten as follows for the slowest-heating particle:

$$\nabla.(k_{pS}\nabla T_{pS}) = \rho_{pS}C_{ppS}\partial T_{pS}/\partial t \tag{26}$$

subject to the surface condition

$$k_{pS}\nabla T_{pS}.\mathbf{n} = h_{fpS}(T_{spS} - T_{bf}(T)) \tag{27}$$

where the bulk fluid temperature T_{bf} depends on location within the system. The following discussion relates to the determination of fluid and particle temperatures.

3.1 Determination of Bulk Fluid Temperature

3.1.1 Simple Models

The simplest approach to determination of the fluid bulk temperature is direct measurement, which has the advantage of realism, although the results are likely to be situation-specific. A more general situation may be addressed by using a model. The literature consists of a number of modelling approaches to determination of fluid temperature, the simplest of which involves the assumption (de Ruyter and Brunet, 1973; Manson and Cullen, 1974) that the fluid temperature increases linearly between inlet and outlet in the heater. This approach is likely to yield a conservative result for the heating section, since the linear curve will predict lower values than the exponential curve joining the two end points (Sastry, 1989a). However, the linear approximation will be non-conservative for situations involving temperature decrease in the fluid, as occurs in the holding and cooling sections. For this reason, Manson and Cullen (1974) considered the situation of exponential temperature decrease in the holding section.

A number of recent studies (Chang and Toledo, 1989; Lee and Singh, 1988) have used the assumption of exponential temperature rise in the heater. This approach is likely to result in a more realistic approximation of fluid temperature than the linear model, although the time constant for such models would be situation-specific. Details of time constants relative to fluid temperature can only be ascertained by more complex models involving energy balances over incremental portions of the processing system.

3.1.2 Energy Balance Models

Two types of approaches have been discussed under this category: the radially well-mixed fluid approach, and the distributed particle residence-time approach. Notably, most of the more recent models (Sastry, 1986; Åström et al., 1988; Chandarana and Gavin, 1989) have used an energy balance approach.

Radially well-mixed fluid approach. In this method, it is assumed for purposes of fluid temperature calculation, that:

(1) Although the particles will in general, possess a size distribution, they will collectively act as a population of particles of equal size.
(2) The fluid medium is perfectly mixed in the radial (but not axial) direction of the process system, and it is, at all times, in contact with a population of particles moving at the same average velocity. It is recognized that in real situations, a distribution of residence times exists.

The primary rationale behind these assumptions is the reduction of the large computation time associated with multiparticle, multidimensional simulations. Assumption (1) corresponds to the definition of a 'mean' particle dimension ($\bar{x}$).

$$\bar{x} = \frac{\sum x_i n_i}{\sum n_i} \tag{28}$$

Simulations by Sastry (1986) have indicated that the influence of average particle size on fluid temperature is slight; consequently the above assumption would be expected to provide a reasonable approximation.

Assumption (2) amounts to definition of an average particle residence time $(\bar{t})$.

$$\bar{t} = \frac{\sum t_i n_i}{\sum n_i} \tag{29}$$

Although a distribution exists in particle residence times, this assumption reduces the computation associated with multiparticle simulation. The rationale is that the influence of variation of particle residence times about the mean value is small. From the standpoint of process safety, the above assumption, with suitably conservative precautions, would be expected to yield reasonably conservative results. This approach (illustrated in Fig. 3), which has been used by Sastry (1986), Åström *et al.* (1988), and Chandarana and Gavin (1989), results in the following energy balance for each incremental section (Δx_{hx}) of the SSHE.

$$m_f C_{pf}(T_\infty^{n+1} - T_\infty^n) = U_{hx} A_{hx}(T_{st} - T_{\infty m}) + h_{hx} A_p n_{hx}(T_{sm} - T_{\infty m}) \tag{30}$$

where:

$T_{sm} = (T_s^{n+1} + T_s^n)/2$
$T_{\infty m} = (T_\infty^{n+1} + T_\infty^n)/2$
$A_{hx} = \pi d_{hx} \Delta_{hx}$

The value of T_s^{n+1} in eqn (30) is determined from the solution to the conduction heat transfer problem for the particle

$$\nabla \cdot (k_{pr} \nabla T_{pr}) = \rho_{pr} C_{ppr} \partial T_{pr}/\partial t \tag{31}$$

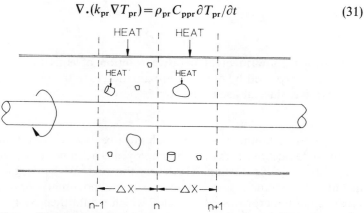

FIG. 3. Illustration of heat balance over incremental section of heat exchanger.

subject to the surface condition

$$k_{pr}\nabla T_{pr}.\mathbf{n} = h(T_{spr} - T_\infty(t)) \tag{32}$$

where the particle in question is the 'representative' one (subscript 'r'), possessing the 'average' dimension and residence time discussed earlier. This problem may be solved by a suitable numerical scheme. Finite difference schemes have been used by Åström et al. (1988), Chandarana and Gavin (1989), and Lee and Singh (1988), while the finite element method has been used by Sastry (1986).

The solution procedure typically involves iteration between eqns (30) and (31) till convergence is attained. A short-cut approach to eliminate iteration would involve the use of suitably small time steps, and the use of the approximation:

$$T_{sm} = T_s^n \tag{33}$$

If this approach is used, the error in the predicted fluid temperature will be a small conservative value. The conservative nature can be demonstrated mathematically by noting that within the heating section:

$$T_s^{n+1} > T_s^n$$

thus use of T_s^n instead of T_{sm} in eqn (30) will result in an increased heat loss from the fluid for each time step.

Within the holding tube, the energy balance for each incremental section may be formulated as:

$$m_f C_{pf}(T_\infty^{n+1} - T_\infty^n) = U_{ht}A_{ht}(T_a - T_{\infty m}) + h_{ht}A_p n_{ht}(T_{sm} - T_{\infty m}) \tag{34}$$

where:

$$A_{ht} = \pi d_{ht}\Delta x_{ht}$$

The problem now involves iterative solution of eqns (34) and (31). If iteration is bypassed by use of approximation (33), the results will not be conservative, since at each time step:

$$T_s^{n+1} < T_s^n$$

consequently, a noniterative approach must be used with caution, and the appropriate safety factors must be employed. The same restriction applies within the cooling section. However, the present discussion will not include this section, since there exists the possibility of mechanical break-up of underprocessed particles, which would then cool faster than expected, yielding an unsafe product.

Distributed particle residence-time approach. This approach would involve use of the assumption that the fluid is radially well mixed, while containing a population of particles of distributed sizes and residence times. The residence-time distributions could be modelled by well-known probability density functions. This approach would possess the advantage of considering the distributions that occur in actual systems, at the expense of inordinate computational effort (albeit less than that for the generalized solution). The computation time could be reduced by considering the particles as spheres, and conducting a one-dimensional simulation, although this would restrict the results to a particular shape. Further, the use of the radially well-mixed fluid assumption would remain, and without solution of the momentum transport equations, any temperature gradients within the fluid would still go unaddressed.

3.2 Determination of Particle Cold-Zone Temperature

Once the fluid medium temperatures are characterised, the particle conduction heat transfer equation remains to be solved for the slowest-heating particle. This has already been represented by eqn (26) subject to boundary condition (27), and can be solved by finite differences or finite elements, as discussed under bulk fluid temperature prediction. By calculating lethalities over each time step, it is possible to obtain the accumulated cold-zone lethality over the process duration, using eqn (1).

4 IMPORTANT UNKNOWN PARAMETERS

While the equations described above can be solved numerically, their accuracy is strongly dependent on accurate information for a number of parameters which determine the rate of heating of the particles, and whether or not a given particle in the group is the slowest heating. These are:

(1) Residence-time distribution (RTD) of particles within heat exchangers and hold tube.
(2) Fluid-to-particle convective heat transfer coefficients.
(3) Thermal properties of particles under process conditions.
(4) Rheological properties of carrier fluids under UHT conditions.

With the exception of particle thermal properties, the above parameters are interrelated, since rheology has a direct bearing on residence-time distribution as well as fluid-to-particle heat transfer coefficient. Some of

the more recent information related to these parameters will be sum-
marised in the following discussion.

4.1 Residence-Time Distribution (RTD)

The concept of residence-time distribution (Danckwerts, 1953) was recog-
nised long ago, when it became understood that materials entering
process vessels in continuous streams did not possess uniform residence
times. The problem assumes a high degree of importance with particulate
foods, because the fastest-moving particle can dictate process design.
Although the RTD concept has been in existence for considerable time,
no data were available for many years for particulate foods in SSHEs. A
number of studies on fluid foods included those of Roig *et al.* (1976) for
plate heat exchangers, and Heppell (1985a) for steam infusion systems.
The only early published study on SSHEs was that of Chen and
Zahradnik (1967) for liquids.

The first studies on RTD of particulates in SSHEs was performed by
Taeymans *et al.*, (1985a), who observed the behaviour of calcium alginate
beads of 6 mm diameter in water. They found that the mean solid phase
residence time was greater than that of the liquid phase, and that, as
the rotational speed of the dasher increased, the average solids residence
time increased. In general, it was noted that the particle RTD in this
situation fell somewhere between plug flow and a perfectly mixed
tank. At low dasher speeds, plug flow was approximated, while at high
dasher speeds, the perfectly mixed tank model was a better descriptor.
Taeymans *et al.* (1985b) noted that as the axial flow rate increased, the
mean residence time of the dispersed (solids) phase decreased and
aproached that of the liquid phase; and that as the solids concentration
increased, the mean residence time of the dispersed phase decreased.
Defrise and Taeymans (1988) reported the development of a model for
description of the $F(t)$ curve, by using a dead-time plus first-order lag type
model.

$$F(t_r) = 1 - [1 + (t_r - T_1)/T_2] \exp\{-(t_r - T_1)/T_2\} \tag{35}$$

where T_1 is the (reduced) lag time corresponding to the reduced residence
time of the fastest particle, T_2 is the (reduced) time constant of the
succeeding exponential curve, and t_r represents the reduced time, defined
as:

$$t_r = t/\bar{t}$$

Also defined was a parameter, (r), defined as the ratio of the reduced mean residence time $(\bar{t}_{dr})$ for the dispersed phase to that for the continuous phase $(\bar{t}_{cr})$:

$$r = \bar{t}_{dr}/\bar{t}_{cr} \qquad (36)$$

It was also noted that, by definition, $\bar{t}_{cr}$ would equal unity, if the mean continuous phase residence time $(\bar{t}_c)$ was used as the basis for nondimensionalisation of time.

Defrise and Taeymans also stated that it could be demonstrated that the parameter, r, could be described by the relationship

$$r = T_1 + 2T_2 \qquad (37)$$

This relation was supported by their experimental data.

One apparently significant finding of this research is that if two SSHEs are operated in series (one for heating and the other for cooling), the mean reduced residence time $(\bar{t}_{dr})$ of the dispersed phase was found to be a minimum if the dasher speeds of the two SSHEs were equal. When experiments were conducted under heating (as opposed to isothermal) conditions, the results were found to be considerably different owing to the temperature-induced change in the properties of the fluid during passage through the system.

Another series of studies that may be valuable in heat transfer modelling, are those reported by Härröd (1988), although they pertain primarily to liquids. One of the key points made is the transition from Couette flow to Taylor vortices as the dasher speed is increased. Härröd demonstrated that if the flow regime within the SSHE was permitted to be laminar, the result would be an instability in the temperature close to the blades at the outlet of the heat exchanger. Thus it is possible, in principle, for fluid to pass through a SSHE without significant heating if vortical flows are not achieved. This in effect, *necessitates* the achievement of vortical flow in SSHE operation. The implications of vortical flow are a high degree of mixing. Defrise and Taeymans (1988), also observed that under conditions where the axial Reynolds number (Re_{ax}) was in the laminar zone, and the rotational Reynolds number (Re_{rot}) was in the turbulent zone, the axial mixing effect (back-mixing) was very high.

The implication of these studies is that, in the SSHE, well-mixed flow is a necessity to ensure stable operation, and to this extent, models based on well-mixed fluid assumption in the SSHE would appear to be justified. The findings of Taeymans *et al.* (1985a) indicate that the fastest-moving particle has a considerably lower residence time than the average velocity fluid.

While the studies of Härröd and Taeymans and co-workers have been useful in developing a basic understanding of SSHE flows, much still remains to be learned for a variety of food products. Given the complexity of the phenomena involved, it would appear prudent to perform RTD studies for each proposed new product and processing system, until a substantial database is established.

Within the holding tube, a number of studies have been conducted using transparent tube sections and model food particles. Nesaratnam and Gaze (1987) showed a relationship between maximum normalised particle velocity (maximum particle velocity/average fluid velocity) and the particle Froude number (Fr_p), defined as:

$$Fr_p = V_f^2 / g d_p [(\rho_p/\rho_f) - 1]^{0.5} \qquad (38)$$

Dutta (1989) conducted studies with spherical polystyrene particles suspended in CMC solution. These studies indicated that the principal factors affecting the mean normalised particle velocity ($V_{nm} = V_{pm}/V_{fm}$) are a nondimensionalised viscosity (μ_{ND}), and the particle Froude number (Fr_p), where

$$\mu_{ND} = \eta V_f^{n-2} / \rho_f d_p^n \qquad (39)$$

Notably, the nondimensional viscosity is non-linearly related to the inverse of the generalised Reynolds number (Re_g) by the relation:

$$Re_g = 1/\{2^{n-3}[(3n+1)/n]^n \mu_{ND}\} \qquad (40)$$

Dutta (1989) found that V_{nm} was a stronger function of μ_{ND} than of Fr_p, although both parameters were found to have significant effects. It was observed that with viscous fluids, more particles were entrained within the flow stream than with low-viscosity fluids. Within the conditions of the study, the standard deviations of the distributions were found to depend on particle concentration. The fastest particle observed in these studies had a normalised velocity of 1·957; less than the theoretical limit of 2·0 for a Newtonian fluid in laminar tube flow, but in excess of the theoretical value for the particular pseudoplastic CMC (carboxymethylcellulose) solution used as a carrier. This effect may be due to 'channelling' phenomena, arising because of the presence of slow-moving particles at the bottom of the tube, which may reduce the effective cross-section and accelerate the fluid flowing above them. These studies were conducted at low particle concentrations owing to the difficulty involved in visualisation of particles at high concentrations; thus it cannot be stated with confidence that channelling phenomena would occur in higher concentration suspensions.

Berry (1989) also conducted studies on cubical rubber particles within holding tubes, and observed the importance of carrier viscosity in determining particle velocities. He also did not report any particles moving faster than twice the mean fluid velocity. These data indicate that a factor of two may represent a safe limit for process design. The cubical particles used in this study showed a greater tendency to clump than the spherical particles studied by Dutta. As with the studies of Dutta (1989) these experiments were conducted using low particle concentrations. As with SSHEs, much still remains to be learned regarding holding tube flows.

One point that remains to be addressed is the influence of system back-pressure on the flow of the slurry through the system. This is not well documented in the academic literature. However, it has been observed in industrial systems employing a downstream pump as a means of back-pressure, that the imbalance between the speeds of the two pumps can lead to oscillatory or pulsing motion through the process system. These phenomena could have significant influences on the RTD within the system.

4.2 Fluid-to-Particle Convective Coefficients
Since the relative velocities of fluids and particles in continuous flow are difficult to measure, it is difficult to estimate the value of the fluid-to-particle convective heat transfer coefficient (h_{fp}). Mathematical modelling studies have indicated that the estimate of h_{fp} can have significant effects on holding tube design if h_{fp} values are low. However, at high values of h_{fp}, the actual assumed value has little effect (Fig. 4).

The conservative approach has typically been to assume zero relative velocity between fluid and particle. Then, by using the Ranz and Marshall correlation (Incropera and deWitt, 1985):

$$Nu = 2 \cdot 0 + 0 \cdot 6 Re^{0 \cdot 5} Pr^{0 \cdot 33} \qquad (41)$$

and assuming zero relative velocity, a Nusselt number of 2·0 is obtained. The simulations of Sastry (1986) overlap this value of Nusselt number. For lack of a sufficient database of information, this conservative approach has been recommended (Sastry, 1989a).

However, there is an increasing body of literature which suggests that h_{fp} values may be considerably higher than predicted from a Nusselt number of 2·0. The earliest reported measurement of h_{fp} in continuous flow was by Heppell (1985b). He immobilised spores of *Bacillus stearothermophilus* within 3·1 mm diameter alginate beads, processed them in a

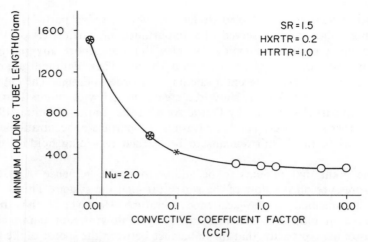

FIG. 4. Effect of dimensionless particle-to-fluid convective heat transfer coefficient (convective coefficient factor $= h_{fp}/h_{wf}$) on minimum required holding tube length. (Adapted from Sastry (1986), with permission from the Institute of Food Technologists.) SR, size ratio = particle size normalized against reference particle size of 0·0236m; HXRTR, heat exchanger residence time ratio = particle residence time/mean particle residence time within heat exchanger; HTRTR, holding tube residence time ratio = particle residence time/mean particle residence time within holding tube.

continuous sterilisation system, and calculated h_{fp} from the survivor count using a mathematical model. The h_{fp} values he reported ranged from 1850 W/m² °C ($Re = 5300$) to 7300 W/m² °C ($Re = 50\,000$).

Zuritz *et al.* (1990) determined h_{fp} values for stationary mushroom-shaped castings immersed in flowing pseudoplastic fluid (aqueous solutions of sodium carboxymethylcellulose; CMC) within a tube. Values of h_{fp} ranged from 548 to 1175 W/m² °C for the range of variables studied. The mean apparent viscosity (as defined by Skelland, 1967) of the fluids used ranged from 2 to 18 Pa s, and fluid temperature was 71°C. However, these experiments did not duplicate the true flow condition within real holding tubes, and consequently the data must be treated with caution.

Sastry *et al.* (1989) determined h_{fp} values in a holding tube situation by using hollow aluminium transducer particles which were allowed to flow within water through a transparent tube of representative dimensions. Temperatures were measured by means of a thermocouple attached to the particle. During these experiments, the thermocouple wire was moved at the same speed as that of an unconstrained particle (the speed of which was determined from preliminary experiments). The reported values of h_{fp} were in the range of 2000 W/m^2 °C for a particle of diameter 0·0239 m within a tube of diameter 0·0381 m. Subsequent data indicated that h_{fp} values were strongly dependent on flow rate and particle-to-pipe diameter ratio, and values of the order of 500 W/m^2 °C were observed for low flow rates and particle/pipe diameter ratios. The values would be expected to be considerably lower for more viscous fluids: Stoforos et al. (1989) determined h_{fp} within tube flow, using liquid crystal-coated particles, and found values that were comparable to those of Sastry et al. (1989).

Snyder (1986) determined h_{fp} between water and stationary shrimp-shaped particles, and found values for forced convection to range from 3478 to 5472 W/m^2 °C, and for free convection to range from 1073 to 1276 W/m^2 °C for heating, and 310 to 391 W/m^2 °C for cooling. Chandarana et al. (1988) have determined h_{fp} under UHT conditions within an experimental device consisting of a chamber within which a silicone cube was immobilised, and the fluid moved over it at slow, controlled rates. Experiments were conducted using various starch solutions, and low values of h_{fp} were obtained. While these studies have the merit of being conducted at UHT conditions, they do not represent the true flow situation within a continuously flowing mixture. Chang and Toledo (1989) also used a similar approach and found mean h_{fp} values for water to range from 239 to 303 W/m^2 °C depending on the relative velocity. For 35% sugar solution and zero relative velocity, h_{fp} values were found to range from 127 to 159 W/m^2 °C, indicating the possible occurrence of significant natural convection effects. These studies are useful to document the dependence of h_{fp} on relative velocity, in situations where the latter is measurable; however, the question of the magnitude or relative velocity within a real process system remains unresolved.

It is clear that further understanding of fluid-to-particle heat transfer is necessary for further development of aseptic processes for particulates. Highly conservative assumptions will result in safe but unappealing product; consequently it is necessary to be *conservative* but *realistic* as well. Results of mathematical models indicate that the assumed h_{fp} value loses its significance above a certain point. However, it is necessary to ensure whether or not a given product, under a given set of conditions, experiences h_{fp} values that are in this range.

4.3 Thermal Properties of Particles under Process Conditions
Recently, Larkin (1989) conducted a number of simulations on heat transfer to particles in continuous sterilisation systems, with the intention

of identifying critical parameters. One of the key findings of the study was that the assumed values of thermal properties played a significant role in the result. Thus, it is critical that accurate data be obtained regarding thermal conductivity of individual particles under process conditions.

The thermal conductivity (k) of foods typically ranges between a low point greater than that of air ($k \approx 0 \cdot 023$ W/m °C) to a high point slightly below that of water ($k \approx 0 \cdot 6$ W/m °C). Since most materials undergoing aseptic processing are likely to be deaerated and to possess high moisture contents, the value of k is likely to be closer to the higher end of the above range. A number of methods are now available to predict thermal properties based on composition. Murakami and Okos (1989) have provided an extensive review of this subject.

While the limits of variation in actual values of k may be established *a priori*, variations may occur due to phase transitions, such as starch gelatinisation or melting of lipids, which may alter the microstructure. This has been demonstrated for starches by Saravacos *et al.* (1989), where gelatinisation has been shown to significantly increase k over a range of temperatures up to 80°C. Therefore it is important to determine changes in k as a function of process conditions, so that these can be incorporated as process design considerations. Unfortunately, data on individual particle conductivities under high-temperature process conditions are largely unavailable.

Choi (1981) determined the thermal properties of tomato juice under high-temperature conditions; however, no studies on particulates were reported. Mosty of the literature on measurement of thermal conductivity of foods relates either to large food samples or materials in bulk. Sweat and Haugh (1974) reported the development of a line source probe for measurement of k for samples of minimum length of 0·0191 m (3/4 in). However, most particulate foods to be processed continuously are of considerably smaller size. Kustermann *et al.* (1981) determined k of individual corn kernels using the probe method. Owing to the small size of the kernels, the probes were threaded into them, and the test duration was limited to 8 s.

Zuritz *et al.* (1989) developed a device based on the approach of Fitch (1935), for the measurement of k for cylindrical samples of 6·4 mm diameter or greater. They used this apparatus to find k for kidney bean cotyledons, which were sanded to achieve the appropriate shape. The study was conducted at atmospheric pressure conditions, and would require adaptation to be applicable to pressurised process conditions.

Kravets and Diehl (1989) developed a bead thermistor method for determining k of samples as small as 5 mm diameter, under process temperatures. The method was reported to possess an accuracy of better than 10% over the 25°C to 125°C range. It is clear that the need for characterisation of variations in k exist, but this will depend on development of appropriate methodologies.

Another parameter with significant impact on sterilisation heat transfer calculations is the specific heat (C_p) of the food material. The critical importance of specific heat in process design has been documented by mathematical models. Like the thermal conductivity, the C_p value is likely to vary within specific limits, with the upper bound being that for water; however, if phase transitions occur, the transition enthalpies can result in 'effective' specific heats that are extremely large over short temperature ranges. Under these conditions, the solid would tend to strongly resist temperature change. This, in effect, necessitates the accurate characterisation of specific heat and phase transitions over the range of process temperatures.

Fortunately, specific heats (both real and 'effective') are somewhat easier to measure than thermal conductivity, owing to sophisticated techniques such as differential scanning calorimetry. It still remains important to test individual food materials for phase transition data before proceeding with simulations.

4.4 Rheological Properties of Carrier Fluids under Process Conditions

While the rheological properties of fluids have been noted to have significant influences on the RTDs and h_{fp} values in process systems, information on the influences of ultra-high-temperature (UHT) and pressurised process conditions on rheological properties is extremely limited. Most studies have relied on rheological characterisation at temperatures below 100°C, followed by extrapolation to higher temperatures, by use of activation energies based on the low-temperature data.

Dail (1989) measured the rheological properties of crosslinked waxy maize starch solutions under aseptic process temperatures, using a specially designed tube viscometer. The solutions were found to be dilatant in 22 out of 23 experiments. The consistency coefficient was found to be significantly affected by temperature, but only marginally by starch concentration, while the flow behaviour index was found to be significantly affected by both variables. One of the reasons for the observed behaviour may have been the continuing gelatinisation of the starch during passage of the solution through the tube viscometer.

Similar results have been observed by Bagley and Christianson (1982), Christianson *et al.* (1982) and Christianson and Bagley (1983), for starches that were either not completely gelatinised or cooked for short times.

The occurrence of dilatancy in carrier fluid is likely to have serious consequences, because of the sharp nature of the velocity profile that occurs for these fluids. The maximum velocity of a fluid during fully developed laminar tube flow may be calculated from the mean fluid velocity by:

$$v_{max} = \frac{(3n+1)}{(n+1)} \bar{v} \tag{42}$$

Dail (1989) reported n values as high as 2·076, which implies that the maximum fluid velocity would be expected to be 2·35 times the mean velocity, resulting in a higher factor of safety than for Newtonian fluid alone. In addition, a dilatant fluid would be expected to be more viscous in zones of high shear (such as boundary layers); consequently h_{fp} values would be adversely affected by such behaviour. These studies imply that if starches are to be used as a thickener for the carrier fluid, complete gelatinisation is necessary prior to aseptic processing. Steffe and Ofoli (1989) have reported preliminary findings in connection with the same studies, to the effect that the no-slip boundary condition is valid, and that strain history effects were important.

Härröd (1989a,b,c) conducted extensive investigations of the rheological behaviour of potato starch pastes over a range of shear rates $(6–450\,s^{-1})$, temperatures $(10–90°C)$, and starch concentrations (3–10%). An extended power-law model was developed to predict the properties of the pastes over the range of conditions tested (Härröd, 1989a). An interesting item of note in the studies of Härröd (1989c) was the observation of thixotropic behaviour at low ($<10\,Pa$) and high ($>150\,Pa$) shear stresses, and rheopexy at intermediate (10–150 Pa) shear stresses. The consequences were discussed by the author, who indicated that in holding tube flows, the occurrence of rheopectic behaviour near the tube wall could cause channelling of fluid at the axis, with greater than expected velocities for the fastest-moving segments.

The above studies underline the need to properly characterize rheological properties under aseptic process conditions. In particular, caution must be exercised in dealing with starch pastes as carrier fluids. While the above studies have provided valuable insight, it is evident that much still remains to be learned in this area.

5 OHMIC HEATING

A recent technology that has attracted interest is ohmic, or electrocon-ductive, heating, where a product may be heated by I^2R energy dissi-pation by passing an electrical current through it. The mechanism of heating is essentially internal energy generation. While the heat transfer problem within the holding section is the same as for conventional process systems, the problem formulation is considerably different within the ohmic heater.

While a number of electroconductive heating patents have existed over the years, the design referred to in the present analysis is that of the Electricity Council Research Centre in Great Britain (Simpson, 1983), which is licensed to APV International Ltd. The design consists of a pipe with electrodes placed within it at various intervals, with the current flowing between the electrodes along the length of the pipe.

5.1 Problem Formulation

As in the case of conventional process systems, the basic problem formulation may be made by considering heat, mass and momentum transfer considerations. Using a rationale similar to that considered earlier in relation to the mass transfer problem, attention may be focused primarily on the energy and momentum transfer problems. The energy transfer equation for the liquid phase during ohmic heating may be obtained from eqn (2), neglecting mechanical energy, viscous dissipation and radiative transport, but retaining the energy generation term:

$$\rho_f C_{pf} \frac{DT}{Dt} = \nabla.(k\nabla T) + q_f''' - q_p \tag{43}$$

The rate of energy trasfer to or from the particles is calculated from eqn (7) as before. The surface temperature of each particle (T_{spi}) must be determined from the conduction energy transfer equation:

$$\nabla.(k_{pi}\nabla T_{pi}) + q_p''' = \rho_{pi} C_{ppi} \partial T_{pi}/\partial t \tag{44}$$

subject to the surface condition

$$k_{pi}\nabla T_{pi}.\mathbf{n} = h_{fpi}(T_{spi} - T_{bf}) \tag{45}$$

Equation (43) must be solved iteratively with a system of equations similar to (44), for each particle in the system. As discussed earlier, in connection with conventional processing, this requires detailed knowledge of particle trajectories and velocities, which translates to simulta-neous solution of the momentum transfer equations for the fluid and each of the particles. Since this may be more easily accomplished by experi-ment or by use of simplifying assumptions, the generalised problem will not be elaborated further; rather the focus will be on the energy transport within fluid and particles. The key unknowns in eqns (43) and (44) are the energy generation rates, q_f''' and q_p''' which depend on the solution of the electrical transport problem in the system.

5.1.1 Electrical Energy Generation

The rate of energy generation per unit volume within a medium of electrical conductivity (σ) can be expressed by analysing an elementary control volume, yielding:

$$q''' = (\nabla V)^2 \sigma \qquad (46)$$

A similar equation has been used by Mizrahi et al. (1975) for studies on electroconductive blanching of corn-on-the-cob. For a two-phase system:

$$q_f''' = (\nabla V)^2 \sigma_f \qquad (47)$$

and

$$q_p''' = (\nabla V)^2 \sigma_p \qquad (48)$$

The energy generation terms can therefore be determined for each incremental volume of the process system, provided the voltage gradient across it is known. For the present situation involving current flow in a tubular conductor, the current flow is constant along the conductor length. The voltage gradient distribution is therefore a function of the distribution of resistances in the system. The resistance of a homogeneous element of thickness Δx (see Fig. 5) could be calculated based on the formula:

$$R = \Delta x / A \sigma \qquad (49)$$

where A is the cross-section area of the conductor. Since the electrical conductivity of foods is a function of temperature, the resistance would be expected to change with location within the system. The temperature-dependence of electrical conductivity has been expressed as (Biss et al., 1987):

$$\sigma_T = \sigma_{ref}[1 + m(T - T_{ref})] \qquad (50)$$

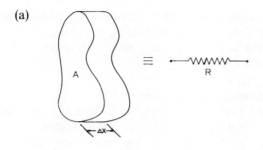

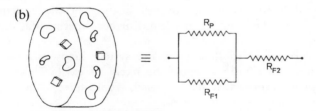

FIG. 5.   Models of equivalent resistances of (a) a homogeneous object, and (b) a solid–liquid mixture.

The electrical conductivity of the solid phase may follow a different pattern: this will be discussed in a succeeding section. For a heterogeneous food mixture, the resistance distribution is composition-dependent, and would vary with the local concentration of continuous and dispersed phases. If the concentration of solid phase within the tube is assumed uniform (Fig. 5), the resistance of each element of volume $A\Delta x$ would vary only with the temperature, the properties of the individual phases, and the orientation and shape of the solid particles. The resistance of each of the incremental volumes would have to be modelled as a combination of series and parallel resistances, and the overall resistance (R) would then be the sum of the resistances of each of the volumetric elements.

$$R = \sum_j R_j \tag{51}$$

Since the resistances and temperature distributions are interdependent, the electrical problem is coupled to the thermal problem, and they need to be addressed in a simultaneous or iterative fashion. An assumption of relevance in this connection is that, although individual fluid and particulate elements undergo transient heating, the overall heat exchange system may be treated as being at steady state with respect to longitudinal temperature profiles.

5.1.2 Problem Simplification and Solution

Since the generalised problem is one of considerable complexity, it is possible to make certain simplifying assumptions regarding fluid mixing to simplify the problem to one involving heat transfer within individual particles. The problem (eqn 44 rewritten for the slowest-heating particle, subject to condition (45)) may then be solved by a suitable numerical procedure. Results of preliminary simulations reported by Sastry (1989b) reveal the importance of particle and fluid electrical conductivities in the overall heating of the system under conditions of constant voltage gradient. Further experimental studies are continuing.

It would be expected that, since the system involves tubular flow, residence-time distributions would be likely to exist. These, and the influence of fluid-to-particle heat transfer, would have to be considered adequately in the modelling process.

5.2 Electrical Conductivity

The critical property influencing the success of ohmic heating is the electrical conductivity (σ). Data on σ are necessary for the entire range of temperatures of concern to aseptic processing. While the σ of a homogeneous food is generally easy to measure, the modelling of the effective resistance of a complex mixture is not as simple. Considerable data on σ are available for milk (although these are generally not at UHT conditions); indeed the value of σ has been used to test for mastitis in cows (Datta *et al.*, 1984). However, much information is needed for a wide variety of carrier fluids.

For liquids, equation (50) provides a reasonable model for prediction of σ. Palaniappan and Sastry (1989) have characterised the electrical conductivity of three commercial juices (tomato, orange and carrot), in the temperature range 25 to 100°C, and found the model to be a reliable descriptor of their behaviour. Further information is needed to address situations involving fine nonionic suspended solids, such as for many commercial sauces. In particular, effects such as particle size and orientation distributions need to be addressed adequately.

For solids with cellular structure, such as fruits and vegetables, the behaviour of σ with temperature is somewhat more complex. Early studies were conducted by Dedek (1946) in connection with beet juices. Brüniche–Olsen (1962) mentioned, in relation to sugar-beet extraction, that beet tissue exhibited a dramatic increase in σ upon heating to certain temperatures. The rate of change of σ was found to be temperature-dependent; as would be expected from kinetic laws. At a relatively low temperature (57°C) the change took 80 to 90 minutes, while at 80 to 85°C, the changes were virtually instantaneous. Heated ('killed') beet tissue was found to possess, upon cooling, a value of σ that was 8 to 15 times greater than unheated tissue. This thermally induced change in σ was attributed to coagulation of protoplasm.

It is to be expected that some other cellular tissue might behave similarly. This has been observed on a more limited scale in studies with potato tissue (Palaniappan et al., 1990). Similar studies need to be conducted for other materials.

The impact of increased electrical conductivity on process design is expected to be significant. This information suggests that for tissue that undergoes significant transitions in electrical conductivity, a preheating treatment may be desirable, prior to ohmic heating, to ensure the maximum value of electrical conductivity during sterilisation.

6 SUMMARY

Continuous sterilisation technology for particulate foods is in its infancy. Much of the current information on the subject has been gained since the mid-1980s. One of the key elements in the development of the technology is the development of a mathematical model. In the United States, the Food and Drug Administration considers mathematical modelling an integral part of the overall program for process filing (Dignan et al., 1989). While mathematical modelling of the transport problems in generality is a major challenge, the use of reasonable simplifying assumptions, and conservative but realistic safety factors, has been shown to result in models that yield helpful information relative to process design.

Despite recent advances, there remains a large body of public domain information that must be gained before the technology gains widespread and routine aceceptance. This has been described as being information on residence-time distributions, fluid-to-particle heat transfer coefficients, and high-temperature rheological and thermal properties. Technologies such as ohmic heating show interesting results, but another major unknown that must be addressed is the electrical conductivity of food materials over the range of process conditions.

Even with the information to ensure process safety, it will be necessary to use models that incorporate mass and momentum transfer considerations in more sophisticated forms to permit processing of complex and unusual products, and to ensure that the processes are optimised. With the widespread interest in this technology, models of increasing capability and sophistication will be likely to be needed in the years ahead.

REFERENCES

Åström, A., Ohlsson, T., Sköldebrand, C. & Falk, C. (1988). Prediction of food quality during continuous heat treatment of particulate products. *Proc. Intl. Symp. Prog. Food Pres. Proc.* Committee for Promotion of Scientific Research of the CERIA. Center for Education and Research of Food and Chemical Industries, Brussels, Belgium, April 12–14, 1988. Vol. 2, pp. 29–38.

Bagley, E. B. & Christianson, D. D. (1982). Swelling capacity of starch and its relationship to suspension viscosity—effect of cooking time, temperature and concentration. *J. Texture Studies*, **13**, 115.

Berry, M. R. (1989). Predicting fastest particle residence time. Presented at the First International Congress on Aseptic Processing Technologies, Indianapolis, IN, March 19–21, 1989.

Bird, R. B., Stewart, W. E. & Lightfoot, E. H. (1960). *Transport Phenomena*. John Wiley, New York.

Biss, C. H., Coombes, S. A. & Skudder, P. J. (1987). The development and application of ohmic heating for the continuous heating of particulate foodstuffs. Unpublished document. APV International Ltd, Crawley, West Sussex, UK; 10 pp.

Brady, J. F. & Bossis, G. (1985). The rheology of concentrated suspensions of spheres in simple shear flow by numerical simulation. *J. Fluid Mech.*, **155**, 105–29.

Brüniche-Olsen, H. (1962). *Solid–liquid Extraction with Particular Reference to Extraction of Sugar from Sugar Beets*. NYT Nordisk Forlag, Arnold Busck, Copenhagen.

Cerny, G. (1989). Studies on inactivation of bacterial spores in particulate foods. Presented at the First International Congress on Aseptic Processing Technologies, Indianapolis, IN, March 19–21, 1989.

Chandarana, D. I. & Gavin, A., III (1989). Establishing thermal processes for heterogeneous foods to be processed aseptically: a theoretical comparison of process development methods. *J. Food Sci.*, **54**, 198.

Chandarana, D. I., Gavin, A., III & Wheaton, F. W. (1988). Particle/fluid interface heat transfer during aseptic processing of foods. ASAE Paper No. 88-6599. American Society of Agricultural Engineers, St. Joseph, MI.

Chang, S. Y. & Toledo, R. T. (1989). Heat transfer and simulated sterilization of particulate solids in a continuously flowing system. *J. Food Sci*, **54**, 1017–23, 1030.

Chen, A. C. Y. & Zahradnik, J. W. (1967). Residence time distribution in a swept-surface heat exchanger. *Trans. ASAE*, **10**, 508–11.

Choi, Y. (1981). Effects of water content and temperature on the thermal properties of tomato juice. M.S. thesis, Purdue University, W. Lafayette, IN.

Christianson, D. D. & Bagley, E. B. (1983). Apparent viscosities of dispersions of swollen cornstarch granules. *Cereal Chem.*, **60**, 116.

Christianson, D. D., Baker, F. L., Loffredo, A. R. & Bagley, E. B. (1982). Correlation of microscopic structure of corn starch granules with rheological properties of cooked pastes. *Food Microstructure*, **1**, 13.

Dail, R. V. (1989). Rheological characterization of crosslinked waxy maize starch solutions under low acid aseptic processing conditions using tube viscometry techniques. M.S. thesis, Michigan State University, East Lansing, MI.

Danckwerts, P. V. (1953). Continuous flow system (distribution of residence times). *Chem. Engr. Sci.*, **1**, 1–13.

Datta, A. K., Puckett, H. B., Spahr, S. L. & Rodda, E. D. (1984). Real time acquisition and analysis of milk conductivity data. *Transactions of the ASAE*, **27**, 1204–10.

Davis, R. H., Serayssol, J. M. & Hinch, E. J. (1986). The elastohydrodynamic collision of two spheres. *J. Fluid Mech.*, **162**, 479.

de Ruyter, P. W. & Brunet, R. (1973). Estimation of process conditions for continuous sterilization of foods containing particulates. *Food Technol.*, **27**, 44–51.

Dedek, J. (1946). Lime salts—a measure of the purification of beet juices. *Socker*, **2**, 357.

Defrise, D. & Taeymans, D. (1988). Stressing the influence of residence time distribution on continuous sterilization efficiency. *Proc. Intl. Symp. Prog. Food Pres. Proc.* Committee for Promotion of Scientific Research at the CERIA. Center for Education and Research of Food and Chemical Industries, Brussels, Belgium, April 12–14, 1988. Vol. 1, pp. 171–84.

Dignan, D. M., Berry, M. R., Pflug, I. J. & Gardine, T. D. (1989). Safety considerations in establishing aseptic processes for low-acid foods containing particulates. *Food Technol.*, **43**, 118–21, 131.

Durst, F., Milojevic, D. & Schonung, B. (1984). Eulerian and Lagrangian predictions of particulate two-phase flows: a numerical study. *Appl. Math. Modeling*, **8**, 101–15.

Dutta, B. (1989). Velocity distributions of model food particle suspensions during holding tube flow. M.S. thesis, Ohio State University, Columbus, OH.

Fitch, D. L. (1935). A new thermal conductivity apparatus. *Amer. Phys. Teacher*, **3**, 135–6.

Garrote, R. L., Bertone, R. A. & Silva, E. R. (1984). Effect of soaking-blanching conditions on glucose losses in potato slices. *Can. Inst. Food Sci. Technol. J.*, **17**, 111–13.

Garrote, R. L., Silva, E. R. & Bertone, R. A. (1989). Effect of surface freezing on ascorbic acid retention in water-blanched potato strips. *J. Food Sci.*, **54**, 1090–1.

Goldsmith, H. L. & Mason, S. G. (1967). The microrheology of dispersions. In *Rheology, Theory and Applications*, ed. F. R. Eirich. Academic Press, New York.

Härröd, M. (1988). Flow patterns, mixing effects and heat transfer in scraped-surface heat exchangers. Ph.D. dissertation, Chalmers University of Technology, Göteborg, Sweden.

Härröd, M. (1989a). Modelling of flow properties of starch pastes prepared by different procedures. *J. Food Proc. Engr.*, **11**, 257–75.

Härröd, M. (1989b). Apparent concentration: a method to predict the flow properties of viscous foods for process applications. *J. Food Proc. Engr.*, **11**, 277–96.

Härröd, M. (1989c). Time-dependent behaviour of starch pastes with food process applications *J. Food Proc. Eng.*, **11**, 297–309.

Hayakawa, K.-I. & Rossen, J. L. (1977). Parametric analyses of simultaneous heat and moisture transfer in dehydrated food subjected to step or ramp functional changes in environmental transfer potentials. *Lebensm. Wiss. u. Technol.*, **10**, 217–24.

Heppell, N. J. (1985a). Comparison of residence time distributions of water and milk in an experimental UHT sterilizer. *J. Food Eng.*, **4**, 71–84.

Heppell, N. J. (1985b). Measurement of the liquid–solid heat transfer coefficient during continuous sterilization of liquids containing solids. Presented at the 4th Intl. Cong. Engr. Food, Edmonton, Alberta, Canada, July 7–10, 1985.

Incropera, F. P. & deWitt, D. P. (1985). *Introduction to Heat Transfer*. John Wiley, New York.

Kravets, R. R. & Diehl, K. C. (1989). Method for measurement of thermal conductivity of small food particulates at thermal processing temperature. Abstract no. 557, presented at the 1989 IFT Annual Meeting, Chicago, IL, June 25–29, 1989.

Kustermann, M., Scherer, R. & Kutzbach, H. D. (1981). Thermal conductivity and diffusivity of shelled corn and grain. *J. Food Proc. Engr.*, **43**, 137–53.

Larkin, J. W. (1989). Critical parameters in aseptic particulate processing systems. Paper no. 89-6554 presented at the 1989 ASAE International Winter Meeting, New Orleans, LA, December, 12–15, 1989. American Society of Agricultural Engineers, St. Joseph, MI.

Lee, J. H. & Singh, R. K. (1988). Determination of lethality in a continuous sterilization system containing particulates. Paper no. 88-6600 presented at the 1988 ASAE International Winter Meeting, Chicago, IL, December 13–16, 1988. American Society of Agricultural Engineers, St. Joseph, MI.

Manson, J. E. & Cullen, J. F. (1974). Thermal process simulation for aseptic processing of foods containing discrete particulate matter. *J. Food Sci.*, **39**, 1084–9.

Mizrahi, S., Kopelman, I. J. & Perlman, J. (1975). Blanching by electroconductive heating. *J. Food Technol.*, **10**, 281–8.

Murakami, E. G. & Okos, M. R. (1989). Measurement and prediction of thermal properties of foods. *Food Properties and Computer-Aided Engineering of Food Processing Systems*, ed. R. P. Singh and A. G. Medina. 1988: NATO ASI Series: Series E: Applied Sciences, 168: 3–48. Kluwer, Dordrecht.

Nesaratnam, R. & Gaze, J. E. (1987). Application of a particle technique to the study of particle sterilization under dynamic flow. Technical Memorandum No. 461. Campden Food Preservation Research Association, Chipping Campden, UK.

Palaniappan, S. & Sastry, S. K. (1989). Experminental studies on electroconductive (ohmic) heating of liquids. Paper no. 89-6553 presented at the 1989 ASAE International Winter Meeting, New Orleans, LA, December 12–15, 1989. American Society of Agricultural Engineers, St. Joseph, MI.

Palaniappan, S. & Sastry, S. K. (1991). Electrical conductivities of selected solid foods during ohmic heating. *J. Food Proc. Engr.*, **14**, 221–36.

Rao, M, A. (1989) Developments in measurement of rheological properties of food dispersions. Food Properties and Computer-Aided Engineering of Food Processing Systems, ed. R. P. Singh and A. G. Medina 1988: NATO ASI Series: Series E, Applied Sciences, 168: 317–9. Kluwer, Dordrecht.

Rao, M. A., Bourne, M. C. & Cooley, H. J. (1981). Flow properties of tomato concentrates. *J. Texture Studies*, **12**, 521–38.

Roig, S. M., Vitali, A. A., Ortega-Rodriguez, E. & Rao, M. A. (1976). Residence time distribution in the holding section of a plate heat exchanger. *Lebensm. Wiss. u. Technol.*, **9**, 255–6.

Saguy, I. & Karel, M. (1980). Modeling of food quality deterioration during food processing and storage. *Food Technol.*, **34**, 78–85.

Saravacos, G. D., Karathanos, V. T., Drouzas, A. E. & Maroulis, Z. B. (1989). Effect of gelatinization of the heat and mass transport properties of starch materials. Paper presented at the Fifth International Congress on Engineering and Food, Cologne, Federal Republic of Germany, May 28–June 3, 1989.

Sastry, S. K. (1986). Mathematical evaluation of process schedules for aseptic processing of low-acid foods containing discrete particulates. *J. Food Sci.*, **51**, 1323–8, 1332.

Sastry, S. K. (1989a). Process evaluation in aseptic processing. In *Developments in Food Preservation—5*, ed. Stuart Thorne. Elsevier Applied Science, London, pp. 177–206.

Sastry, S. K. (1989b). A model for continuous sterilization of particulate foods by ohmic heating. Paper presented at the Fifth International Congress on Engineering and Food, Cologne, Federal Republic of Germany, May 28–June 3, 1989.

Sastry, S. K., Heskitt, B. F. & Blaisdell, J. L. (1989). Convective heat transfer at particle–liquid interface in aseptic processing systems. *Food Technol.*, **43** 132–6, 143.

Schwartzberg, H. G. & Chao, R. Y. (1982). Solute diffusivities in leaching processes. *Food Technol.*, **36**, 73.

Simpson, D. P. (1983). Apparatus for heating electrically conductive flowable media. US Patent No. 4,417,132.

Skelland, A. H. P. (1967). *Non-Newtonian Flow and Heat Transfer*. John Wiley, New York.

Snyder, G. (1986). Mathematical model for prediction of temperature distribution in thermally processed shrimp. M.S. thesis, University of Florida, Gainesville, FL.

Steffe, J. F. & Ofoli, R. Y. (1989). Food engineering problems in rheology and non-Newtonian fluid mechanics. In *Food Properties and Computer-Aided Engineering of Food Processing Systems*, ed. R. P. Singh and A. G. Medina. NATO ASI Series E: Applied Sciences, Vol. 168: 313–16. Kluwer, Dordrecht.

Stoforos, N. G., Park, K. L. & Merson, R. L. (1989). Heat transfer in particulate foods during aseptic processing. Abstract no. 545, presented at the 1989 IFT Annual Meeting, Chicago, IL, June 25–29, 1989.

Sweat, V. E. & Haugh, C. G. (1974). A thermal conductivity probe for small food samples. *Trans. ASAE*, **17**, 56–8.

Taeymans, E., Roelans, J. & Lenges, J. (1985a). Residence time distributions in a horizontal SSHE used for UHT processing of liquids containing solids. Presented at the 4th Intl. Cong. Engr. Food, Edmonton, Alberta, Canada, July 7–10, 1985.

Taeymans, E., Roelans, J. & Lenges, J. (1985b). Influence of residence time distribution on the sterilization effect in a scraped-surface heat exchanger used for processing liquids containing solid particles. In *International Union of Food Science and Technology (IUFOST) Symp. Aseptic Proc. Packag. Foods Proc.*, September 9–12, Tylosand, Sweden, 100–7.

Tomasula, P. & Kozempel, M. F. (1989). Diffusion coefficients of glucose, potassium and magnesium in Maine Russet Burbank and Maine Katahdin Potatoes from 45 to 90°C. *J. Food Sci.*, **54**, 985–9, 1046.

Zuritz, C. A., Sastry, S. K., McCoy, S. C., Murakami, E. G. & Blaisdell, J. L. (1989). A device for measuring the thermal conductivity of small food particles. *Trans. ASAE*, **32**, 711–18.

Zuritz, C. A., McCoy, S. C. & Sastry, S. K. (1990). Convective heat transfer coefficients for irregular particles immersed in non-Newtonian fluids during tube flow. *J. Food Engr.*, **11**, 159–74.

Chapter 7

THE APPLICATION OF TIME–TEMPERATURE INDICATOR TECHNOLOGY TO FOOD QUALITY MONITORING AND PERISHABLE INVENTORY MANAGEMENT

JOHN HENRY WELLS

Department of Biological and Agricultural Engineering,
Louisiana State University,
Baton Rouge, LA, USA

and

R. PAUL SINGH

Department of Agricultural Engineering,
Department of Food Science and Technology,
University of California,
Davis, CA, USA

1 INTRODUCTION

A time–temperature indicator is a device that monitors the combination of time and temperature, exhibiting a change in color (or other physical characteristic) in response to the temperature history to which it is exposed. This definition includes those devices that have been developed from a theoretical basis (a programmed rate reaction), as well as those that have been developed from empirical consideration (an observed phase change). There exists a wide range of devices that could be classified as time–temperature indicators. For example, an ice cube could be used as time–temperature indicator, since the rate at which the ice cube melts is a direct result of the time–temperature exposure history. Similarly, an indicator could be made from a temperature–sensitive chemical (or enzymatic) reaction, where the products of reaction could be monitored to gauge the temperature exposure history.

Indicators that have been introduced commercially utilize a variety of concepts to monitor changes in temperature with time. These concepts

271

include the use of bacteria or enzymes that interact with a substance to change the solution chemistry, chemical substances that polymerize to form new substances with different physical properties, capsules that rupture upon freezing, thereby releasing liquid dyes when thawed, oils that diffuse along a paper or fabric wick in proportion to temperature, and devices that mechanically deform as temperature fluctuates.

Time–temperature indicators have been used primarily to monitor temperature conditions during the handling of pharmaceuticals, blood plasma, and temperature-sensitive vaccines. In addition to monitoring the viability of medical supplies, a potential application for time–temperature indicators lies in monitoring quality changes in perishable foods. Recent investigations have confirmed that time–temperature indicators can be used to monitor and predict temperature–related changes in food quality during storage and distribution. The use of time–temperature indicators as food quality monitors has a potentially important application in the area of perishable inventory management.

This review outlines the historical developments and recent advances in time–temperature indicator technology. State-of-the-art time–temperature indicating systems are described, and the motivation for using indicators in food quality monitoring is discussed. Finally, the food distribution chain is examined, and an application of time–temperature indicators to perishable inventory management is presented.

2. HISTORICAL OVERVIEW OF TIME–TEMPERATURE INDICATORS

2.1 Development of Time–Temperature Indicator Technology
Earliest work on a simple device that could be used to monitor time and temperature in research surroundings was reported by Andersen (1949). However, it is believed that 'the first practical time–temperature indicator offered to the frozen food industry' was developed by Renier et al. (1962). This device was developed because 'the lack of an adequate quality reserve monitoring control scheme for frozen foods has been a source of problems to many'. Renier et al. (1962) believed that a time–temperature indicator must be able to monitor specific time–temperature relationships in frozen products and cautioned that for proper use in applications of food quality monitoring, indicator response would need to be calibrated to the specific changes in food quality.

Guadagni (1963) reported on a laboratory evaluation of the device developed by Renier *et al.* and observed:

Unfortunately, the (time) temperature response of different frozen foods varies considerably. Hence, it is necessary to know the (time) temperature response of both the indicator and the food in question. With this information, it should be possible to make a rough estimate of possible quality changes from device readings.

The time–temperature indicator was commercially developed by Honeywell, but the findings of these evaluations are now irrelevant (Honeywell no longer manufactures a time–temperature indicator). In historical retrospect, it seems the Honeywell device may have been slightly ahead of its time. Several years later the device was mentioned in a proceedings discussion (Van't Root, 1973):

H. W. SYMONS—Mr. Van't Root said he did not know why the Honeywell Time–Temperature Integrator is no longer manufactured. The last time I purchased one of these integrators from Honeywell I was told that the demand was insufficient for them to continue manufacture.

Interest in developing a time and temperature monitor continued as Hu (1971) reported the development of an indicator that utilized oxygen permeation through a plastic film. Since the rate of oxygen transmission through a film is temperature-dependent, by enclosing an oxygen reactive solution within a sealed pouch, the indicator would record the effect of time and temperature in the products of the reaction. The result of reaction was a change in solution color (red to clear). Hu (1971) demonstrated film combinations that could be used in storage temperatures from 5·5 to 55°C and discussed possible applications to monitoring storage of semi-perishable military rations.

Bengtsson *et al.* (1972) reviewed the literature attempting to systematize the time–temperature tolerance data for frozen food by defining the variability of such data for practical use in estimating quality loss during frozen storage. It was hoped that by developing an indicator that conformed to time–temperature relationships in frozen food, the unacceptable performance that had plagued previously developed indicators would be overcome. After presenting 95% confidence interval bands for different groups of food and different quality criteria, Bengtsson *et al.* concluded:

Taking into account the considerable variability in time–temperature response of product quality, it appears that an accurate time–temperature integrator–indicator would probably be more useful for giving information about the quality of the 'handling' in the freezer chain than about the quality of individual products.

Other ideas and uses of time–temperature indicators were expressed by Schoen and Byrne (1972). Schoen and Byrne examined 44 patented and unpatented 'defrost' indicators and stated that the 'ideal' indicator for frozen foods should reliably inform an individual when to discard a product. It was pointed out that no 'ideal' time–temperature indicator had yet been developed because of the subjectivity in defining food quality and the difficulty in deciding which relevant storage variables an indicator should measure (i.e. ambient temperature, air velocity, heat capacity, initial temperature, etc.). They cautioned that an 'ideal' indicator would be limited as a food quality decision-making tool because of incorrect interpretations. Schoen and Byrne concluded:

> In order to use any indicator as a decision-making tool, it is important to determine what product attributes or characteristics we are asking the indicator to measure and then to be aware that the question of false positives and negatives must be carefully considered. This is one reason why many people in the frozen food industry are inclined to consider the whole subject of indicators at this time as a monitoring tool rather than a decision-making tool.

The false positive (and false negative) indications that Schoen and Byrne referred to are indicator responses that may falsely indicate product quality changes that do not actually exist (and not indicate changes that do exist).

Hayakawa and Wong (1974) investigated the performance of commercially available time–temperature indicators in the context of their theoretical correlations with quality change reactions. Bryne (1976) reviewed commercially available time–temperature indicators describing these devices as defrost indicators, time–temperature integrators, or time–temperature integrator/indicators. It was pointed out that certain time–temperature indicators lose the ability to accurately respond if stored for relatively long periods of time before they are activated and put to use. Byrne stated that simple time–temperature indicators do not require the precision and accuracy of recording thermometers. Additionally, he challenged the manufacturers of time–temperature indicators to develop a 'means for arresting the action (indicator response) at any given point so that records could be collected from many locations over extended periods without field observers'.

Kramer and Farquhar (1976) (with related discussion of Labuza (1976), Witonsky (1976), and Hayakawa (1976)) documented the performance of commercially available and prototypical time–temperature indicators. The indicators investigated represented a new generation of devices that favored response at lower temperatures with rates of change increasing with temperature, opposed to the ('ideal') defrost-type indicators, previously discussed. Kramer and Farquhar determined that the indicators evaluated could be used in the food industry but that some improvements in method of activation, scaling, readout, and reliability were still required. It was also proposed that when using temperature indicators with most frozen foods, an indicator's 'point of expiration should coincide with time–temperature accumulation of one year at $-20°C$'.

An investigation of the performance of a chemical time–temperature integrating device was reported by Arnold and Cook (1977). Their findings concluded that there existed a lack of reproducibility between devices of the same make and model. Schubert (1977) proposed a method of calculating quality changes in frozen food products from temperature history during storage. The theoretical response of a time–temperature indicator based on capillary liquid transport was compared with hypothesized food quality levels for different temperature functions.

The design and development of a biological time–temperature indicator (I-POINT Temperature/Time Monitor) was discussed by Blixt and Tiru (1976). The enzyme/substrate/pH-indicator response mechanism of this time–temperature indicator was presented and was claimed to be 'superior to purely chemical or physical indicating methods and devices' because it more closely responded to the biological changes that occur in food systems.

Fields and Prusik (1983) explained the operating principles of the LifeLines Freshness Monitor. They envisioned the incorporation of this indicator into a food 'inventory rotation index', suggesting that 'appropriate charts could be developed which would correlate quality levels of different products to the indicator index number, so that products with excessive quality loss due to thermal abuse could be identified'.

Manske (1983) outlined the motivation and criteria that were the basis for the 3M Monitor Mark time–temperature indicator. It is cited that 'one of the most widespread causes of quality loss in perishable products is temperature abuse during distribution'. This, coupled with the 'increased levels of product quality consciousness and awareness of product liability', had set the stage for the development of a low-cost device to monitor the thermal history of perishable food products.

The performance of commercially available time–temperature indicators has been examined by several investigators (Hayakawa and Wong, 1974; Sanderson-Walker, 1975; Arnold and Cook, 1977; Farquhar, 1977 and 1982). Although these studies had been conducted to evaluate the performance of time–temperature indicators under known temperature conditions, Wells and Singh (1985) pointed out that previous studies had provided useful data about the end-point measures of indicator response but lacked information regarding the kinetic interpretation of the indicator scale readings. In light of the interest in 'shelf-life kinetics', Wells and Singh evaluated four commercially available time–temperature indicators in an effort to revise the information on indicator response in conditions that simulated frozen food transport. The study concluded that indicators could be used to monitor temperature conditions during frozen transport, but because of high response variability in the indicators examined, statistical sampling and inspection procedures must accompany any implementation of time–temperature indicators. In later studies, Singh and Wells (1987a) reiterated the need for statistical sampling and proposed a framework to develop operating characteristics curves for the interpretation of indicator response in decisions relating to inventory management.

2.2 Classification of Time–Temperature Indicators

Several classification schemes for time–temperature indicators can be found in the literature. Schoen and Byrne (1972) categorized proposed and patented indicators based on the information provided by the indicator response. They proposed six categories: (1) go/no go without delay, (2) go/no go with delay, (3) time/temperature integrators, (4) real-time recorders, (5) multi-temperature go/no go, and (6) multi-temperature with time element. This classification was strictly based on the response information obtained from each indicator. For example, a 'go/no go without delay' type of indicator would provide a discrete response (go or no go) immediately after a preset single or combined effect of time and/or temperature had been achieved.

Later, Byrne (1976) simplified this classification scheme by placing the various time–temperature indicating devices into three groupings: (1) defrost indicators, (2) time–temperature integrators, and (3) time–temperature integrating indicators. The basis for this three group classification was a combination of response information and device function. According to Byrne, the 'integrators' respond to the accumulated effect of time and temperature (a functional basis); and the difference between 'integrators' and 'integrating indicators' was one of scale interpretation and quantization (an informational basis).

Kramer and Farquhar (1976) stated that all indicators were of two types: (1) defrost indicators and (2) time–temperature integrators. The basis for this categorization was strictly device-functional, with the 'defrost indicator' responding to the single effect of temperature and the 'time–temperature integrators' responding to the accumulated effect of time and temperature.

The classification of time–temperature indicators has evolved from an informational basis to a functional basis. There has, however, been an important oversight in the functional-based categorizations mentioned to this point. Consider the classification scheme of Kramer and Farquhar (1976). They define 'defrost indicators' as those devices that respond when temperature conditions are such as to cause a frozen product to begin to thaw. This type of device only responds to a limited portion of the temperature exposure history, namely that temperature above a specified threshold temperature. In contrast, the 'time–temperature integrator' would operate continuously at all temperatures to which it was exposed. The difficulty with this two-group classification is that it ignored the type of device that would respond to the combined influence of time and temperature only after a specific temperature threshold had been exceeded. Byrne (1976) alluded to this kind of device by pointing out that certain time–temperature integrators start to react as soon as some activating temperature has been reached. Thus, there exist time–temperature integrators, and more generally time–temperature indicators, that respond to either the full temperature exposure history or the partial temperature history.

Wells and Singh (1985) characterized the performance of four commercially available time–temperature indicators (Table 1) and noted a functional classification for time–temperature indicators based on temperature history. The two classes of time–temperature indicators suggested were: (1) partial-history indicator (devices that do not respond unless some temperature threshold is exceeded), or (2) full-history indicator (devices that respond continuously, independent of a temperature threshold). The difference in the way the full- and partial-history indicators respond to the same temperature history is shown in Fig. 1. Because a full-history indicator responds to the complete range of exposure temperatures, this type of device provides a common means of comparing different temperature histories. The convention of designating a time–temperature indicator as either a partial-history or a full-history indicator will be used throughout the remainder of this review.

TABLE 1
INDICATOR PERFORMANCE CHARACTERISTICS (WELLS AND SING, 1985)

	'A'	'B'	'C'	'D'
Classification	Partial-history	Full-history	Partial-history	Partial-history
Response mechanism	Fluid capillary	Enzyme reaction	Liquid diffusion	Fluid capillary
Response scale	Linear 0–6 h	Color references 0, 1, 2, 3	Logarithmic 0–10	Linear 0–1000 (degree-min)
Means of activation	Hand	Hand/mechanical	Hand	Hand
Preconditioning	Yes	No	Yes/No	Yes

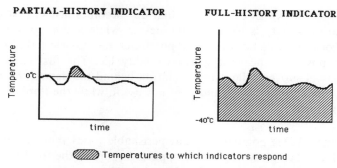

PARTIAL-HISTORY INDICATOR   FULL-HISTORY INDICATOR

▨ Temperatures to which indicators respond

FIG. 1.   Types of time–temperature indicators.

2.3 Time–Temperature Indicators and Food Quality Assurance

For many years the prevailing thought has been that time–temperature indicators were unsuitable for monitoring time–temperature-related changes in food quality or for use in inventory management. Schoen (1983) stated that time–temperature indicators 'can be used at any point in the distribution chain as a decision-making tool, a monitoring tool, or an informational tool'. Furthermore Schoen advocated that indicators were best used only as monitoring tools to determine heat abuse problems in distribution and handling. Schoen emphasized that no direct inference about product quality should be made from arbitrary indicator readings, and that an indicator should not be trusted in deciding whether a product was acceptable or unacceptable.

Earlier Sanderson-Walker (1975) had discussed various aspects of the cold chain and called for an improvement in the quality of frozen foods through implementation of quality assurance procedures during distribution and storage. Previously the use of open dating and time–temperature indicators had been suggested as a means to maintain the delivery of high-quality frozen products to the consumer (Sanderson-Walker, 1979). Sanderson-Walker stated that the 'sell-by' date, required in many countries, actually detracted from proper temperature control and product management because of false assurances that the date provided. The author conceded that the use of time–temperature indicators could be an aid in quality assurance but concluded that the cost of indicators, even when used to a limited extent, was prohibitive. It was also hypothesized as to what the consumer behavior would be with regards to a device that clearly indicated product quality. Sanderson-Walker stated:

There would seem to be only three possible reactions. The intending purchaser could rummage for the package with the most quality life still intact, in which case first in first out becomes last in first out. A second possibility is to ignore the device, while a third possibility is that conscience dictates that the purchaser should select the package which possesses the least residual quality life. The first category of purchasers subverts the whole intention behind the device; the second is oblivious to the device and does not use it; while the third probably does not exist.

Farquhar (1981) pointed out that perishable foods (both refrigerated and frozen) have grown to be an important part of the food supply in western countries. He stated that human and mechanical factors were responsible for breakdowns in proper handling procedures, resulting in loss of temperature control and accelerated quality deterioration. Four quality control/quality assurance tools were proposed for use in perishable distribution: (1) spot temperature checks; (2) time–temperature recorders; (3) open dating; and (4) time–temperature indicators. Time–temperature indicators were believed to be the most promising quality control tool available.

Rose (1981) speculated that the use of time–temperature indicators had been limited because the requirements demanded by potential user were not being met in indicator design. He reported that potential users required time–temperature indicators to be economically feasible, to produce a clear and irreversible response, to relate directly or indirectly to the quality of the product being monitored, and to 'allow corrective action to be taken during the distribution process so that product waste can be minimal'. The corrective action requirement represented a new perspective on time–temperature indicator usage and was contrary to the philosophy of the previous decade, that an indicator should identify a product as acceptable/unacceptable. This approach also presented the notion that indicators might be most effectively used by shippers and suppliers of frozen food rather than by consumers.

The complexity of the frozen food distribution system was detailed by Farquhar (1982). The quality control procedures, including spot temperature checks, use of time/temperature recorders and open dating, were compared with the use of time/temperature indicators as product handling monitors. Two schemes incorporating time–temperature indicators to monitor the handling of fish and beef throughout the distribution chain were proposed. Blixt (1983) reiterated the weakness of 'date-stamping' (open-dating), stating that it only indicates total storage time, and not the combination of time and temperature that crucially influences quality loss during distribution of perishables.

Farquhar (1983) proposed the use of time–temperature indicators in various aspects of the distribution of frozen and refrigerated seafood. Laboratory testing, sensory analysis, and physical inspection were stated to be neither practicable nor cost-justified as quality assurance procedures in the retail and food service level of seafood distribution. Farquhar proposed an alternative scheme for ensuring proper handling of perishable products. The proposed scheme favored the use of time–temperature indicators as an integral part of a buyer's specification and utilized indicator response to predict the product's shelf life.

The prospect of using time–temperature indicators in food distribution management was detailed by Wells et al. (1987). These authors presented a methodology by which indicators could be used to help establish a basis for distribution action (e.g., product shipment, recall, price restructuring) of frozen foods. The approach used a graphical representation of food quality in the form of a contour plot of quality for known time and temperature combinations. The response of a time–temperature indicator was superimposed on the plot, and regions of action and non-action were defined based on sensory responses for a specific quality attribute. The graphical representation called attention to the need for distribution action based on food quality as estimated by the length of time in storage and indicator response. Individual contour graphs would be needed for each combination of indicator model and quality attribute. This was the first work published to formally systemize a method to use time–temperature indicators in food distribution management.

3 PRESENT TIME–TEMPERATURE INDICATOR TECHNOLOGY

Time–temperature indicators have been used to a limited extent within the food industry as temperature history monitors, but have not been adopted widely in commercial use as food quality monitors. The use of time–temperature indicators has been limited because of their high cost, poor durability, lack of reliability, inability to measure appropriate quality parameters, and the lack of a method to use indicator response in inventory management (Farquhar, 1977; Wells, 1987). During the last decade, however, several advances have taken place to reduce indicator cost and increase measurement reliability, and many individuals within the food industry now believe that the stage has been prepared for widespread commercial use of time–temperature indicators. Recently, the authors were able to survey current indicator technology and evaluate commercially available devices with respect to response and functionality (Singh *et al.*, 1984, 1986; Singh and Wells, 1987a). The indicators examined during these studies are described and discussed below according to the functional classification of each indicating device.

3.1 Partial-History Time–Temperature Indicators
Partial-history time–temperature indicators are devices that do not respond unless exposed to temperatures above (or below) a predetermined threshold. Partial-history indicators yield either a limited response or extended response in conjunction with temperature exposures that violate the threshold settings. Because the partial-history indicator responds only to fluctuations in temperature above (or below) certain thresholds, this type of indicator is generally used in applications of temperature monitoring.

3.1.1 *MonitorMark Thaw Indicator*
The MonitorMark Thaw Indicator (Packaging Systems Division Laboratory/3M, St Paul, MN) is a partial-history time–temperature indicator that responds irreversibly when temperatures rise above a preset threshold. Several models of the thaw indicator are available from the manufacturer, with each model having a different threshold or activation temperature. The MonitorMark Thaw Indicator is shown in Fig. 2(a) and consists

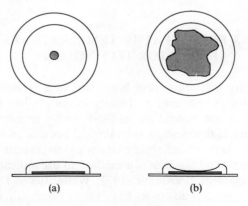

(a)   (b)

FIG. 2.   MonitorMark Thaw Indicator.

of an adhesive-backed circular base with a paper blotter containing a crystalline dye and domed over-housing of heavy paper. The crystalline dye has a melting point corresponding to the activation temperature of the indicator. When the heavy paper dome is depressed it is placed in contact with the blotter containing the dye. As the temperature exceeds the melting point of the dye, the liquid dye diffuses into the over-housing, thus giving a visual indication that the temperature exposure has exceeded the threshold (Fig. 2(b)). The thaw indicator can be used to identify temperature conditions that would be considered abusive or detrimental to product quality.

3.1.2 MonitorMark Freeze Indicator

The MonitorMark Freeze Indicator (Packaging Systems Division Laboratory/3M, St Paul, MN 55144) is a partial-history time–temperature indicator that responds irreversibly when temperature exposure falls below a preset threshold. This indicator is available from the manufacturer in a model that will register a response when exposed to temperature below $0°C$, or for other temperatures on special request. The Monitor-Mark Freeze Indicator is constructed with a 2-mm (O.D.) glass capillary exposed to atmosphere at one end, and attached to an 8-mm (O.D.) spherical glass bulb at the other end. The capillary and bulb are enclosed in a $75 \times 8 \times 10$-mm high plastic housing laminated to a pressure-sensitive adhesive backing (Fig. 3). The indicator is made up of four working fluids, one in the bulb and three in the capillary. As the indicator is exposed to temperatures below $0°C$, one of the capillary fluids freezes and contracts in volume, thereby allowing a second colored liquid to pass into the bulb by molecular affinity. As a result the liquid in the bulb

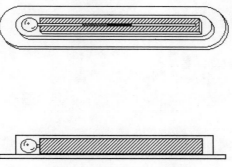

FIG. 3.   MonitorMark Freeze Indicator.

becomes colored showing that the indicator has been exposed to a temperature below 0°C. The working fluids within the bulb and capillary are proprietary. A potentially important application for the Monitor-Mark Freeze Indicator is in monitoring storage temperatures of products that are subject to chilling injury.

3.1.3 MonitorMark Extended Response Indicators

The MonitorMark Extended Response Indicator (Packaging Systems Division/3M, St Paul, MN) is shown in Fig. 4. This partial-history indicator consists of five parts layered from the bottom as follows: 88- by 19-mm cardboard rectangle; a 28- by 12-mm pad containing a blue dye within a carrier substance; a plastic slip-tab for isolating the dye; a 7-mm blotter paper wick; and another 88- by 19-mm cardboard rectangle with five window cutouts. The bottom piece has a pressure-sensitive adhesive backing and the remaining surfaces are encased in transparent plastic film.

Prior to activation, the MonitorMark Extended Response Indicator must be stored at a temperature lower than the carrier substance's melting temperature (the indicator response temperature). The indicator can be attached to a product with the adhesive backing and prepared for

FIG. 4. MonitorMark Extended Response Indicator.

response by removing the slip-tab. Removal of the slip-tab brings the pad and wick in contact. The dye remains contained within the pad until the carrier substance undergoes phase change due to temperature exposure above the response temperature. Upon phase change, the carrier substance and dye enter the wick and begin to diffuse along its length, moving more rapidly along the wick at high temperatures. Indicator response is measured by reading the distance the dye front has migrated past the windows in the indicator.

The response of the MonitorMark Extended Response Indicator to a variable temperature treatment is shown in Fig. 5. The extended response nature of this indicator is seen as the indicator does not reach a full-scale response until after a second high-temperature exposure (Wells and Singh, 1985). During the +20°C and +5°C steps, the MonitorMark Extended Response Indicator responded very rapidly and then continued to respond even when moved back to the −18°C storage condition. Although the −18°C temperature was lower than the response temperature of the indicator, continued response (creeping effect) was a result of a combination of temperature close to the indicator response temperature and a continued, but slowed, diffusion of the dye already in solution within the paper wick. This indicator has an important application to the estimation of shelf-life reduction due to temperature exposures above certain critical thresholds.

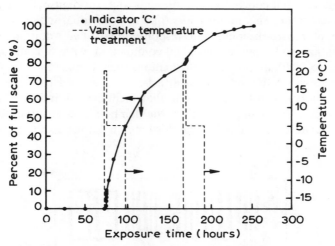

FIG. 5. Time–temperature response of the MonitorMark extended response indicator to variable temperature treatment (Wells and Singh, 1985).

3.2 Full-History Time–Temperature Indicators

Full-history time–temperature indicators are devices that respond continuously to all temperature exposure conditions. Because of this characteristic, the full-history time–temperature indicator can be used as a common means of monitoring and comparing different temperature exposures. Several different indicator models are available from their respective manufacturers, each having a different response rate and temperature-sensitivity range. For example, one indicator model might achieve a full-scale response after just a few days, while another model of the same indicator would expire only after several months of storage at the same temperature. The different response characteristics are useful in selecting indicators for applications of monitoring quality changes in frozen and refrigerated foods. Wells and Singh (1988a) examined two types of full-history time–temperature indicators and reported extensively on several models of each indicator. A general description and sample of indicator response is summarized below.

3.2.1 *LifeLines Freshness Monitor*

The LifeLines™ Freshness Monitor (LifeLines Technologies, Morristown, NJ) is shown in Fig. 6. The LifeLines indicator is an adhesive-backed paper label (102 × 37 mm) consisting of three distinctive regions of bar-code. The first coded region represents an eight-digit number unique to each indicator. This number identifies an individual indicator for the purpose of record keeping and response reporting. Additionally, the identification code can be used in conjunction with a computerized database to attribute product information, such as manufacture date, to the item to which the indicator is attached. The second bar-code region on the indicator is a two-digit code that identifies the indicator model. The model identification specifies the temperature-sensitivity of the indicator material contained in the third region, known as the 'indication band'.

FIG. 6.   LifeLines™ Freshness Monitor.

The 'indication band' is that portion of the LifeLines indicator that responds to temperature history and is composed of a narrow strip of polydiacetylene monomer (Anonymous, 1986). This compound is continuously undergoing a temperature-sensitive polymerization reaction that changes the optical density of the indicating band and results in a darkening of the material that proceeds more rapidly with higher temperatures (Fields and Prusik, 1983). In effect, the darkening is an analog monitor of the time and temperature exposure, integrating the time–temperature function according to the rate of the reaction. The LifeLines indicator has no independent means for activation; therefore, once the indicator has been manufactured, the device is poised for temperature-history response. In practice, when an indicator is attached to a food product, it must be inspected immediately to establish a baseline response from which relative response measurements can be determined.

The response of the LifeLines indicator can be monitored only with a hand-held microcomputer and optical light wand obtained from the manufacturer (Fig. 7). The hand-held microcomputer measures the

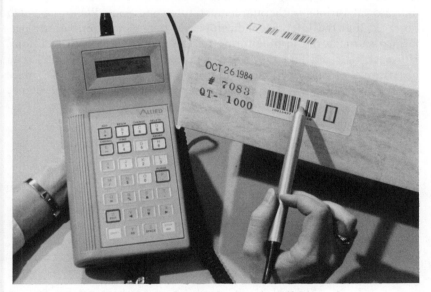

FIG. 7.   Hand-held computer for monitoring the LifeLines time–temperature indicator.

percentage of light reflected by the indication band, electronically recording this measurement to the nearest 1% reflectance. The indicator
changes from 100% reflectance (a faint blue-white color) to 0% reflectance (completely black) at a rate governed by the temperature-sensitivity
of polymerization (Fields and Prusik, 1983). Additionally, the hand-held
unit can read the bar-code containing the identification and model
numbers, and indicator response, identification code, and model number
can be transferred to a personal computer with proprietary software to
generate indicator response reports.

The indicator lacks a means of being inspected without the aid of the
optical scanner, and while inspection with the scanner is not tied to the
visual acuity of the observer, conditions such as insufficient charge in the
microcomputer batteries, fouling of the optical portal, and angle of
incidence at which the wand is held does influence the recorded indicator
response (Singh et al., 1986). The manufacturer suggests that a series of
five scans be taken on a single indicator during one inspection and that
average responses be used in further analysis.

Other characteristics of the LifeLines monitoring system, including the
response of different indicator models, were detailed by Wells and Singh
(1988a). Figure 8 shows the response for one model of the LifeLines
indicator at various isothermal temperature conditions. Wells and Singh
observed that the LifeLines indicators and microcomputer/scanner performed satisfactorily in monitoring refrigerated temperature conditions.
However, they did find that a small percentage of the individual scan
observation on the LifeLines indicators (approximately 1 in 300) were
recorded as 'null scans'. The null scans reported a value of 0% reflectance

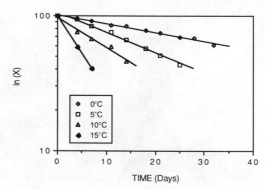

Fig. 8.   Semi-log plot of the response of the LifeLines Freshness Monitor model
57 to isothermal storage (Wells and Singh, 1988a).

even though repeated scans and visual observation would verify a much higher reflectance value. The manufacturer claims to have corrected this situation with the addition of a new microcomputer scanner that uses advanced laser technology.

3.2.2 I-POINT Time/Temperature Monitor

The I-POINT® Time/Temperature Monitor (I-POINT Biotechnologies A.B., Reston, VA) is shown in Fig. 9. The I-POINT indicator consists of an inner transparent plastic pouch with two compartments and an outer rectangular casing (62×25 mm) clear on one side with an adhesive backing on the other. One compartment of the inner pouch contains a pH indicator dye and enzyme solution, and the other a lipid substrate in fluid suspension (Blixt and Tiru, 1976). The two compartments of the inner pouch are initially separated with a thin barrier that seals enzyme and substrate in their respective compartments.

When the barrier seal is broken by applying external pressure to one of the compartments, and the contents of the two compartments are mixed the indicator is said to be 'activated'. Enzymatic hydrolysis of the lipid substrate follows initiating an irreversible change in solution pH, which

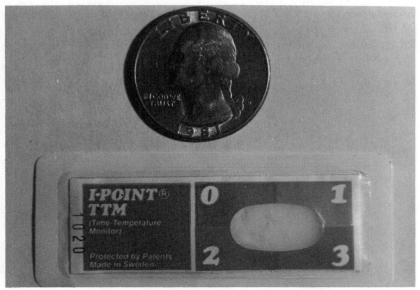

FIG. 9.   I-POINT® Time/Temperature Monitor.

in turn is reflected as a change of solution color by the pH indicator dye.
The temperature-sensitive hydrolysis reaction causes the solution pH
(and thus indicator color) to change continuously in time once the
indicator has been activated. The rate of change is regulated by temperature and substrate concentration.

The color change is visually compared to a paper color scale, which is
in place between the inner pouch and the clear side of the outer casing.
An oval window in the paper covering allows for easy comparison of the
solution color to a visual standard printed on the comparator scale. As
the indicator responds, the color is seen to change from green, to yellow,
to brown-red, to red, corresponding to four discrete increments (0, 1, 2,
and 3) printed on the color scale. At the present time the I-POINT
indicator must be inspected manually; however, an experimental electronic monitoring system to detect and record indicator response has
been described by Witt *et al.* (1987) and Singh and Hsu (1988).

The response of an I-POINT indicator to several isothermal temperature conditions is shown in Fig. 10. Wells and Singh (1988a) observed
that the I-POINT indicator responded more rapidly than expected
from the manufacturer's data. The differences in indicator response
can be attributed in part to discrepancies in the perception of the
observer during inspection. That is, the ambient lighting conditions
under which the I-POINT indicators are inspected and the visual acuity
of the observer will influence the judgment of indicator color change.
Discrepancies between manufacturer data and experimental findings for
the I-POINT indicator were also observed by Dolan *et al.* (1985).

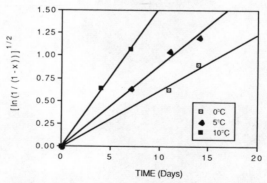

FIG. 10. Plot of the Gaussian transformation of the response of the I-POINT
Time/Temperature Monitor model 2220 to isothermal storage (Wells and Singh,
1988a).

Development of an electronic color detector and definition of the I-POINT response scale in terms of an electronic signal would eliminate discrepancies in visual judgments (Witt *et al.*, 1987).

4 KEEPING QUALITY OF PERISHABLE FOODS

For the purpose of this review, the term 'perishable food' will refer to an item that uses refrigerated or frozen storage as a means to aid in the preservation of desirable characteristics inherent to a product. All food products, regardless of preservation technique, will eventually deteriorate; however, the keeping quality of frozen and refrigerated foods is particularly sensitive to the temperature of the storage environment. Fruits and vegetables, for example, that are marketed as fresh products require refrigerated conditions to limit the biological functions of respiration and transpiration (Wills *et al.*, 1981); and meat, fish, and poultry products preserved by freezing need controlled temperature conditions to avoid a proliferation of resident microorganisms and to retard biochemical changes that result from enzymatic activity (Desrosier and Tressler, 1977).

4.1 Storage Temperature and Changes in Food Quality
The keeping quality of perishable foods is a highly complex subject that has received a great deal of attention in the literature. Research has shown that the primary factors contributing to the keeping quality of perishable foods are storage temperature, initial product composition and quality, processing techniques, and the packaging materials and processes (Fennema *et al.*, 1973; Goodenough and Atkin, 1981). Additionally, extensive research has been reported as to the kind of quality changes that occur in foods stored in refrigerated and frozen conditions. Typically, the major quality changes that occur during storage of frozen foods result from physical and chemical changes caused by oxidation of lipids, denaturation of proteins, discoloration of product, sublimation of ice, and recrystallization of ice crystals (Singh and Wang, 1977). The review study by Singh and Wang included the results of earlier work that showed that unduly high temperature exposure, steady or fluctuating, produces cumulative adverse effects on frozen food quality. The physical characteristics of products with unstable texture, such as ice cream, gels, and many plant tissues, are particularly susceptible to fluctuating temperatures. McNutt and Lee (1974) found that freeze/thaw cycles have an adverse effect on certain ready-to-eat prepared foods that contain sauces and gravy.

The books by Van Arsdel *et al.* (1969) and Jul (1984) reviewed the results of storage investigations on the keeping quality of frozen foods. These reviews document the influence of storage temperature on the length of time that frozen fruits, vegetables, and meats may be stored. A similar type of comprehensive review for the keeping quality of fresh fruits and vegetables, dairy products, and low-moisture foods is available in a book by Labuza (1982).

Results of temperature abuse on frozen foods are illustrated in Fig. 11. In the example shown, there is clear evidence of severe dehydration (freezer burn). Products that were individually quick frozen are no longer free-flowing as they have become fused together. Quality abuses such as these are due to temperature variations during distribution and storage (Londahl, 1983). Less dramatic, but no less severe, quality abuses can occur from temperature mishandling of chilled foods.

The important physical and chemical changes that influence the keeping quality of perishable foods are dependent on both residence time and temperature exposure. A longer storage time, or a storage

FIG. 11.   Frozen product with severe freezer-burn that has become fused together.

TABLE 2

SUMMARY OF TEMPERATURES IN FROZEN FISH HAULED IN MECHANICALLY REFRIGERATED TRUCKS (FOLEY AND LENTZ, 1968)

Truck company	No. of loads checked	Trip length (av. days)	Loading temp. (°C)			Unloading temp. (°C)			Increase during transit (°C)
			High	Low	Av. (5 pts)	High	Low	Av. (5 pts)	
A	28	3½	−17·7	−22·3	−20·2	−11·8	−16·5	−14·2	6·0
B	13	3	−20·2	−21·8	−21·0	−9·7	−16·5	−13·1	7·9
C	12	1	−16·2	−18·9	−17·1	−8·9	−14·5	−11·7	5·4
D	7	3	−18·3	−20·9	−19·5	−10·9	−15·9	−13·6	5·9
E	7	2½	−18·9	−23·0	−21·1	−14·4	−17·8	−17·6	3·5
F	6	3½	−14·9	−21·8	−18·7	−11·1	−16·6	−13·9	4·8
G	4	2½	−16·0	−20·0	−17·9	−13·6	−17·9	−16·1	1·8
H	3	2	−12·4	−15·4	−13·9	−10·2	−12·8	−11·3	2·6
I	1	4	−21·1	−21·7	−21·2	0	−14·4	−8·0	13·2
J	1	1	−18·9	−20·6	−20·1	−12·2	−15·6	−14·4	5·7
K	1	2	−16·7	−24·4	−21·3	−17·2	−18·3	−17·8	3·5
Average all loads	83	3	−17·5	−21·3	−19·4	−10·8	−16·2	−13·8	5·6

temperature higher than recommended standards, adversely affects food quality, reducing the length of time that a product can be stored. Adverse temperature exposures often occur as products are transported from one storage facility to another.

Londahl (1983) found that in an average of 45% of all in-transit spot checks conducted in five European countries, temperature of frozen product was above $-15°C$ despite a recommended maximum temperature of $-18°C$. Increases in product temperature can result from wide variations in the temperature of mechanically refrigerated trucks used in distribution. Foley and Lentz (1968) studied the transport of frozen fish in Canada and showed that in an average of 83 loads ranging from 1 to 4 days in length, the product temperature increased by over 5°C, with maximum temperature increases of 13°C (Table 2). Such increases in product temperature contribute heavily to product deterioration and shelf-life reduction.

4.2 Food Quality Evaluation Techniques
The term 'quality' is used as a gross measure of the deterioration that has occurred in a food item. While 'quality' has no scientific meaning of its own, from the perspective of the consumer, 'quality' can be referenced to specific desirable characteristics or attributes that are inherent in a food. The sensory expectations that an individual establishes for a food product can be expressed in terms of the presence of desirable characteristics within the product. Thus, an item with a greater amount of a desirable characteristic would be perceived to be a higher-quality product, whereas an item with a lesser amount of that same characteristic would be considered a lower-quality product. This simplistic approach to consumer acceptance and quality does not account for the interactions between various attributes, but is useful in simplifying the notion of food quality for the purpose of mathematical description and analysis.

Often a desirable attribute of food quality can be quantified with empirical or analytical techniques. Analysis of chemical or microbial components that contribute to changes in the perception of a desirable characteristic would constitute an analytical technique, while monitoring changes in the magnitude of a characteristic with human subjects would constitute an empirical technique. Various sensory and objective evaluation methodologies can be used to study the extent of change in desirable quality attributes. Time-dependent studies of the quality changes in foods have been the basis for establishing a product's shelf life (Dethmers, 1979).

Much of the research undertaken to evaluate frozen food quality has been aimed at identifying the shelf life of a product. The definition of shelf life suggested by the International Institute of Refrigeration is 'practical storage life' (PSL). PSL is defined as 'the period of frozen storage after freezing of an initially high quality product during which the organoleptic quality remains suitable for consumption or the process intended' (International Institute of Refrigeration, 1986). PSL, as interpreted from the definition, is a measure of consumer acceptance.

Figure 12 shows the pronounced effect that temperature has on PSL of frozen products. In general, warmer storage temperatures decrease the PSL, except for certain items which exhibit a lengthened PSL at increased storage temperature (i.e. vacuum-packaged sliced bacon shown in curve 1 of Fig. 12). This unusual phenomenon is referred to in the literature as 'reverse stability' (Fennema et al., 1973).

The relationship between PSL and temperature can be used to calculate shelf-life losses that occur during distribution and storage. Table

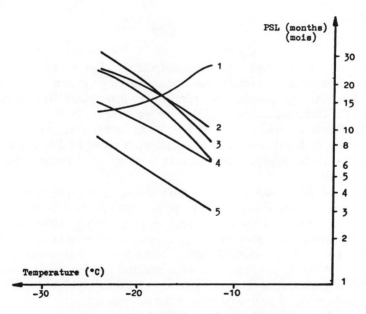

FIG. 12.   Practical storage life (PSL) for different frozen foods: (1) vacuum-packaged sliced bacon; (2) carrots; (3) beef cuts; (4) green beans; (g) fatty fish (International Institute of Refrigeration, 1986).

TABLE 3

EXAMPLE OF CALCULATING SHELF LIFE LOSS ALONG THE FREEZER CHAIN (INTER-
NATIONAL INSTITUTE OF REFRIGERATION, 1986)

1 Links of the cold chain	2 Average temperature	3 Storage time (days)	4 PSL (days)	5 PSL loss (% per day)	6 Loss (%)
Producer	−23	40	420	0·238	9·5
Transport	−20	2	350	0·286	0·6
Cold store	−25	190	480	0·208	39·9
Transport	−18	1	300	0·333	0·3
Wholesale	−23	30	420	0.238	7·2
Transport	−15	1	230	0·435	0·2
Display cabinet					
center	−20	20	350	0·286	5·8
upper layer	−12	6	180	0.556	3.4
Transport	−8	1/6	120	0·833	0·1
Consumer	−18	50	300	0·333	16·5
Total loss of PSL in		340			83·6

3 illustrates an example of such a calculation. For each stage in the
distribution chain, an average temperature and storage time are assumed.
The PSL for the assumed temperature is determined from a figure
such as is discussed above, and the storage time is divided by the PSL
to determine the percentage of loss in the PSL that occurs during
each stage of distribution. The losses for each phase of distribution can
be summed to express the cumulative effect of storage time and
temperature.

A host of specific sensory evaluation procedures and statistical analysis
techniques have been developed to define product shelf life in terms of
quality differences. These definitions employ sensory difference tests
(discrimination methods) and a strict statistical criteria for shelf-life
failure. One popular shelf-life failure procedure is 'just noticeable difference' (JND). In this type of test, a trained sensory panel compares
treatment and control samples by means of a difference test (i.e. triangle
or paired comparison) to determine if the samples are noticeably different
(Van Arsdel et al., 1969). The noticeable difference between experimental
and control samples is determined 'considering all things' and is not
referenced to a specific quality attribute. Testing is usually terminated when

TABLE 4

ERAGE TEXTURE JUDGMENTS AND HEDONIC RATINGS ($N = 5$ FOR SENSORY PARAMETERS; $N = 21$ FOR HEDONIC RATINGS) (SCHUTZ et al., 1972)

Carrot samples and treatment[a]	Flexibility	Hardness	Chewiness	Juiciness	Hedonic rating
itside (1)[b]	4·0[c]	4·8	5·2	3·2	1·5
itside (2)	3·0	4·4	5·6	2·8	2·1
itside (3)	1·4	5·4	4·6	4·8	5·5
esh carrot	1·4	4·4	4·8	4·2	5·4
)en, no sun (1)	2·2	5·6	5·6	3·4	5·3
)en, no sun (2)	2·0	5·4	5·0	4·4	5·4
)en, no sun (3)	2·2	4·8	5·6	3·8	5·4
)en, no sun (5)	3·8	4·8	5·0	4·0	4·1
eezer (1)	5·6	2·6	2·6	5·4	1·7
eezer (2)	5·0	2·2	4·0	6·4	1·2
eezer (3)	6·6	1·6	2·4	6·6	1·3
eezer (5)	6·4	2·2	4·2	6·6	1·5
astic bag (1)	1·4	5·8	5·0	4·2	4·4
astic bag (2)	1·0	6·4	5·4	5·0	5·1
astic bag (3)	2·8	5·2	4·4	4·2	5·2
astic bag (5)	1·2	6·2	4·8	4·8	5·7
ld water (1)	1·2	6·2	5·2	3·8	5·3
ld water (2)	1·2	5·2	4·4	4·4	4·6
ld water (3)	1·4	5·6	4·6	5·0	5·1
ld water (5)	1·0	4·8	3·4	4·4	5·1
pboard (1)	1·6	6·0	4·8	3·8	5·1
pboard (2)	2·0	4·6	4·8	3·8	5·6
pboard (3)	1·4	5·4	4·6	4·8	5·5
pboard (5)	2·8	5·2	5·2	4·2	4·2

reatments took place under the following storage conditions: *outside*, exposed to the sun; zen in the refrigerator; unwrapped in the *cupboard*; in a *plastic bag* in the refrigerator; in rigerator, packed in air-tight *water*-filled container; in the *open* air, protected from the sun; d, *fresh*, no treatment.

Jumber in parentheses refers to total days in storage.

= low degree of characteristic; 7 = high degree of characteristic.

a difference, at a predetermined level of statistical probability, is established between experimental and control products. The level of statistical probability can be specified such that it will call attention to a quality difference that may be of commercial significance (Dethmers, 1979).

TABLE 5

FREQUENCY OF TERMS USED IN FINAL DESCRIPTIVE ANALYSIS SESSION—HAMBURGER (NUMBER OF PARTICIPATING JUDGES: $N=9$) (SINGH *et al.*, 1984)

Descriptors	Frequency of use	Descriptors	Frequency of use
Flavor		*Texture*	
Flavor intensity	4	Dryness	5
Meat flavor	5	Moisture	2
Old meat flavor	3	Juiciness	5
Rancidity	5	Greasy	2
Aftertaste	6	Coarse	3
Metallic	0	Crumbly	3
Cardboard flavor	3	Chewiness	5
Cooked flavor	0	Rubberiness	5
Salty	0	Gumminess	1
		Hardness	0
		Firmness	2
Aroma		Easy to bite	2
Overall aroma intensity	3	Amount of gristle	1
Greasy	2		
Rancid	4		
Meaty	2		

Note. Samples compared had been stored 168 days at $-35°C$ and $-12°C$.

In general, the results of storage studies that use difference tests, such as JND, are correlated with the expected length of time a product can be stored (PSL). That is, JND can be thought of as a highly sensitive acceptability measure. Difference testing procedures, however, do not provide information about either the extent or rate of change in product quality (an attribute measure). The aim of a testing methodology to monitor quality changes in perishable food should include procedures to measure the extent of attribute changes, while remaining sensitive to noticeable changes that could economically impact the industry.

Schutz et al. (1972) used an attribute-based approach in an investigation of the texture of raw carrots. Carrots, subjected to various storage treatments and abusive conditions, were evaluated by trained and untrained sensory panels. The hedonic response to carrot texture obtained from the untrained panel were correlated with the 'degree of sensory characteristic' obtained from the trained panel (Table 4). Regression analysis of the three textural attributes rated by the trained panel yielded a correlation equation that accounted for 83% of the variability in average hedonic response of the untrained panel. These results provide strong experimental evidence that attribute monitoring can be an effective means of indicating consumer product acceptance.

One of the difficulties of attribute monitoring has been the correct identification of product characteristics that will change during storage. Often accelerated studies are used to identify product quality attributes, but since this method requires either high-temperature exposure or repeated temperature cycling, the kind and extent of quality changes identified may be vastly different from what is observed during isothermal storage at temperatures in the range recommended for a particular product. In the storage study conducted by Singh et al. (1984), trained panelists were asked to identify terminology that characterizes quality changes in frozen hamburger after extended constant temperature storage (Table 5). This evaluation was motivated by the observation that quality attributes found to change during accelerated testing were not observed to change during isothermal storage. The selection of appropriate sensory attributes for frozen food storage studies is further discussed by Wells and Singh (1988b).

4.3 Quality Monitoring with Time–Temperature Indicators
Storage studies have shown that full-history time–temperature indicators can be used to monitor changes in certain attributes or characteristics that describe food quality. This research provided evidence that commer-

cially available full-history time–temperature indicators can be used with various perishable and semi-perishable foods, including dairy, meat, fish, bakery, and fruit and vegetable products (Mistry and Kosikowksi, 1983; Campbell *et al.*, 1986; Singh and Wells, 1985; Singh *et al.*, 1984 and 1986). In these investigations, responses of several indicator models were correlated with sensory and objective measures of food quality when both indicator and food were exposed to the same temperature conditions. The success of these storage studies have been due in part to a better understanding of the perception of food quality and its methods of measurement, in addition to sustained efforts on the part of indicator manufacturers to improve the reliability and functionality of their products.

Mistry and Kosikowski (1983) investigated the use of time–temperature indicators as quality control devices for fluid milk. This research concluded that a combination of different models and types of indicators could be used to predict milk spoilage. Mistry and Kosikowski, however, did not examine the use of time–temperature indicators as monitors of the growth patterns of different microorganisms. Earlier work by Ratkowsky *et al.* (1982) had shown that growth rates of specific organisms observed in foods could be monitored with electronic temperature sensors coupled to a microprocessor. An electronic time–temperature indicator was developed and demonstrated by this work, but complexity and cost has limited the use of electronic indicators to research applications.

Singh *et al.* (1984) examined the use of full-history time–temperature indicators in monitoring quality changes in several frozen foods. Reporting on the results of this study, Singh and Wells (1985) showed that the I-POINT model 3015 was correlated with sensory score of rancidity and TBA number in frozen hamburger stored at $-12°C$ (Fig. 13). In addition, high statistical correlations were found between indicator response and ascorbic acid loss in frozen strawberries (Singh and Wells, 1987b). The response of the I-POINT indicator model 1020 was significantly correlated with changes in strawberry firmness and total ascorbic acid for products stored at $-12°C$. The relationship between firmness, ascorbic acid, and indicator response is shown in Fig. 14.

Zall *et al.* (1984) used the LifeLines Freshness Monitor to track quality changes in UHT sterilized milk. These researchers correlated a sensory 'freshness score' obtained from an expert panel with time–temperature indicator response. Singh *et al.* (1986) confirmed the use of time–temperature indicators with UHT sterilized milk by correlating changes

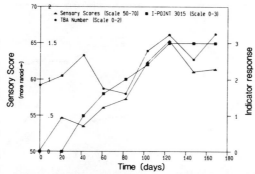

FIG. 13.   Comparison of mean response of the I-POINT model 3015 and mean sensory evaluations of rancidity an TBA number in frozen hamburger patties (Singh and Wells, 1985).

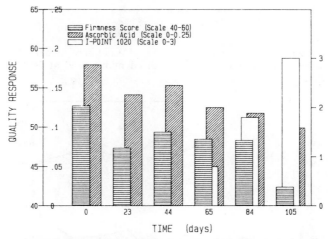

FIG. 14.   Comparison of changes in frozen strawberry firmness score and total ascorbic content, and the response of the I-POINT model 1020 indicator during −12°C constant temperature storage (Singh and Wells, 1987b).

in the sensory attributes 'whiteness' and 'coconut flavor' with the response of two different LifeLines models. Figures 15 and 16 show the relationship between indicator response and the observed changes in UHT milk. Results of this investigation demonstrated that certain models of time–temperature indicator could function at ambient temperatures.

Wells and Singh (1988c) studied the relationship between the quality changes in fresh produce (i.e. lettuce and tomatoes) and the response of

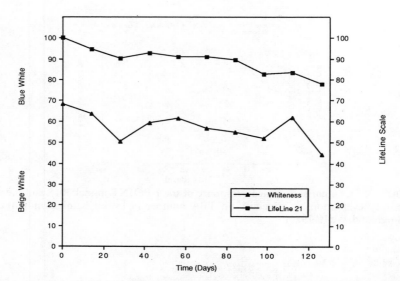

FIG. 15. Comparison of mean response of LifeLines model 21 and mean sensory score of whiteness in UHT sterilized milk stored at 20°C (Wells and Singh, 1988c).

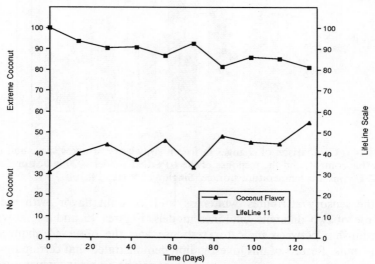

FIG. 16. Comparison of mean response of LifeLines model 11 and mean sensory score of coconut flavor in UHT sterilized milk stored at 5°C (Wells and Singh, 1988c).

full-history time–temperature indicators. Sensorial textural and flavor changes of fresh tomatoes were evaluated and changes in tomato firmness were significantly correlated with the response of both the I-POINT model 2340 and the LifeLines model 57 (Figs 17 and 18, respectively). While none of the monitored quality characteristics of lettuce was correlated with indicator response, Wells and Singh pointed out a relationship between the shelf life (as defined by the termination of sensory testing) and the response of the I-POINT model 2340 (Fig. 19). This suggested that the I-POINT model 2340 could be used to identify lettuce that was nearing the end of its practical shelf life, the point beyond which a product is unfit for consumption.

Grisius *et al.* (1987) found a high statistical correlation between microbial growth in pasteurized milk and the response of both the LifeLines and I-POINT time–temperature indicators (Table 6). Total aerobic count was significantly correlated to the continuous response of the LifeLines Inventory Freshness Monitor over a wide variety of constant and variable temperature histories. Grisius *et al.* also asserted

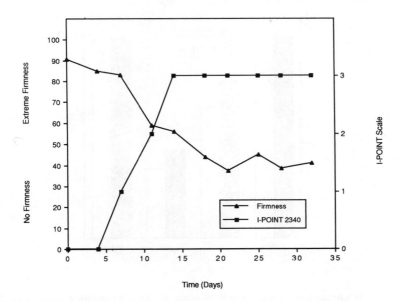

FIG. 17. Comparison of mean response of I-POINT model 2340 and mean sensory score of tomato firmness at 15°C storage (Wells and Singh, 1988c).

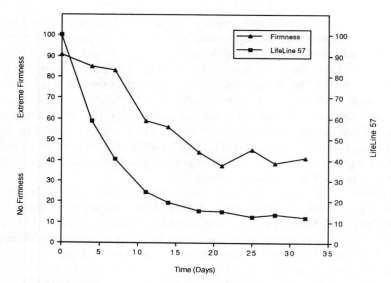

FIG. 18. Comparison of mean response of LifeLines model 57 and mean sensory score of tomato firmness at 15°C storage.

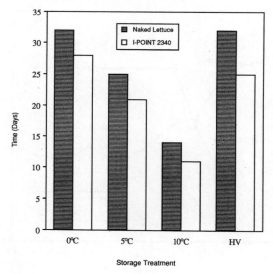

FIG. 19. Comparison of the length of time to observe a color change of 2 (red-brown) in the I-POINT model 2340 and the termination of sensory testing for naked lettuce (Wells and Singh, 1988c).

TABLE 6

CORRELATION COEFFICIENTS AND SIGNIFICANCE LEVELS OF CORRELATIONS BE-
TWEEN STORAGE TIME, TIME–TEMPERATURE INDICATOR RESPONSE, AND SELECTED
MICROBIAL COUNTS AT EACH CONSTANT TEMPERATURE TREATMENT (GRISIUS *et
al.*, 1987)

	Correlation coefficients and significance levels					
	Total counts		Spore formers		Psychrotrophics	
Time	0.951^a	***	0.308	n.s.	0.923	***
	0.981^b	***	0.918	**	0.965	***
	0.985^c	*	0.948	n.s.	0.875	n.s.
I-POINT TTM						
2140	0.905	***	0.094	n.s.	0.722	*
	0.794	*	0.910	**	0.908	**
	0.926	n.s.	0.825	n.s.	0.871	n.s
2180	0.828	**	0.295	n.s.	0.943	***
	0.890	**	0.901	**	0.848	*
	0.965	*	0.823	n.s.	0.715	n.s.
2220	0.841	*	0.291	n.s.	0.951	***
	0.935	**	0.890	**	0.865	*
	0.989	*	0.921	n.s.	0.686	n.s.
2340	0.680	*	0.244	n.s.	0.755	*
	0.871	*	0.663	n.s.	0.751	n.s.
	0.823	n.s.	0.888	n.s.	0.498	n.s.
LifeLine						
57	−0.940	***	−0.171	n.s.	−0.897	***
	−0.973	***	−0.926	**	−0.963	***
	−0.962	*	−0.988	*	−0.893	n.s.

^{a} Correlation coefficient for 0°C storage treatment.
^{b} Correlation coefficient for 5°C storage treatment.
^{c} Correlation coefficient for 10°C storage treatment.
Levels of significance designated as:
* $p < 0.05$.
** $p < 0.01$.
*** $p < 0.001$.
n.s.   not sigificant.
       $p > 0.05$.

that I-POINT indicator, which initiates a discernible response only after
a predetermined time and temperature combination has been achieved,
could be used to estimate injury recovery and germination of psychrotrophic organisms. Figure 20 shows the comparison between discernible
color change from green to yellow for the I-POINT model 2140 and the

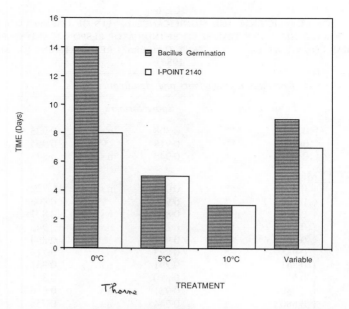

FIG. 20.   Comparison of the length of time to observe a discernible color change from 0 to 1 (green to yellow) in the I-POINT model 2140 and detection of the presence of psychrotrophic bacteria in pasteurized milk (Grisius *et al.*, 1987).

detection of the presence of psychrotrophic bacteria in pasteurized milk. The length of time to observe the color change in the indicator slightly precede the detection of psychrotrophic bacteria.

Prediction of the changes in food quality from the response of time–temperature indicators was discussed by Campbell *et al.* (1986). These researchers suggested that if significant correlations existed between indicator response and observations of food quality at several isothermal conditions, a regression equation could be used to estimate food quality based on indicator response. Campbell *et al.* demonstrated the use of such an equation to predict the sensory quality of refrigerated salad from the response of a full-history indicator.

Likewise, Grisius *et al.* (1987) observed that the response of one model of the LifeLines Freshness Monitor was correlated to microbial changes in pasteurized milk stored at 0°C, 5°C, and 10°C. Figure 21 shows the correlation of milk data and the simple regression equation that described 80% of the variability in total aerobic counts in terms of indicator response. Wells and Singh (1986a) pointed out that the regression

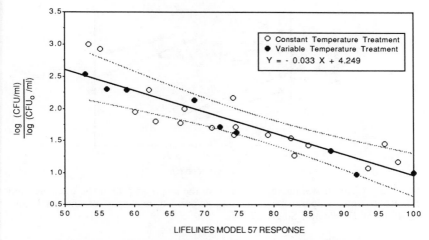

FIG. 21.   Plot of normalized total count enumeration and response of lifeline indicator model 57 for constant and variable temperature treatments (Grisius *et al.*, 1987).

approach to quality monitoring was limited in that individual indicator models need to be calibrated to a particular attribute of food quality. Additionally, this work presented evidence that a regression model developed under controlled isothermal conditions may prove to be systematically inaccurate when employed for fluctuating temperature conditions. This limitation was overcome with the introduction of a generalized mathematical approach to quality monitoring and shelf-life prediction (Singh and Wells, 1987a). The generalized approach was based on the principles of chemical kinetics, and the theoretical derivation to support prediction model is fully detailed by Wells (1987) and Wells and Singh (1988d).

The mathematical structure of chemical kinetics is often used to describe the quality deterioration of perishable food products. Wells and Singh (1988a) showed that the effect of temperature on the indicator response can also be described with Arrhenius kinetics (Fig. 22). Because of the similarities in modeling indicator response and changes in food quality, Wells and Singh (1988a) proposed that kinetic information be used as the basis selecting a particular indicator model for quality monitoring applications. The criteria for indicator selection required that both activation energy and a reference rate constant be approximately matched to that of the food quality attribute to be monitored. A

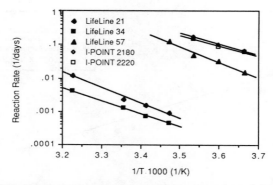

FIG. 22. Effect of storage temperature on the response rate of the LifeLines and I-POINT time–temperature indicators expressed in terms of the Arrhenius relationship (Wells and Singh, 1988a).

TABLE 7

ACTIVATION ENERGY AND SELECTED RESPONSE CHARACTERISTICS FOR THE LIFE-LINES AND I-POINT TIME–TEMPERATURE INDICATORS (WELLS AND SINGH, 1988a)

Indicator model		E_{AR} (kcal/mol)	Temp. (°C)	Time (days)	Response[a]
LifeLines	21	21·3	15	20	95%
	34	17·8	15	20	99%
	57	21·3	15	20	18%
I-POINT	2180	14·3	10	6	Color 2
	2220	14·0	10	12	Color 2

[a] Response of LifeLines indicators is given in percentage reflectance of LifeLines scale; response of the I-POINT indicators are given in the units of the I-POINT color scale.

summary of the activation energies and selected response characteristics for the LifeLines and I-POINT indicators is given in Table 7.

5 QUALITY MODELING WITH TIME–TEMPERATURE INDICATORS

Previous efforts in mathematical modeling and prediction of tempera-ture-related changes in food quality required explicit knowledge of the temperature history. Time–temperature indicators provide implicit knowledge of the temperature history, providing information previously unavailable without the aid of expensive recording thermometers or data acquisition systems. The background for modeling perishable food quality and the mathematical basis for using time–temperature indicators to predict changes in food quality are summarized below.

5.1 Modeling of Food Quality Changes

The literature on the keeping quality of perishable foods provides ample evidence of a direct relationship between storage time and temperature, and changes in food quality. Time–temperature related changes in food quality arise from an interaction of several poorly understood deterioration mechanisms. Development of a comprehensive mathematical model that describes each interacting mechanism is virtually impossible; however, various mathematical expressions, usually posed in the form of a differential equation, have been used to describe the rate of change in a predominant quality characteristic for known temperature conditions.

Earliest interest in the mathematical modeling of food quality loss was motivated by the observation that frozen foods stored in isothermal conditions did not have the same shelf life as products stored at fluctuating temperatures (Hicks, 1944). Hicks believed that temperature influence on the rate of quality change was expressed as a simple exponential relationship (i.e. linear plot of natural logarithm of rate versus temperature) and developed an equation to predict the effective mean temperature for a diurnal temperature fluctuation. The effective mean temperature was the constant temperature necessary to bring about the same quality change observed during a known temperature fluctuation. Hicks presented an equation to determine the effective mean temperature for a regular sinusoidal temperature function. Schwimmer *et al.* (1955) extended this work to derive a set of equations that described the effective temperature for other periodic temperature fluctuation (i.e. square and sawtooth functions). The assumption of a simple exponential relationship between temperature and rate of quality change lead to a straightforward series solution from which the results could be tabulated.

Schubert (1977) derived a set of equations to predict the effective mean temperature for periodic temperature fluctuations based on a mixed linear and exponential relationship between temperature and rate of quality change. The empirical function used to describe the temperature effect on the rate of quality change had three experimentally determined parameters, but could be reduced in complexity by assuming a narrow range for the temperature fluctuation. The concept of an effective temperature was generalized to random variable temperature conditions by

Labuza (1979). Labuza described the influence of temperature on the rate of food quality loss in a form adapted from chemical kinetic theory.

The chemical kinetics approach to the mathematical modeling of changes in food quality had been advocated previously by Kwolek and Bookwalter (1971). They argued that the kinetic model was the most general and widely applicable mathematical formula to describe the influence of temperature on the rate of quality loss. The primary characteristic of the chemical kinetics approach is that the rate of quality loss is an exponential function of the reciprocal of absolute temperature (the Arrhenius relationship). Saguy and Karel (1980) concurred with the recommendation of the kinetic model in food quality modeling, but other researchers (cf. Moreno, 1984) have preferred modified forms of the model with additional parameters.

A methodology for computer simulation of food quality changes during frozen storage was introduced by Singh (1976). Singh presented a computer algorithm to predict changes in food quality based on a simulated temperature history during storage. The Arrhenius relationship provided a means of estimating the rate of quality change for a small calculation step in the prediction algorithm.

A graphical representation of the temperature history/food quality relationship as described by the kinetic model was presented by Wells *et al.* (1987). The graphical representation of the time–temperature/quality relationship is shown in Fig. 23. In this three-dimensional representation, the sensory scores of hamburger rancidity were predicted by the kinetic model and depicted as a surface. The graphical representation was

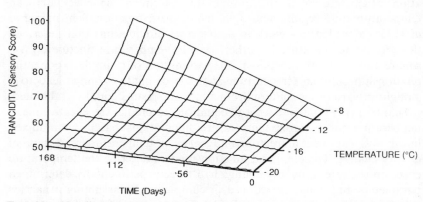

FIG. 23. 'Quality-response surface' for sensory score of rancidity in frozen hamburger patties (Wells *et al.*, 1987).

developed in the context of monitoring time–temperature related quality changes in frozen foods with the aid of time–temperature indicators.

5.1.1 Mathematical Structure of Chemical Kinetics

Chemical kinetics is the study of the rate and mechanism by which one chemical species is converted to another (Smith, 1970). The rate of a chemical reaction is measured as the mass of a product produced (or reactant consumed) per unit time, while the mechanism of a reaction is the sequence of individual chemical events that produce the overall result of the observed reaction. Determining the mechanism of a chemical reaction is a difficult task, and the reaction mechanisms for only a few very simple systems are known. The study of chemical kinetics, however, has provided a powerful mathematical structure that can be used to systemize and model experimental observations.

The general form of the kinetic model is motivated by considering the following chemical reaction:

$$a\text{A} + b\text{B} \underset{k_b}{\overset{k_f}{\longleftrightarrow}} c\text{C} + d\text{D} \tag{1}$$

where A and B are the reactants of the reaction; C and D are the products of the reaction; a, b, c, and d are the stoichiometric coefficients for the reactants and products; and k_f and k_b are the forward and backward reaction rate constants. In the case of the given reaction, A reacts with B at a rate of k_f to form two products, C and D, which in turn react at a rate of k_b to re-form the original reactants. The standard equation that defines the rate of loss of reactant B is

$$-\frac{\text{d}[B]}{\text{d}t} = k_f[A]^\alpha[B]^\beta - k_b[C]^\gamma[D]^\delta \tag{2}$$

where $[A]$, $[B]$, $[C]$, and $[D]$ denotes the concentration (mass per unit volume) of reactants and products; t is time; α, β, γ, and δ are the reaction orders with respect to each product or reactant.

Equations (1) and (2) describe an elementary chemical reaction that results from a collection of individual mechanism events. Since the precise mechanisms of most chemical reactions are poorly understood, the practical use of eqns (1) and (2) would seem to be limited. From a mathematical standpoint, even if the concentration of each reaction component could be measured as a function of time, eqn (2) could not be solved as there would still be six unknowns (k_f, k_b, α, β, γ, δ). Labuza (1984) pointed out that most texts on chemical kinetics suggest that reaction conditions be chosen such that either the forward or backward reaction is predominant and that the concentration of one or more species is so high that their change in concentration is negligible. Thus, if $k_b \ll k_f$ and the concentration of reactant A is very high, the rate of conversion (loss) of reactant B would be denoted as:

$$-\frac{d[B]}{dt} = k[B]^n \qquad (3)$$

where k is the pseudo rate constant and n is the reaction order. Equation (3) is the mathematical model used in chemical kinetics to describe the rate of a reaction as influenced solely by concentration. The true mechanism of the reaction is ignored by this expression and additional factors that affect the rate of the reaction (e.g. temperature) are not included.

The temperature dependence of the rate at which the reaction progresses may be described by the Arrhenius relationship. The Arrhenius relationship is used in chemical kinetics to describe the variation in reaction rate with respect to absolute temperature and is based on a thermodynamic argument. The form of the Arrhenius relationship is:

$$k = k_0 \exp\left(-\frac{E_A}{R_g}\frac{1}{T}\right) \qquad (4)$$

where k_0 is a constant, independent of temperature (referred to as the pre-exponential factor), E_A is the reaction activation energy, R_g is the ideal gas constant, and T is the temperature at which the reaction occurs as measured on an absolute scale. The primary parameters of the Arrhenius relationship are the pre-exponential factor and the activation energy. The pre-exponential factor is the magnitude of the reaction rate independent of temperature, and the activation energy describes the temperature-sensitivity of the reaction. The solution to the combination of eqns (3) and (4) fully describes a reaction in terms of concentration and temperature.

The overall changes in food quality (i.e. taste, aroma, and appearance) that occur during storage result from the combination of changes within the individual food components. Changes in individual food components arise from the interaction of several deterioration mechanisms (i.e. chemical, enzymatic, and microbial processes). From this standpoint, the chemical kinetics approach appears to be a good basis for a model to describe overall changes in an attribute of food quality. Hill and Grieger-Block (1980) demonstrated the use of the kinetic model to successfully predict time- and temperature-related changes for predominant quality attributes of several refrigerated and frozen foods.

5.1.2 Methods of Estimating the Kinetic Parameters

The general time-temperature-dependent kinetic model given by the combination of eqns (3) and (4) is:

$$-\frac{dB}{dt} = k_0 \exp\left(-\frac{E_A}{R_g}\frac{1}{T}\right) B^n \tag{5}$$

Equation 5 has three parameters (n, k_0, and E_A) that must be derived from experimental data. To simplify the solution to eqn (5) the reaction order, n, is generally assumed to take an integer value. Three different analysis methods can be used to determine the remaining kinetic parameters from experimental data collected during a storage study investigation. The different analysis methods are discussed below.

Two-step linear regression method. The kinetic parameters E_A and k_0 may be determined from concentration changes monitored during isothermal storage by sequentially applying linear regression of eqns (3) and (4). Such an analysis is possible by assuming the reaction order to be an integer value. Quality changes in most foods have been observed to follow either a zero-order ($n=0$) or a first-order ($n=1$) reaction (Labuza, 1982). However, losses in certain vitamins during storage can be modeled with second- or higher-order reaction (Singh, 1976).

The mathematical notations for an isothermal reaction modeled with zero-order ($n=0$) or first-order ($n=1$) kinetics are given by:

$$-\frac{dB}{dt} = k \tag{6a}$$

$$-\frac{dB}{dt} = kB \tag{6b}$$

where eqns (6a) and (6b) denote a zero-order ($n=0$) or first-order ($n=1$) reaction, respectively. The analytical solutions for eqns (6a) and (6b) may be found by separation of variables and integration over the time interval 0 to t. The resulting equations:

$$B = B_0 - kt \tag{7a}$$

$$\ln(B) = \ln(B_0) - kt \tag{7b}$$

are in the form of a simple linear model. Equations (7a) or (7b) may be used in regression anaysis of food quality measurements [B or ln(B)] on time to obtain an estimate of the specific reaction rate, k, for the particular isothermal condition in which the quality changes were observed.

As stated earlier, the influence of temperature on the reaction rate can be described with the Arrhenius relationship. The Arrhenius relationship may be expressed in a linear form with a natural logarithmic transformation of eqn (4). The linear form of the Arrhenius expression is:

$$\ln k = \ln k_0 - \frac{E_A}{R_g} \frac{1}{T} \tag{8}$$

The parameters $\ln k_0$ and E_A/R_g can be determined from regression analysis of the natural logarithm of isothermal reaction rate against the reciprocal of the corresponding absolute temperatures. Rate constants from three or more isothermal conditions are needed to properly conduct the regression analysis. The activation energy is calculated by multiplying the slope of the regression equation by the ideal gas constant.

Non-linear regression method. The parameters for the kinetic model can be estimated using non-linear regression (Arabshahi and Lund, 1985; Cohen and Saguy, 1985; Haralampu et al., 1985). The non-linear procedure involves simultaneous solution of eqns (3) and (4) without determining individual rate constant values. The non-linear form for the zero-order and first-order reactions are given, respectively, by:

$$B_{ij} = B_0 - k_0 t_{ij} \exp\left(-\frac{E_A}{R_g} \frac{1}{T_j} \right) \tag{9a}$$

$$B_{ij} = B_0 \exp\left[k_0 t_{ij} \exp\left(-\frac{E_A}{R_g} \frac{1}{T_j} \right) \right] \tag{9b}$$

where the subscripts 'i' and 'j' indicate the time and temperature of the corresponding quality measurement. Data on quality changes during storage can be coded into a computer data array, and the kinetic parameters determined using the SAS NONLIN procedure (SAS Institute Inc., 1982) or the BMDP P3R procedure (University of California, 1983).

Shelf-life analysis method. Lai and Heldman (1982) developed an expression to determine the activation energy for food quality change based on product shelf life. The relationship between shelf life and temperature is based on kinetic theory and has the form:

$$\ln t_Q = \ln b + \frac{E_A}{R_g} \frac{1}{T_{ref}} \tag{10}$$

where t_Q is the product shelf life and b is a function of the Arrhenius pre-exponential factor, initial and end point quality magnitude. Equation (10) is dependent on reaction order only in the b parameter, thus the activation energy for the quality changes that gives rise to a shelf-life criterion can be obtained by plotting natural logarithm of shelf life against the reciprocal of absolute temperature. The slope of the resulting curve will be equal to the ratio E_A/R_g. Equation (10) may be rewritten in terms of the ratio of shelf life, t_Q, to a reference shelf life, $t_{Q,ref}$, thus rendering the expression completely independent of reaction order. The resulting equation is:

$$\ln \frac{t_Q}{t_{Q,ref}} = \frac{E_A}{R_g} \left(\frac{1}{T} - \frac{1}{T_{ref}} \right) \tag{11}$$

where $t_{Q,ref}$ is the product shelf life at an arbitrarily chosen reference temperature, T_{ref}.

Lai and Heldman (1982) used a least squares fitting technique on eqn (11) to document the activation energy for the shelf-life criteria of several common frozen foods. A summary of the values of activation energy and the PSL for the products reviewed by Lai and Heldman are given in Table 8. Equation (11) can be generally applied to estimate the activation energy, E_A, from storage stability data presented in the literature (Tressler *et al.*, 1968; Van Arsdel *et al.*, 1969; Labuza, 1982; Jul, 1984). A tabulated listing of the activation energies for quality changes in various refrigerated and semi-perishable foods may be found in a book by Labuza (1982).

5.2 Method of Predicting Changes in Perishable Food Quality

The structure of the kinetic model can be used to describe both time–temperature indicator response and changes in food quality. If the indicator response at a constant reference temperature and the activation energy for that indicator model are known, a constant temperature equivalent can be predicted for any interval between successive indicator

TABLE 8
KINETIC INFORMATION OF FROZEN FOODS (LAI AND HELDMAN, 1982)

Product	Activation energy (kcal/mol)	PSL Days ($-18°C$)	References	
Beef	13·34	206	Van Arsdel	(1969)
	14·81	258	Van Arsdel	(1969)
roasts	12·63	368	Tressler	(1957)
ground	8·68	153	Van Arsdel	(1969)
Lamb	13·24	320	Tressler	(1957)
Pork	26·75	316	Van Arsdel	(1969)
sausage	16·12	119	Tressler	(1957)
roasts	7·18	194	Tressler	(1957)
Turkey	15·34	181	Van Arsdel	(1969)
Chicken	20·20	282	Van Arsdel	(1969)
Eggs	25·44	297	Van Arsdel	(1969)
Butter	8·81	271	Van Arsdel	(1969)
Fatty fish	11·70	60	Van Arsdel	(1969)
	10·78	185	Tressler	(1957)
Lean fish	10·17	95	Van Arsdel	(1969)
	9·78	283	Tressler	(1957)
cod	13·97	163	Lane	(1964)
cod (canned)	10·94	193	Lane	(1964)
halibut	9·76	163	Young	(1950)
	9·33	420	Lane	(1964)
haddock (fillet)	12·73	282	Tressler	(1957)
pollock (fillet)	15·33	181	Tressler	(1957)
Smoke fish	10.73	79	Van Arsdel	(1969)
Lobster	13·10	192	Tressler	(1957)
Shrimp	11·28	316	Tressler	(1957)
Asparagus	16·15	239	Tressler	(1957)
	10·51	292	Van Arsdel	(1969)
Beans, snap	16·15	239	Tressler	(1957)
Beans, lima	16·12	379	Tressler	(1957)
Broccoli	16·12	379	Tressler	(1957)
Brussel sprouts	16·15	239	Tressler	(1957)
Cauliflower	16·12	379	Tressler	(1957)
Corn, on cob	12·56	219	Tressler	(1957)
Corn, cut	12·85	653	Tressler	(1957)
Carrots	12·85	653	Tressler	(1957)
Mushrooms	15·56	201	Tressler	(1957)
Peas	16·12	379	Tressler	(1957)
	5·88	302	Van Arsdel	(1969)
Pumpkin	12·85	653	Tressler	(1957)
Spinach	16·12	379	Tressler	(1957)
	13·48	474	Van Arsdel	(1969)

TABLE 8 (contd)

Product	Activation energy (kcal/mol)	PSL Days (−18°C)	References	
Squash	12·85	653	Tressler	(1957)
Apricots	15·56	201	Tressler	(1957)
with A.A.	16·12	420	Tressler	(1957)
Peaches	15·56	201	Tressler	(1957)
with A.A.	16·12	420	Tressler	(1957)
Raspberry	12·72	327	Tressler	(1957)
sugared	12·80	456	Tressler	(1957)
Strawberry, sliced	12·80	456	Tressler	(1957)

A.A., ascorbic acid.
Tressler = Tressler and Evers (1957).
Van Arsdel = Van Arsdel et al. (1969).

inspections. In turn, the constant temperature equivalent can then be used to estimate the amount of food quality change expected during that same interval. The following discussion will detail the derivation of the equivalent temperature prediction and estimation of the food quality changes based on time–temperature indicator response.

5.2.1 Equivalent Temperature Prediction

The kinetic reaction models can be used to describe the response of full-history time–temperature indicators. Wells and Singh (1986b) characterized the response of a LifeLines time–temperature indicator with a first-order kinetic model, and Taoukis and Labuza (1987) used a first-order model in conjunction with a Gaussian type transformation to describe the response of the I-POINT indicator. The expression that describes indicator response as a first-order reaction ($n = 1$) is:

$$-\frac{dR}{dt} = k_{R,\text{ref}} R \tag{12}$$

where $k_{R,\text{ref}}$ is the kinetic model rate constant for the indicator response at some isothermal reference temperature T_{ref} ($k_{R,\text{ref}}$ is referred to as the response rate constant). The response rate constant may be determined from eqn (12) by separation of variables, and integrating the expression over the length of time it takes the indicator to respond to one-half of the original scale. The resulting expression:

$$-\int_{R}^{R/2} \frac{1}{R} \, dR = k_{R,\text{ref}} \int_{0}^{t_{R/2}} dt \tag{13}$$

can be simplified to yield an analytical result for the response rate constant at the given reference temperature. The solution for the response rate constant at the reference temperature is:

$$k_{R,\text{ref}} = \frac{\ln(2)}{t_{R/2}} \tag{14}$$

where $t_{R/2}$ is the length of time it takes the time–temperature indicator to achieve a response of one-half of its original response value. Observation of indicator half-life, $t_{R/2}$, would be necessary to establish the response rate constant for a particular indicator at the temperature recommended for a perishable food product.

The general temperature-dependent equation that describes indicator response with a first-order kinetic model is:

$$-\frac{dR}{dt} = k_{0R} \exp\left(-\frac{E_{AR}}{R_g}\frac{1}{T}\right)R \tag{15}$$

where the temperature-dependence of the indicator response rate constant follows the Arrhenius relationship. For any time interval, t_{n-1} to t_n, the differential equation (eqn 15) may be solved by separation of variables to yield the expression:

$$-\int_{R_{n-1}}^{R_n} \frac{1}{R}dR = \int_{t_{n-1}}^{t_n} k_{0R}\exp\left(-\frac{E_{AR}}{R_g}\frac{1}{T}\right)dt \tag{16}$$

where R_{n-1} and R_n are the indicator responses at the times t_{n-1} and t_n, respectively.

In general, the integral on the right-hand side of eqn (16) cannot be solved explicitly as the temperature history for the interval, t_{n-1} to t_n, is unknown. Integrating the left-hand side of eqn (16) and dividing the expression by $k_{R,\text{ref}}$ will yield:

$$\frac{\ln(R_{n-1}) - \ln(R_n)}{k_{R,\text{ref}}} = \int_{t_{n-1}}^{t_n} \frac{k_{0R}}{k_{R,\text{ref}}}\exp\left(-\frac{E_{AR}}{R_g}\frac{1}{T}\right)dt \tag{17}$$

where the response rate constant, $k_{R,\text{ref}}$, had been determined from the observation of the half-life response (eqn (14)).

The response rate constant, $k_{R,\text{ref}}$, may also be expressed as:

$$k_{R,\text{ref}} = k_{0R}\exp\left(-\frac{E_{AR}}{R_g}\frac{1}{T_{\text{ref}}}\right) \tag{18}$$

from the Arrhenius relationship. Combining eqns (17) and (18), and reducing the exponential expression with the law of exponents gives the result:

$$\frac{\ln(R_{n-1}) - \ln(R_n)}{k_{R,ref}} = \int_{t_{n-1}}^{t_n} \exp\left[-\frac{E_{AR}}{R_g}\left(\frac{1}{T} - \frac{1}{T_{ref}}\right)\right] dt \qquad (19)$$

where the solution to the integral expression is given in terms of successive indicator response values and the response rate constant of the indicator. An alternative form of eqn (19) is the expression:

$$\frac{\ln(R_{n-1}) - \ln(R_n)}{k_{R,ref}} = \int_{t_{n-1}}^{t_n} U(T)\, dt \qquad (20)$$

where the temperature-dependent function $U(T)$ is given by:

$$U(T) = \exp\left[-\frac{E_{AR}}{R_g}\left(\frac{1}{T} - \frac{1}{T_{ref}}\right)\right] \qquad (21)$$

in which temperature, T, is a continuous time-varying parameter.

An equivalent temperature (denoted as T_{eq}) can be defined such that the function $U(T_{eq})$ takes on a constant value. From eqn (21) it follows that:

$$U(T_{eq}) = \exp\left[-\frac{E_{AR}}{R_g}\left(\frac{1}{T_{eq}} - \frac{1}{T_{ref}}\right)\right] \qquad (22)$$

where $U(T_{eq})$ is now a constant.

Evaluating eqn (20) for the interval t_{n-1} to t_n at the equivalent temperature, T_{eq}, will result in the expression:

$$U(T_{eq}) = \frac{\ln(R_{n-1}) - \ln(R_n)}{k_{R,ref}(t_n - t_{n-1})} \qquad (23)$$

Equation (23) is a solution for the unknown function $U(T)$ evaluated at $T = T_{eq}$, expressed in terms of the observation of successive indicator responses, the elapsed time between indicator inspections, and the response rate constant for the indicator at a reference temperature. It follows that the equivalent temperature, T_{eq}, can be determined from eqns (22) using the solution of eqn (23) for $U(T_{eq})$ in terms of measured indicator response for an interval. The resulting expression for the equivalent temperature is:

$$\frac{1}{T_{eq}} = \frac{1}{T_{ref}} + \frac{\ln[U(T_{eq})]}{(-E_{AR}/R_g)} \qquad (24)$$

or

$$T_{eq} = \left[\frac{1}{T_{ref}} + \frac{\ln[U(T_{eq})]}{(-E_{AR}/R_g)} \right]^{-1}$$

where T_{eq} is the constant temperature that is necessary to cause the equivalent indicator response that resulted from an unknown temperature exposure during the time interval between t_{n-1} and t_n.

The equivalent temperature, T_{eq}, differs slightly from the effective mean temperature as previously discussed (Hicks, 1944; Schwimmer et al., 1955; Labuza, 1979). The effective mean temperature is determined from the change in food quality by inverting an expression of quality as a function of time and temperature and solving for the temperature parameter. This procedure required explicit knowledge (or assumption) of the quality change during the storage interval, or the temperature function for that interval, so that the quality change could be estimated. In order to calculate the effective mean temperature, the food quality would have to be observed experimentally (possibly requiring destruction of food samples) or predicted theoretically (based on the temperature history recorded by a data acquisition system).

The equivalent temperature, on the other hand, is calculated based on the observed response of a time–temperature indicator and the elapsed time between indicator inspections. For small time intervals between inspections, or conditions of constant temperature storage, the equivalent temperature predicted by the time–temperature indicator is approximately equal to the effective mean temperature calculated from the change in food quality. The authors propose that the equivalent temperature be used to approximate the effective mean temperature, thereby providing a method to predict the changes in food quality without knowledge of the specific temperature function.

5.2.2 Estimation of Food Quality Change

As previously stated, change in food quality can be described with either a zero-order ($n=0$) or first-order ($n=1$) kinetic model. The following derivation will examine changes in food quality described by a zero-order reaction model. A parallel analysis for the first-order reaction model was given by Wells and Singh (1988d).

The general temperature-dependent expression that describes food quality change as a zero-order kinetic reaction is:

$$-\frac{dQ}{dt} = k_{0Q} \exp\left(-\frac{E_{AQ}}{R_g} \frac{1}{T} \right) \tag{25}$$

where Q is a measure of an attribute of food quality; k_{0Q} is pre-exponential factor for the quality change model; and E_{AQ} is the activation energy of the quality attribute.

Separating the variables and evaluating the integral for the quality change Q_{n-1} to Q_n, that occurs during the time interval t_{n-1} to t_n will yield the expression:

$$\int_{Q_{n-1}}^{Q_n} dQ = -\int_{t_{n-1}}^{t_n} k_{0Q} \exp\left(-\frac{E_{AQ}}{R_g}\frac{1}{T}\right) dt \qquad (26)$$

Solving integrals in eqn (26), and dividing both sides of the equation by the rate constant at a reference temperature, $k_{Q,\mathrm{ref}}$, will result in the expression:

$$\frac{Q_n - Q_{n-1}}{k_{Q,\mathrm{ref}}} = -\int_{t_{n-1}}^{t_n} \frac{k_{0Q}}{k_{Q,\mathrm{ref}}} \exp\left(-\frac{E_{AQ}}{R_g}\frac{1}{T}\right) dt \qquad (27)$$

where the rate constant, $k_{Q,\mathrm{ref}}$, is given by the Arrhenius expression:

$$k_{Q,\mathrm{ref}} = k_{0Q} \exp\left(-\frac{E_{AQ}}{R_g}\frac{1}{T_{\mathrm{ref}}}\right) \qquad (28)$$

with T_{ref} chosen as the same reference temperature used to determine the previously discussed response rate constant. Combining eqn (27) with eqn (28) and simplifying the expression with the law of exponents will result in an equation of the form:

$$\frac{Q_n - Q_{n-1}}{k_{Q,\mathrm{ref}}} = -\int_{t_{n-1}}^{t_n} \exp\left[-\frac{E_{AQ}}{R_g}\left(\frac{1}{T} - \frac{1}{T_{\mathrm{ref}}}\right)\right] dt \qquad (29)$$

where the right-hand side of eqn (29) is of similar form to that of eqn (19).

Raising the integrand in eqns (29) by the power E_{AR}/E_{AR} (i.e. raising the integrand to the power of one) will give the equation:

$$\frac{Q_n - Q_{n-1}}{k_{Q,\mathrm{ref}}} = -\int_{t_{n-1}}^{t_n} \left\{\exp\left[-\frac{E_{AQ}}{R_g}\left(\frac{1}{T} - \frac{1}{T_{\mathrm{ref}}}\right)\right]\right\}^{E_{AR}/E_{AR}} dt \qquad (30)$$

which with exponential algebra will yield:

$$\frac{Q_n - Q_{n-1}}{k_{Q,\mathrm{ref}}} = -\int_{t_{n-1}}^{t_n} \left\{\exp\left[-\frac{E_{AR}}{R_g}\left(\frac{1}{T} - \frac{1}{T_{\mathrm{ref}}}\right)\right]\right\}^{E_{AQ}/E_{AR}} dt \qquad (31)$$

Equation (31) may then be written in terms of the temperature-dependent function $U(T)$ (eqn (21)), and expressed as:

$$\frac{Q_n - Q_{n-1}}{k_{Q,\mathrm{ref}}} = -\int_{t_{n-1}}^{t_n} \{U(T)\}^W dt \qquad (32)$$

where

$$W = \frac{E_{AQ}}{E_{AR}} \tag{33}$$

is the ratio of the activation energy of the quality change to the activation energy of the indicator response.

If the activation energy of the indicator response, E_{AR}, is equal to that of the quality change, E_{AQ}, then the left-hand side of eqn (32) is equivalent to eqn 20. Thus, for $W = 1$ the quality change for the interval t_{n-1} to t_n is directly proportional to the change in time–temperature indicator response observed during the same interval. In the cases where $W \neq 1$, the quality change for the interval can be estimated by substituting $U(T_{eq})$ (eqn (23)) into eqn (32) to derive a generalized mathematical structure to estimate food quality change based on indicator response measurements at the beginning and end of an interval. In effect, the equivalent temperature is an approximation of the effect that the temperature function has on the change in food quality during the storage interval (i.e. the equivalent temperature is an estimate of the effective mean temperature for the interval).

Wells and Singh (1988d) verified the equivalent temperature method of quality prediction for mature green tomatoes stored in non-isothermal conditions. Figure 24 compares changes in tomato firmness predicted from a LifeLines model 57 time–temperature indicator to the changes observed by a sensory panel during the study. Over the duration of the study, the predicted values were not significantly different from the

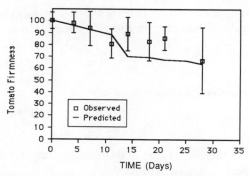

FIG. 24. Comparison of the sensory scores of tomato firmness and scores predicted from the mean response of the LifeLines model 57 during variable temperature treatment (Wells and Singh, 1988c).

observed scores. The equivalent temperature method of predicting changes in an attribute of food quality based on the response of time–temperature indicators is very promising. The limitations of this method and a means to determine the error associated with the equivalent temperature approximation are discussed by Wells (1987).

5.2.3 Definition and Estimation of Remaining Shelf Life

Research into the storage stability of perishable foods has been aimed at identifying the length of time that an item can remain in storage, a product's shelf life. The shelf life of a product is commonly interpreted on the basis of storage time and temperature, but alternatively may be thought of in terms of product quality. The quality prediction model derived above can be related to the quality based interpretation of the shelf life to predict reduction in the shelf-life potential based on temperature exposure during storage and distribution.

The earlier-mentioned definition of PSL for frozen foods suggested that shelf life is the length of time a perishable product can be stored before the quality changes that accrue during storage result in an unacceptable product. This would imply that there is some limiting threshold of quality beyond which a product would be unsuitable for consumption.

Assuming that the time- and temperature-dependent changes in a characteristic of food quality can be satisfactorily predicted with the kinetic model, it would follow that a quality-based interpretation of shelf life can be expressed mathematically in the form of a kinetic model. The general form of the zero-order kinetic model was given in eqn (25). When evaluated at a reference temperature, the integral form of the zero-order quality change model is:

$$-\int_{Q_0}^{Q_{th}} dQ = \int_0^{t_{Q,ref}} k_{Q,ref}\, dt \tag{34}$$

where the limits of integration Q_0 and Q_{th} represent the initial and threshold levels of the specific quality characteristic, and $t_{Q,ref}$ represents the length of time that it takes the quality characteristic to change from its initial value to the undesirable threshold.

The quality rate constant, $k_{Q,ref}$, may be removed from the integral which then can be solved to give the quality-based definition of shelf life (the length of time, $t_{Q,ref}$, necessary to bring about a change in quality from the initial quality, Q_0, to some undesirable quality threshold, Q_{th}, at a constant reference temperature, T_{ref}). The shelf life of a product at a reference temperature is denoted mathematically as:

$$t_{Q,ref} = \frac{Q_0 - Q_{th}}{k_{Q,ref}} \tag{35}$$

where the magnitude of a desirable characteristic of food quality is assumed to be decreasing (e.g. $Q_0 > Q_{th}$).

During the storage and distribution of food products, temperature conditions may be encountered that give rise to increased rates of quality change. Thus, the threshold quality, Q_{th}, that defines the end point of the shelf life will be achieved at some elapsed storage time other than $t_{Q,ref}$. For any level of quality, Q_n, between the initial and threshold quality levels, shelf life may be expressed as the sum of the product's equivalent age and remaining shelf life. This relationship is denoted as:

$$t_{Q,ref} = A_{e,n} + A_{r,n} \tag{36}$$

where $A_{e,n}$ and $A_{r,n}$ are the equivalent age and remaining shelf life, respectively.

The equivalent age, $A_{e,n}$, represents the length of time that would be necessary to bring about the same level of quality, Q_n, if the product had been stored at the reference temperature chosen for $k_{Q,ref}$. Mathematically the equivalent age is given by:

$$A_{e,n} = \frac{Q_0 - Q_n}{k_{Q,ref}} \tag{37}$$

for a zero-order reaction.

The remaining shelf life, $A_{r,n}$, represents the length of time for food quality to change from the observed level, Q_n, to the threshold level, Q_{th}, if the product is stored at the reference temperature. The remaining shelf life is given by:

$$A_{r,n} = \frac{Q_n - Q_{th}}{k_{Q,ref}} \tag{38}$$

for a zero-order reaction. The remaining shelf life and equivalent age functions are complementary and both functions of quality.

For the time interval t_{n-1} to t_n the change in remaining shelf life, ΔA_r, may be expressed as:

$$\Delta A_r = A_{r,n} - A_{r,n-1} = \frac{Q_n - Q_{n-1}}{k_{Q,ref}} \tag{39}$$

Equation (32) may be substituted into eqn (39), resulting in a single equation that is independent of the initial assumption of reaction order. Substitution and rearrangement of the equation yields:

$$A_{r,n} = A_{r,n-1} - \int_{t_{n-1}}^{t_n} [U(T)]^W \, dt \qquad (40)$$

which can be used on interval-wise bases (t_n to t_{n-1}) evaluated at $T = T_{eq}$ to estimate the remaining shelf life of a product based on the initial estimate of remaining shelf life:

$$A_{r,0} = t_{Q,ref} \qquad (41)$$

and indicator response values.

The result of the above derivation provides a generalized mathematical model to predict food quality and remaining shelf life from the response of a full-history time–temperature indicator. The use of the formula presupposes that the activation energy and reference rate constants for both the indicator and food quality attribute are known, and that it holds true only for situations of continuous quality deterioration. The quality prediction model would not be valid in situations where temperature (or other conditions) cause a discontinuity in the deterioration function. Examples of a discontinuity in quality deterioration would include thawing in frozen foods, excessive proliferation or sporulation of microbial contaminates, changes in product composition caused by protein denaturation, or mechanical injury due to product damage or loss of package integrity.

6 PERISHABLE INVENTORY MANAGEMENT

Substantial evidence has been presented in the literature to relate time–temperature indicator response to changes in perishable food quality. However, very little attention has been given to the use of these relationships in perishable inventory management. The following discussion will examine the means of utilizing food quality prediction based on time–temperature indicator response in decisions relating to inventory management.

6.1 Perishable Food Distribution

Perishable inventory control theory and issue policy has been discussed within the management science and operations research literature. Earliest work in this area documented research on management of inventory depletion without regard to specific application (Derman and Klein, 1958, 1959). Recent investigations in this area have focused on the class of inventory problems related to the issuance of whole blood from a central blood bank (Pegels and Jelmert, 1970; Pierskalla and Roach, 1972). A review of perishable inventory theory by Nahmias (1982), and an overview of blood inventory management theory and practice by Prastacos (1984), document a number of methodological contributions that could be applied to any perishable commodity.

Research in perishable inventory management has been conducted considering the inventory items to have a fixed finite storage life or a uniform and constant deterioration rate. Current procedures in inventory issuance do not compensate for varying deterioration rates. This is considered to be a serious limitation when applying previous research results to management of perishable food inventories. The following analysis examines the food distribution system and suggests an appropriate inventory issue policy that utilizes the prediction of remaining shelf life from time–temperature indicators.

6.1.1 Food Distribution and the Inventory Stockpile

Perishable foods move from 'manufacture' to 'consumption' via a transportation and storage network called the 'distribution system' or 'distribution chain'. For the purpose of this discussion, 'consumption' will be defined as the delivery of a food item to a consumer from a retail outlet (a consumer purchase); and 'manufacture' will be considered to be the point

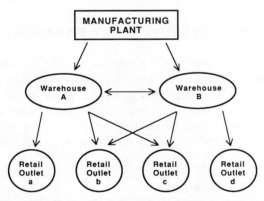

FIG. 25. Perishable food distribution chain consisting of manufacturing plant, warehouses, and retail outlets (Wells, 1987).

in the processing of a food such that the item is suitable for retail purchase. Processors and suppliers have little control over the destiny of perishable foods beyond consumption at the retail outlet. However, since most food items are ultimately destined for a consumer's dining table, the food inventory within the distribution system must be managed in such a way as to deliver the highest-quality product possible.

A typical distribution system is encompassed by temporary storage within the manufacturing plant, shipment of products to one or more centralized warehouses, and transport of the warehouse inventory to the point of retail sales. A simplified perishable distribution system is shown in Fig. 25. After a sufficient number of items have been processed and accumulated in temporary storage at the manufacturing plant, a truck-load, or other convenient shipping quantity (a so-called product 'lot') is delivered to a centralized warehouse for longer-term storage. At the centralized warehouse the arrival of a product lot is recorded, and the number of 'stock keeping units' (SKU) entering storage is recorded. An SKU is usually a quantity of items less than the amount contained in a product lot and represents the smallest number of individual items that can be supplied to a retail location and/or other warehouses. A typically SKU would be the so called 'case lot'.

The contents of a warehouse vary with each inventory transaction. Items are dispersed in quantities to satisfy the demand for items needed at the retail outlets (or other warehouses), and are received into storage to replenish items that have been distributed. The inventory within a warehouse is dynamic in that items are dispersed and received in unequal quantities and at different times. At any given point in time, an accumulation of items in excess of those demanded at other locations would constitute an inventory 'stockpile'. The flux of inventory within the stockpile is not constant and is subject to both fluctuation and uncertainty. Accordingly, a warehouse manager is faced with two types of management problems: (a) stockpile replenishment, and (b) stockpile depletion.

The 'stockpile replenishment problem' is concerned with quantity and timing of the inventory delivery to a warehouse. The solution to the problem is motivated by consideration of the cost of inventory storage and the cost to order and deliver the items to the storage location (Silver, 1981; Nahmias, 1982). It is usually assumed that an adequate supply of inventory items either exists or can be manufactured at some location within the distribution system and that the items needed to replenish the inventory can be delivered after a relatively short, well-defined period of time (Liao and Khumawala, 1984). However, for many perishable food items these assumptions do not hold true as supplies of raw material for processing or manufacture may be available only on a seasonal or irregular basis. The processing of perishable fruits and vegetables, for example, is seasonal because of the nature of these commodities, while meat and poultry products may be available on an irregular basis since shifting market prices may deem alternative use of the product more profitable. Further consideration of the stockpile replenishment problem in the context of perishable foods is beyond the scope of this presentation.

When the inventory supply at one of the retail locations (or other warehouses) is depleted, or nearly depleted, replenishment stock is ordered from the inventory stored at a centralized warehouse. The centralized warehouse that receives the inventory order is obligated to supply the inventory from the items that are stored within its stockpile or obtain the necessary items from another warehouse if its supply is depleted.

The number of case lots contained in a single shipment distributed from a warehouse is usually less than the number received in a shipment from the manufacturer. Additionally, the timing of the shipments may be such that several lots are received from the manufacturer prior to the distribution of product to retail locations or other warehouses. Since there is a difference in quantities of units received and dispersed from the warehouse inventory, and the timing of these shipments varies, an arbitrary inspection of the inventory will show that the stockpile contains items that have originated from different product lots. The different lots were manufactured at different times, and thus the items within the inventory stockpile would be of different ages. The question then arises as to which items in the inventory stockpile should have the highest priority for shipment. The choice of which stockpile items to issue, or an appropriate policy to establish shipment priority, leads to the 'stockpile depletion problem'.

6.1.2 Perishable Inventory Depletion

The 'stockpile depletion problem' was formulated by Derman and Klein (1958) as a way of determining an optimal sequence to remove items from a stockpile with units of varying ages. It was assumed that an item issued from the stockpile had a field life that was a known function of the age of the item, and that an item was issued in response to a specific demand when previously issued items had expired or been consumed. The assumptions in the problem formulation meant that the total field life of the stockpile was dependent upon the sequence in which items were removed from the stockpile. An inventory issue policy was considered an optimal policy when the total field life of the entire stockpile was maximized.

The general approach to the inventory depletion problem has been to determine the conditions of the field-life function such that either the last-in first-out (LIFO) or the first-in first-out (FIFO) policy gives rise to the optimal issue sequence (Derman and Klein, 1959; Pierskalla, 1967a,b; Nahmias, 1974; Albright, 1976). A FIFO policy implies that items be issued in the order of decreasing age beginning with the oldest item in supply. Thus, the oldest item in inventory (first into storage) will be the first to be issued (first out of storage). Conversely, a LIFO policy implies that items be issued in the order of increasing age beginning with the youngest item in stock. Both in LIFO and FIFO policies are time-based issue policies in that items held in inventory are issued according to the length of time that an item has been in storage.

The LIFO and FIFO issue policies have been shown to be optimal for perishable inventories that exhibit deterioration functions (utility functions) of specific mathematical form (Derman and Klein, 1959). Items that have utility functions that are concave are optimally issued under a LIFO policy, and items with functions that are convex are optimally issued with the FIFO policy. The use of these policies holds only for stockpile items that deteriorate with the same, uniform deterioration function. Since the keeping quality of perishable foods is dependent on storage temperature, inventory deterioration will be nonuniform unless all items in the stockpile have been exposed to the same temperature conditions. Because temperature fluctuations may occur during storage and distribution, the FIFO issue policy, widely used in the food industry, may be inappropriate.

6.1.3 Classic View of Perishable Inventory Management
The stockpile depletion problem as presented in the management science literature is stated as follows (Bomberger, 1961):

An operation requires a stockpile of items to be issued to satisfy some specified demand. The field life of an item is a known non-negative function, $L(S)$, of the age, S, of the item being issued. The problem is to determine the order of issue (issue policy) which maximizes the total life of the stockpile. Such a policy is called optimal.

The formulation of the classic inventory depletion problem includes two key assumptions: (1) the field life of an item is a known function of its age;

and (2) an optimal issue policy is one that maximizes the total life of the stockpile. The assumptions of the stockpile depletion problem and the results of previous research are important in establishing the characteristics of an appropriate issue policy for perishable foods.

Items within an inventory stockpile will have different ages because of the varying quantities and timing of replenishment and distribution shipments. Compounding this problem, stockpile items with different ages may have originated from more than one replenishment source. Thus, the items within the stockpile may not only have different ages, but may also have had different histories of transportation and storage. In addition to different sequences of transportation and storage, items within the stockpile may have been stored for different lengths of time at other locations prior to arriving at the current storage location.

For example, an inventory stockpile may consist of items that have been delivered directly from the manufacturing plant and items that had first been stored at another warehouse and later reallocated to the present location. Each different distribution pathway will undoubtedly have exposed the products to a slightly different temperature history. Thus, while the items within the stockpile may be of the same age (as measured from time of manufacture), because of the different distribution routes, the items probably would have experienced different temperature histories.

As previously discussed, research has established a relationship between temperature history and the shelf life of perishable foods. Because of this, the field life of a perishable food (the time it can be stored subsequent to issue) is not solely dependent on the age of the inventory but is more closely related to the cumulative time and temperature exposure. The field life can be expressed as a function of its age only if the complete temperature history of the product is known. That is the shelf life of two items will be the same only if both items have experienced the same temperature history. Even slight temperature fluctuations during the storage of some frozen foods can cause noticeable changes in the shelf life compared with a product of the same age that has been stored under strict isothermal conditions (Van Ardsel et al., 1969). Therefore, the age of a perishable food item has little bearing on the field life (shelf life) of the product if storage temperature did not remain consistent throughout the distribution system.

For the general perishable inventory problem, the objective of an optimal issue policy is to maximize the total life of a stockpile. In the case of a perishable food stockpile, this objective also seems desirable because of high fixed and operating costs related to frozen and refrigerated storage. In addition, maximizing the life of a stockpile at a centralized site would result in increased distribution flexibility for deliveries to satellite storage locations and possible increased demand satisfaction among multiple retail locations. On the other hand, an inventory issue policy that maximizes the total life of the stockpile without constraints on product quality may give rise to issuance of items that fail to meet certain minimum quality standards. Imposing a penalty cost for the disposal or remanufacture of items that fail to meet the quality threshold could alter the classic view of an optimal inventory policy.

6.1.4 Appropriate Issue Policy of Perishable Foods
The FIFO issue policy is commonly used to determine the order in which frozen and refrigerated foods are dispersed from a storage location. Food quality change has been observed to deteriorate along either a decreasing linear or decreasing concave decay function (i.e. zero-order or first-order kinetic model). When the inventory depletion problem is studied for such a decay function, the inventory issue policy that meets the classic objective of maximizing the total life of the stockpile is the LIFO policy. Thus, the LIFO issue policy would be considered the optimal inventory issue policy for a stockpile in which all items deteriorated with this class of function.

The conflict between the theoretically optimal LIFO policy and the widely used FIFO policy can be understood by examining how each policy affects the issued item. Adherence to the FIFO issue philosophy from manufacture to consumption amounts to the issuance of items in ordered sequence of decreasing age as measured from time of manufacture, while adherence to the LIFO policy will issue items in order of increasing elapse time from manufacturer (i.e. the FIFO policy will require issue of the oldest items, while the LIFO policy will require issue of the most recently processed items). If a LIFO issue policy (the theoretically optimal policy) was placed into effect, a portion of the accumulation in the inventory stockpile would never be distributed since a more recently manufactured product would preempt the issue of any older items. The product remaining within the stockpile that could not be issued would eventually become unsuitable for consumption. The FIFO issue policy does not have the problem of stockpile obsolesence since the oldest items within the inventory would take highest issue priority.

When all items within the distribution system deteriorate with the same uniform decay function, use of the FIFO issue policy will outperform the LIFO issue policy with respect to the issuance of products with uniform quality. That is, when all items within the inventory stockpile deteriorate in the same manner, the use of a FIFO issue policy will give rise to the shipment of items with the most consistent quality. One can argue that uniform product quality is substantially important in determining the issue priority of perishable foods. Given that a food item does not deteriorate to a point that exceeds the quality threshold that defines end of shelf life, a product of consistent quality would be preferred to a produce of inconsistent quality. Certainly consumers of brand-name foods continue to purchase these products because of the reasonable surety of consistent quality. While consistent product quality is often thought of as uniform manufacturing standards and careful selection of raw materials, an inappropriate choice of which item to issue from the inventory stockpile could negate whatever quality consistency that has been attributed to that product. An inappropriate issue policy could inadvertently retain an item that with additional storage would result in a product grossly inferior to the quality of the issued item had the issued product remained in storage for the same period of time.

When elevated or irregular temperature exposures occur during transit or storage, a time-based issue policy (such as FIFO or LIFO) is unable to compensate for the increased deterioration, and the uniformity in the quality of the product distribution from the stockpile may be compromised. Ideally, an appropriate inventory issue policy for perishable foods would seek to manage the quality of the inventory in such a way that the product is delivered to the consumer in the most quality-consistent manner possible. Several researchers have supported the notion of quality-based inventory management for perishable foods (Schoorl and Holt, 1982, 1985; Shewfelt, 1986).

6.2 Quality-Based Inventory Management

The mathematical relationship between time–temperature indicator response and food quality change provides the means by which product inventory can be issued based on the estimated quality rather than the elapsed storage time. Such a scheme would establish a framework to justify taking action to expedite the shipment of heat-abused product from the warehouse and would call attention to any segment of the distribution chain that was deficient in temperature-maintenance procedures.

6.2.1 Shortest Remaining Shelf Life (SRSL) Issue Policy

An alternative to the time-based issue policy would be to determine issue priority on the maximum expected field life as calculated from the estimated quality change. The precise field life of a perishable food is unknown since the product may be consumed (eaten) at any time subsequent to issue. However, because food quality continues to change until the product is consumed, the maximum expected field life can be derived in terms of the amount of quality change that is acceptable prior to final consumption. Thus, the maximum length of time the product can be stored (when held at an isothermal reference), such that the food quality will not deteriorate beyond an unacceptable threshold, would constitute the maximum expected field life. The maximum expected field life is equivalent to the derived definition of remaining shelf life (eqn (38)).

The authors have proposed an inventory issue policy based on remaining shelf life as estimated from time–temperature indicator response (Wells and Singh, 1989). The proposed policy, the shortest remaining shelf life (SRSL) issue policy, would establish issue priority for stockpile items in the sequence from shortest to longest remaining shelf life. The SRSL issue policy would retain the items with the greatest amount of quality reserve within the stockpile and expedite issue of the items which could not withstand an additional period of storage. In effect, the SRSL issue policy would allow inventory items that have undergone the greatest amount of quality change to move most rapidly through the food distribution system.

Wells and Singh (1989) demonstrated that items issued under the SRSL policy were of equal or higher average quality, with less quality variation at time of issue, than items issued under the FIFO and LIFO policies. In this investigation, inventory transaction records for frozen broccoli were studied, and computer simulation was used to explore the influence of issue policy on the quality and consistency of products distributed from an inventory stockpile. The simulation study examined system performance for variations in storage temperature, initial quality of replenishment inventory, and issue priority as scheduled according to the FIFO, LIFO, and SRSL policies.

The average quality at time of issue as influenced by changes in initial product quality for $-18°C$ storage temperature is shown in Fig. 26. No significant differences between average product quality at issue for the SRSL and FIFO policies were found. The variation in quality at time of issue as influenced by changes in initial quality level is shown in Fig. 27. The choice of inventory issue policy is seen to have an effect on quality

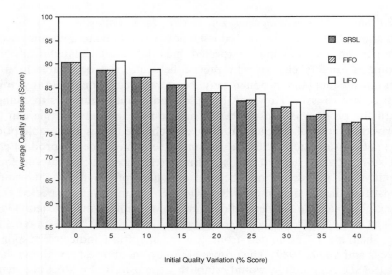

FIG. 26.   Average quality of frozen broccoli at time of issue for the SRSL, FIFO, and LIFO issue policies as influenced by the variation in quality of replenishment stock ($-18°C$ storage) (Wells, 1987).

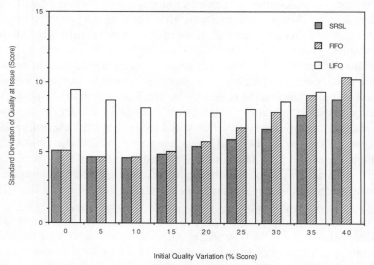

FIG. 27.   Standard deviation of the average quality of frozen broccoli at time of issue for the SRSL, FIFO, and LIFO issue policies as influenced by variations in quality of replenishment stock ($-18°C$ storage) (Wells, 1987).

variation of the issued products with the SRSL issue policy giving the least variation. Wells and Singh concluded that for conditions of variable temperature storage or for variations in the quality of replenishment inventory the SRSL issue policy significantly reduced the variation in quality at time of issue as compared to the FIFO issue policy.

6.2.2 Distribution Decision Support and the SRSL Issue Policy
The SRSL inventory issue policy lends itself to implementation of addition logistical and quality constraints in the context of a computer-based decision support system. The SRSL issue policy provides the framework to implement supplemental decision criteria regarding inventory quality and remaining shelf life, in addition to ranking the stockpile items for shipment priority. Additional decision criteria could reflect constraints on distribution logistics and/or premium quality standards. For instance, in situations where logistics of delivery are such that lengthy transit time is required, an appropriate distribution constraint could be:

$$A_{r,n} > A_{r,min} \qquad (42)$$

where $A_{r,n}$ is equal to the remaining shelf life of the product to be issued, and $A_{r,min}$ is equal to the length of time that is required to deliver the shipment plus the length of storage required at the destination. The constraint of eqn (42) would require that the remaining shelf life of a product be greater than the length of time it takes to travel the distance to the destination that placed the inventory order, plus the shelf-life expectation prior to consumption. The remaining shelf life, of course, is conditional on the maintenance of the isothermal reference temperature and changes at a rate that varies with the actual storage temperature maintained subsequent to the issue decision.

Similarly, a constraint could be placed on food quality if an item of higher quality would command a higher price at a retail outlet compared with items of a lesser quality. The constraint on food quality could be implemented within the SRSL issue policy as a threshold of premium quality. Since food quality is estimated in calculation of shortest remaining shelf life by comparing the estimated quality to the limiting value of the premium quality threshold, stockpile items could be segregated into groupings of premium and non-premium items. Items that met the requirements of premium quality could be distributed to preferred retail locations or marketed separately from items that did not meet the premium standard, thereby leading to increased profits.

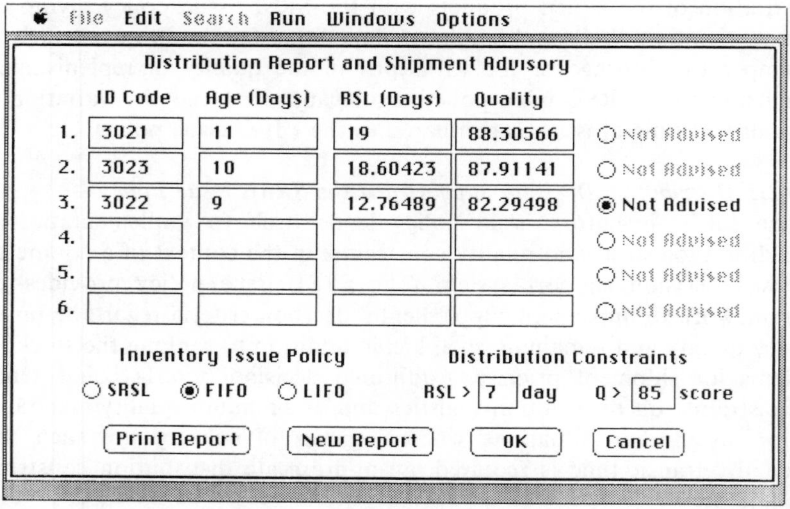

336   J. H. WELLS and R. P. SINGH

FIG. 28. Screen graphic of the revised issue priority based on the FIFO policy and the shipment advisory based on unmet distribution constraints (Wells and Singh, 1987a).

In general, the SRSL issue policy would provide the means to incorporate any logistic constraints of minimum remaining shelf life and/or an established threshold of premium quality into a decision support system. The decision support system could be used by warehouse managers to make more informed decisions regarding inventory shipments. Implementation of an inventory management system to provide distribution decision support can be easily facilitated with an advanced microcomputer system. The microcomputer provides both the environment to conduct the calculations required for food quality and remaining shelf life prediction and the means to structure the information relevant to inventory management.

The design and evaluation of a microcomputer-based inventory management system was discussed by Wells and Singh (1987a). The computer-based inventory management system was conceived to fulfill three objectives: (1) to provide for distribution decision support based on time–temperature indicator response; (2) to provide a means of calculating quality predictions based on indicator responses; and (3) to facilitate simulation of the effect of known temperature histories on indicator response and food quality changes. The decision support aspect of the microcomputer system allows different inventory lots to be compared based on SRSL, FIFO, or LIFO issue policies, subject to constraint on remaining shelf life or food quality. Wells and Singh (1987a) developed microcomputer software to demonstrate an implementation of the inventory management system. An example of the computer screen graphic that shows the distribution report and shipment advisory is shown in Fig. 28. The software has proved to be a valuable aid to research and teaching with a separate software package developed for computer-aided instruction in simulation of quality changes of frozen and refrigerated foods (Wells and Singh, 1987b).

7 FUTURE APPLICATIONS OF TIME–TEMPERATURE INDICATOR

Temperature mishandling during storage and distribution of perishable foods, and the resulting loss in quality, have a tremendous economic impact on the frozen and refrigerated food industry. As distribution routes become longer with increased international trade in perishable food, problems with the loss of quality due to temperature mishandling will continue to be acute, necessitating management procedures that promote delivery of consistently high-quality products. Increased consumer awareness of the relationship between health and nutrition will also predicate the implementation of more strict quality-control procedures during perishable food distribution. Time–temperature indicators are anticipated to play an important role in the development of comprehensive quality assurance programs and inventory control practices applicable to the food industry.

7.1 Technical Limitations

At the present time perhaps the most serious limitation to the widespread use of time–temperature indicators is the great deal of manipulation and meticulous hand-work necessary to accomplish indicator activation, attachment, and inspection. Technological development will be required to combine indicator fabrication, attachment, and initial inspection into the continuous processing environment. Advances aimed at overcoming these concerns could possibly be achieved by adopting present packaging technology and machine vision systems. Data collection and information flow is also a potential problem as logistical systems become increasingly complex and decentralized.

The response scale and qualitative interpretation of certain types of time–temperature indicators remains troublesome. Further complicating response and interpretation is the fact that prevailing environmental conditions (i.e. light, temperature, humidity, etc.) can influence the perception and measurement of the indicator response. Continued progress is needed to develop electronic sensors for indicator measurements that can withstand harsh treatment in varying temperature extremes. Problems relating to a means for attachment of time–temperature indicators to product containers under conditions of high humidity or low temperatures also limits their use.

7.2 Future Research Needs

A substantial need relating to the implementation and use of time–temperature indicators in quality assurance and inventory management is user education. Effective means are required to educate shippers, suppliers, warehouse managers, and consumers as to the proper handling of perishable foods. Simulation of logistical networks disguised in the cloak of an animated computer game may have potential for the purposes of education.

There is a need for computer-aided inventory management systems that integrate a quality-based management scheme using time–temperature indicators into conventional management systems that track inventory position, log sales and ordering activity, and forecast shipment demand. Basic and applied research in the area of management and decision science is needed to examine how time–temperature indicators and quality monitoring can be used with advanced scheduling techniques such as just-in-time manufacturing and production. Other systems analyses are needed to determine relevant economic and quality criteria for product culling and inventory disposal.

Continued development of monitoring systems for perishable foods is directly linked to the scientific understanding of consumer acceptance and quality perception. Producers and processors will need to identify specific product attributes that are influenced by storage time and temperature and determine kinetic relationships between these attributes and the storage environment. Additional work to define indicator response in term of kinetic structures parallel to that of specific quality attributes is needed. Questions of food safety must also be examined in relation to quality monitoring, especially in the light of increased interest in the use of modified-atmosphere packaging.

ACKNOWLEDGEMENTS

The authors greatly appreciate the financial support provided by the U.S. Army Natick Research, Development and Engineering Center, from contract nos. DAAK60-83-C-0100, DAAK60-84-C-0076, and DAAK60-85-C-0111. The technical support contributed by the contract officers from Natick's Food Engineering Division was also appreciated.

REFERENCES

Albright, S. C. (1976). Optimal stock depletion policies with stochastic lives. *Management Science*, **22**, 852–7.

Andersen, A. A. (1949). A defrosting indicator for frozen foods. *Food Technol.*, **3**, 357–8.

Anonymous (1986). Polydiacetylenes spur activity from commercial to theroretical. *Chemical & Engineering News*, **64**, 33–7.

Arabshahi, A. & Lund, D. B. (1985). Considerations in calculating kinetic parameters from experimental data. *J. Food Process Engineering*, **7** 239–51.

Arnold, G. & Cook, D. J. (1977). An evaluation of the performance claimed for a chemical time/temperature integrating device. *J. Food Technol.*, **12**, 333–7.

Bengtsson, N., Liljemark, A., Olsson, P. & Nilsson, B. (1972). An attempt to systemize time–temperature tolerance data as a basis for the development of time–temperature indicators. *Intl. Inst. Refrig. Bull. Suppl.*, **2**, 303–11.

Blixt, K. G. (1983). The I-point TTM—a versatile biochemical time–temperature integrator. IIR, Commission C2 Preprints, 16th International Congress of Refrigeration, pp. 629–31.

Blixt, K. G. & Tiru, M. (1976). An enzymatic time/temperature device for monitoring the handling of perishable commodities. *Develop. Biol. Stand.*, **36**, 237–41.

Bomberger, E. E. (1961). Optimal inventory depletion policies. *Management Science*, **7**, 294–303.

Byrne, C. H. (1976). Temperature indicators—the state of the art. *Food Technol.*, **30**, 66–8.

Campbell, L. A., Morgan, R. G. & Heldman, D.R. (1986). Correlation of commercial time–temperature integrating polymer performance with refrigerated food quality. Presented at the Institute of Food Technologists' 46th Annual Meeting & Food Expo, Dallas, TX, June.

Cohen, E. & Saguy, I. (1985). Statistical evaluation of Arrhenius model and its applicability in prediction of food quality losses. *J. Food Processing and Preservation*, **9**, 273–90.

Derman, C. & Klein, M. (1958). Inventory depletion management. *Management Science*, **4**, 450–6.

Derman, C. & Klein, M. (1959). A note on the optimal depletion of inventory. *Management Science*, **5**, 210–13.

Desrosier, N. W. & Tressler, D. K. (1977). *Fundamentals of Food Freezing*. AVI Publishing, Westport, CT.

Dethmers, A. E. (1979). Utilizing sensory evaluation to determine product shelf life. *Food Technol.*, **33**, 40–2.

Dolan, K. D., Singh, R. P. & Wells, J. H. (1985). Evaluation of time–temperature related quality changes in ice cream during storage. *J. Food Processing and Preservation*, **9**, 253–71.

Farquhar, J. W. (1977). Time–temperature indicators in monitoring the distribution of frozen foods. *J. Food Quality*, **1**, 119–23.

Farquhar, J. W. (1981). Monitoring food handling by time/temperature devices. *Refrig. Science and Technol.*, 1981–4, 517–24.

Farquhar, J. W. (1982). Monitoring food handling using time and temperature devices. *Intl. J. Refrig.*, **5**, 50–4.

Farquhar, J. W. (1983). Time/temperature monitoring of frozen and refrigerated seafood products. IIR, Commission C2 Preprints, 16th International Congress of Refrigeration, pp. 621–8.

Fennema, O. R., Powrie, W. D. & Marth, E. H. (1973). *Low Temperature Preservation of Foods and Living Matter*. Marcel Dekker, New York.

Fields, S. C. & Prusik, T. (1983). Time–temperature monitoring using solid-state chemical indicators. Paper presented at the 16th International Congress of Refrigeration, Paris, July.

Foley, M. A. & Lentz, C. P. (1968). Survey of temperatures in frozen fish shipped by road. *Can. Inst. Food Technol. J.*, **1**, 123–5.

Goodenough, P. W. & Atkin, R. K. (1981). *Quality in Stored and Processed Vegetables and Fruit*. Academic Press, London.

Grisius, R., Wells, J. H., Barrett, E. L. & Singh, R. P. (1987). Correlation of full-history time–temperature indicator response with microbial spoilage in pasteurized milk. *J. Food Processing and Preservation*, **11**, 309–24.

Guadagni, D. G. (1963). Time–temperature integrator: a laboratory evaluation. *Frosted Food Field*, **36**, 42–4.

Haralampu, S. G., Saguy, I. & Karel, M. (1985). Estimation of Arrhenius parameters using three least squares methods. *J. Food Processing and Preservation*, **9**, 129–43.

Hayakawa, K. (1976). Letter. *Food Technol.*, **30**, 40.

Hayakawa, K. & Wong, Y. F. (1974). Performance of frozen food indicators subjected to time variable temperatures. *ASHRAE J.*, **16**, 44–8.

Hicks, E. W. (1944). Note on the estimation of the effect of diurnal temperature fluctuations on reaction rates in stored foodstuffs and other materials. *J. of the Council for Scientific and Industrial Research, Australia*, **17**, 111–14.

Hill, C. G. & Grieger-Block, R. A. (1980). Kinetic data: generation, interpretation and use. *Food Technol.*, **34**, 56–66.

Hu, K. H. (1971). Time–temperature indicating system 'writes' status of product shelf-life. *Food Technol.*, **26**, 56–8, 60, 62.

International Institute of Refrigeration (1986). *Recommendations for the Processing and Handling of Frozen Foods*, 3rd edn. IIR, Paris.

Jul, M. (1984). *The Quality of Frozen Foods*. Academic Press, New York.

Kramer, A. & Farquhar, J. W. (1976). Testing of time–temperature indicating and defrost devices. *Food Technology*, **30**, 50–3, 56.

Kwolek, W. F. & Bookwalter, G. N. (1971). Predicting storage stability from time–temperature data. *Food Technol.*, **25**, 51–63.

Labuza, T. P. (1976). Letter. *Food Technol.*, **30**, 34.

Labuza, T. P. (1979). A theoretical comparison of losses in food under fluctuating temperature sequences. *J. Food Science*, **44**, 1162–8.

Labuza, T. P. (1982). *Shelf-Life Dating of Foods*. Food and Nutrition Press, Westport, CT.

Labuza, T. P. (1984). Application of chemical kinetics to deterioration of foods. *J. Chemical Education*, 61, 348–58.

Lai, D. & Heldman, D. R. (1982). Analysis of kinetics of quality change in frozen foods. *J. Food Process Engineering*, **6**, 179–200.

Lane, J. P. (1964). Time–temperature tolerance of frozen seafoods I. Review of some of the recent literature on the storage life of frozen fishery products. *Food Technol.* **18**, 156–62.

Liao, W. M. & Khumawala, S. B. (1984). Sensitivity study of the economic-order-quantity model. In *Computer Models for Production and Inventory Control*, ed. H. Bekiroglu. Simulation Series 12(2):55–68. Simulation Councils, Inc. (The Society for Computer Simulation), La Jolla, CA.

Londahl, G. (1983). Market needs for temperature and time–temperature monitoring devices. Unpublished report.

Manske, W. J. (1983). The application of controlled fluid migration to temperature limit and time temperature integrators. IIR, Commission C2 Preprints, 16th International Congress of Refrigeration, pp. 632–5.

McNutt, J. W. & Lee, F. H. (1974). Effect of freeze–thaw cycle on meal; ready-to-eat, individual, 1966 prototype. Technical Report Series FL-183, US Army Natick Laboratories, Natick, MA.

Mistry, V. V. & Kosikowski, F. V. (1983). Use of time–temperature indicators as quality control devices for market milk. *J. Food Protection*, **46**, 52–7.

Moreno, J. (1984). Quality deterioration of refrigerated foods and its time–temperature mathematical relationships. *Intl. J. Refrigeration*, **7**, 371–6.

Nahmias, S. (1974). Inventory depletion management when the field life is random. *Management Science*, **20**, 1276–83.

Nahmias, S. (1982). Perishable inventory theory: a review. *Operations Research*, **30**, 680–708.

Pegels, C.C. & Jelmert, A. E. (1970). An evaluation of blood-inventory policies: a Markov chain application. *Operations Research*, **18**, 1087–98.

Pierskalla, W. P. (1967a). Optimal issuing policies in inventory management—I. *Management Science*, **13**, 395–412.

Pierskalla, W. P. (1967b). Inventory depletion management with stochastic field life functions. *Management Science*, **13** 877–86.

Pierskalla, W. P. & Roach, C. D. (1972). Optimal issuing policies for perishable inventory. *Management Science*, **18**, 603–14.

Prastacos, G. P. (1984). Blood inventory management: an overview of theory and practice. *Management Science*, **30**, 777–800.

Ratkowsky, D. A., Olley, J., McMeekin, T. A. & Ball, A. (1982). Relationship between temperature and growth rate of bacteria cultures. *J. Bacteriology*, **149**, 1.

Renier, J. J., Morin, W. T., *et al.* (sic) (1962). Time temperature indicators. *Intl. Inst. Refrig. Bull.*, Annexe 1962-1, 425–35.

Rose, R. E. (1981). Quality assurance in the cold-chain use of an enzymatic time/temperature monitor during transport and storage of refrigerated fish. *Refrig. Science and Technol.*, 1981-4, 483–6.

Saguy, I. & Karel, M., (1980). Modeling of quality deterioration during food processing and storage. *Food Technology*, **34**, 78–85.

Sanderson-Walker, M. (1975). Frozen food: management of the distribution chain. *Food Manufacturer*, **50**, 25, 26, 28, 34.

Sanderson-Walker, M. (1979). Time–temperature monitoring and quality inspection: practical considerations for the quick-frozen food manufacturer. *Intl. J. Refrig.*, **2**, 97–101.

SAS Institute Inc. (1982). *SAS User's Guide: Statistics*, 1982 edn. SAS Institute, Cary, NC.

Schoen, H. M. (1983). Thermal indicators for frozen foods. IIR, Commission C2 Preprints, 16th International Congress of Refrigeration, pp. 589–92.

Schoen, H. M. & Byrne, C. H. (1972). Defrost indicators: many designs have been patented yet there is no ideal indicator. *Food Technol.*, **26**, 46–50.

Schoorl, D. & Holt, J. E. (1982). Fresh fruit and vegetable distribution—management of quality. *Scientia Horticulturae*, **17**, 1–8.

Schoorl, D. & Holt, J. E. (1985). A methodology for the management of quality in horticultural distribution. *Agricultural Systems*, **16**, 119–216.

Schubert, H. (1977). Criteria for application of T-TI indicators to quality control of deep frozen products. *Science et Technique du Froid IIF-IIR*, 1977-1, 407–23.

Schutz, H. C., Damrell, J. D. & Locke, B. H. (1972). Predicting hedonic ratings of raw carrot texture by sensory analysis. *J. Texture Studies*, **3**, 227–32.

Schwimmer, S., Ingraham, L. L. & Hughes, H. M. (1955). Temperature tolerance in frozen food processing: effective temperatures in thermal fluctuating systems. *Industrial and Engineering Chemistry*, **47**, 1149–51.

Shewfelt, R. L. (1986). Postharvest treatment for extending the shelf life of fruits and vegetables. *Food Technol.*, **40**, 70–2, 74, 76–8, 80, 89.

Silver, E. A. (1981). Operations research in inventory management: a review and critique. *Operations Research*, **29**, 628–45.

Singh, R. P. (1976). Computer simulation of food quality during frozen food storage. *International Institute of Refrigeration Bull*, Supp. 1976-1, 197–204.

Singh, R. P. & Hsu. (1988). Unpublished report. Department of Agricultural Engineering, University of California, Davis, CA.

Singh, R. P. & Wang, C. Y. (1977). Quality of frozen foods—a review. *J. Food Process Engin.*, **1**, 97–127.

Singh, R. P. & Wells, J. H. (1985). Use of time–temperature indicators to monitor quality of frozen hamburger. *Food Technol.* **39**, 42–50.

Singh, R. P. & Wells, J. H. (1987a). Development, evaluation and simulation of an automated stock management system utilizing time–temperature indicators. Report prepared for US Army Natick Research, Development & Engineering Center, Natick, MA, May. (Contract No. DAAK60-85-C-0111).

Singh, R. P. & Wells, J. H. (1987b). Monitoring quality changes in stored frozen strawberries with time–temperature indicators. *Int. J. Refrig.*, **10**, 296–300.

Singh, R. P., Wells, J. H., Dolan, K. D., Gonnet, E. J. & Muñoz, A. M. (1984). Critical evaluation of time–temperature indicators for monitoring quality changes in stored subsistence. Report prepared for US Army Natick Research & Development Center, Natick, MA. September. (Contract No. DAAK60-83-C-0100).

Singh, R, P., Barrett, E. L., Wells, J. H., Grisius, R. C. & Marum, W. (1986). Critical evaluation of time–temperature indicators for monitoring quality changes in perishable and semi-perishable foods. Report prepared for US Army Natick Research & Development Center, Natick, MA. January. (Contract No. DAAK60-84-C-0076).

Smith, J. M. (1970). *Chemical Engineering Kinetics*, 2nd edn. McGraw-Hill, New York.

Taoukis, P. S. & Labuza, T. P. (1987). A systematic approach to using time–temperature indicators as shelf life monitors of food products. Presented at the Institute of Food Technologists' 48th Annual Meeting & Food Expo, Las Vegas, NV, June.

Tressler, D. K. & Evers, C. F. (1957). *The Freezing Preservation of Foods*, 3rd edn. AVI Publishing, Westport, CT.

Tressler, D. K., Van Arsdel, W. B. & Copley, M. J. (1968). *The Freezing Preservation of Foods*, 4th edn. AVI Publishing, Westport, CT.

University of California (1983). *BMDP Statistical Software*, ed. W. J. Dixon. University of California Press, Berkeley, CA.

Van Arsdel, W. B., Coply, M. J. & Olson, R. L. (1969). *Quality and Stability of Frozen Foods. Time–Temperature-Tolerance and its significance*. Wiley–Interscience, New York.

Van't Root, M. J. M. (1973). Is it feasible to measure the time–temperature history of frozen foodstuffs? *Proceedings 13th Intl. Congress Refrig.*, Vol. 4, IIR, Paris, pp. 445–51.

Wells, J. H. (1987). A computer-based inventory management system for perishable foods. D. E. Dissertation, Graduate Division, University of California, Davis, CA. July.

Wells, J. H. & Singh, R. P. (1985). Performance evaluation of time–temperature indicators for frozen food transport. *J. Food Science*, **50**, 369–71, 378.

Wells, J. H. & Singh, R. P. (1986a). Influence of temperature fluctuation on time–temperature indicator response. ASAE Paper No. 86-6559. December.

Wells, J. H. & Singh, R. P. (1986b). Evaluation of full-history time–temperature indicators. ASAE Paper No. 86-6002.

Wells, J. H. & Singh, R. P. (1987a). Design and evaluation of a microcomputer-based inventory management system for perishable foods. Presented at the Institute of Food Technologists' 48th Annual Meeting & Food Expo, Las Vegas, NV, June.

Wells, J. H. & Singh, R. P. (1987b). A computer aided demonstration of food quality change. ASAE Paper No. 87-6570.

Wells, J. H. & Singh, R. P. (1988a). Response characteristic of full-history time–temperature indicators suitable for perishable food handling. *J. Food Processing and Preservation*, **12**, 207–18.

Wells, J. H. & Singh, R. P. (1988b). Sensory attributes appropriate in frozen food storage studies. Unpublished report, Dept. of Agricultural Engineering, University of California, Davis.

Wells, J. H. & Singh, R. P. (1988c). Application of time–temperature indicators in monitoring changes in quality attributes of perishable and semiperishable foods. *J. Food Science*, **53**, 148–52, 156.

Wells, J. H. & Singh, R. P. (1988d). A kinetic approach to food quality prediction using full-history time–temperature indicators. *J. Food Science*, **53**, 1866–71, 1893.

Wells, J. H. & Singh, R. P. (1989). A quality-based inventory issue policy for perishable foods. *J. Food Processing and Preservation*, **12**, 271–92.

Wells, J. H., Singh, R. P. & Noble, A. C. (1987). A graphical interpretation of time–temperature related quality changes in frozen food. *J. Food Science*, **52**, 436–9, 444.

Wills, R. B. H., Lee, T. H., Graham, D., McGlasson, W. B. & Hall, E. G. (1981). *Postharvest*. AVI Publishing, Westport, CT.

Witonsky, R. J. (1976). Letter. *Food Technol.*, **30**, 34–5.

Witt, C., Smith, N., Singh, R. P., Wells, J. H. & Zhao, J. (1987). A color detector for an integrating time–temperature indicator. ASAE Paper No. 87-6058.

Young, O. C. (1950). Quality of fresh and frozen fish and facilities for freezing, storing and transporting fishery products. *Food Technol.*, **4**, 447.

Zall, R., Chen, J. & Fields, S.C. (1984). Evaluation of automated time–temperature monitoring systems in measuring freshness of UHT milk. Presented at the Ninth Annual Eastern Research Highlights Conference, Washington, DC, November.

INDEX